HOW TO START, FINANCE, AND MANAGE YOUR OWN SMALL BUSINESS
Revised Edition

Joseph R. Mancuso

A FIRESIDE BOOK
Published by Simon & Schuster
New York London Toronto Sydney Tokyo Singapore

F

FIRESIDE
Simon & Schuster Building
Rockefeller Center
1230 Avenue of the Americas
New York, New York 10020

Copyright © 1984 by Prentice-Hall, Inc.
First Fireside Edition 1992

Manufactured in the United States of America

10 9 8 7 6 5

Library of Congress Cataloging-in-Publication Data

Mancuso, Joseph
How to start, finance, and manage your own small
business.
Includes index.
1. Small business–Management   2. Small business–
Finance.   I. Title
HD 62.7.M365   1984   658′.022   84-13411
ISBN 0-671-76356-3

Contents

Preface   v

I STARTING A SMALL BUSINESS

1 Who Is the Entrepreneur?   3

2 The Entrepreneur's Quiz   15

3 Building an Entrepreneurial Team   25

II FINANCING A SMALL BUSINESS

4 Venture Capitalists   37

5 What Is a Business Plan?   53

6 Raising New Money   78

III MANAGING A SMALL BUSINESS

7 Managing the Small Enterprise   93

8 Leading the Small Enterprise   **111**

9 Preparing for Failure   **129**

APPENDIXES

A Information Questionnaire   **143**

B Associations of Value to Small Business   **148**

C Sample Business Plans   **193**

    Index   **387**

Preface

The objective of all dedicated employees should be to thoroughly analyze all situations, anticipate all problems prior to their occurrence, have answers for those problems, and move swiftly to solve these problems when called upon. . . . However . . . when you are up to your ass in alligators, it is difficult to remind yourself that your initial objective was to drain the swamp.

This book was written to appeal both to students and to practicing small business people. It focuses on the three-step process of starting, financing, and managing a business of your own. The emphasis is more with the starting and financing aspects because these topics are unique to small companies. Although managing a small business is not necessarily the same as managing a large one, it's not unduly different either. The same fundamental principles of "managing" apply, regardless of the size of a business.

The starting and financing process is what makes a small business unique. Because of this uniqueness, entrepreneurship can be separated from all other aspects of business management. An entrepreneur starts businesses where none previously existed. In the past, he may have been labeled a hustler, but the American capitalistic system has legitimized him under the umbrella of the French-derived word *entrepreneur*. The first chapter of this book asks and answers the question "Who is an entrepreneur?"

All successful business starters have to raise money at some time in the business's growth. Chapter 4 of this book is labeled Venture Capitalists; several entrepreneurs, however, claimed it would be better labeled "Russian Roulette." The central part of this book addresses the heart of the financing issue, and for that matter, the heart of the business: the business plan. Sample business plans are offered in order to give an overview of how they can be interpreted. Entrepreneurs have claimed that the best preparation for writing business plans of their own is reading several other plans. Learning by this example or case approach is more commonly preferred to learning by reading guidelines and prose.

What makes this book different is its unique focus on the entrepreneur and the business plan. On the one hand, it can serve as a practical and useful guide to existing enterprises; on the other, it can also serve as a textbook on starting, financing, and managing aspects of business management. It should have a special appeal for new venture initiation courses or the Small Business Institute programs that deal with entrepreneurs. It is ideally suited for project courses dealing with small businesses where one of the requirements of the course is to develop a business plan. As a guide to a team of consultants working in a small business, this book should be an ideal complement to the development of a business plan for a specific entrepreneurial enterprise.

The third and final segment of the book deals with the management issues of a small business. This part of the book presents management concepts that focus on small, not large, businesses. Those areas where a difference in practice exists between large and small businesses are singled out for particular attention.

Managing an ongoing growth-oriented business, whether your own or someone else's, requires unique management expertise. Just because an individual was a successful manager in a larger business is no guarantee that the management skills are transferrable to a small venture.

Venture management has been a popular phrase to describe the internal operations of a small business. The final part of the book deals with venture management issues. The intent is to highlight the management skills that are needed by a small businessperson in order to grow the small business into a big business.

The business plans in Appendix C are reproduced as they were written prior to the actual effort to raise venture capital. Except for the changes indicated, they are actual plans, and any errors or shortcomings were also present in the original documents. Some facts have been disguised to protect identities where necessary, however. The essence of each plan has been retained.

HOW TO START, FINANCE, AND MANAGE YOUR OWN SMALL BUSINESS

Revised Edition

I

STARTING A SMALL BUSINESS

1

Who Is
The Entrepreneur?

Not so long ago, to have been called an entrepreneur would have been cause for a duel. It meant that you were overly aggressive and probably not terribly trustworthy. Entrepreneur was a synonym for hustler; it used to symbolize the least attractive aspects of American capitalism. It certainly meant that you were not the kind of person with whom "good" people associated.

Today, that view is somewhat dated; and the volumes of scholarly literature on the subject of entrepreneurship and the accomplishments of great entrepreneurs have given respectability to the label. The importance of the start-a-business process has been brought into focus by the societal impact of major U.S. industrial companies which grew out of nothing. These industrial empires, which were created by great entrepreneurs, have become the backbone of the economy of the richest country in the world. Just as the phrase "Yankee Doodle" was turned from a cynical downgrading of earlier Americans into a national cry of colonial unity, "entrepreneur" has become the rallying symbol of the free enterprise system. It is not really difficult to understand how such a view became prevalent.

To create a business from nothing—and to succeed at it—requires motivation and perseverance bordering on obsession. It sometimes requires ruthlessness. It nearly always means neglecting your family and taking long absences from home. All of this could easily be interpreted as antisocial behavior, and none of it is good for a person's reputation. Yet an entrepreneur does all of this and more.

In Webster's *Seventh New Collegiate Dictionary,* the entrepreneur is defined as: "(en-tre-pre-neur, F. fr, *entreprendre,* to undertake); one who organizes, manages, and assumes the risks of a business or enterprise—en-tre-pre-neur-ship/n." In *The Achieving Society,* by David McClelland of Harvard University, the entrepreneur is defined as "someone who exercises some control over the means of production and produces more than he can consume in order to sell (or exchange) it for individual (or household income."[1] In *The Organization Makers,* by Collins and Moore, the entrepreneur is identified as "a man who has created out of nothing an ongoing enterprise."[2]

The foregoing puts the present day entrepreneur in perspective but it does little to explain how he gets that way in the first place. That's a puzzling issue with no once-and-for-all answer. Although clues and trends exist to explain his behavior, no irrefutable cause and effect relationship has been established. A better understanding of his motivations and behavior is available from knowledge of his early development.

THE EARLY DEVELOPMENT OF ENTREPRENEURS

Most entrepreneurs enjoy talking about their childhood. And most of the time, their recollections of their early years are honestly interesting, if not downright fascinating. They were interesting and unusual children. It is during childhood that entrepreneurial tendencies first begin to show themselves: As early as age four or five, entrepreneurs-to-be are peddling "lemonade" on the sidewalk at a penny a glass. At eight or nine they're delivering newspapers to earn money for a new bike. In their early teens they like to collect coins or rocks or stamps or photographs. These activities may be fun, but they are always aimed toward profit and growth. By the time they reach high school they may actually be running their own businesses—on a small scale, of course. In short, most entrepreneurs were enterprising children who had their courses already set toward future enterprises. These basic characteristics emerged very early in life.

The first-born child is the oldest in the family and the most likely to become an entrepreneur. Vance Packard, in an article titled, "The First, Last, and Middle Child: The Surprising Difference," highlights various studies, especially one by behavioral scientist Dr. Stanley Schacter, which show that first-borns far outnumber later-born children in almost every ranking of achievement. First-born children are overly representative in *Who's Who* and they virtually dominate most achievement rankings in the United States culture. George Washington, Abraham Lincoln, Thomas Jefferson, Woodrow Wilson, Franklin D. Roosevelt—all were first-born children. Of the first twenty-three astronauts to go on U.S. space missions, twenty-one were either the eldest or only children. This is remarkable when you consider that later-born children outnumber first-borns by two to one in the general U.S. population. In a recent analysis of 1,618 Merit Scholarship winners, 971 were first-born children.[3]

Later in the article, Packard indicates that the first-born children are most likely to accept the parents' standards, to be traditionally oriented, and to call themselves religious. It's the later-born who are likely to rebel against the parents' standards. The firstborn tend to be entrepreneurs.

The entrepreneur's obsessive need to achieve may often be traced to his relationship with his father. If they have a "good" relationship, even if dad was not a great success, the son strives to prove himself and to make dad proud. Dad's subtlest signs of approval, such as a nod or a half-smile, are his most cherished rewards. A surprisingly large number of entrepreneurs are the offspring of self-employed fathers. Thus many entrepreneurs imitate their fathers and soon become self-employed. The free spirit

[1] D. McClelland, *The Achieving Society* (New York: Van Nostrand, 1961).

[2] O. Collins and D. Moore, *The Organization Makers* (Ann Arbor: University of Michigan, 1970).

[3] Vance Packard, "The First, Last, or Middle Child: The Surprising Difference," *Reader's Digest,* December 1969.

and the independence of self-employment is molded into many young entrepreneurs-to-be and can never be totally suppressed in their later careers.

In cases where the father-son relationship is less cordial—even strained—the son may be out to "get the old man" by achieving a greater level of success in order to prove that he's the better man. Finally, if the father was not present—because of death, divorce, or desertion—during the entrepreneur's childhood, the son may have been forced to assume the provider's role in the family. Inheriting a great deal of responsibility at an early age can speed along maturity and, with it, the entrepreneurial tendencies. Very seldom, it seems, does the entrepreneur ever have what we would consider your average, run-of-the-mill, subdued Oedipal relationship with his father.

The above discussion of the entrepreneur's early childhood development uses the pronoun he; consequently the female version of this unique person is relegated to a second place. That is the way it is today. The hard facts are that starting, financing, and managing a small business have traditionally been men's work—the female of the species has chosen not to try her hand in this arena. But this may not be the way of the future.

Early evidence indicates that more women are becoming interested in the entrepreneurial process. Hence, this is potentially one of the discipline's most significant changes of the future. The societal changes created by the women's liberation movement are reappearing in the small business community, and the historical traits and characteristics of male entrepreneurs which have existed for centuries may well change in the near future. The change may have to do with a growing number of women who seek to start, finance, and manage a small business of their own. It is too soon yet to determine whether female entrepreneurs will also be overwhelmingly first-born or only children. It is too soon, also, to know whether they will follow their self-employed mothers as entrepreneurs.

ENTREPRENEURIAL TRAITS

One of the initial scholarly studies of entrepreneurship, *The Enterprising Man*[4], concluded that entrepreneurs have a lower educational base than their counterparts in larger businesses and that often they were not college graduates. This pioneering study of about 100 small businessmen in Michigan indicated that the average age of the entrepreneur at the time of the study (1950s) was 52. Twenty percent of the entrepreneurs studied were immigrants to the U.S.A. Moreover, 35% were sons of immigrants; hence, the surprising conclusion was that 55% of the entrepreneurs studied in Michigan in the 1950s, were either foreign born or first generation Americans.

About 20% of this sample in Michigan were college graduates. While this percentage was about the same as that of college graduates in the general Michigan population, it was less than half of the 57% of executives in larger companies who held college degrees. The other interesting finding was that about one quarter of the sample had fathers who were self-employed. This sample by Collins and Moore was representative of businesses founded after World War II and this data became the foundation of further small business research in the 1960s and 1970s.

The studies conducted in the 1960s by Professor Edward Roberts of the Sloan School at The Massachusetts Institute of Technology characterized the Boston entrepreneur differently from the earlier Michigan study. Roberts was studying the typical entrepreneur who had founded a new technological enterprise along Route 128 in

[4] O. Collins, and D. Moore, *The Enterprising Man* (Ann Arbor: University of Michigan, 1964), p. 36.

Boston.[5] The difference between the Boston and the Michigan groupings was most evident in the educational attainment and age of the entrepreneur. Roberts concluded that the average age was closer to 35 years and that the average educational attainment of those in the sample was a master's degree.

These studies by Roberts and Collins and Moore initiated a series of follow-up studies designed to uncover the traits of entrepreneurs. Although there were some differences in these studies, there were more similarities than differences between the Michigan and Massachusetts samples. Further, Professor Arnold Cooper of the Krannert Graduate School of Industrial Administration at Purdue University published another study of the entrepreneurs located around Palo Alto, California.[6] This work in the San Francisco Peninsula generally agreed with the data gathered in Robert's Boston Studies. All three of these studies concluded that entrepreneurs do have certain common traits and characteristics.

My own work was conducted in the late 1960s and early 1970s in the New England area.[7] My conclusions and findings support some of the earlier studies, but they deny certain other findings. Moreover, my research delved a little deeper than the other studies did into the issue of what makes an entrepreneur tick. Although the demographic data of background characteristics is interesting and valuable, the underlying psychological motivations were of more interest to my work. Conclusions about mean age were of only casual interest to my research—which focused on "why."

Alfred North Whitehead once said, "The greatest invention of all is the invention of inventing inventions." If that is the case, the person who introduces an invention to the world—the entrepreneur—must share that greatness. Much has been written about the entrepreneur—his desires, his motivations, and his characteristics—but most of this literature has been the result of deep scientific investigation that, in my opinion, has neglected the "human" side of the issue.

Actually, it is very difficult to study the entrepreneur. Many, if not most, are absorbed into the business world and eventually cannot be separated from the whole. This is especially true of the majority of entrepreneurs whose ventures fail. Therefore, most previous studies have been made only of successful entrepreneurs. The results mentioned earlier (Roberts, Collins and Moore and Cooper) were performed on *existing* entrepreneurial companies—a factor which implies a certain degree of success.

Many of these prior studies were conducted on the scientific basis of statistically sampling a directory of small businesses within the region. The small companies which responded to the questionnaire, to phone calls, or to visits provided the input data for the research. These results were then analyzed and eventually published. Unfortunately, small businesses which started and failed do not maintain an identity (such as a telephone number or an address) for the convenience of follow-up academic research. Moreover, when one recalls that the vast majority of entrepreneurial businesses do fail, this no longer becomes an issue of insignificant proportions. Hence, I claim that most of this earlier research is primarily valid for somewhat "successful" entrepreneurs, and that the differences introduced by my research are partially caused by my inclusion of failure in the initial sample. My study, although it lacked statistical sampling procedures, included all types of entrepreneurs—winners and losers. In fact,

[5] E. B. Roberts, "Entrepreneurship and Technology," *Research Management,* July 1968, p. 53.

[6] Arnold C. Cooper, *The Founding of Technologically Based Firms,* The Center for Venture Management, Milwaukee, Wisconsin.

[7] J. R. Mancuso, *Fun 'n' Guts, The Entrepreneur's Philosophy,* Reading, Mass.: Addison-Wesley, 1973.

several of the entrepreneurs in my study were both winners and losers, depending upon which of their several companies were used as criteria.

THE NEW RESEARCH

During the late 1960s and early 1970s, I have worked directly with more than 250 entrepreneurs in a variety of businesses and industries. I was their confidant and sounding board. I shared their failures and successes. I was their consultant, regardless of the nature of the circumstances.

I have worked with winners and losers alike, although each time I began a consulting relationship I was confident that I was working with a winner. But of course this was not always the case. If nothing else, my experience has taught me that it is nearly impossible to predict what makes a "successful" entrepreneur. It is a good deal easier to predict what causes an entrepreneur to fail.

These conclusions about entrepreneurial motivation are mine alone. They are not based on any sensible sampling or interviewing, nor are they based on any statistical fact gathering. You might call these opinions my "gut" reaction after working hand-in-glove with so many different entrepreneurs.

My data agreed with Roberts' earlier studies in both the age and education category. Obviously, it contradicted some of the findings in the earlier studies of Collins and Moore. My research concluded the average age of the entrepreneur was between 30 and 35 years, and that this age was slowly moving down towards a 30 year old average. In fact, a good many of the entrepreneurs I studied and worked with actually started their businesses while in their middle or late twenties. The data on the master's degree was also overwhelming. More than half the group I studied held a master's degree in either business or a technical discipline.

Now this does not mean that these individuals were brilliant students. In fact, the opposite might be the case. It does, however, indicate a certain level of respect for education—a level that ends abruptly when it comes to taking that extra time to gain a doctorate. For some unexplainable reason, the master's degree is the most popular terminal degree for the New England entrepreneur. Outside of a few professors who turned entrepreneur, almost no one chooses to start a business after he has persevered long enought to obtain a doctorate. Rather, these individuals choose to profess at a university rather than to practice by founding a new business enterprise.

This observation is not meant to knock all academics in one damaging blow, but it is helpful in pointing out that little assistance in becoming a better entrepreneur is offered by most academic programs of study leading to a terminal academic degree. Rather than being academically brilliant, the entrepreneur has too much energy to wait at the university before applying his new found talents in the real world. He does, however, maintain a cordial though not intimate relationship with academia. Of course, there are exceptions to the rule, and An Wang of The Massachusetts Institute of Technology (MIT), founder of Wang Laboratories in Massachusetts, is one of the popularly cited exceptions.

The entrepreneurs I worked with were overwhelmingly the first-born children of self-employed fathers. They were holders of the master's degree and were married when they started their businesses in their early thirties. However, many business men and women also hold master's degrees, and, in their middle thirties, they are working for someone else. These business executives have no business of their own—nor do they have a desire to have one. They are perfectly content with the role of the employee. So, possessing this unusual set of individual characteristics is not enough to be labeled an entrepreneur. In fact, most individuals who possess the unusual grouping

7

of characteristics are *not* entrepreneurs; rather, they are successful business executives employed in American industry. An entrepreneur must also have the energy, enthusiasm, and positive mental attitude which create the burning inner desire to be your own boss. You've got to be able to go twenty-five hours a day, if need be, to make the business work— and that takes energy. If you don't have it, all the Wheaties, Ovaltine, and little blue pills in the world aren't going to help.

And just having the magic set of personal characteristics is not enough to be classified as an entrepreneur, either. Just as the earlier research into leadership eventually concluded that there was no single set of personal characteristics that assured leadership ability, the same is true of entrepreneurs. Possessing the traits does not make one an entrepreneur, for this chicken-and-egg question begins with the finding that existing, not aspiring, entrepreneurs have these traits. I judge that the same conclusion will be forthcoming in the future research about entrepreneurs. Hence, being short, fat, and ugly doesn't necessarily help or hinder a person as a leader or an entrepreneur. Although an appreciation of "typical" personal characteristics of entrepreneurs is interesting, only a deep seated inner drive to start a business from nothing can classify a person as a bonafide entrepreneur. And, as yet, all of the research to date, including my own, has failed to uncover the primary sources of motivation prompting a human being to found a new business enterprise.

ENTREPRENEURIAL CHARACTERISTICS

I often invite outside guests to speak to the college students in my course in entrepreneurship and venture management at Worcester Polytechnic Institute (WPI). My purpose is to expose my students to a broader view of the entrepreneurial universe than I alone can offer. One of these speakers, Anthony "Spag" Borgatti, founder of Spag's Department Store, New England's leading discount center in Shrewsbury, Massachusetts, is, to my mind, an excellent example of the entrepreneur as an individualist. Every year he repeats, "A small business is not an institution. It's a way of life, and the best teacher of life is personal experience. There is no book; you sort of observe and make your own way." In another incident, after the course was completed, one of my students came to me and said, "I've listened to every one of our guest speakers, successful and unsuccessful, but I can't figure out the pattern for success. Each speaker was so different." As soon as he completed his sentence, he realized that he had just answered his own question.

Besides being strong individualists, every entrepreneur is a born optimist. To them the bucket is never half-empty but always half-full. This trait sometimes goes so far that it becomes an unrealistic perspective. However, it takes undying optimism to survive the false starts, near failures, and disappointments that every entrepreneur faces every day. They seek out opportunities—and when they don't exist—they create them. Entrepreneurism is an synonym for optimism. Because of this natural trait, they avoid problems while seeking solutions. Employees of entrepreneurs should keep these basic and fundamental entrepreneurial characteristics in mind in their day-to-day work. Instead of bringing the entrepreneur/boss problems for his resolution, bring him opportunities for his consideration. Entrepreneurs have enough problems of their own.

A popular misconception about an entrepreneur concerns his willingness to accept risks or to gamble. Because of this, many people have been curious about the behavior entrepreneurs would exhibit at a horse race. Would they bet on the 20 to 1 shots, on the odds-on-favorites, or on some complicated version of the daily double?

In my work with entrepreneurs, I asked questions designed to learn the answer to the horse racing riddle. This answer was a bit surprising.

Somehow, most people guess that the entrepreneur would be betting on the 10 to 1 shot—you know, the chance to make a killing. They are dead wrong, according to my findings. On the other hand, they would not bet on the house favorite, either. The odds are too short.

Entrepreneurs seem to thrive on the 3 to 1 shot—a gamble they judge to be exciting but realistic. Even when our discussions left the remote topic of horse racing, the entrepreneurs' attitudes remained about the same. They played for the realistic but achievable odds in their business enterprise as well. They set reasonable and obtainable objectives—and then they attain or exceed their goals.

The philosophy which holds at the track also holds in business. They prefer to bet on the 3 to 1 shot, but then to stand at the rail, shouting and yelling frantically for the chosen one to run faster. All the noise and commotion seems to help, because the 3 to 1 shots do come in every so often—and it seems to be more frequent with the support of someone cheering them on. Contrary to popular belief, entrepreneurs are not big gamblers or "high rollers."

Their willingness to accept risk is one area of increasing academic inquiry. Although they are unwilling to gamble on long shots, they are more willing to take a chance if their individual skills can affect the probability of success. They love to bet a few dollars on a hole of golf or to wager on a tennis match. These risks involve their skill and they aren't beyond overestimating their abilities—not by a long shot.

The Irish Sweepstakes, the State Lottery System, or a roll of the dice are events of pure chance. These are seldom as inviting as a contest of skills to justify a wager. As a matter of fact, on the premise that some of my own individual traits are common to entrepreneurs, I'm the only person I know who can make the following claim. I have never bought an Irish Sweepstakes ticket or a State Lottery ticket, nor have I ever bet on a sporting event. I have never been to or bet at a horse race or a dog race. In my mind the risk/reward ratio is too poor. Do you know anyone who can honestly make that statement?

Every student of entrepreneurship has, at one time or another, speculated about what motivates a person to leave a good job and security to start his own business. Some say that they are basically insecure and must prove their worth on their own. Some say they just can't work for someone else; that they have to be their own bosses. Others claim that they are bored by the slow pace in a large company and hunger for more action. It has even been suggested that they are motivated by a nagging spouse or by the desire to keep up with the Joneses.

Any or all of these factors may influence an entrepreneur's decision to strike out on his own, but more often than not it is the realization that as long as he is working for someone else, his employer is earning at least 25 percent more than he is paying. Why, asks the entrepreneur, shouldn't he be getting all he is worth?

But don't be misled. It's not the money they are interested in as much as the autonomy of deciding how to allocate their worth. They don't like just anyone mixing in such a personal matter. Money, in fact, is a poor reason to go into business, and is probably the reason behind most of the failures. Deciding to go into business solely to make money is a mistake. Most successful companies are founded by someone with an idea and a dream. Making money and accumulating wealth are usually the by-products for accomplishing some nobler goal. You need an idea or a dream to provide the push for success.

There is another "personal characteristic" that can make or break an entrepreneur, given all the other factors I've mentioned—his spouse. If venture capitalists could get to know every client's spouse, they'd have a far better indication of the client's likelihood of success. The reason I write spouse and not wife is simple. When I'm writing this material, *wife* is clearly the most appropriate but, when you are reading it, *spouse* may well be a better choice.

Without a doubt this so-called personal characteristic is undergoing a great deal of change. During my research in the late 1960s and early 1970s, I found that less than one percent of all entrepreneurs were female. A rare incidence or two of a woman founding or managing a small business was always good material for a local newspaper story. The industries were typically food (Betty Crocker, Sara Lee), cosmetics (Helena Rubenstein), fashion, and clothes—areas where women seem to have more knowledge than men, as well as a natural aptitude. This is not a chauvinistic attitude; merely a reflection of the progress being made by women in the field of management.[8] To me the breakdown in this last stronghold of male superiority will occur when the female sex becomes involved in venture capital. When this transition occurs, probably by 1980s, the ratio of men and women entrepreneurs could approach a more even distribution. There is only one woman today who acts as a venture capitalist and that statistic must change dramatically before women significantly impact the entrepreneurial world.

But by the 1980s I wouldn't be surprised to find that more than 10% of all entrepreneurs are female. The evidence is starting to accumulate even now. However, even though the vast majority of providers to the American family are still men, the wife may often be the power behind the throne.

I've toyed with various methods of displaying a wife's value to a small firm on a balance sheet. I would rank her right below "cash" when she's an asset, and just below "trade payables" when she's a liability. What would you say; can you find a better place for the wife on the balance sheet? Which way does she tip the balance? It's a life and death question which must be addressed during the start-a-business-process.

According to my research, almost all entrepreneurs are married, as compared to a smaller percentage of non-entrepreneurs. Entrepreneurs need the continuity and stability that marriage can provide. It isn't easy being married to an entrepreneur. You have to live with insecurity and change (often for years), and put up with broken dates, forgotten birthdays, burned dinners, deep depressions, and a multitude of other hardships. But show me an entrepreneur whose wife is content and willing to help her husband, and—much more often than not—I'll show you success. An understanding wife gives assurance, consolation, advice, encouragement, and love. And she may often help with the business herself, for little or no pay! With all that going for you, how can an entrepreneur help but succeed?

Another unusual trait of entrepreneurs is their displeasure at making out expense reports—and when they do they are usually incorrect or incomplete. It's not because they're trying a little petty thievery, either—quite the contrary. It's just very had for entrepreneurs to separate the company's finances from their personal finances, so they tend to treat the company's money as their own and vice versa.

You see, the entrepreneur/boss signs all the checks, and the impact of having more or less money in the company checking account is an everyday sensation. As a result, they don't fill out expense reports, and they often don't report many of their personal expenses. I've known entrepreneurs to carry this to an extreme, holding several dozen uncashed pay checks rather than deplete the company checking account during tough periods.

The only paperwork chore an entrepreneur despises more than filling out his

[8] My friend, Donald Dible, *Up Your Own Organization,* published by The Entrepreneur Press in 1972, claims a female entrepreneur is known as an entrepreneuse.

expense report is signing an employee's expense report. It's a failing of many entrepreneurs that they can't understand why every employee doesn't have their same desire to conserve the company's cash. Putting down every $4.25 cab fare or $1.95 lunch galls the hell out of them. As an employee of a small business, remember this wisdom about expense accounts, for it seems to be one of the infallible findings.

MANAGEMENT STYLE

In managing any business enterprise, a delicate balance exists between delegating and abdicating. It is a problem that plagues all businessmen in both profit and nonprofit enterprises. Entrepreneurs accomplish most tasks better and faster than their employees. It stands to reason: They have all the facts at their disposal, and they also have the authority, so there's no need to communicate with others in order to resolve the problem. They know what to do, so they just do it—and they do it at least three times faster and better. Hence, the issue of delegating is even more difficult in an entrepreneurial for-profit venture.

Sometimes all of this knowledge and authority vested in one person is bad—or at least not all good. Management theory teaches that authority and responsibility should always be in harmony. Yet there is often a serious imbalance between them in a small business. With all of this power vested in one person, the individual often tends to be in a hurry, to decide and do rather than to think, plan, and delegate. Given a choice between doing and thinking, an entrepreneur almost always chooses to do. This is one of the causes of an entrepreneur's mangerial ineffectiveness. They are poor delegators.

Such behavior not only eats up the valuable time of the leader, who should be involved in other, more productive tasks, but it also tends to destroy employee morale. Managing requires "skill in accomplishing tasks through other people." Entrepreneurs have difficulty in managing people. They have neither the patience nor the inclination to get down to the nitty-gritty of motivating an employee to perform. Perhaps it's because they tend to be more creative, or perhaps they're too self-centered, or perhaps they're too busy. Whatever the reason, they're not good at delegating, and when they do give power to a subordinate they usually abdicate and become totally uninvolved—unless they have to jump back in to put out the fire.

The same problem shows up in the sports world. A good player does not necessarily make a good manager. On the other hand, many great managers never attained great stature as players. Sport consists of a competitive game; and after each game a winner is declared—but this is not so in the competitive world of small business. Some of the findings in sports are transferable to other management disciplines. Small business seems to be such a case. Although only a few will agree on who was the greatest athlete, there is fairly good evidence to suggest that the most successful sports managers were not great players. For instance, the men below were not great players, but they are generally considered to be among the top of the list as managers:

Basketball	Red Auerbach
Football	Vince Lombardi, George Allen
Baseball	John McGraw, Casey Stengel

A great manager is seldom a great individual performer in the specific sport, whereas entrepreneurs are universally great as individual performers. It's rare to find them successful as managers, as teachers, or as trainees. Often the ease of performing well with a minimal effort stands in the way of a teacher. Often a teacher lacks the proper patience and self-discipline to bring the younger players along. "But how can that be?" you may ask. The reason is simple. The skills needed to be a good manager are not the same skills needed to be a good player. In business, the skills needed by an entrepreneur are not the same skills needed by a manager.

Some of the most successful entrepreneurs, like Edwin Land of Polaroid, have recognized their managerial limitations early in the game and hired others to fill the gaps. As a bonus, this allows the entrepreneur to capitalize on his own strengths and thus benefit his company even more. In Land's case, he maintains control of product decisions while leaving the day to day management operation to others.

Keeping the above traits in mind, an entrepreneur has a choice of either ignoring these findings or using them to his advantage. Naturally, a successful entrepreneur desires to have everything going for him, and this is how he overcomes the numerous insurmountable obstacles. A way of capitalizing on the entrepreneur's inherent inability to delegate is to select this talent in your partners or key employees. Below is a framework for an entrepreneur to use in picking a first mate.

The First Mates

	Stupid	Bright
Energetic	0	0
Lazy	0	X

Use this matrix when selecting an entrepreneur's management team.

"Energetic Stupid" is a poor choice, because he's forever starting new projects, talking out of turn at meetings, and asking the same question three times. And if he is really energetic he'll drive the whole company—and you—crazy.

The second choice, "Energetic Bright," has personality characteristics similar to your own. However, he's also a poor choice for your varsity. This "smart guy" usually alienates his peers on his way up the ladder. But you shouldn't keep him on the junior varsity solely because of his peers' distrust. If a person with these traits isn't his own entrepreneur, he'll soon be frustrated and develop ulcers. That's the reason to reject him—ulcers. Team members must be healthy.

The third choice, "Lazy Stupid," is the poorest of all, because the few tasks he actually finishes are done badly. He shouldn't even be in your company, never mind being chosen as a member of the management team.

The fourth choice, and bless this type, because companies are built around them, is "Bright and Lazy." He works well with the entrepreneur and doesn't try to surpass his energies. He'll let the entrepreneur put in more hours than he does so that they'll develop a mutual respect. He can be awfully clever at thinking of ways to get out of work and at getting others to do it for him. He's the best choice for your first mate—and then let him pick the varsity.

An entrepreneur who is able to understand his limitations is often better able to deal with his deficiencies. The business is all the better when these insights are used to advantage. Others need to develop insights into entrepreneurs as much as entrepreneurs need to develop insight into themselves. One of the quickest methods of gaining valuable insight into an entrepreneur is to learn the nature and style of his personal heroes.

Nearly every profession has its heroes. Visit any graduate school of law and you'll find portraits of Daniel Webster, Clarence Darrow, and other luminaries of the legal profession hanging in the halls. In the medical schools there are bound to be portraits of Hippocrates, Pasteur, or Paul Dudley White. These men are the universal heroes of their professions.

Do you know the name of the president of General Motors, General Foods, General Electric, or General Mills? I'll give you a hint: None of them are generals. In business, there are no universal heroes. The presidents of the biggest U.S. corporations are uncelebrated and unknown. The only portraits on the business school walls are those of the faculty.

Heroes in business are personal heroes. Nearly every entrepreneur has one—a man whose career he has followed, a man whom he admires and tries to emulate. The chosen idol may be only the neighborhood druggist or the operator of a taxicab, but he's a hero to an entrepreneur somewhere. Discover the identity of an entrepreneur's hero and you'll learn a lot about him. His ability to follow or parrot an inspiring person or message is unusual. Entrepreneurs understand their self-defined mission, and these heroes are often instrumental during the pursuit of the chosen destiny.

During the upward climb from a small business to a bigger enterprise, the style and manner of thinking of the entrepreneur's hero often plays a subconscious role. When an entrepreneur is backed into a corner and has no answer, he'll often muse, "What would so-and-so do in this case?" Most of the time he'd conclude that so-and-so just wouldn't get himself in such a pickle. But, putting that consideration aside, the entrepreneur often looks to the style of his hero in order to solve unsolvable dilemmas. During the upward climb, the entrepreneur often suffers from great exhilarations and depressions. The upward struggle is so energy-sapping that it creates unusual personality traits within would-be normal entrepreneurs.

One weakness to which many entrepreneurs are prone is the tendency to "fall in love" too easily. They go wild over new employees, products, suppliers, machines, and methods. Anything new excites them. These "love affairs" usually don't last long; many are over as suddenly as they begin, rather like a sudden summer shower. The problem is that during these affairs, the entrepreneur may alienate some people, be stubborn about listening to opposite views, and lose his objectivity. It's a dangerous trait if it's practiced with intense passion. A good medicine for this disease is to spend a few moments a day recalling past infatuations. While you're daydreaming about your past love affairs, extend the practice to just old fashioned daydreaming about anything at all. You see, daydreaming isn't all bad, as it tends to sharpen your subconscious ideas and, in turn, stimulate your hunches.

This tendency to be intuitive is not all bad, however. The process of guessing right and betting on hunches is a positive feature known as the entrepreneur's intuition. Rather than destroying the sensations of pursuing new, novel problem-solving methods, a wiser entrepreneur would only seek to control or modify his intuitive impulse. A careful program of checks and balances—which is monitored by a good financial officer or an active board of directors—can accomplish this objective. Ignoring the intuition could relegate one of the positive features of entrepreneurs to a neutral status. The controlling mechanism takes some prior planning to get established, but having a monitoring function in place prior to a crisis is the issue of an ounce of prevention versus a pound of cure. Organizing to capitalize on intuitive hunches while avoiding false love affairs is a trait well worth acquiring.

Most entrepreneurs are well organized when it comes to planning the use of their time and getting chores done. They all have a system. Some keep index cards or a notepad "jotter" in their inside jacket pocket on which they list the things to do.

They tick them off one by one as they're done. Others keep a neatly arranged "to do" list on their desks with about fifteen items listed. The first four or five items are usually crossed off. Still another type stuffs all of his pockets with little scraps of paper of every description on which he records ideas, things to do, and shopping lists. To keep track of what's been done, he changes the slips from one pocket to another pocket.

Take away his system, and you'll throw the poor chap off his stride for days. But don't knock it. Entrepreneurs almost universally possess the ability to tackle far more than the ordinary guy, and it's usually because they're superorganized.

The foregoing comments have been offered as insight into the riddle, "What makes an entrepreneur run?" Why is he more at home in his swivel chair than in his living room? What makes him willing to lose his wife, his wits, and even his wad—not once, but three or four times? Why can't he be happy working for someone else? Why does he always have to go it alone? What's with him, anyway? When the other kids were out playing ball, why was he busy hustling lemonade? When his friends were dating cheerleaders, why was he organizing rock concerts? Or marketing grandmother's pickle recipe? Or inventing a better fly swatter? Is he really smarter than the rest of us? Or just crazy?

What I concluded during my research was that, strangely enough, entrepreneurs do share many traits—too many to be purely coincidental. And, when I started to dig deeper, I hit on all kinds of weird phenomena.

The Entrepreneur's Quiz

Who is the entrepreneur? What molds him and what motivates him? How does he differ from the nine-to-fiver, and where are those differences most telling? Why will one brother set out to build a business, while another aspires to promotions and perks? Why does one stay up nights working on a business plan, while the other brags about his pension plan? Is it brains? Or luck? Is it hard work? Or does it just happen?

When most people think of entrepreneurs, names like Henry Ford, or Edwin Land, or even Famous (Wally) Amos automatically come to mind. But in fact, American entrepreneurs number in the millions. Of the fifteen million businesses in this country, over eleven million are operated as sole proprietorships. And while not all of these businesses can be labelled "entrepreneurial ventures," the dictionary definition of an entrepreneur is "one who manages, organizes, and assumes the risk of a business or enterprise."

Why then do we think of the entrepreneur in almost mythical terms? The answer is easy. Like the cowboys of the old American West, the entrepreneur represents freedom: freedom from the boss, freedom from the timeclock, and, with a lot of hard work and more than a little luck, freedom from the bank.

More importantly, entrepreneurs are the backbone of the free enterprise system. When an entrepreneur gambles on his skills and abilities, everyone stands to win. New and innovative products and services created by entrepreneurs constantly revitalize the marketplace and create thousands of new jobs in the process. One need look no further than the light bulb, the automobile, or most recently, the personal computer to see how entrepreneurs can change the country's way of life. What's more, nothing keeps a big corporation on its toes like an entrepreneur nipping at its heels—and its markets.

So who is the entrepreneur? Anyone who's ever looked at a problem and seen an opportunity, as well as a solution, is a likely prospect. The same goes for anyone who feels his ambition is being held in check by corporate red tape. But then it takes more than just cleverness and frustration to get an entrepreneurial venture off the ground. It takes guts, an indefatiguable personality, and nothing short of a total dedication to a dream. On top of that, it takes the kind of person who can call working 90 hours a week fun.

While there is no single entrepreneurial archetype, there are certain character traits which indicate an entrepreneurial personality. In this quiz we've tried to concentrate on those indicators. So if you've ever wondered if you have what it takes to be an entrepreneur, here is your chance to find out.[1]

THE ENTREPRENEURIAL ROOSTER

The tale begins with a farmer who has a chicken farm and the chickens have stopped laying eggs. The farmer, disgusted, "fires" all his roosters. He goes to the rooster market to get a new bunch, and while he is looking around he is approached by a short, suspicious-looking fellow who says: "I hear you're looking for about 40 new roosters, but I think you're crazy because it just so happens that I've got a real deal for you. Over here in the corner I've got a skinny little 'entrepreneurial' rooster. He can keep your whole hen house happy and they'll soon be laying eggs again." The farmer just laughed. "A rooster *that* size? Do you know how many hens I have?" But when the man offered the farmer a thirty-day money-back guarantee, he figured he really couldn't go wrong and decided to give the rooster a tryout.

After a few days, sure enough, the farmer saw that his hens were smiling, happy, and laying eggs. After about the tenth day, the farmer saw that his ducks, who lived next door to the chicken coop, were *also* smiling, happy, and laying eggs.

A few days after that, the farmer noticed that his eight-foot high pet ostrich was *also* smiling, happy, and laying eggs. Then, about a week later, the farmer noticed that his *cows* were giving twice as much milk as they used to. The farmer couldn't believe it—this skinny little rooster was single-handedly saving his farm from bankruptcy.

However the farmer, remembering his thirty-day money-back guarantee, still kept his eye on the rooster, just in case. On the morning of the 29th day, he looked out from his bedroom window, but he didn't see the rooster. He went outside and looked around, but the rooster was nowhere in sight. But far off in the desert the farmer saw a black cloud. He hopped into his pickup truck and drove off in that direction. When he got nearer, he saw a flock of vultures circling a limp form lying on the ground. "I *knew* he couldn't keep up that pace," the farmer thought. There the rooster lay, his tongue out and his head to one side; he was dead as a doornail.

The farmer felt that the rooster's death was a tragedy, a waste of an unusual kind of drive and spirit. But he also remembered that he could collect on the guarantee because the rooster was not going to be able to perform on the 30th day. He went over to pick the rooster up, throw him in the back of the truck and take him back to the farm. Just as he reached down, the rooster turned his head, pecked the farmer on the hand and said, "Cut it out and take a walk—this is the only way I can get those damn vultures!"

[1] This entrepreneurial profile was developed from a series of questionnaire analyses performed by The Center for Entrepreneurial Management, Inc. Founded in 1978, the Center is the world's largest non-profit association of entrepreneurial managers with over 2,500 members.

QUIZ

1. How were your parents employed?
   a. Both worked and were self-employed for most of their working lives.
   b. Both worked and were self-employed for some part of their working lives.
   c. One parent was self-employed for most of his or her working life.
   d. One parent was self-employed at some point in his or her working life.
   e. Neither parent was ever self-employed.

2. Have you ever been fired from a job?
   a. Yes, more than once.
   b. Yes, once.
   c. No.

3. Are you an immigrant, or were your parents or grandparents immigrants?
   a. I was born outside of the United States.
   b. One or both of my parents were born outside of the United States.
   c. At least one of my grandparents was born outside of the United States.
   d. Does not apply.

4. Your work career has been:
   a. Primarily in small business (under 100 employees).
   b. Primarily in medium-sized business (100-500 employees).
   c. Primarily in big business (over 500 employees).

5. Did you operate any businesses before you were twenty?
   a. Many.
   b. A few.
   c. None.

6. What is your present age?
   a. 21–30.
   b. 31–40.
   c. 41–50.
   d. 51 or over.

7. You are the _____ child in the family.
   a. Oldest.
   b. Middle.
   c. Youngest.
   d. Other.

8. You are:
   a. Married.
   b. Divorced.
   c. Single.

9. Your highest level of formal education is:
   a. Some high school.
   b. High school diploma.
   c. Bachelor's degree.
   d. Master's degree.
   e. Doctor's degree.

10. What is your primary motivation in starting a business?
    a. To make money.
    b. I don't like working for someone else.
    c. To be famous.
    d. As an outlet for excess energy.

11. Your relationship to the parent who provided most of the family's income was:
    a. Strained.
    b. Comfortable.
    c. Competitive.
    d. Non-existent.

12. You find the answers to difficult questions by:
    a. Working hard.
    b. Working smart.
    c. Both.

13. On whom do you rely for critical management advice?
    a. Internal management teams.
    b. External management professionals.
    c. External financial professionals.
    d. No one except myself.

14. If you were at the racetrack, which of these would you bet on?
    a. The daily double—a chance to make a killing.
    b. A 10-to-1 shot.
    c. A 3-to-1 shot.
    d. The 2-to-1 favorite.

15. The only ingredient that is both necessary and sufficient for starting a business is:
    a. Money.
    b. Customers.
    c. An idea or product.
    d. Motivation and hard work.

16. At a cocktail party, you:
    a. Are the life of the party.
    b. Never know what to say to people.
    c. Just fit into the crowd.
    d. You never go to cocktail parties.

17. You tend to "fall in love" too quickly with:
    a. New product ideas.
    b. New employees.
    c. New manufacturing ideas.
    d. New financial plans.
    e. All of the above.

18. Which of the following personality types is best suited to be your right-hand person?
    a. Bright and energetic.
    b. Bright and lazy.
    c. Dumb and energetic.

19. You accomplish tasks better because:
    a. You are always on time.
    b. You are super organized.
    c. You keep good records.

20. You hate to discuss:
    a. Problems involving employees.
    b. Signing expense accounts.
    c. New management practices.
    d. The future of the business.

21. Given a choice, you would prefer:
    a. Rolling dice with a 1-in-3 chance of winning.
    b. Working on a problem with a 1-in-3 chance of solving it in the time allocated.

22. If you could choose between the following competitive professions, your choice would be:
    a. Professional golf.
    b. Sales.
    c. Personnel counseling.
    d. Teaching.

23. If you had to choose between working with a partner who is a close friend and working with a stranger who is an expert in your field, you would choose:
    a. The close friend.
    b. The expert.

24. In business situations that demand action, clarifying who is in charge will help produce results.
    a. Agree.
    b. Agree, with reservations.
    c. Disagree.

25. In playing a competitive game, you are concerned with:
    a. How well you play.
    b. Winning or losing.
    c. Both of the above.
    d. Neither of the above.

Scoring

1. a–10	8. a–10	14. a–0	20. a–8
b–5	b–2	b–2	b–10
c–5	c–2	c–10	c–0
d–2		d–3	d–0
e–0			
2. a–10	9. a–2	15. a–0	21. a–0
b–7	b–3	b–10	b–15
c–0	c–10	c–0	
	d–8	d–0	
	e–4		
3. a–5	10. a–0	16. a–0	22. a–3
b–4	b–15	b–10	b–10
c–3	c–0	c–3	c–0
d–0	d–0	d–0	d–0
4. a–10	11. a–10	17. a–5	23. a–0
b–5	b–5	b–5	b–10
c–0	c–10	c–5	
	d–5	d–5	
		e–15	
5. a–10	12. a–0	18. a–2	24. a–10
b–7	b–5	b–10	b–2
c–0	c–10	c–0	c–0
6. a–8	13. a–0	19. a–5	25. a–8
b–10	b–10	b–15	b–10
c–5	c–0	c–5	c–15
d–2	d–5		d–0
7. a–15			
b–2			
c–0			
d–0			

1. The independent way of life is not so much genetic as it is learned, and the first school for any entrepreneur is the home. So, it's only natural that a child who has grown up in a home where at least one parent is self-employed is more likely to try

his hand at his own business than a child whose parents were in, say, the civil service. Our own research has shown this to be the case more than two-thirds of the time. Some good examples of this are Howard Hughes and New York real estate tycoon Donald Trump, both of whom parlayed modest family businesses into major fortunes.

2. This question is tricky because the independent-thinking entrepreneur will very often quit a job instead of waiting around to get fired. However, the dynamics of the situation are the same; the impasse results from the entrepreneur's brashness and his almost compulsive need to be right. Steven Jobs and Steven Wozniak went ahead with Apple Computer when their project was rejected by their respective employers, Atari and Hewlett-Packard. And when Thomas Watson was fired by National Cash Register in 1913, he joined up with the Computer-Tabulating-Recording Company and ran it until a month before his death in 1956. He also changed the company's name to IBM. The need to be right very often turns rejection into courage and courage into authority.

3. America is still the land of opportunity and a hotbed for entrepreneurship. The displaced people who arrive on our shores (and at our airports) every day, be they Cuban, Korean, or Vietnamese, can still turn hard work and enthusiasm into successful business enterprises. Fifteen years ago, Korean born entrepreneur K. Philip Hwang worked his way through college by sweeping the floors of a Lake Tahoe casino. Last March, Hwang took his company, TeleVideo, public, and his personal stock holdings are now valued at over $750 Million. Though it is far from a necessary ingredient for entrepreneurship, the need to succeed is often greater among those whose backgrounds contain an extra struggle to fit into society.

4. I've heard it said that "inside every corporate body, there's an entrepreneur struggling to escape." However, small business management is more than just a scaled down version of big business management. The skills needed to run a big business are altogether different from those needed to orchestrate an entrepreneurial venture. While the professional manager is skilled at protecting resources, the entrepreneurial manager is skilled at creating them. An entrepreneur is at his best when he can still control all aspect of his company. That's why so many successful entrepreneurs have been kicked out of the top spot when their companies outgrew their talents. Of course, that isn't always a tragedy. For many, it offers the opportunity (and the capital) to start all over again.

5. The enterprising adult first appears as the enterprising child. Coin and stamp collecting, mowing lawns, shoveling snow, promoting dances and rock concerts are all common examples of early business ventures. The paper route of today could be the Federal Express of tomorrow.

6. The average age of entrepreneurs has been steadily shifting downward since the late 50s and early 60s when it was found to be between 40 and 45. Our most recent research puts the highest concentration of entrepreneurs in their thirties, but people like Jobs and Wozniak of Apple Computer, Ed DeCastro and Herb Richman of Data General, and Fred Smith of Federal Express all got their businesses off the ground while still in their twenties. Although we look for this data to stabilize right around 30, there are always exceptions which leave us wondering. Computer whiz Jonathon Rotenberg is just such an exception. He currently presides over the 8,500 member Boston Computer Society, is the publisher of the slick magazine *Computer Update,* and earns up to $1,500 a day as a consultant. In 1978, Rotenberg's advice was solicited by the promoter of an upcoming public computer show. After conferring several times on the phone, the promoter suggested they meet for a drink to continue their discussions. "I can't," Rotenberg replied. When asked, "Why not?" Jonathan

answered, "Because I'm only 15." An established entrepreneur, Rotenberg is now all of 20 years old.

7. The answer to this question is always the same. Entrepreneurs are most commonly the oldest children in a family. With an average of 2.5 children per American family, the chances of being the first child are only 40%. However, entrepreneurs tend to be the oldest children more than 60% of the time.

In an interesting aside (and we're not quite sure what it means), a Mormon Church official has revealed that in cases of polygamous marriages, the first sons of the second or third marriage are generally more entrepreneurial than the first child of the first marriage.

8. Our research concluded that the vast majority of entrepreneurs are married. But then, most men in their 30s are married, so this alone is not a significant finding. However, follow-up studies have shown that most successful entrepreneurs have exceptionally supportive wives. (While our results did not provide conclusive results on female entrepreneurs, we suspect that their husbands would have to be doubly supportive.) A supportive mate provides the love and stability necessary to balance the insecurity and stress of the job. A strained marriage, the pressures of a divorce, or a strained love life will simply add too much pressure to an already strained business life.

It's also interesting to note that bankers and venture capitalists look a lot more favorably on entrepreneurs who are married than on entrepreneurs living with their mates without the benefit of clergy. And this is more of a pragmatic attitude than it is a moralistic one. A venture capitalist remarked to us the other day that "if an entrepreneur isn't willing to make a commitment to the woman he loves, then I'll be damned if I'm going to make any financial commitment to him."

9. The question of formal education among entrepreneurs has always been controversial. Studies in the 50s and 60s showed that many entrepreneurs, like W. Clement Stone, had failed to finish high school, not to mention college. And Polaroid's founder, Edwin Land has long been held up as an example of an "entrepreneur in a hurry" because he dropped out of Harvard in his freshman year to get his business off the ground.

However, our data concludes that the most common educational level achieved by entrepreneurs is the bachelors degree, and the trend seems headed toward the MBA. Just the same, few entrepreneurs have the time or the patience to earn a doctorate. Notable exceptions include An Wang of Wang Laboratories, Robert Noyce and Gordon Moore of Intel, and Robert Collings of Data Terminal Systems.

10. Entrepreneurs don't like working for anyone but themselves. While money is always a consideration, there are easier ways to make money than by going it alone. More often than not, money is a byproduct (albeit a welcome one) of an entrepreneur's motivation rather than the motivation itself.

11. These results really surprised us because past studies, including our own, have always emphasized the strained or competitive relationship between the entrepreneur and the income-producing parent (usually the father). The entrepreneur has traditionally been out to "pick up the pieces" for the family or to "show the old man," while at the same time, always seeking his grudging praise.

However, our latest study showed that a surprising percentage of the entrepreneurs we questioned had what they considered to be comfortable relationships with their income-producing parents. How do we explain this? To a large extent, we think it's directly related to the changing ages and educational backgrounds of the new entrepreneurs. The new entrepreneurs are children of the fifties and sixties, not the children of the Depression. In most cases they've been afforded the luxury of a college education, not forced to drop out of high school to help support the family. We think that the entrepreneur's innate independence has not come into such dramatic conflict with the father as it might have in the past. We still feel that a strained or competitive relationship best fits the entrepreneurial profile, though the nature of this relationship is no longer so black and white.

12. The difference between the hard worker and the smart worker is the difference between the hired hand and the boss. What's more, the entrepreneur usually enjoys what he's doing so much that he rarely notices how hard he's really working. I've always believed that a decision is an action taken by an executive when the information he has is so incomplete that the answer doesn't suggest itself. The entrepreneur's job is to make sure the answers always suggest themselves.

13. Entrepreneurs seldom rely on internal people for major policy decisions because employees very often have pet projects to protect or personal axes to grind. What's more, internal management people will seldom offer conflicting opinions on big decisions, and in the end the entrepreneur makes the decision on his own.

Outside financial sources are also infrequent sounding boards when it comes to big decisions because they simply lack the imagination that characterizes most entrepreneurs. The most noble ambition of most bankers and accountants is to maintain the status quo.

When it comes to critical decisions, entrepreneurs most often rely on outside management consultants and other entrepreneurs. In fact, our follow-up work has shown that outside management professionals have played a role in *every* successful business we've studied, which wasn't the case when it came to unsuccessful ventures.

14. Contrary to popular belief, entrepreneurs are not high risk takers. They tend to set realistic and achievable goals, and when they do take risks, they're usually calculated risks. They are very confident in their own skills and are much more willing to bet on their tennis or golf games than they are to buy lottery tickets or to bet on spectator sports. If an entrepreneur found himself in Atlantic City with just ten dollars in his pocket, chances are he'd spend it on telephone calls and not in slot machines.

15. All businesses begin with orders, and orders can only come from customers. You might think you're in business when you've developed a prototype or after you've raised capital, but bankers and venture capitalists only buy potential. It takes customers to buy products.

16. Like billionaire Daniel Ludwig, many entrepreneurs will adamantly state that they have *no* hobbies. But that doesn't mean that they have no social life. In fact, the entrepreneur is a very social person and, more often than not, a very charming person. (Remember, an entrepreneur is someone who gets things done, and getting things done often involves charming the right banker or supplier.) And while he will often only talk about things concerning himself or his business, his enthusiasm is such that anything he talks about sounds interesting.

17. One of the biggest weaknesses that entrepreneurs face is their tendency to "fall in love" too easily. They go wild over new employees, products, suppliers, machines, methods, and financial plans. Anything new excites them. But these "love affairs" usually don't last long; many of them are over almost as suddenly as they begin. The problem is that during these affairs, entrepreneurs can quite easily alienate their staffs, become stubborn about listening to opposing views, and lose their objectivity.

18. The answer to this question is easy: "bright and energetic," right; Wrong. The natural inclination is to choose "bright and energetic" because that describes a personality like your own. But stop and think a minute. You're the boss. Would you be

happy or, for that matter, efficient as someone else's right-hand man? Probably not. And you don't want to hire an entrepreneur to do a hired hand's job.

That's why the "bright and lazy" personality makes the best assistant. He's not out to prove himself so he won't be butting heads with the entrepreneur at every turn. And while he's relieved at not having to make critical decisions, he's a whiz when it comes to implementing them. Why? Because, unlike the entrepreneur, he's good at delegating responsibilities. Getting other people to do the work for him is his speciality!

19. Organization is the key to an entrepreneur's success. This is the fundamental principle on which all entrepreneurial ventures are based. Without it, no other principles matter. Organizational systems may differ, but you'll never find an entrepreneur who's without one. Some keep lists on their desks, always crossing things off from the top and adding to the bottom. Others use notecards, keeping a file in their jacket pockets. And still others will keep notes on scraps of paper, shuffling them from pocket to pocket in an elaborate filing and priority system. But it doesn't matter how you do it, just as long as it works.

20. The only thing an entrepreneur likes less than discussing employee problems is discussing petty cash slips and expense accounts. Solving problems is what an entrepreneur does best, but problems involving employees seldom require his intervention so discussing them is just an irritating distraction. Expense accounts are even worse. What an entrepreneur wants to know is how much his sales people are selling, not how much they're padding their expense accounts.

21. Entrepreneurs are participants, not observers; players, not fans. And to be an entrepreneur is to be an optimist, to believe that with the right amount of time and the right amount of money, you can do anything.

Of course, chance plays a part in anyone's career—being in the right place at the right time; but entrepreneurs have a tendency to make their own chances. I'm reminded of the story about the shoe manufacturer who sent his two sons to the Mediterranean to scout out new markets. One wired back: "No point in staying on. No one here wears shoes." The other son wired back: "Terrific opportunities. Thousands still without shoes." Who do you think eventually took over the business?

22. Sales gives instant feedback on your performance; it's the easiest job of all for measuring success. How does a personnel counselor or a teacher ever know if he's winning or losing? Entrepreneurs need immediate feedback and are always capable of adjusting their strategies in order to win. Some entrepreneurs brag that they play by the rules when they're winning and change the rules when they're losing. Although we don't endorse it (look what happened to John DeLorean), when it works it's known as the win/win strategy.

23. While friends are important, solving problems is clearly more important. Oftentimes, the best thing an entrepreneur can do for a friendship is to spare it the extra strain of a working relationship. By carefully dividing his work life and his social life, the entrepreneur insures that business decisions will always be in the best interest of his business.

24. Everyone knows that a camel is a horse that was designed by a committee, and unless it's clear that one person is in charge, decisions are bound to suffer from a committee mentality.

25. Vince Lombardi is famous for saying, "Winning isn't everything, it's the only thing," but a lesser known quote of his is closer to the entrepreneur's philosophy. Looking back at a season, Lombardi was heard to remark, "We didn't lose any games last season, we just ran out of time twice."

Entrepreneuring is a competitive game and an entrepreneur has to be prepared to run out of time, occasionally. Walt Disney, Henry Ford, and Milton Hershey all experienced bankruptcy before experiencing success. The right answer to this question is *c*, but the best answer is the game itself.

Your entrepreneurial profile

225–275 . . . . .Successful Entrepreneur[2]

190–224 . . . . .Entrepreneur

175–189 . . . . Latent Entrepreneur

160–174 . . . . Potential Entrepreneur

150–159 . . . . Borderline Entrepreneur

Below 149 . . . . .Hired Hand

[2] The CEM member profile is 234

Building An Entrepreneurial Team

THE ENTREPRENEUR'S LIFE CYCLE

Having a business of your own is not too different from having a child. You experience many of the same emotions and problems. And, as with a child, starting one is half the fun. However, only being a business starter is less than one half of the job. The hard part is to make a business successful.

All successful small businesses start with an idea and proceed through the classic entrepreneur's life cycle. Below is a life cycle for entrepreneurs.

Stage	I	The entrepreneur's early development
Stage	II	The idea stage
Stage	III	The start-up problem
Stage	IV	The venture financing
Stage	V	The growth crisis
Stage	VI	The maturity crisis
Stage	VII	The impossible transition

One of the interesting aspects of small business is the team built around the entrepreneur. A talented entrepreneur recognizes that the central fact of management is "accomplishing tasks through other people." An ineffective entrepreneur tries to do everything himself. This raises the classic issue of delegating, which is often contrary to the entrepreneur's natural tendencies.

The vast majority of successful small companies were built around an entrepreneur team and not a single entrepreneur. In fact, partnerships are an increasingly effective method of balancing each entrepreneur's strengths and weaknesses to produce a well-balanced top management team.

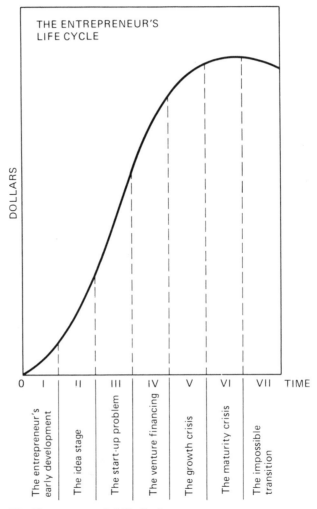

The Entrepreneur's Life Style

Some of the most successful companies were launched by two equal partners who complement one another. Rolls and Royce, the founders of the prestigious British motor car company bearing their names, were totally opposite in philosophies and lifestyles. One was Mr. Inside and the other Mr. Outside, but together they were an effective entrepreneurial team. The same holds for the largest consumer goods company, Proctor & Gamble. The team allows balance and strength to exist in the enterprise. The stronger the team, the more powerful the company. It's the synergistic concept of two plus two being equal to five.

Franklin Delano Roosevelt summed up the process this way, "I'm not the smartest fellow in the world, but I can sure pick smart colleagues." He claimed: "Because I'm not so smart, I have to surround myself with real talent." The entrepreneur who can adopt this same philosophy will select the following members of the team.

1. Partners
2. Lawyers
3. Accountants
4. Bankers
5. Consultants
6. Board of Directors—Angels
7. Advertising Agencies
8. The Controller

Following is a commentary on the roles of these team members. I shall also try to provide insight into the process of building a team of professionals.

PARTNERS

A partner can be a blessing or a curse. Whether you take one, or more, into your business venture depends on your needs for additional depth in management, marketing, technology, or financing.

Selecting your business partners is not much different from choosing your wife, and it should be done with the same care. More, perhaps, because the wrong partner can put the entire venture in jeopardy. Marriages are relatively easy to start. A marriage license and a blood test only cost a few dollars. If one fails, you can try again. In business it's not so easy.

I advise finding a partner whose talents complement your own, but whose business philosophy, personality, and background differ. The most successful companies are formed with two partners whose combined abilities give depth to the enterprise, and whose differing backgrounds serve as a buffer against excesses of any kind. You both may disagree and you both may have conflicts, but usually they are over business issues rather than personalities. A good marketing/financial man is an ideal partner for a strong production/engineering type, but two optimists or two pessimists can kill a business before it has a chance to get off the ground. The outside and inside philosophy has also been applied to David Packard, former Secretary of Defense (Mr. Outside) and to his equally talented, but less outgoing partner, William Hewlett (Mr. Inside). Even the discount retail revolution was launched by a partnership and not a lone entrepreneur, Two Guys, from Harrison.

Once you have selected your partner, you should immediately agree to disagree. From my experience in mediating between partners, I never become concerned about disagreements. They are akin to fights between alley cats: After all the scrapping, the only result seems to be more cats. The success of a partnership depends on arriving at sensible business decisions through cooperation and equal participation.

Every partnership should have a "godfather." Not the kind made famous in Mario Puzo's novel about the underworld, but one who is trusted and respected by both partners and who can serve as a mediator to help resolve conflicts. This helps unstick the sticky problems in the 50–50 partnerships.

This "godfather" should be unbiased; he should have little or no vested interest in the company. He can be a business acquaintance, a friend, a college professor, or someone respected in the technology of your business. Bring him into the picture right at the beginning and keep him abreast of what goes on so he can understand the causes of any problems.

If you're lucky and if the situation is very unusual, you may never require him to do more than settle minor disputes or serve as a sounding board for new ideas. If worst comes to worst, however, and you must dissolve the partnership, the "godfather" may be the only one who can keep the pieces together long enough for the company to gain its equilibrium and survive. Remember, nothing lasts forever. But the business, if it survives at all, will most likely outlive the partnership.

LAWYERS

How to Form Your Own Corporation Without a Lawyer for Under $50, a book written by Nick Peterson, seems to imply that incorporating a small business can be a homemade process. I don't disagree. It can be done cheaper on your own, but I suggest that the first step in starting a business game is to see a lawyer. Not just so he or she can incorporate the business to avoid the legal disadvantages in a proprietorship, but to begin a long relationship. Selecting a proprietorship as the form of your new business can leave you and your assets exposed to law suits by unsatisfied creditors. Using a corporate format will strongly discourage unsecured creditors from suing any individual of the management to collect unsecured unpaid corporate bills. A corporation will seldom protect an individual from repaying secured bank debt, as almost all banks require a small business person to sign two ways—first, as the president of the corporation and second, as an individual. Hence, secured creditors such as banks, receive payment from either the corporation or the individual responsible for the management of the business. Unsecured creditors, traditionally known as the accounts payable, are legally discouraged from pursuing any management individual to collect unsecured debts. This level of legal protection for a corporation is not available to a sole proprietor, and often the small business person is responsible for all debts, secured and unsecured. It's not the money you save that counts but the headaches you avoid by having competent legal advice from the beginning. I say step one in the start-a-business-process is to see a good lawyer. You can still buy Ted Nicholas's book, but I would not recommend any homemade legal advice.

The lawyer is one of the critical elements in any business. He or she is a full-fledged team member and many times he captains the team. Hence, he or she must be well qualified. I'd suggest going into the city to select your lawyer and choosing the Securities and Exchange Commission (SEC) which regulates security markets, or corporate specialist at one of the prestigious law firms. Your lawyer will know how to take companies public, how to set up tax shield stock plans, and how to keep all the liabilities to a minimum (Form and Name of the Enterprise). One good lawyer is worth a dozen bad ones; a good lawyer is one of the most important and critical players on your management team.

ADVERTISING AGENCIES

Most entrepreneurs tend to avoid advertising agencies or they put off hiring one until they hit an impasse in their marketing plans. Then it may be too late. I believe in finding a good, small (no more than ten men) agency early.

With advertising agencies, unlike law firms or public accounting firms, the largest is not always the best for the small businessman. With a small agency, you'll get the attention—and probably plenty of it—of the top man.

The agency is often a junior member of the team but they should be selected early. An integrated corporate communications concept for letterheads, business cards, envelopes, and logos will establish a corporate identity that blends well together. It makes a big difference when all the corporate communications are well coordinated from the beginning. It avoids the embarrassment of not looking professional or of not being taken seriously.

Once you've found the right advertising agency, give them their head. Don't tell them what colors *you* like. Be candid and honest, and give them all the information you can about your product and your markets—but don't impose your artistic talents. The more you give them, the more they'll be able to give you.

When it comes to agency compensation, don't rely on the old fifteen percent of the media costs method. This old method of compensating for agency efforts was very simple. Most approved media will allow an accredited agency to deduct a 15% discount very much like the airlines allow a travel agency a 15% discount. Hence, an advertising agency that annually placed $100,000 of media billing for a client would be indirectly compensated by paying the various media $85,000 while billing the client the published rates of $100,000. First of all, it's impossible for an agency to work profitably on a straight commission basis unless your media expenditures are considerable. Remember, they're in business to make a profit, too. Furthermore, it tends to create a conflict of interest for the agency, since it is to their advantage if your advertising dollars go into a commissionable media. The best course for your company may be direct mail or some other noncommissionable medium. Do you want the agency working for your company or for the commissionable advertising media? There is a possible conflict between what is good for the media and what is good for the client. An agency that is singularly reimbursed for commission media, print or electronic, may be unreceptive to designing brochures or trade literature because the printing commissions may be less than the earned discount from the commissionable media. An estimate of the annual advertising budget should be the foundation for determining an agency's compensation. This allows a fuller, fairer choice of the optimal allocations between commissionable and noncommissionable activities.

The most practical and fairest method of agency compensation is a monthly retainer fee which amounts to about ten percent more than the commissions they would receive on annual forecasted commissionable media expenditures. This method eliminates the conflict of interest and lets the agency worry about what's best for you, not about what's best for them.

ACCOUNTANTS

Another person you'll want to get on board at the earliest moment is a top-flight certified public accountant (CPA). Numbers are the language of business management, and intelligent decisions require an understanding of the quantitative factors involved.

If you have hopes for expansion or for going public, line up one of the big accounting firms. A merely adequate accountant is suicide. A big, well-known firm immediately lends credibility to your numbers; and, when the time comes for that public offering, three years of audited statements from one of the big names adds plenty of status. Don't worry about a big firm being too expensive. Most of them have separate divisions for small businesses. They'll install a one-write check system (which can save hours of work and improve your accuracy) and an accounts-payable voucher register (so you'll know who you owe money to), proof of your receivables (so you'll know who owes you money), and set up all the necessary financial systems to help you avoid unnecessary false starts.

_ Next, introduce your lawyer and your accountant to your banker. There will be plenty of decisions where their functions overlap, so they should know one another from the outset.

BANKERS

Pick a banker, not a bank. If he is with a large bank, or a bank with a captive small business investment company (SBIC), so much the better. Many bankers are really venture capitalists in disguise and they can be sources of valuable financial assistance.

Here again, forget the big titles and pick a young loan officer or assistant vice president: Then gain his confidence. Supply him or her with detailed pro forma cash flow projections to show what your cash needs will be. Simply stated, this is a cash plan which estimates the future incoming cash and subtracts the estimated future cash needs of the business. The difference will be the estimated future cash needs (or excess cash) generated by the business. Then meet or exceed your projections. Getting financial aid will be easy from then on.

In working with your friendly banker you'll soon learn that he expects you to countersign your company's bank debt personally. Don't let it throw you. It's the only way he or she has to certify your numbers and your confidence in what you're doing. But don't take this responsibility lightly, either. It's easy for you to be overly optimistic, and that can get you into a lot of trouble. Before you sign that note, take a good, hard look at those figures again. That signature on the back of the note isn't an autograph—unless you become very, very famous. The countersignature on a bank note means that you, as an individual, are personally responsible for the debts. In the event that the business goes into bankruptcy and is unable to meet the financial obligation which bears your countersignature; the lender can seek the difference between what is collected and what is owed from you as the countersigner of the debt.

If you have inventory and/or receivables, you may be able to avoid the countersignature; or you may at least be able to limit your personal vulnerability by assigning them to the bank. If the worst happens and the bank has to go after your security, it is better that the bank secures the company's inventory, not your wife's diamond ring. Some states protect your home from creditors or bankers trying to collect against a bankrupt company under the Homestead Act. The Homestead Act originated years ago to protect farmers who often lost their farms when they were unable to meet the payments for large farm equipment. The states individually passed legislation in the 1800s that protected a person's primary residence from creditors other than the principal mortgage holder. But, to gain this level of additional protection, a short two-page document must be filed prior to any seizure attempts by creditors. It's all very complicated, very legal and it varies from state to state. But all of these issues point out the reason you selected a good lawyer first. Ask your lawyer how to do it, that's why lawyers are paid so well.

BOARD OF DIRECTORS

There is no doubt that the most crucial single personification of an entrepreneur's management team is the board of directors. A board of directors is charged with establishing policy level decisions. A well-balanced board of directors adds depth to a small, under-staffed enterprise. When the board is composed of respected business advisors who meet periodically and debate policy and develop corporate strategies, then the company is operating on a solid foundation.

Unfortunately, too many small businesses do not have actual board of directors. The entrepreneur who is concerned with day to day activities often ignores the potential advantages of establishing a balanced board of directors. The board of directors is often comprised of a wife and father who never influence business issues. They are rubber stamps in the true sense of the word.

Whether to choose accountants, lawyers, bankers, or others to serve on the board of directors is a puzzle with no single answer. Rather, the answer depends on the other talents of the individuals and on the needs of the company. The only group who consistently offers a universal appeal as board members is a group affectionately labeled "angels." These seasoned investors/businessmen are often the nucleus of a good working board of directors.

Angels are hard to find, but they do exist. They're those marvelous people who descend from the heavens just to invest in small companies. No, they're not supernaturals. Usually they are just successful, wealthy businessmen, who, instead of putting their money in the stock market, investing in mutual funds, or buying savings bonds, invest a portion of their wealth in young businesses.

This is the best sort of investor/director. Such an individual usually joins the team at the founding level and stays with the company until it makes a public offering. Often he makes useful contacts for the company. When more money is needed, he is usually the first to step forward. Most angels have invested between $100,000 and $200,000 in several small businesses, keeping their stake in each venture below $50,000. They are likely to be the only nonemployee investors in the companies. To top it off, they're usually the salt of the earth: nice people—but smart. As venture capitalists, they are better to do business with than with any other alternative. They don't value their advice as highly as a professional venture capitalist, even though it's usually better; they don't value their money as highly as a professional venture capitalist, because they don't have large fixed costs for offices and the like. Compared to doctor and lawyer money, angels are seldom nervous or irrational over business problems as they grew up in business, not in law or medicine. If you can find one (in a city the size of Boston there are probably only 100 angels), you can't go wrong by bringing him into the financing arrangements. Then go the extra step to involve him in a balanced board of directors who meet monthly and debate business policies vigorously.

MANAGEMENT CONSULTANTS

Entrepreneurs, more then other businessmen, rely on other people—such as professional management consultants, college professors, other company presidents, or anyone else who can intelligently offer advice and objectivity.

These people serve as sounding boards for the entrepreneur's ideas and help him weigh alternatives before making the final decision. In other fields—such as government, the military, and even sports—these sounding boards exist internally in the form of staff assistants.

Since small businesses can't afford droves of staff assistants, they have to rely on external sources; and this has led to the emergence of professional management consultants for small businesses. The management consultant (M.C.) is usually a person with a broad range of knowledge in the management of businesses, and he applies that experience to your problems in order to guide you in the right direction. Ultimately, the decision is always yours; but the M.C. plays a vital role in helping you see flaws and correct them before you implement the plan. The M.C. is often the source for new creative concepts, too.

In order to demonstrate the emergence of the management consultant, I counted the number of consulting firms listed in the Yellow Pages in various cities and noted their increase over the years. The results are shown in Table 3-1 presented on page 43. Apparently there is no other means to prove this point, as neither the government nor any association compiles statistics on the number of management consulting firms by city. I believe the data demonstrate the growth, and thereby the value, of the service.

Strangely enough, many small businesses use the services of management consultants successfully. They can often provide the frosting on the cake, but should never be over-extended to provide the cake. That's the job of the entrepreneur. This is often confusing or misunderstood by a struggling small businessperson who is unsure of the economic return from a small business consultant. If the business succeeds, it's because of the entrepreneur, not the adviser. The same if it fails. The consultant only provides help, guidance and assistance, and he is never the pivotal difference between success and failure in a small growing enterprise. That's the job of the entrepreneur.

Table 3.1 Number of Management Consultant Firms in Yellow Pages by Year

City	1951	1960	1963	1964	1965	1969	1970	1974	1975	1976	1981	1988
Boston	17		60			178				365	450	560
Chicago					268		449				675	640
Los Angeles		112			225		337	340				833
Philadelphia					108		158		182			246
Washington, D.C.				111						401	435	593

MANUFACTURER'S REPRESENTATIVES

The manufacturer's representative or rep is the mainstay of the sales force of most small businesses. They are independent businessmen, entrepreneurs in their own right, peddling the merchandise of several manufacturers rather than just one.

Reps don't add to a company's fixed costs. They're paid on a commission basis according to what they sell. Because of this, a small company can afford to maintain a respectable sales force without incurring large fixed overhead costs.

The rep is also a valuable source of industry intelligence. He is a kind of mercenary soldier, stomping through the industrial mud as a commissioned member of several armies. If anyone knows what's going on, he does. He's the sage of his industry.

When you latch onto a good rep (there are some poor ones), hold onto him—even when it's time to hire an inside man. Many companies make special arrangements with their best reps to keep them on. It's good for the company; and it's good for the rep, who lives in fear of selling himself right out of a good line. If a rep performs too well in a territory, many small companies get confused and suddenly believe that the best alternative would be to fire the rep and hire a direct salaried salesman. A manufacturer may eventually decide that a certain territory is lucrative enough to support a full time company employee. This cost efficient decision will occur at different levels for different companies and products. A cost efficient decision is elusive in practice but easily explained in theory. It's elusive because the opening assumption usually proves to be misleading. The question is, given the same sales in both cases, when is an independent, commissioned agent less expensive than a salaried full-time company salesman? The answer is, of course, when less commissions are paid to the agents than salary which would have been paid to the salesmen, for a given level of sales. Whenever the crossing point occurs for a sales territory, it is commonly thought to be more cost efficient to replace the commissioned agent with a salaried employee. But always watch out for the assumptions.

It is useful to clarify this issue in the early stages of business growth, for many small companies begin with manufacturer's representatives and eventually shift to full time company paid salesmen. The issue is, "What are the trade-offs in making these decisions?" They are both qualitative and quantitative reasons to prefer one type of sales force to another.

The qualitative advantages of each are listed below.

Manufacturer's Representatives:

1. A commissioned agent who receives compensation only when he sells something.
2. Usually the representative firm has a number of persons covering a single territory instead of just one person.
3. A manufacturer's representative also sells products for other manufacturers, and this can help them in merchandising complementary products.
4. The nature of their specialization makes them knowledgeable about their territory and their customers.
5. The marketing effort by a team of experienced reps is usually more efficient than a headquarters directed effort at identifying and merchandising.

Company Salesmen:

1. Loyalty undoubtedly rests with the single employer and is not scattered among many manufacturers.
2. Willing to invest effort to develop new products or to maintain service to customers, both of which may be less income productive than pursuing other activities.
3. More efficient above a certain sales volume.
4. Able to develop better inside managers by having them initially perform at field sales.
5. Able to control sales activities better.

THE CONTROLLER

Show me a successful small company with great growth potential and I'll show you a company with a talented financial man keeping his thumb on the cash flow—the company controller. This is the person who passes on all company expenditures. He's also the one who manages to get the quarterly audit done, in spite of last quarter's foolish mistakes.

When given the chance, he'll vote "no" 80 percent of the time. He frustrates everyone with his pessimism, and is accused of throwing cold water on every good idea. Production doesn't like him because he refuses to sign purchase orders. Sales doesn't like him because he gives them a hard time about expense reports.

The controller is never popular—he doesn't smile or tell jokes—but he's the one person in the company who can provide the balance it needs. With him, there's temperance. Without him, there could be a drunken spending spree that might cripple a small, young company or a growing old one. This financial genius, along with the first mate,[1] are the two most crucial picks in your draft of management talent. Let's call them the first two rounds of the draft, or the number one and two draft picks.

Entrepreneurs often make fatal mistakes in selecting the financial specialist. This is especially true of the Boston Route 128 technical types. Typically, they are unfamiliar with finance, as compared to their extensive engineering and technical knowledge. Hence, in selecting the financial genius, they often rely on those with college degrees rather than on those with proven experience on the job.

Consequently, technical entrepreneurs hire business school MBAs (Masters in Business Administration) the way some large firms hire minority groups. It's the thing to do—especially if those hired are finance majors. Entrepreneurs tend to be infatuated with the MBA—the brash kid in his late twenties who knows all the answers and all the buzz-words, like "game plan" and "M.B.O."—Management by Objectives, a managing technique made famous by Mr. Peter Drucker.

The trouble with most of today's business school graduates is that they have more answers than there are questions. It may sound strange, but too many solutions can create a problem Furthermore, it's claimed they get too much money and change jobs too often.

In my experience with MBAs in small business, I have found that they spend most of their time analyzing their employer and the company. The ones who excel in small business management are running their own companies. They won't work for entrepreneurs; they *are* entrepreneurs. Think twice before you offer an unusually high salary for a would-be soothsayer.

If you must hire one of the new MBAs, try to find one who is in his second or third job. A little experience under his belt could do you a lot of good. A person with an MBA in finance or marketing, who is looking for his third job and who has some small company experience, could be the right medicine for your company. This is especially true for retail businesses because of the unique nature of retailing. In retailing, it's often best to wait until the MBA is past the age of 40, regardless of the number of previous jobs. A certain maturity plus an MBA is extremely powerful medicine, even for certain sick businesses.

[1] See my comments and The First Mate Chart on page 17.

FINANCING A SMALL BUSINESS

Venture Capitalists

Venture capitalists are the people whose business is investing money in starting and expanding businesses. However you feel about them, venture capitalists play a vital role in the founding and eventual success—or failure—of many entrepreneurial ventures.

Usually the relationship between entrepreneurs and their venture capitalists is tense. Beneath the outward cordiality and camaraderie, the sentiment is often one of mutual mistrust. You can't blame either of them, really. The venture capitalist, on the one hand, has what must be one of the world's toughest jobs: evaluating the potential of businesses that, in reality, are little more than pro forma cash flows and an entrepreneur's dream. It's a risky business. On the other hand, the entrepreneur knows he is going to make the venture capitalist wealthy beyond his fondest hopes, and so he finds it hard to understand the need for so much unnecessary deliberation.

Attracting venture capital has been called a form of Russian Roulette, or the "You bet your company" game. Both venture capitalists and entrepreneurs play the game, each with his own tools. Venture capitalists bet on people and managements; but entrepreneurs judge that people and managements are unreliable and so choose to bet on products and technologies. Thus the competition is between players with different combat weapons. It's an exciting contest. The entrepreneur tries to build a company and prove his point. The venture capitalist tries to make money by backing highly speculative enterprises. It isn't difficult to understand why the two don't fit comfortably together.

Entrepreneurs are poor venture capitalists, and vice versa, but each needs the other. They can coexist peacefully, even profitably, so long as each recognizes the other's objectives. Many big deals have resulted from such recognition. However, these views of the venture capital/entrepreneur relationship are not in concert with the views of most small business people. Before you disagree with my notions on venture financing, let me make one thing perfectly clear. My views are in the minority. Most venture capitalists don't agree with my position. Most don't believe in the prime criteria being the chosen product area; they don't believe in premature public stock offering.[1] They don't like what I have to say on this issue, period. But I am reporting the situation as I have seen it through the eyes of the entrepreneur—and we can't both be right!

The vast majority and also the better venture capitalists subscribe to the axiom, "We bet on top flight management." They repeat it over and over, and they mean it down deep—they bet on people. The background, education, and experience of the management are the pivotal inputs for their investment decisions. I prefer to judge the product, the product concept, and the general product area. By this I mean the nature of the product and the market. Later in this text I shall refer to this by the fancy term, the nature of what the business takes to market. In that commentary, I nickname this the heart of the business. The product area is on target when customers are willing to exchange cash for your product or service time and again, and it costs you very little to produce or provide it. I say you have a winning product area. I say it's even more crucial than the pedigree of your management team.

I claim venture capitalists are wrong—and I stand firmly behind that claim. I believe that an uneasiness exists between venture capitalists and entrepreneurs at all venture stages. My reasons are straightforward. Each is in a different business; each is from a different school; each plays a different ballgame with different rules. Most venture capitalists have seldom had to raise money for a new business enterprise. True, the good ones have had to raise money for their venture portfolios—but not for a new business enterprise, not for something with a product or a service concept. They have raised investment funds, a few of them, for a cause and a concept. I claim that difference is vital.

Entrepreneurs are poor venture capitalists and venture capitalists are poor entrepreneurs. I claim each should recognize that this phenomenon is as infallible as the more popular notion that entrepreneurs are poor managers and managers are poor entrepreneurs. The transition between venture capitalists and entrepreneurs is shaky at best. That doesn't mean that we shouldn't admire and respect a good venture capitalist. I do, very much. It is truly an unusual talent that enables a person to make money by investing in other people. But that doesn't make a venture capitalist a good entrepreneur.

HOW TO RAISE VENTURE CAPITAL

Given the preceding relationship between entrepreneurs and venture capitalists, how do they manage to coexist peacefully, and, at times, seem to prosper? Given the number of times a venture capitalist is told an exaggeration, how does he manage to believe the next entrepreneur looking for money? How does an entrepreneur raise money to launch or keep afloat a new exciting business? The answer, I claim, rests in part with the ever-improving skills of entrepreneurs seeking money. I call this skill broken-field running. A broken field runner is so much more colorful and effective than a straight-ahead plunger because he's always only an inch from danger and a second away from success. He remains totally visible as he cuts, spins, and turns during his mad dash toward the goal.

[1] A stock offering is generally considered premature if the stock fails to perform in the after market. In other words, if a stock is originally issued at $10.00 per share and is actually selling at $5.00 per share several months later, the offering is considered premature.

Here is the core reason I believe broken-field running is a necessary part of the entrepreneurial process. I can cite a handful of companies which have succeeded despite the company management: They have made all the management mistakes possible; they have hired the wrong banker, lawyer, and accountant; and yet they have succeeded. I can also cite companies that have failed—companies that have made limited management mistakes. Here's the vital difference: Almost every situation that has failed has attracted funds. That's how it qualified to be a failure. Without funds, a business doesn't become a company or even become recognized: The business without funds dies at the idea stage. Millions of businesses do that every year! To be classified as a failure you first have to have started. Otherwise your business will remain just an idea.

What is broken-field running? Raising venture capital often parallels trying to make a touchdown through the best defense in the league. It takes fancy footwork to work your way over that goal line.

Let's say you want to raise $250,000 for 25 percent of your company in a private placement. A private placement of funds into a business is any type of equity financing which is not considered a public (open to everyone) stock offering. First, you must get a venture capitalist lukewarm about your situation. No one will be really enthusiastic after only one visit. I've heard that Digital Equipment Corporation (DEC) of Maynard, Massachusetts shopped around for quite awhile before American Research and Development Corporation (ARD) finally committed itself to the tune of $70,000, an investment which, rumor has it, is worth $300,000,000 today.

Venture capitalists see dozens of deals a day, so it will not be easy to turn them on to your proposition. Besides, they are like sheep. They'd rather follow than lead. An entrepreneur has to be the sheep dog to keep the pack moving.

Once you've gotten the first party lukewarm, the remaining strategy must be planned carefully.

One strategy that usually works begins on the second visit, when you say, "I know you're not in a position to go first in this package, but I have a proposition that should interest you. I already have other investors subscribed for the first $200,000. You can have the last $50,000. You don't have to sign anything—just give me a verbal commitment contingent on my getting the other $200,000 first."

If he agrees, then repeat your story to anyone else who seems to be lukewarm and proceed to sell the last $50,000 five times. You have to deal from strength—and that takes broken-field running skills. The example may be a little farfetched, because someone has to go first. He's the one who counts and the hardest one to find—not a sheep but a true *venture* capitalist.

This is the man who'll set the pace for the rest of the deal. Once he has spoken up, or at least said, "Well, maybe," ask him for some sort of tentative percentages and terms. And after you've negotiated the terms, get a letter of intent for his share of the investment which details the terms of the placement. You may have to make a few concessions to him, but once you have his pledge on paper—or even verbally—your placement is in the bag and you should have the rest within two months. Touchdown!

Always talk to potential investors as if your deal is all but closed and you may have to eliminate two or three investors from the package. Never act as if you need their help or you'll be tackled before you reach midfield; rather, suggest that this one time you'll accept their money. I can't overemphasize the need to deal from strength in order to succeed as a broken-field runner.

Venture capitalists have a batting average of less than two successes in ten tries. Consequently, they are understandably familiar with failing: It's a common part of their business. Failure happens much more frequently than success. The entrepreneur, however, gets only one attempt—or possibly two—at success. If he fails, it's all over—at least for awhile. Now that's a whopping big difference.

To have the opportunity to fail is the yearning of the would-be entrepreneur. Lord Tennyson claimed, " 'Tis better to have loved and lost than never to have loved at all." Loving and starting businesses are both tricky processes. I offer no advice about loving. But in order to start a business successfully, an entrepreneur must treat a venture capitalist as a resource, just as he treats accountants, lawyers, consultants, and bankers. You never fully oblige yourself to a resource; rather, you employ it as long as it produces more than it costs. Someday it may be replaced, so don't grow totally dependent on it—at least no more dependent than on any other resource.

A statement of a venture capitalist I admire is more in keeping with my views. He said, "Don't think of this process as me giving you money to start your business; it is more appropriately thought of as you giving your stocks to buy some of my money." That's the right philosophy; and I urge every aspiring entrepreneur to consider those thoughts before disagreeing with me and arguing with the views of the venture capitalists.

Venture capitalists always claim that they bet on management when making an investment. They'd like you to believe that the people involved—your investors, future investors, and the board of directors included—form the axis about which your success revolves. Here is the second place I disagree with traditional venture capitalists.

I'll take exception to making investments based on management's abilities. A good product is what I choose to bet upon. I've seen plenty of talented men, who had no trouble raising venture money, fall flat with poor products; and I've seen some no-talents succeed on the strength of a good product.

Right now, at the first stages of your new venture, remember that the most important ingredient is the customers for the product—or service—not the talents of the employers. Good people will be easy to find once the product has been proven in the marketplace. Don't let the venture capitalists scare you in this issue. If they're so smart, how come they succeed in only about two out of ten ventures?

This is a chicken and egg debate to some degree. I claim the product and the market must possess two fundamental ingredients in order to warrant a venture investment. The venture capitalists claim the quality and depth of the management are the criteria for when to invest. My two fundamental product and market ingredients are:

1. Many, many customers must be willing to exchange cash for your product (market ingredient).
2. There must be a large difference between your product's selling price and the product total cost (product ingredient).

In other words, many customers must be willing to buy your product in large quantities and to pay a high relative price for it. In the event your business is a service business, such as a retail store,[2] this translates into:

1. Many customers must shop at your store (market ingredient).
2. These customers must pay much more for your merchandise than you pay for it (product ingredient).

_____

[2] Incidentally, there are three ingredients necessary for success in any type of retail business: 1) location, 2) location, and 3) location.

These are the preferred criteria for successful investing and for successful small businesses. The difference between this view and the financier's philosophy can be explained to some degree. Venture capitalists often claim the quality of management is most precisely gauged by their expertise in selecting the proper market and product. A "good" management, they claim, would necessarily select a product and market which fully agrees with my two fundamental product and market ingredients above. So, the difference may be partially a semantic one. But then again, so-called good management may not select winning formulas for product and market.

Of the several hundred small firms I've worked with, the product area chosen has made the difference. The pattern for a success unfolds when someone discovers or identifies a product which has enormous demand—you know, a product for which customers are willing to exchange cash. Ray Stata and Matthew Lorber, the cofounders of Analog Devices, Inc. in Norwood, Massachusetts, started this business when they were both pushing thirty. Their product was a full line of operational amplifiers (op-amps) sold to the electronics industry. Matt and Ray claim they started all wrong with too little capital, the wrong lawyer, banker, and accountant. Their initial selection of top managers provided only one person who lasted beyond five years. Yet, in 1983, from a beginning in 1966, Analog Devices will ship and bill over $250,000,000 worth of operational amplifiers and employ in excess of 1,000 people. Their product, with the aid of hindsight and the market and several prudent product decisions, continually pulled them over the hump during the many initial start-up crises. The enterprise may make all the classic management mistakes, but the strength of the product pulls the business over the hill. Good management can fail with a poor product, so choose both the product and the market wisely.

THE STRUCTURE OF VENTURE CAPITAL

The name of the game for every entrepreneur is "Raising Money." For all but a chosen few, it's the hardest part of starting a business—and the most rewarding when you are successful at it.

People who invest in new business enterprises run the gamut from public investors to private doctors and lawyers to "angels" and institutional investors. Each has his own special characteristics and peculiarities with which every entrepreneur should be familiar.

At the end of the spectrum is the "itchy" money. These are the nonprofessionals who invest with high expectations for quick profit and provide little, if any, management assistance. At the other end are the professionals who seem to worry little about their money but who pride themselves in the caliber of help and advice they can give the management. Somewhere between these two extremes lies the happy medium.

Table 4.2 Types of Money Sources

		Value Investor Places on Their Advice	
		High	Low
Speed that investor seeks return on capital	Fast	Professional venture capitalists	Friends and relatives
	Slow	Institutional money sources	Angels

There are nearly as many methods of financing entrepreneurial ventures as there are entrepreneurs and venture capitalists. All venture financings, however, proceed through the same three stages—from seed money (initial money) to private financing to public offering. Any of these steps can be multifaceted; and having a number of substeps within a stage has recently become common. The entrepreneur must adapt his company structure and financial needs to meet the needs of the investors at each stage. Investors seldom adapt for companies.

Seed money financing is the most thrilling and exciting stage of any new venture. Here the investor takes the biggest gamble by supplying long money at long odds in search of a long gain, usually with a basis no more concrete than an idea or a dream.

The danger that lurks at the seed stage involves the natural tendency of the entrepreneur to look to friends and relatives for his seed money. The number of fathers, uncles, and neighbors who have backed new business ventures is legion. Because most entrepreneurs are inexperienced and unfamiliar with the foot-work necessary to raise venture capital, they all too often take this route, and all too often it proves catastrophic. Venture capitalists seek to make money by investing in new businesses, but even they frequently fail to evaluate start-up situations properly. If the professionals have trouble, how can Uncle Bert do better?

If you really believe you have "such a good deal" to offer your friends and relatives, you shouldn't have much trouble convincing a professional venture capitalist. Remember, you have to live with friends and relatives for a long time. Coexistence could be tough if you lost their money. So seek your capital from the professionals—venture capitalists and angels—especially the seed money. If your venture is successful, you can always invite your friends and relatives to buy stock later—and sleep better in the meantime.

If you follow the course taken by most entrepreneurs, you will not start out with a public stock offering. By definition, then, you will be making a private placement; and you will have to negotiate most of the following terms with the individual investors, regardless of which type you deal with:

1. Registration rights and timetables for selling the investor's stock. This would allow the investors to know in advance the mechanisms for selling their stock in a public stock registration, and provide an easier feeling during the duration of the investment.

2. Seats on the board of directors, frequency of financial statements, and right of inspection of books. These monitoring functions keep investors informed (board), aware of financial changes (statements), and secure in being told the entire story (books).

3. Piggyback features of investors' stock to allow them to participate in a registration at a formula-determined cost. This relates to # I as above as it also allows investors to sell off their stock during a public stock offering at predetermined favorable financial terms.

4. Working capital, net worth, and dividend restrictions. The first two restrictions are offered to keep the company financially healthy, and the third dividend is to prevent the stockholders from unfairly draining cash from the business.

5. Key-man life insurance for you; property and product liability insurance for the company. Insurance is another form of protection for the business.

6. Employment and salary agreements for key personnel. This can be ever so crucial if it's actually implemented before a dramatic shift in personnel.

7. Structure of the capital between debt and equity to keep the company financially healthy.

8. Call or conversion aspects of the stock or debt, including preemptive rights, or, in other words, offering new stock to old stockholders first; penalty and prepayment provisions for changing the debt-equity structure.

Most investors prefer to invest capital as part equity (stock) and part debt (loan). The equity money provides a base on which the company can build, and the debt money allows the investor to exercise controls over the company's financial activities without being involved on a day to day basis. Debt money offers the investor the added benefits of being returned with the interest if the venture is successful.

In negotiating these "boiler-plate" provisions, remember that the investor is entitled to certain considerations. Usually, an investor's requests are reasonable. Entrepreneurs may be caring for the garden, but the investor is providing the fertilizer. Enough of the right type of fertilizer can do wonders for your seeds, even with poor gardening skills. These investors want to make sure that the crop comes in, too. It is also a good idea to enlist the aid of your lawyer and accountant in drafting the provisions of your deal. They'll catch negotiable contractual agreements that you'll miss, such as what will happen if the new funds fail to materialize.

All investors have their own special needs and reasons for making an investment. Your major decision and greatest effort should go toward choosing the right type of investor for your needs. If yours is a high risk situation but one with potentially large rewards, you'll probably do best with "itchy" money. If your situation is relatively stable and secure, the institutional investor might be your best choice.

Pick the "right" money and you're on your way. The "wrong" money can mean plenty of headaches. Once you've found it, though, don't haggle unnecessarily over terms; and keep in mind that what's good for the investor can't hurt you. Remember, after a successful private placement of capital into your company by the venture source, you're both stockholders in the same company.

A PUBLIC STOCK OFFERING

The entrepreneur who stays with his company through the growth crisis is only slightly less rare then the entrepreneur who manages to get his new venture off the ground in the first place. The rate of entrepreneurial attrition between those first exhilarating days of the start-up and the time when a company is finally out of the woods and on its way to maturity is legend. From this, one might assume that it's all downhill after the venture capital is salted away in the bank. But they'd be dead wrong.

If actuarial figures existed on the life expectancy of the business that reaches maturity, I believe they would indicate that it can expect to survive for a good many years. But the crises are not at an end—not by any stretch of the imagination.

Every entrepreneur secretly dreams of the day when his company can go public. Selling those seemingly worthless pieces of paper for real money by just talking to an underwriter is the myth that nightly emerges in a soon-to-be-public entrepreneur's dreams. It's a blessed event that comes after a long, trying, and often painful gestation. It makes all your past problems disappear, just as the memory of labor pains disappear for the new mother. When the baby comes, you forget the pain.

What does a public offering do for the company? It gives it status; it's a scorecard to show the public that you've done more things right than wrong. Most important, however, is the fact that a public offering provides equity capital, that magic potion that allows the entrepreneur to operate unprofitably while increasing his volume. Furthermore, fresh infusions of capital create a fine mist that clouds the real profit potential of the enterprise. Lack of capital amplifies the entrepreneur's mistakes. Excess new capital covers them up.

Wall Street has an unwritten rule that says a "good" company shouldn't go public until it has reached at least a million dollars in profits on ten million dollars in sales. Most "good" small companies try to adhere to that rule. If capital is short, try to raise it privately and put off that public offering as long as possible.

Small businessmen whose enterprises survive and thrive may find it necessary to seek external financing from investors having more substantial and varied capital resources than commercial banks and the SBA. There is a new set of obstacles on this road to economic growth.

The access of small companies to public markets, particularly in the early 1950's, encouraged the formation of venture capital—money that was available for innovation and small business growth in the hope that some of the funds invested could be recovered within two to five years.

Venture capitalists, however, like all investors, found that the years following 1969 were difficult ones. They were forced to cut back on investments in many new ventures, because without a lively secondary public market for resale of these securities, underwritings do not take place. Without underwritings, there are no investments, and the economy suffers. Table 4.3 illustrates the precipitate decline in public offerings and money raised for companies having net worth of $5 million or less.

Making a public stock offering means selling some of your firm's equity through an underwriter to many small investors. Although major books are written on this topic, I'll try to explain it all in a paragraph or two. Your firm needs new funds and you have decided not to have a private placement. Hence, you are going public with your firm's stock. In turn, your firm will be dealing with the Securities and Exchange Commission (S.E.C.), and your financial information will be in the public domain.

Your first step is to locate the underwriter—the financial firm which will actually "buy" a block of stock from you and sell or distribute it to their many customers. One of your key tasks in this process is to negotiate the specific price at which you'll sell this stock. Usually it's a multiple of earnings. The multiple of earnings is also known as the price-earnings ratios (P/E) and it is simply price per share divided by the earnings per share (EPS) of common stock. The negotiation centers around what the multiple should be in your case. The entrepreneur will argue for a high multiple in order to sell the stock at as high a price as possible. The underwriter, who is paid in numerous ways, will scrap to have the initial offering price as low as possible. The underwriter will mention the "after market"—which is the price per share and the volume of shares to be traded in the over-the-counter (OTC) market. Here is a specific instance.

Example:

1. Company's 12-months after tax earnings on profits are $500,000.
2. Company desires to raise $1,000,000 in a public stock offering, after all legal, accounting, and underwriting fees.
3. This is an initial public stock offering of a growing small retail chain of stores which now has 500,000 shares authorized and issued.
4. The company claims that the multiple of earnings should be 25 and that the total valuation of the company should be $12,500,000. Hence, they are negotiating to sell 8% of the company's stock for $1,000,000.
5. The underwriter declares that companies similar to this firm have earnings multiples closer to 15 times earnings. Hence, the underwriter will seek to value

the total business at $7,500,000. Thus, to raise the needed $1,000,000, they would have to sell 12½% of the common stock.

6. In case the company's position is won and the earnings multiple is 25, the price per one share of the common stock would be:
    8% of 500,000 shares = 40,000 shares to be sold for $1,000,000.
    Hence, the price for one share of stock would be $25.

7. In case the underwriter's position is won, and the earnings multiple is 15, the price per one share of common stock would be:
    12½% of the 500,000 shares = 62,500 shares to be sold at $15 per share.

If one looks at the two cases above, one can see that the price of the stock at the initial public offering could vary between $15–$25 per share, depending upon the prevailing argument. What are the ramifications of each possibility?

The obvious result of the first choice is the dilution (selling a greater share of the company stock than necessary) of the entrepreneur if the stock is underpriced at the initial public offering. In this case, the entrepreneur is selling the stock too cheaply. On the other hand, in the second case, the stock price will tend to fall from the initial offering price if it is initially overpriced. The underwriter will argue, and incidentally he is correct; and the initial investors will be excited about their purchase as they'll each experience a net gain immediately after buying the stock if it is not initially overpriced. The action in the after market (which occurs immediately after the public offering) then, is to be considered in either case.

The price of the initial sale of stock is a very subjective matter. In a later section of this book, I will comment further on this topic. However, when considering whether to raise money via a public stock offering, remember that the viability of the financing is a factor of 1) The strength of the business; 2) The condition of the stock market. Although the strength of the business can vary a good deal over time, it seldom fluctuates as much as the condition of the stock market. This is especially true of the third market, known as the over-the-counter market (OTC) or the pink sheets, where most small companies trade their stock. In fact, in the late 1980s, as many as several thousand small companies held their initial public stock offering in a one year period. In the mid-seventies, fewer than a dozen firms held their initial stock offering in a twelve-month period. Hence, the condition of the market can vary dramatically.

When you do finally take your company public, I can offer two important pieces of advice. First, don't jump at the first underwriter who makes an offer. Although the financial community generally advises against "shopping your deal," I think it's advisable to line up a few alternative underwriters in the event of unexpected trouble with the prime underwriter. On the other hand, you shouldn't shop your package all over the lot, attempting to create an auction environment in order to raise the stock multiple and per share offering price. In fact, the Securities and Exchange Commission (SEC) gets very upset if your deal is shown to more than thirty-five potential investors. This figure includes anyone shown the deal, not just those who eventually invest. Again, these rules change every few years, so consult your professional advisors and also discuss an I.P.O. (initial public offering market) within your state.

Finally, going public can make the entrepreneur rich—at least on paper. Except in rare cases, the principals can't sell their stock in the first public offering; but every entrepreneur likes to count his shares, multiply them by the public offering price and use the electronic calculator to estimate his worth. During all those years in the cellar, when he fought and struggled to build the company, he never really knew the value of his venture. Now, there is a realistic measure; and it feels good just to have a firm answer—even if it is only a momentary one.

Table 4.3 Certain Federal Securities Offering Alternatives

		Rule 504	Rule 505	Rule 506	Section 4(2)*
I	Limitation on Amount Sold	$500,000.	$5,000,000.	None.	None.
II	Limitation on Number of Offerees	No Limit.	No Limit.	No Limit.	No specific numerical limit but cannot rise to level of public offering.
III	Limitation on Number of Purchasers	No Limit.	35 non-accredited purchasers. Unlimited number of accredited purchasers.	35 non-accredited purchasers. Unlimited number of accredited purchasers.	No specific numerical limit but cannot rise to level of public offering.
IV	Qualifications for Purchasers or Offerees	None.	None.	All non-accredited purchasers must be sophisticated.	All offerees and purchasers must be sophisticated and/or must be able to bear the economic risk.
V	Prohibition on Advertising and General Solicitation	Yes, except for certain state-registered offerings.	Yes.	Yes.	Yes.
VI	Mandatory Disclosure	None specified.	None specified if all investors accredited. If non-accredited investors, disclosure requirements vary.	None specified if all investors accredited. If non-accredited investors, disclosure requirements vary.	None specified but must furnish or make available same kind of information as registration would provide.
VII	Financial Statement Requirements	None specified.	Yes, but requirements vary.	Yes, but requirements vary.	None specified but see box immediately above.
VIII	Limitations on Issuer	Not available to 1934 Act reporting companies or investment companies.	Not available to investment companies or issuers disqualified under certain provisions of Reg. A.	None.	None.
IX	1934 Act Reporting Obligations Triggered	Not unless 500 or more shareholders and $3,000,000 or more in total assets.	Not unless 500 or more shareholders and $3,000,000 or more in total assets.	Not unless 500 or more shareholders and $3,000,000 or more in total assets.	Not unless 500 or more shareholders and $3,000,000 or more in total assets.
X	SEC Filings	Yes, Notices.	Yes, Notices.	Yes, Notices.	No.
XI	Resale Restrictions	Yes, except for certain state-registered offerings.	Yes.	Yes.	Yes.

*There is considerable uncertainty concerning the precise factors requisite to the availability of the Section 4(2) exemption, and there are numerous, sometimes conflicting, court decisions interpreting that exemption. Accordingly, the factors specified in this column of the table should be viewed with some caution.

	Section 4(6)	Rule 147	Reg. A	Form S-18
I	$5,000,000.	None.	$1,500,000.	$5,000,000.
II	No Limit.	No Limit.	No Limit.	No Limit.
III	No Limit.	No Limit.	No Limit.	No Limit.
IV	All purchasers must be accredited investors.	All offerees and purchasers must be residents of single state.	None.	None.
V	Yes.	No.	No.	No.
VI	None specified.	None specified.	Yes.	Yes.
VII	None specified.	None specified.	Unaudited financial statements for two fiscal years.	Audited financial statements for two fiscal years.
VIII	None.	Must be organized and doing business in state where securities offered and sold.	Unavailable for sale of oil or gas or mineral rights and to investment companies.	Unavailable to investment companies, insurance companies and 1934 Act reporting companies.
IX	Not unless 500 or more shareholders and $3,000,000 or more in total assets.	Not unless 500 or more share holders and $3,000,000 or more in total assets.	Not unless 500 or more share holders and $3,000,000 or more in total assets.	Yes, but reporting obligations reduced for first year.
X	Yes, Notices.	No.	Yes, Offering Statements.	Yes, Registration Statement.
XI	Yes.	Yes, Out-of-state resales prohibited for nine months.	No.	No.

SELECTING THE UNDERWRITER

An early step in making a public offering is the selection of an underwriter—the firm that actually peddles your stock. It is difficult to generalize about the best method of selecting one. Each situation is different, and each underwriter has certain advantages and disadvantages for each situation. The most crucial aspect of the selection is to match your company's financial needs to your underwriter's capabilities.

Talk to several underwriters before making a choice. You'll be "in bed" with them for some time and it's a difficult relationship to revoke. At the same time, shopping your deal to a dozen underwriters may scare away the good guys.

Underwriters are compensated in many ways. They often receive warrants and options to buy your stock at lower prices in the future, in addition to the underwriting discount. Be sure to understand all the levels of compensation before closing your deal. Your underwriter will choose the best form of public offering from several alternatives, depending on your financial needs and on the condition of the stock market at the time of your offering.

Going Public

If you're thinking of taking your company public while the window is still wide open, you'll have to comply with both federal and state securities laws, as well as investing considerable time and money to make it happen. Table 4.4 highlights some of your options.

An excellent 60 booklet, *A Businessman's Guide to Capital-Raising Under the Securities Laws,* by Michael M. Coleman and Irving P. Seldin, offers a valuable appendix dealing with the new and popular Regulation D and form S-18. This booklet is available from:

Packard Press
1528 Walnut St.
Suite 2020
Philadelphia, PA 19102
(215) 236-2000

Table 4.4   Equity Capital Raised by Companies with a Net Worth of Under $5M

Year	Number of Offerings	Millions of Current Dollars
1968	358	745.3
1969	698	1,366.9
1970	198	375.0
1971	248	550.9
1972	409	896.0
1973	69	159.7
1974	9	16.1
1975	4	16.2
1976	29	144.8
1977	13	42.6
1978	21	89.3
1979	81	506.5
1980	237	1,401.0
1981	306	1,760.0
1982	112	617.0
1983*	500*	2,000.0*

*estimated

SHARING THE WEALTH

As soon as an enterprise becomes successful, many entrepreneurs want to "share the wealth" with some key employees by making the company's stock available to them over a period of time at highly favorable prices. It's a nice thing to do. It's always well intended. A qualified stock option plan can give a valued employee an opportunity to increase his net worth substantially. Recently, employee stock option trusts—ESOPs—have become popular because of their positive tax benefits. They can also tie an employee to a company for a long time, in return for the promise of future capital gains. Although the concept has been known for more than 20 years, the employee stock ownership plan has generated little interest until recently. In the past few years alone, ESOPs have increased approximately tenfold. Much of this enthusiasm derives from the restrictions that the Employee Retirement Income Security Act of 1974 (ERISA) imposes on other forms of deferred compensation and from the impetus that Congress provides for the adoption of ESOPs. Although ESOPs possess corporate financing capabilities not available to other plans, the consequences of using ESOPs as a financing tool can be unattractive.

The most important legislation is the Tax Reduction Act of 1975, which gives an additional 1% investment tax credit to the corporation adopting an ESOP. Moreover, legislation is pending that will give additional benefits to companies that adopt such a plan. Congress has provided this incentive because it believes that ESOPs will ease the expected capital shortages. Although the ESOP results in employees becoming investors in their corporation, most discussion of ESOPs as financing tools focuses on using leverage in the ESOP. By this borrowing (i.e., leverage), a corporation can raise large amounts of money quickly and easily. We've all heard the promise of repayment of debt with pretax dollars contributed by the company to an employee stock ownership trust (ESOT—the trust that holds the assets of the plan—as opposed to ESOP, which refers to the written plan). This is the promise, and its appeal is all positive for the small businessperson.

Although it does provide cash flow to the company beyond that provided by a straight loan, the ESOP also dilutes the earnings per share and the owners' equity per share. The ESOP's real financing promise lies in its use as a means of providing liquidity to existing shareholders, so such a plan is most likely to provide financing help to the present shareholders instead of to the corporation.

The ESOP is similar to a profit-sharing plan, since contributions can be made in cash or stock and are allocated to participants in proportion to their compensation. There are major dissimilarities between a profit-sharing trust and an ESOT. The corporation may make contributions to an ESOT whether or not the corporation has profits. The ESOT is *required* to invest primarily in corporate securities, whereas a profit-sharing plan is merely *permitted* to invest largely in company securities.

An ESOT is designed to invest primarily in the company's common stock, but it can invest in other securities. Although it is unclear how much of an ESOT can be invested in noncompany securities, it is likely that a 50% level will be permitted before its tax qualifications is endangered.

Distributions from the ESOP when the employee retires or leaves must be made solely in the employer corporation's stock. This is required because the primary purpose of an ESOP is to give employees ownership of qualifying company securities. Retirement benefits are only an incidental benefit.

An additional 1% investment tax credit (ITC) is available for 1976 and 1977 to companies with an ESOP. The Tax Reduction Act of 1975 provides this benefit solely to companies with ESOPs as long as the credit flows to the trust, vests immediately, and gives voting rights to participants on the stock purchased. This feature has been instrumental in causing companies such as General Motors Corporation to strongly consider adopting such a plan. More important, this extra 1% ITC may be only the beginning of a series of tax breaks for companies with an ESOP.

The ESOP can be used as a financing and liquidity tool, unlike any other deferred compensation plan. The 1974[3] Pension Reform Act permits the ESOT to borrow money from a bank, have the loan guaranteed by the corporation, and repay the debt out of company contributions to the ESOT. Although this ability to borrow may be helpful to some corporations, it is not a cure-all.

To better understand an ESOP, we should seek legal guidance. The laws are changing so fast that any of my guidance may already be out of date. Issuing stock in any form to employees is an extremely delicate issue with complex legal overtones. The ESOPs encourage employee ownership of business, but even prior to the first ESOP, entrepreneurs were sharing the wealth via stock options or reduced rate employee stock purchase plans.

If you do offer your key men stock options, which I recommend, please don't offer them advice on when to exercise their options. Consider what would happen if you were asked, "off the record," to predict the company's future to an employee who was trying to decide when to exercise his option. Naturally, you're going to paint a rosy picture, based on your optimistic nature. But what if something goes sour and the stock price takes a nosedive? Then to make matters worse, what if you're forced to let that employee go? Now he doesn't have a job, and all of his savings are tied up in a depressed stock. And don't forget that he is your friend. Such a situation can be unsettling on a fellow's psyche. It's much wiser to send him to a professional for that kind of advice. You stay out of it.

Finally, it might interest you to know that a study by Professor Arnold Cooper of Purdue University of new companies in Palo Alto, California showed that more than half of them were founded with money generated from stock option programs of other entrepreneurial companies. Your stock option plan could eventually finance some new competition, too. It's a two-edged sword.

Throughout a public offering, you are regulated by the Securities Act of 1933 which prohibits your promoting or selling stock before it is properly registered. Ignoring this rule is the fastest way to foul up an offering—and your company. Your lawyer and underwriter will explain the requirements in detail. Listen hard. It's important.

Finally, the success of your offering may depend on your underwriter, so be sure there is no mismatch before you jump for the much-needed, fresh, new, money transfusion.

SELLING THE BUSINESS

Many entrepreneurs decide not to take their company public. They put it on the market in one lump instead of in thousands of small pieces. In many respects this can be more desirable than a public offering. The net effect is the same, especially if the buyer, as is often the case, is a larger public company. There is a fresh source of capital, and the entrepreneur gets either cash (better than the first public offering) or stock in the purchaser's company. The drawback is that he becomes an employee (or may not even have a permanent job with the larger company) and loses at least some of the control.

[3] In 1980, these laws were altered to further increase the appeal of ESOPs and ESOTs. We would suggest checking with legal counsel for the latest laws.

In selling a small business, one very important problem is how to determine its value so that the seller gets what he deserves, and the buyer gets what he pays for. The following are the three methods generally used to determine the market value of a small company.

Liquidation Value

This is the value that would be assigned to a business being sold in order to satisfy its creditors. Tangible assets, such as land, usually have a liquidation value close to their market value. Inventories, on the other hand, are usually valued at about twenty percent of cost.

In order to determine the liquidation value, all of the assets are assigned distressed values, and the debts are totaled. Most assets sold under duress are discounted from their fair market value. This is especially true for retail stores which reduce prices dramatically for the going-out-of-business sale. The difference between the distressed value of the assets and the actual value of the liabilities is the liquidation value. This method is used only if a company is in serious financial trouble or is exceptionally heavy with assets.

Book Value

Book value is what is shown on the books as net worth, or stockholders' equity. It is determined by subtracting the book value or net worth of the assets from the book value of the liabilities. It can also be determined by adding profits earned, or by subtracting losses incurred, from the initial total capital investment in the company. In practice, book value is seldom used, although I believe it is as realistic an approach as any to measuring a small company's worth.

Market Value

This is the most common—and the trickiest—method of evaluating a small company. Simply stated, market value is the value a willing buyer would pay a willing seller. If the selling company's stock is publicly traded, its value is the traded per share price multiplied by the number of outstanding shares. When selling a company, however, that calculation doesn't mean that someone will pay the existing per share price for every single share. It often happens that the price is inflated or deflated when only a small part of the outstanding stock (float) is traded on the open market. The per share price does suggest a ballpark price/earnings ratio (the price per share, P, divided by the earnings per share, E). A P/E ratio of about 20 is common for a small growth company. However, this method of evaluation applies only when the stock is publicly traded.

As an example of the complicated figuring that is involved in selling a closely held small company, let's review the case of a client in the chemical business who recently sold his company. It had annual sales of about $1,000,000 and earned about 10 percent profit after taxes, or $100,000. Both the book value and the assets value were approximately $250,000. There was no debt. The buyer claimed the business was worth $1,000,000 (after-tax earnings of $100,000 multiplied by the price/earning ratio of 10). His estimate of the valuation was based solely on the company's earning potential.

My client refused the offer, calling attention to an important fallacy in this technique of valuation. The business, he pointed out, had a net worth of $250,000. Therefore, it had about a quarter of a million dollars of borrowing power. Technically, he could borrow that $250,000, declare a bonus after taxes of $125,000 in cash, and not affect the company's future earning power, except for a small interest charge. According to the buyer's valuation technique, this transaction wouldn't change the market value of the company. In this case, my client would be $125,000 better off and the business would suffer an interest burden on the borrowed funds ($250,000) which could impair its future earnings. In turn, this could be used to reduce the valuation of the business. So my client placed a value of $1,200,000 on the company—the original $1,000,000 plus $200,000 for the net worth. In the final negotiations, his argument held water, and he got a compromise of $1,100,000.

5

What Is a Business Plan?

HOW TO DESIGN A BUSINESS PLAN

A document written to raise money for a growing company is known as a *business plan*. The most popular types are written for entrepreneurial companies seeking a private placement of funds from venture capital sources. Internal venture management teams of larger companies also write business plans. Although these venture plans seldom circulate to external private placement sources, they do progress upward within the organization for approval by corporate management.

Modest differences exist between the entrepreneurial plan and internal venture group plan. The major difference rests in the enterprise's risk and reward structure and not in the reading or writing of the document. The objectives of both types of plan are the same—launching a new business or expanding a promising small business. The ultimate responsibility for success or failure in one case rests with an entrepreneur/ venture capitalist and in the other with a manager/vice president. But no matter what its origin, the document that consummates the financing is called the business plan. In both cases, the document must be thorough and well done to be successful in securing new capital.

The vast majority of business plans are prepared by entrepreneurs seeking venture capital. New venture groups within large companies are expanding their activities, but they do not approach the number of existing small companies seeking the same goal. As a comparison, there are about 14 million small businesses in the United States while only several thousand larger companies exist in the country. In addition, start-up companies, which still appear despite current depressed economic conditions, require a special breed of entrepreneurial business plan. This third category of brand new companies is the least common source of business plans.

The term *business plan* is the more formal name for the document; however, many within the financial and legal communities prefer the nickname *deal*. Although the latter is crude and a bit harsh, it does have shock value, which makes it a realistic and descriptive phrase. Some financiers carry this nicknaming one step further and compare the fund raising process to the television program "Let's Make a Deal." In any case, the word *deal*, which embodies the excitement of the chase, becomes *business plan* when the chase is successfully completed.

The Business Plan [1]

Why should you go to the trouble of creating a written business plan? There are three major reasons.

1. The process of putting a business plan together, including the thought put in before beginning to write it, forces you to take an *objective, critical, unemotional* look at your business project in its entirety.
2. The finished product—your business plan—is an operating tool that, properly used, will help you manage your business and work toward its success.
3. The completed business plan is the means for communicating your ideas to others and provides the basis for your financing proposal.

The importance of planning cannot be overemphasized. By taking an objective look at your business, you can identify areas of weakness and strength, pinpoint needs you might otherwise overlook, spot problems before they arise, and begin planning how you can best achieve your business goals. As an operating tool, your business plan helps you to establish reasonable objectives and figure out how to best accomplish them. It also helps you to red-flag problems as they arise and aids you in identifying their source, thus suggesting ways to solve them. It may even help you avoid some problems altogether.

In order for it to work, it is important that *you* do as much of the work as possible. A professionally prepared business plan won't do you any good if you don't understand it thoroughly. This understanding comes from being involved with its development from the very start.

No business plan, no matter how carefully constructed and no matter how thoroughly understood, will be of any use at all unless you use it. Going into business is rough—over half of all new businesses fail within the first two years of operation; over 90 percent fail within the first 10 years. A major reason for failure is lack of planning. The best way to enhance your chances of success is to plan and follow through on your planning.

Use your plan. Don't put it in the bottom drawer of your desk and forget it.

Your business plan can help you avoid going into a business venture that is doomed to failure. If your proposed venture is marginal at best, the business plan will show you why and may help you avoid paying the high tuition of business failure. It is far cheaper not to begin an ill-fated business than to learn by experience what your business plan could have taught you at a cost of several hours of concentrated work.

Finally, your business plan provides the information needed by others to evaluate your venture, especially if you will need to seek outside financing. A thorough business plan automatically becomes a complete financing proposal that will meet the requirements of most lenders.

[1] Copyright permission granted by Andy Bangs of Upstart Publishing, Portsmouth, NH 03801. Excerpted from *The Business Planning Guide*, Osgood and Bangs. Reprinted with permission.

Preparing a Business Plan For Lenders or Investors[2]

This is a true story. In the late 1960s a sightless entrepreneur raised two million dollars at luncheon with the partners of one of New York's most prestigious investment banking firms. The purpose was to launch a new company whose objective was to merge computer technology and education to solve social problems I don't mean the partners of the investment banking firm set off after lunch to raise $2 million. I mean that following the dessert, the entrepreneur left the luncheon with a certified check for two million in his hands. Nothing like it has happened in the annals of venture capital, before or since, so don't hold your breath until it happens again!

The late 1960s were fascinating times on Wall Street. Venture capital could be raised for any purpose via a public offering. The stock price of any new company from 1967 to mid-1969 went up. One prospectus from that era described the background of a man and his wife, each about 23 years of age, who intended to use the proceeds of the public offering to identify and promote a new business. The prospectus, or business plan, provided no more information than that. The public poured millions of dollars into small underwritings to launch companies whose names they did not know. Little or no due diligence was performed by the brokerage firms that were underwriting these new issues. Today, when most of the new companies of the late 1960s and their underwriters are out of business and the public is reluctant to return to a stock market that cost so dearly, the process of launching a new company is considerably different.

As the 1960s passed into the early 1970s, private venture capital firms became the primary source of start-up and expansion capital. The new issue public market was laid to rest. For example, in 1974, the only new issue I can remember was that of a small firm whose business was liquidating brokerage firms. Between 1975 and 1976 there were a handful of new issues and in 1977 and 1978, perhaps twenty. The few private venture capitalists, beaten about their wallets by the stock market's decline, began to demand substantially more information from entrepreneurs about their objectives, the costs of achieving those objectives, and myriad other details. In addition, someone had to take the blame for the huge portfolio losses. Rather than blaming themselves for their Koros, Ubris, and Ate, as would the good Spartans carrying their dead on their shields, the venture capitalists of the early 1970s pinned the blame on the entrepreneurs. They told them, in effect: "I'll finance your company, but I have to own most of the stock and I must have voting control of the board." This did not encourage new company formation, although a few interesting enterprises were launched between 1973 and 1975, which will be discussed later. The primary effect of this attitude was to reduce the number of new companies launched in the early 1970s, shrink the number of venture capitalists, and usher in competitive government programs to assist in new company formation. For specifics, see *Upfront Financing,* John Wiley & Sons, Inc., New York, New York.

The venture capital industry is new, immature, and seemingly in perpetual transition. This industry is constantly trying to grasp and absorb the various changes that affect it. Entrepreneurs are not aware of this. All too frequently entrepreneurs think that a venture capitalist is J. P. Morgan or Jacob Schiff reincarnate: very wealthy, ultra-conservative, and poised to press a buzzer under the desk that will call in a runner with the bags of cash to pour on the table for the entrepreneur to scoop up. Not true! Venture capitalists are intelligent young men and women seeking to simultaneously recommend to their investment committees the next Syntex, Polaroid, or

[2] Reprinted from A. David Silver, *Upfront Financing,* John Wiley & Sons, Inc., New York, New York, 1982. Used by permission.

Xerox and prevent erosion of capital in their fund through portfolio demise. Therefore, when an entrepreneur and a venture capitalist meet, the entrepreneur should bear in mind the following ideas.

1. The venture capitalist wishes that the information he or she is given by the entrepreneur is true.
2. The venture capitalist, if sold, must resell the idea to his or her investment committee and must be given the facts with which to do so.
3. The venture capitalist has twenty other situations on his or her desk, each competing for time and attention.
4. Venture capitalists make judgments about a new company's projections based on their recollection of past projections, both realized and unrealized.

The latter is a process similar to the description in Plato's *Republic* of the Artisans in the cave chained in place all day staring at shadows. They are not permitted to turn around and see the shadowcaster; they can only stare straight ahead at the shadow. But they must form judgments about the shadowcasters based on the shadows.

Similarly, venture capitalists literally stare at projections all day, unable to see the actual future operating statement numbers. If the projections remind the venture capitalist of the sales and earnings trend to Intel, City Investing, or Teledyne, he or she will be inclined to dig into the deal. If they evoke memories of Stirling Homex or Viatron, the venture capitalist will not be so inclined.

The uncertainty surrounding the entrepreneur is the ability to realize the projections. He or she may be merely a good projection maker and a lousy accomplisher. The venture capitalist does not know which. Herein lies a duel: The venture capitalist tries to attack the business assumptions on which the projections are based to determine their credibility, *i.e.*, the ability of the entrepreneur to make the projections come true. The entrepreneur jabs with upside potential. The venture capitalist counters with downside risk. The projections are dissected to their most minute ratio to try to see if the business plan has credibility. The battle lasts on into the night for day after day, until finally the seller and buyer become joined in their enthusiasm for the new business and have but to agree on a price in order to complete the funding.

This all sounds a bit romanticized, and yet there is no denying that raising money is a battle in the war called Wealth. It is but an early battle in a three to five year war and the entrepreneur has far less experience in fighting it than the venture capitalist. Knowing how to prepare a credible business plan helps put the two on an equal footing.

THE FIVE MINUTE READER

Business plans are comprehensive documents that often require several months to compile. Although they vary in length and complexity, the process of writing them requires the coordination of external legal, financial, and accounting assistance. In addition, the internal analysis of manufacturing, finance, and marketing must coincide with the external activities; this coordination adds to the time required for a preparation. Spending $2,000 to $20,000 for outside services to prepare a business plan is typical. The prepayer intuitively believes that the plan's thoroughness and sophistication reflect on the enterprise's likelihood of success. Consequently, there is a tendency to do the plan well and sometimes to do it and redo it.

Despite all this care during the preparation, most business plans are not read in detail from cover to cover. Although five weeks may have been required to compile it, potential investors will initially invest only *five minutes* in reading it. A venture capitalist who receives a dozen plans a day—hundreds annually—simply does not have enough time to read through each one. In fact, a leading venture capitalist at a large Boston bank claims he never reads any plan. "They all say the same thing and it's never true," he comments, "so I never read them."

In spite of this, you should not conclude that a business plan is unnecessary; it is essential to raising new money for internal or external entrepreneurs. The business person without a plan will be immediately conspicuous and will be turned away by a venture capitalist. The fact of financial life is unlikely to change, even though the plan may not be read initially, the entrepreneur must write one, if for no other reason than to prove that he eventually can do it. It will be read from cover to cover if you are successful in writing it.

Multiple exposures are often given to a single business plan, one of the reasons hundreds of deals arrive at a single venture capitalist's office. An entrepreneur in dire need of funds will often mail the plan to a long list of venture capitalists. Such lists are available from several sources. This multiple exposure, frequently described as "shopping the deal," often seriously weakens rather than improves the chances of raising the needed capital. On the other hand, not showing the plan to anyone assures failure. A thin line exists between exposure to too few or too many potential investors. Incidentally, the Security Exchange Commission (SEC) frowns on exposing a deal to more than thirty-five potential investors. This issue is in constant flux; first you must comply with the federal government's regulations for an offering, and secondly you must comply with each state's so-called blue sky offering laws. Just as you'd guess, these two regulatory bodies (state and federal government) don't always have common laws. For instance, in Massachusetts, a deal can only be shown to 25 potential investors while the federal limit is 100 potential investors. Hence, both rules must be observed. Also, these rules vary depending upon the amount of money you seek. Lately, it's been significantly more attractive to raise less then $500,000 within any consecutive twelve-month period to avoid costly registration problems. Check with your lawyer on this issue as the guidelines are constantly changing.

The number of deals reviewed by a venture capitalist depends upon his or her reputation, which, in turn, depends upon past success. There are now about 1,000 venture capital firms in the United States and a little better than one-half are also SBIC's, small business investment companies regulated by the federal Small Business Administration (SBA). The number of successes contained within a single venture capital portfolio seldom exceeds one in ten or, in baseball language, a batting average of .100. A typical million dollar venture portfolio might be invested in ten companies. Although only one winner is the average, the typical portfolio would have five businesses that are essentially bankrupt; two or three marginal firms with little real potential; and one or two firms with a chance to become a big winner. The pattern reveals the dangers of the venture business and demonstrates the crucial nature of a single winner.

A venture capitalist heading up the largest bank-owned Small Business Investment Company (SBIC) in Boston believes the batting average is a poor measure of a venture capitalist's performance. "The batting average which is so often quoted by academicians," claims this venture capitalist, "mixes up the singles, doubles, and home runs. A better average would be the slugging average or, in baseball terms, an average that weighs the home run and triple more than the single and double." In either case, he argues that the ultimate criterion is always based on a Return on Investment (ROI) analysis. For instance, the typical venture source previously mentioned, with

10 investments of $1,000,000 each, will have committed $10,000,000 to their portfolio. If all the investments eventually turn sour save one, the batting average will be .100. However, if the one success produces a $20,000,000 gain on the original $1,000,000 investment, or a 20 times return, the slugging average would be calculated at 2:1 or $20,000,000 returned on the $10,000,000 invested. This, according to one of the venture capitalists in Boston, accounts for the confusion in analyzing the industry. One success could actually count much higher than a grand slam home run.

Writing For A Five Minute Reader

The primary problem in writing a business plan is making it comprehensive and shaping it for the reader for whom it is intended—the prospective investor with five minutes to read it. The entrepreneur should accept the inevitable: A potential investor will initially invest only five minutes to read a plan; therefore, the plan should be adapted to this time span.

Many authors concerned with the writing of business plans focus on checklists, blank sample forms, and tables of contents. As guides, they help catch items that might be overlooked because they force a full and balanced consideration of the many intertwined issues. In the appendices of this book are a number of actual table of contents of business plans as well as an actual business plan that secured bank debt for a solar industries business in New Hampshire. Excerpts of a business plan, or a table of contents from a typical plan, or a checklist can be useful guides and are strongly encouraged.

A central message of how-to-write-a-plan advice is that you should tailor the document to meet the needs and desires of the potential investors. This sound advice does not mean that you should exaggerate, lie, or inflate the sales projections. It does mean that you should emphasize items of special interest for a specific potential investor. In some cases, a business plan is written in modular form, the appropriate modules being combined to appeal to the characteristics of the investor. A single plan rarely suffices for all possible uses. However, every plan eventually has its moment and is given a once-over lightly.

Insight into what happens to a plan when it finally reaches the top of the pile is scarce. What happens during the five minutes the venture capitalist examines the plan? How is it read? How is it analyzed? An understanding of the reading and interpretation process may help to direct the writing style and the focus of the plan. On the basis of field research involving several dozen venture capitalists and several hundred entrepreneurs, I have concluded that all knowledgeable investors use the precious five minutes of reading time in about the same way.

HOW A BUSINESS PLAN IS READ

In order to determine how a business plan is analyzed, I conducted in-depth interviews over the past three years with two dozen venture capitalists and twice as many others (including bankers, lawyers, accountants, and consultants) in the financial community. The reading process is naturally a private affair between the company and the money source. Each source prides itself in the sophistication it has developed for analyzing investment opportunities. I spent several days actually observing several venture sources; and, as an investor in several entrepreneurial companies, I have read hundreds of business plans.

Almost everyone, the study revealed, analyzed the plans in the same way; the initial five minute reading is a good average if all the plans that are never read are excluded. The following steps are typical of the reading process (less than a minute is invested in each step):

Step 1.   Determine the characteristics of company and industry.
Step 2.   Determine the terms of the deal.
Step 3.   Read the latest balance sheet.
Step 4.   Determine the caliber of the people in the deal.
Step 5.   Determine what is different about this deal.
Step 6.   Give the plan a once-over lightly.

Determine the Characteristics of Company and Industry

Each venture capitalist has preferred areas for investment. Some like high technology and others like low technology; some others like computers; others like consumer goods; and still others prefer publishing. A single venture capitalist is seldom at ease in every industry, just as a single entrepreneur cannot manage with equal skill in diverse industries. The venture capitalist's area of expertise is developed over the years and is based upon past successes; success in a particular industry will cause him to be receptive to deals in the same industry. Consequently, many of the potential investors may never read a business plan beyond Step 1, regardless of the terms of the deal, if they have little interest in the industry.

Consequently, it is well worth your time to be careful in selecting the venture capitalists who will read and analyze your plan. Several good venture capital guidebooks exist that not only identify venture capital sources but highlight their industry preferences. These are listed in the appendix.

Every potential investor also factors the current glamour of the specific industry into the analysis. Are there any larger publicly traded companies in the same industry? If so, how high is the stock price earning multiple (P/E ratio) of these firms? Or, better yet, is there a larger company that is extremely successful in this industry? How well has it done? Companies find it easier to raise funds when another company has pioneered successfully. For example, in the computer industry the Data General Corporation could point to Digital Equipment Corporation; in the consumer goods industry, many smaller companies have pointed to Avon Products or Alberto-Culver. A specialty chemical company that eventually failed, Lanewood Laboratories, Inc., raised $500,000 based on a business plan that pointed to Lestoil. The B.L.T. Company in the appendix, the carwash gas station, successfully raised over $1,000,000 just after Robo-Wash went public with an initial offering. However, B.L.T. went bellyflop in less than 2 years.

Industry glamour rises and falls much like the length of women's skirts. Ten years ago the glamour field was electronics, followed by franchising, and then by computers. Currently the glamour field is energy, and tomorrow it will be genetic engineering. Despite the obvious problems with financial fads, everyone accepts them as a reality. They exist and they do make a difference; if one's industry is momentarily glamourous, one's chances of securing funds suddenly increase.

The reason for the glamour is important. Investors must hope to get out of their investments eventually. They must become liquid again to be able to invest in the next business, as that is their business. So, determining the salebility (glamour) of an industry before investing is crucial. Otherwise, no other financial source will buy out their investments and they will be locked into a business.

After the potential investor examines and evaluates the industry, he or she will quickly categorize the company within the industry. The potential investor will determine the following six facts about the company.

1. annual sales for the past twelve months
2. profit or loss for last year
3. number of employees
4. share of market
5. degree of technology
6. geographic location of facilities

The fundamental value of carefully highlighting these items in a front page summary of the business plan is that it saves time.

Depending upon his or her interpretation of these facts, the investor will soon be able to determine whether the company matches the venture capitalist's profile of an ideal investment. Is it too large or small? Is it too far away? There are numerous acceptable reasons for not making the investment. Seldom, if ever, is a venture capitalist faulted for the investments not made. More often and more intense is the criticism of the investments he or she actually selected. The sequence in Step 1 is first to check the industry and then to check the company.

Determine the Terms of the Deal

How much of a company is being "sold for what price" are the terms of the deal. The peripheral issue is the form (debt or equity) of the deal being offered. Many venture firms strongly prefer convertible debt (or debt with warrants) to a straight equity deal. Their profit-seeking structure may require the venture firm to generate annual income to pay current overhead, in addition to the capital gains expected from the capital portfolio. Naturally, these firms would prefer interest-bearing debt to help cover this overhead, and a few of them will discourage deals that do not satisfy this basic requirement. In these cases, form is not a peripheral issue; but in the majority of cases the more substantive issue of "how much for how much" is of more concern.

Accordingly, a well-done business plan informs the reader of the following financial items on the first page. Other items should also be included in this summary, such as number of employees, geographic location, types of products, annual sales, and profits.

A. Percentage of company being sold (after dilution)
B. The total price for this percentage of the company (per share figures also included)
C. The minimum investment (number of investors sought)
D. The total valuation (after the placement) being placed on the company
E. The terms of the investment
   1. Common stock
   2. Preferred stock
   3. Debt with warrants
   4. Convertible debentures
   5. Subordinated convertible debt
   6. Straight debt

Following is a more complete explanation of these last six terms.

1. *Common stock:* Common stock is the term used to describe the documents that represent the value on the books of the business. When the funds are initially put into a company, common stock is known as capital stock. These certificates of common stock describe the ownership of the company.

2. *Preferred stock:* This is a special category of stock which, in some ways, is preferred or treated better than simple common stock. Most of the time, preferred stock has certain advantages, such as guaranteed dividends or prior rights in a liquidation, and it is a separate category above common stock.

3. *Debt with warrants:* The debt of a company is simply an obligation to repay a certain amount of money over a certain period of time at an agreed-upon rate. In the simplest terms, it's a loan. Some loans are risky, and a high interest rate is not enough to make the loan financially attractive. Hence, stock warrants are attached to the debt to sweeten the attractiveness of the investment. Warrants are the right or privilege to buy shares of common stock at a fixed price within a specified time period. If the price of the common stock rose above the predetermined stock warrant price within the time period, the holder of the warrant could opt to exercise the warrant. If, for instance, the warrant was at $3.00 per share and the stock was trading at $5.00 per share, a holder of 1,000 warrants could buy stock from the company for $3,000 and supposedly resell the same stock for $5,000, less appropriate commissions. Hence, a warrant is like a stock option and it has some value. The value is only realized after the warrants are exercised and the stock is sold.

A classical example of a debt with warrants type of investment occurred in the mid-1960s. Fred Fideli of the Worcester-based firm State Mutual Life Assurance Company traveled to Chicago in order to evaluate a growing chain of hamburger stands. Although only 100 units were operating at this time, after personally visiting about 75 of the chains, Fideli offered a loan of $750,000 with an interest rate of 7½% to this business now headed up by the famous entrepreneur, Ray Kroc. In addition, to sweeten the financial attractiveness of this loan, Fideli obtained warrants to purchase 10% of the common stock of the chain.

About ten years later, State Mutual had received full payment for its loan, exercised the warrants on the company, and sold the stock in the public market. Rumor has it that this conservative life insurance company realized about $12,000,000 in turn for making this loan. The McDonald's Corporation was the most successful of all of State Mutual's investments.

4. *Convertible debentures:* A debenture is a loan and it is a type of debt. The convertible feature allows the debt holder to choose whether or not to convert the remaining outstanding debt into stock. For instance, a five year note for $500,000 at 10% simple annual interest, payable monthly, is a form of debt. The convertible feature would add the possibility that the note holder could convert any remaining debt into common stock at a specific price. Consequently, when and if it becomes attractive, a note holder could trade in the remainder of the debt for common stock at a predetermined price. The difference between this technique and debt with warrants is simple. Under convertible debts, the note holder may not retrieve all the loan before purchasing the stock. In the case of debt with warrants, all of the debts must be repaid and, in addition, the note holder is given warrants which he may or may not exercise. Consequently, most venture capitalists prefer a debt with warrants rather than convertible debts.

5. *Subordinated convertible debt:* This is a special class of debt. The adjective *subordinated* refers to the ranking in event of liquidation of this debt as compared

to other forms of debt. Subordinated debt is usually senior to any equity but subordinated to any other debt, especially bank borrowing. In case of bankruptcy or liquidation, subordinated debt is paid after all other debts, usually including trade payables, are satisfied. The stockholders are traditionally the only group of investors with lower priority than holders of subordinated debts. The convertible feature remains the same as described in 4 above. The difference between 4, convertible debenture, and 5, subordinated convertible debentures, is only that 5, subordinated convertible debentures, is also subordinated to other debt.

Following is a common possible ranking of rights in a bankruptcy.

1. certain IRS liens
2. secured creditors
3. unsecured creditors (trade payables)
4. subordinated debt
5. stockholders

6. *Straight debt:* This is simply a loan or debenture—an obligation to pay back an amount of borrowed funds at an agreed-upon rate over an agreed-upon time period. There are two basic forms of straight debt: secured and unsecured. Secured debt is further backed up by an asset that is pledged to guarantee the payment of the debt. In the event of default, the secured lender would seize the pledged asset to recover the outstanding debt. A house mortgage is a good example of secured debt. Any debt without an asset pledged as collateral is considered unsecured debt.

This information is most helpful if it is presented both clearly and quickly to the potential investor. There is a considerable amount of detail and there are intricacies in every business plan and the terms mentioned only cover a few points of interest.

Unfortunately, many deals do not spell out these financial details plainly. The short time invested by a venture capitalist in looking over the plan is spent in digging out these pieces of needed information. If they were clearly stated at the beginning, potential investors could spend more time analyzing the plan's more positive selling features (such as product literature). A summary sheet saves everyone's time and increases an interested reader's enthusiasm.

Finally, after the terms are known, the follow-up analysis focuses on these related issues; depending upon the specifics, the following may also be included in the summary.

How does the price per share of this placement compare with the founder's price per share?

Are the founders reinvesting in this placement?

What was the value of the company at the last placement and why has it changed?

How will the new funds be used, and, more specifically, will they be used to repay old debts or to undertake new activities that, in turn, will increase profitably?

Read the Latest Balance Sheet

A current balance sheet is usually located at the end of the written business plan, just before the appendix and future estimates of (*pro forma*) cash flow and income statements. The most current balance sheet is often the first page of the financial exhibits; and often it is also the *only* financial page glanced at during an initial reading of a business plan. This historical document exposes the company's history, whereas most other financial documents in the appendix describe the company's future hopes.

Much preferred to any pro forma analysis is a one-minute process for interpreting the balance sheet and income statement. (Merrill, Lynch, Pierce, Fenner & Smith publishes a free twenty-four page brochure, *How to Read a Financial Report*, which contains greater detail on the same subject. Call any of their local offices to receive this free brochure.) The following four-step process, which is used to read a balance sheet from the top down, offers most of the financial information needed to make a quick evaluation of the deal.

      A—Determine liquidity
      B—Determine debt/equity structure
      C—Examine net worth
      D—Examine assets and liabilities

A—Determine liquidity. Check working capital or current ratio, each of which measures about the same thing. Working capital is equal to current assets minus current liabilities, while the current ratio is current assets divided by current liabilities. Below is a typical balance sheet illustrating these relationships.

Cash	$ 50,000
Accounts Receivable	200,000
Inventories	+ 250,000
Total Current Assets	$500,000
Accounts payable	$250,000
Notes payable (within one year)	75,000
Accrued expenses payable	100,000
Federal income tax payable	+ 25,000
Total Current Liabilities	$450,000

Working Capital=$50,000 ($500,000-$450,000)
Current ratio = 1.1 ($500,000/$450,000)

A firm's working capital should be positive while the current ratio should be greater than 1 (those two statements say the same thing in different words). A current ratio closer to 2 indicates a more financially stable company. A company with less than a positive $100,000 of working capital will be tight on cash. A quick check will determine the firm's payroll, and then relating payroll to cash (or working capital) will place the firm's needs for cash in a better perspective. For instance, if the firm above needs $100,000 per month for payroll, its cash is only two weeks of payroll and its working capital is only half a month of payroll. This analysis indicates the firm's need for cash and is a fair indication of how well they are doing.

B—Determine long term debt/equity structure. It is important to remember that the debt/equity ratio is equal to total debt divided by total equity. The ratio reveals how much credit a debt source (such as a bank) has already extended to the company. In addition, it offers insight into the remaining borrowing power of the company. A 400 percent debt/equity ratio, where a lender advances three dollars for every equity dollar, is a ballpark upper limit for this ratio. Seldom will debt sources advance three long term debt dollars for every equity dollar in a small company. Consequently a debt/equity ratio of 3:1 is rare, while a ratio of 1:1 usually indicates the company has some borrowing power remaining.

The numerator usually consists of long term debt, such as bonds or mortgages, and never includes current liabilities (due within one year), such as accounts payable.

The denominator is tangible net worth or owner's equity at the time of the placement. This is not to be confused with the initial investment of the owners, which may have been made some time ago. Many times, small companies have unusually high (larger than one) debt equity ratios. This often indicates that outside assets other than those on the company's balance sheet are securing the debt. A wealthy owner may have countersigned the bank note or pledged an asset in order to obtain more debt. The debt/equity ratio often uncovers this discrepancy. In the following example, the debt/equity is 2/3.

C—Examine net worth. The potential investor extracts from the balance sheet the amount of money initially invested in the firm, which is the initial capitalization provided by the founders. The cumulative profits (or losses) that are contained within retained earnings offer another benchmark of the company's success to date. These two items added together algebraically determine a company's current net worth. Below is a typical balance sheet:

Long term debt (current portion that is due this year is shown under current liabilities)	$100,000 Line 1
Capital stock (initial capitalization)	+ 250,000 Line 2
Retained earnings (profit or loss to date)	(100,000) Line 3
[3]*Owner's equity* (combines capitalization and retained earnings)	150,000 Line 4

$$\frac{\text{Line 1}}{\text{Line 2} \pm \text{Line 3}} = \frac{\text{Debt}}{\text{Equity}} = \frac{\$100}{\$150} = .667 = 2/3$$

A prospective investor interprets this information by noting that the founders began the company with $250,000 and that they have lost $100,000 since its inception. The company has a long term interest-bearing note that was probably awarded when the company was founded and was based upon the initial capital of $250,000. A further check to determine what, if anything, is offered as security for the long term debt would follow by examining the footnotes to the balance sheet. However, due to the losses to date, the company probably has little remaining borrowing power. The investor will make a quick check to determine which assets (accounts receivable, inventory, and fixed assets) are pledged to secure any of the debt. Free and unencumbered assets would indicate more borrowing power.

Remember the debt to worth ratio is only one factor to consider in determining a business's borrowing power. There are three other issues of concern to any lending source. First and foremost is the ability to repay the loan. This vital element is a function of the two other variables mentioned: (a) the strength of any personal endorsements and (b) the profitability of a business enterprise.

As a rule of thumb, a debt source will allow the following amounts of debt shown in column 2 to be secured against the assets shown in column 1.

[3]Owners equity is what is initially put in to start the company plus or minus the earnings to date, which is equal to Line 2 + Line 3.

COLUMN 1	COLUMN 2
Asset As It Appears on Balance Sheet	Percentage of Balance Sheet Value Which Can Be Borrowed Against
Cash or marketable securities 100%	
Accounts receivable 75–85%	of those under 90 days (Percentage will depend upon market value, not on book value)
Inventory. 20–30%	
Fixed assets. 75%	(Percent will depend upon market value, not on book value)

D–Examine assets and liabilities. A potential investor will quickly check to be sure all assets are real (tangible), and then he or she will check liabilities to verify that debt is owed to outsiders, not to insiders (such as notes to stockholders). This determination also hinges on the reputation of the accounting firm that prepared the financial statement. An unaudited, company-generated financial statement is seldom even interpreted, since the investor needs some independent assurances that the financial reporting is accurate. Without this assurance, investors will undoubtedly pass over the deal, at least at the initial reading.

By examining the asset categories, investors check to be sure soft assets (such as good will, patents, or trade secrets, formulas, or capitalized research and development) are not large or unreasonable. For some unexplained reasons, small companies often choose to capitalize research and development (R & D) or organizational expenses rather than write off these expenses during the period in which they occur. This practice is frowned upon by all potential investors because it distorts the balance sheet, impairs future earnings, and is a sure sign of danger. If this "asset" is large, it can dampen an investor's interest. Furthermore, entrepreneurs, and friends and relatives of entrepreneurs, often choose to make their initial investment in small companies as debt rather than equity. This makes these founders feel more secure because it offers some protection in the event of bankruptcy. By making a quick check, a potential investor uncovers the identity of the company's creditors and the amount of the debt.

This four-step process (A through D) usually takes less than one minute of reading time from beginning to end. In the initial reading of the business plan, potential investors are not probing the balance sheet in depth but are searching for red flags. Before an investment is consummated the balance sheet, income statement, and pro formas will be analyzed in considerable detail. However, during the first glance, the balance sheet analysis and a quick look to determine the magnitude of last year's sales from the profit-and-loss statement are the extent of the financial investigation. The balance sheet, along with a magnitude of sales, provides sufficient data to judge whether or not a more detailed financial investigation is warranted.

Determining the Caliber of the People in the Deal

This step, most venture capitalists claim, is the single most important aspect of the business plan. A potential investor begins by examining the founders, board of directors, current investors, outside professionals (accountants, lawyers, bankers, consultants, directors) in hopes of uncovering a familiar name. The reputation and "quality" of the team are the issues in this measure. Unfortunately, this is a subjective area and, as such, is open to a wide range of individual interpretations; what is good to some is not so good to others. Because it is subjective, opinions and assessments fluctuate dramatically.

Potential investors usually know someone associated with the company (at least they will know someone who knows someone), and this person will set the tone for the whole deal, regardless of his affiliations with the company. Even if he is only a small investor, the company loses its identity and the business plan becomes known as "John Smith's deal" around the office. These known insiders become the links for further information sought by the potential investors.

Consequently, the reputation of *all* the individuals surrounding the business is of serious concern in securing additional funds. For start-up deals or for situations where the company is unknown to the potential investors, a number of questions are asked in order to determine management's abilities. This format is about the same for both internal and external businesses. However, internal venture teams are greatly assisted when the project directors are highly regarded by corporate management. Many times this *golden boy syndrome* becomes the crucial variable in approving new corporate funds. Here are the issues.

> What is the track record of founders and managers, including where they worked and how well they performed in the past? Without a doubt, this is the single most significant ingredient when assessing management's abilities.

> How much balance and experience does the inner management team possess? How long have the members worked together, and what is the degree of balance among marketing, finance, and manufacturing represented by the operating managers?

> Who is the financial man (or bank or accountant) and what are his credentials? Potential investors much prefer a deal with one strong full-time financial type. He speaks their language and is more at home with money than products. Potential investors like to envision this financial type as a caretaker for any newly arrived funds.

Determine What is Different About This Deal

This difference is the eventual pivotal issue on whether or not a specific venture capital firm chooses to invest. The same holds true for obtaining headquarters approval for internal venture management teams in larger companies.

Is there an unusual feature in the product? Does the company have a patent, an unusual technology, or a significant lead over competition? Is this a company whose critical skill rests in marketing, manufacturing, or finance? Does the company's strength match the skills needed to succeed in this industry? Or is there an imbalance? What is different about this company, and how much better is its product? The answers to these questions are the investor's chief concerns.

Does the company have the potential to open up a whole new industry, such as Polaroid, Xerox, IBM, Digital Equipment Corporation, McDonald's or Hewlett-Packard did? Or is this a modest idea with limited future growth? A venture capitalist needs a return of greater than ten times his or her investment just to stay even (one in ten succeed). He or she is seldom intrigued with companies that hold a marginal advantage over competing firms or products. In essence, this is what Rooser Reeves has called the Unique Selling Proposition (U.S.P.)! Good ideas or products that are better than others attract capital. Marginal improvements do not possess enough potential to offset the risks inherent in a new business venture.

Give the Plan a Once-Over Lightly

After this analysis, the final minute is usually spent thumbing through the busines plan. A casual look at product literature, graphs, unusual exhibits, samples, letters of recommendation, and letters of intent is the purpose of this last check. Seldom, if ever, are new opinions formed during the final minute. However, the fact that every-one engages in this leafing through process supports the argument for unusual en-closures. A product pasted on a page, a letter with a meaningful letterhead, or an unusual chart or two can be helpful in maintaining interest. Although enclosures will not make the big difference in the final analysis, an eye-catching enclosure can extend the readership of a business plan.

After this final step, the analysis is over and the investors decide whether to obtain more information or to return the plan. Ninety-nine times out of a hundred, the deal is turned down. A few investors make phone calls at this stage, and then re-ject the deal after a detail or two is confirmed. But it is important to remember that deals are actually turned down during the first reading even though the act of formal rejections is postponed a few additional days.

THE PLAN PACKAGE

Most entrepreneurs assume that a positive relationship exists between time invested in reading the plan and the likelihood of obtaining capital. "If they would only read my plan," mumbles the unsuccessful entrepreneur, "they would be chasing me in-stead of vice versa." With this goal in mind, and assuming that the product is only as good as the package, business plans are often dressed in their Sunday best, in leatherbound jackets sometimes costing over ten dollars each.

In research with several dozen venture capitalists, I conducted some small tests to determine the method used to select a single business plan from a group of five to ten. Several deals were randomly placed on a table and the investors were asked to examine only the covers of the business plans before selecting which of the half dozen plans they would read first. The plans that received the most initial attention were not the ones with pretty covers; instead the company name was more crucial. Next in importance was the geographical location of the company. The third element was the thickness of the plan; the shorter plans received more attention.

In these tests, nothing else was revealed about any of the business plans other than what appeared on the cover. The position of the deals on the tables was random, and I observed each venture capitalist as he or she glanced over the deals. To conclude, I have ranked the variables in descending order of importance:

1. company name,
2. its geographic location,
3. length of business plan, and
4. quality of cover.

The next question I explored was, "How can an entrepreneur increase the like-lihood that a capitalist will read a business plan once past the cover?" Should the entrepreneur send it along in installments with the final chapter first, or should he or she send along a summary? In my research, I concluded that summaries and "mini-plans" are not effective documents. A teaser summary that is not an integral part of the plan only delays the eventual reading of the entire plan, and the teaser is often vague or incomplete. It is much better to have the entire document available to each and every potential investor and highlight the plan with a succinct and informative summary page as the first page of the business plan.

Two additional variables were uncovered that help to determine a plan's eventual reading and, to a lesser extent, the likelihood that a venture capitalist will make an investment. The first is the method of dispatching the plan. The second is the *preselling*, which precedes the plan. Months may be spent preparing the plan, but only a few minutes are spent deciding how to deliver it. The naive entrepreneur follows the suicidal path of a blind mass mailing. Armed with a directory and helped by a secretary, the plan is mailed with a form letter to a sampling from the directory. This wastes everyone's time and the entrepreneur's money because this procedure never works.

Another bad approach for the entrepreneur is to make a personal visit with the business plan tucked under his arm. This humble, straightforward approach is like going to a doctor as an unreferred patient. Everyone asks, "Who sent you?" The key man is often away from his office or unable to see the visitor, who then begins to feel like an intruder.

The best method of delivering a business plan is through a third party. Unless the entrepreneur is already established and successful, a third-party referral adds credence to the plan and, as a result, increases the likelihood that it will be read. Anyone from the following groups is acceptable as long as the reputation and liaison with the venture capitalist are positive (it need not be the same person for each potential investor): consultants, bankers, lawyers, accountants, or other entrepreneurs.

The second level of improvement—a good job on *preselling*—is invaluable. If the potential investors are told about the exciting company six months before the plan arrives and then about current developments each month for the intervening six months, they will be more receptive to reading the plan when it finally arrives. *After all, the best time to raise money is when it isn't needed.* The same holds for arousing potential investor interest. A well-managed company planning to expand will invest time in such preselling often and early. The preselling is as important as any aspect of the process.

The same person should both presell and eventually deliver the plan. With the company name and address and location clearly spelled out on the cover page, it should be hand-carried by a mutual friend to a select group of venture capitalists.

If the process is depressing, always remember that the two most successful venture capital deals in the Northeast were turned down a number of times before receiving a "yes." In 1958, Digital Equipment Corporation (DEC) finally convinced American Research & Development to invest about $70,000. Rumor has it that the investment today is worth over $500 million.

A spin-off from DEC occurred in 1968 when three engineers in their twenties approached Fred Adler, a New York attorney, who agreed to a modest investment in a struggling new company known as Data General Corporation. It is rumored that the four principals each made in excess of $10 million within four years of launching this venture. The rewards are high for those who play and win. Unfortunately, those who play lose most of the time, and plans of this type significantly outnumber the winners.

Explaining the format for reading a business plan suggests that the document's preparations should be based on the process that will inevitably be used to read and interpret the plan. Whether the writer is an internal or external entrepreneur, it is his responsibility to put the company's best foot forward once the business is underway. Thus, a well done business plan will be tailored to the reader.

The definition of a "good" business plan is one that raises money; a "bad" plan does not attract investors. It is that simple; but the entrepreneur must remember that the terms "good plan" and "good business" are not synonymous. A good plan may raise money, but the business may still fail. However, a bad plan almost always means business failure. In order to succeed in reaching the more crucial objectives of a profitable business, a good plan plus a good business is required.

The five-minute process is so cold in concept that it may seriously alienate many business people. The business becomes part of life and the plan becomes the essence of the business. Hence, to add a degree of warmth and a bit more understanding to the central aspect of small business, actual business plans should be interpreted against the above process.

While dealing in this abstract area remember a quotation that links entrepreneurs and venture capitalists.

The men who manage men, manage the men who manage things, *but*, the men who manage money manage the men who manage men.

Pecking order	Ease of handling	
	Venture capitalist	*Entrepreneur*
1. Money	High	Low
2. Men	Medium	Medium
3. Things	Low	High

WRITING A BUSINESS PLAN

The business plan is such a personal document that actual hard advice on its proper preparation is like giving any extremely personal counsel. Usually this type of guidance is not specific enough to be of applied value. Yet there are some common, helpful ideas that can and should be embodied in a business plan.

The most important first stage of development for a business plan is the development of the table of contents. This should be done before any serious writing occurs. The process of then subdividing the actual writing of each module that appears in the table of contents is an extremely common practice. Although sub-dividing is an efficient and reasonable practice, any plan that is developed by the modular approach runs the risk of appearing pieced together. Naturally, this nonintegrated business plan risks the substantial danger of lacking an overall thrust.

The purpose of writing a business plan is to raise capital by the direct sale of securities to one or more private investors. The transaction is exempt from registration with the Securities and Exchange Commission (SEC) provided that it conforms to certain SEC established laws. Very often a business plan does not seek to sell equity but rather to arrange for long term debt financing.

In many cases, particularly in the past few years, the condition of the public stock market prohibits companies from securing new financing through an initial sale of common stock. In the late 1960s it was not uncommon to have several thousand small companies *go public*; but the early and middle 1970s were years when this figure fell from several thousand to fourteen or sixteen per year. In those lean years the only viable alternative was the long term debt market. These facts give some indication of why the development of the business plan should be integrated with the needs of the financial markets.

To offer guidance in writing a business plan, a typical table of contents follows.

A.1   History of the Company

A.2   Business Summary

A.3 Manufacturing Plan

A.4 Production and Personnel Plan

A.5 Products and Services

A.6 Marketing and Sales

A.7 Competition

A.8 Research and Development

A.9 Management

A.10 Financial Reports Supplied by the Company and Accompanying Explanations, Footnotes

A.11 Capitalization or Equity Structure

A.12 Capitalization or Debt Structure

History of the Company

A. Date and place, including state of incorporation as well as preincorporation organizational structure.

B. Founding shareholders and directors.

C. Important changes in the structure of the company, its management, or its ownership. Set forth predecessor companies, subsidiaries, and divisions in an easy to understand manner.

D. Company's major successes or achievements in the field to date.

Business Summary

A. Principal products or services.

B. Describe the unique features of the business and the products. Compare these objectively with the competition. Give specific goals on annual sales growth and profits and relate to actual past performance.

C. Detailed breakdown of sales or services for the current year and for the past five years. Indicate the cost of goods sold and the pretax profit by product line for all products or services that contribute more than 10% in pretax profits.

D. Breakdown of sales by industries, including the U.S. (military versus nonmilitary) and export.

E. Product brandnames, price ranges, and quality.

F. Capital goods versus consumer goods. How cyclical or seasonal?

G. Describe patents, trademarks, and other trade advantages such as geographic or labor advantages. List expiration dates, if any, and impact on sales, profits, and marketing strategy.

H. Give the statistical record of the industry or subindustry in which company operates, with an evaluation of its prospects.

I. Maturity of the product line. Discuss the problems of technological obsolescence and product line, and the problems of competition.

J. Describe any technological trends or potentialities within the business environment that might be favorable or unfavorable to the company.

Manufacturing Plan

A. Fill in data below.

    1. Plant location.
    2. Square feet.
    3. Number of floors.
    4. Type of construction.
    5. Acres of land.
    6. Owned or leased.
    7. Lease value.
    8. Annual rent expires.

B. Describe levels of current operations. Estimate the capacity and the current percentage utilization of plant and equipment.

C. List auto equipment, including delivery trucks, number of vehicles, and whether rented or owned. What are the lease arrangements?

D. Describe the company's depreciation policies. How are they accounting for wear on their assets? Over what time period and at what rate are these assets being depreciated?

E. What manufacturing and/or office equipment is leased?

F. Condition and description of plant equipment (enclose evaluation if possible):

    1. List major equipment.
    2. Condition.
    3. Location.
    4. Owned or leased.
    5. Value estimate.

G. Is the plant layout efficient? Describe.

H. What is the general housekeeping condition?

I. Is the operation job-shop or mass-production oriented? Do they build custom products per individual jobs or is it a mass-produced product that can be manufactured under large cost-efficient methods, and inventoried?

J. Incremental increase in space and equipment required for $1,000,000 increase in sales. For each major increment of expansion in revenue is an equal, more, or less increment necessary in facilities, people, and equipment?

K. Logic for plant location(s).

L. What future capital expenditures for plant and machinery are planned? How will they be financed?

M. What major capital improvements have been made in the past few years? What was their cost and how were they financed?

N. Any sale of assets planned—on what basis, cash or deferred payments?

O. Number of shifts being worked daily. Percentage of overtime. Breakdown by departments. Economics of a two or three shift schedule.

Production and Personnel Plan

A. Brief description of manufacturing operation.

B. Number of personnel (breakdown by functions).

C. Union affiliation. State address and representative.

D. Strike history.

E. Turnover and morale.

F. Labor market (description of important skills) and competition for labor.

G. Percentage of labor content in cost of goods sold by product.

H. Fringe benefits provided and their cost percentage to wages.

I. Does the company rate itself as a low-cost, high-cost, or average-cost employer? What is the unemployment rate based upon the business's past hiring, and firing practice charged to the company by the state government?

J. Steps being taken to improve production methods.

K. Are competent people assigned to production planning?

L. Describe quality control procedures.

M. Unit costs versus production levels, detailing fixed and variable costs.

Products or Services

A. Principal suppliers, location, product, volume, officers dealt with.

B. A brief description of significant materials and supplies, including availability. Are the storage and material handling facilities adequate?

C. Are purchase economies available? Are purchase discounts available?

D. Are make-or-buy decisions made?

E. What is the average inventory turnover within the company's industry? Explain any deviations for your firm.

F. Does the finished inventory have a shelf-life?

G. Methods of inventory valuation.

H. Current inventory status of distributors and ultimate users.

Marketing and Sales

A. Describe the market. History, size, trend, and your product's position in the market. Identify sources of estimates and assumptions.

B. Is the market at the take-off stage? Project the market back five years and forward five years.

C. Where are the products sold, and who is the essential end user?

D. Are the products sold by salaries or commissioned sales force, by distributors, by brokers, or?

E. Are accounts receivables sold, discounted, or pledged? If so, to whom, at what discount, with or without recourse, and so forth? If receivables are pledged to a loaning source, either the lender or the borrower actually receives the cash. If they are discounted, the lender gives a percentage of the receivables at the moment they are pledged as collateral. Resource means that the lender can recover any bad debt on an uncollectable receivable from the borrower, thus lowering the lender's risk.

F. Number of customers or active accounts, and the amount of accounts receivable due over 90 days.

G. How many customers make up 80% of the sales? Please list.

   1. Principal customers.

   2. Location.

   3. Product.

4. Volume.

5. Percent of Company's Sales.

6. Officer Dealt With.

H. Describe any special relationships with customers.

I. Describe pricing policies with respect to all product lines. How sensitive are prices to costs?

J. Current backlog and current shippable backlog. The shippable backlog can be shipped and billed immediately upon completing the manufacturing of the product.

K. How many purchase orders are on hand at present (dollar amount)?

L. Warranties on present products (enclose copies).

M. Advertising: annual budget and media used (enclose recent copy).

N. Is business seasonal? If so, explain peaks in production, sales, and so forth.

O. Selling costs as a percentage of revenues. How will these vary with more or less sales volume?

P. Customer primary motivation to purchase your product: price, delivery time, performance, and so forth.

Q. Are any proposed government regulations expected to affect your market?

Competition

A. List major competition, location, sales earnings, percent of market, and strengths and weaknesses.

B. Nature of competition: cut-throat or permissive, poorly or well financed.

C. Competitive advantages; disadvantages. Be specific.

D. Is new competition entering the field?

E. Compare your company's prices with those of the competition.

F. Share of the business you receive by market area.

G. Describe service arrangements and service experience.

H. Describe advertising and promotional efforts. Discuss the importance of brand names and trademarks.

I. Independent firms, publications, or outside agencies which have evaluated your firm against competitors.

J. Effects of regulatory agencies, including government.

Research and Development

A. Amount of percentage of sales spent per annum in the past five years and projected. Compare with competitors. Detail any capitalized R & D costs.

B. Number of employees in this area. Advanced college degrees.

C. Detail product developments and R & D that is not related to specific products or services, which is basically research and not development.

D. Percent of current sales generated by past R & D.

E. State any new field your firm comtemplates entering: Is it complementary to the present product or service line?

F. List any outside consulting R & D relationships such as firms, universities, individuals, and so forth, and state the percentage of total R & D budget let to outside sources.

G. Funding and its consistency from government sources.

Management

A. Is an organization chart included?

B. Are résumés included?

C. Are references included?

D. Have credit and personal investigation checks been performed?

E. Analysis of reputation, capabilities, and attitude. Analysis of team: one man show, executive turnover, morale.

F. Profit consciousness: Is there an on-going profit improvement plan? An executive incentive program?

G. Innovative ability. Be specific. How is creativity fostered?

H. Schedule of past, current, and proposed salaries and other compensation for each member of management and/or owners, including bonuses, fee arrangements, profit sharing, and so forth. Please list.
1. Key personnel.
2. Annual salary.
3. Bonuses, fees, and so forth.

I. If a stock option or other management incentive plan is in effect, provide an outline.

J. How are salary increases for management controlled?

K. Directors—other than officers and employees: Please list.
1. Name and identity.
2. Compensation.
3. Shares of stock owned.
4. Common or preferred.

L. Life insurance on officers (amount and company).

M. Enclose any contract or proposed contract between the firm and any member of management, any stockholder, or any outside consultant.

Financial Reports Supplied By the Company and Explanations

A. Reports.
1. Audited annual reports for the past five years, including balance sheets, profit and loss statements, and statements of sources and applications of funds.
2. Current financial reports, with officer's statements as to material changes in condition.
3. Pro forma balance sheets giving the effect of the proposed financing on a quarterly basis for two years.
4. Month by month projections of profit and loss, cash receipts, and disbursements for the two year period.
5. Yearly projections of revenues and earnings for five years.
6. Analysis of sales by markets, products, and profits.
7. Record of the industry or subindustry in which the company operates to contrast with the performance of the specific business.

B. Describe accounting principles regarding depreciation, R & D, taxes, inventories, and so forth.

C. Are the tax returns of the company and its subsidiaries for the past five years included?

D. If the business is seasonal, explain its cycle and relate it to the company's financial needs.

E. Discuss the aging of accounts receivable and accounts payable.

F. List the losses from bad debts over the past five years.

G. Describe the trend and give percentages for the following:

    1. Sales, increases or decreases.
    2. Cost of goods sold.
    3. Overhead, fixed and variable.
    4. Selling expenses.
    5. Research and development.
    6. Taxes.
    7. Pretax and after-tax profit margins.
    8. Return on total capital, including long term debt.
    9. Return on total equity.
  10. Industry trends in each of the above areas.

H. Does the balance sheet contain hidden or undervalued assets or liabilities?

I. Discuss any nonrecurring items of income or expense in recent financial statements.

J. Describe the company's profit improvement plan.

K. What years' tax returns have been audited?

L. Are all taxes paid?

M. Are there any disputes between the company and any taxing authority?

Capitalization: Equity

A. Total shares authorized: Common___Preferred___.

B. Total shares outstanding: Common___ Preferred___.

C. Describe principal terms, including voting rights, dividend payments, conversion features, and so forth, for each class of stock.

D. If a private company, list all shareholders. If a public company, list all shareholders who directly or indirectly control more than 5% of the outstanding voting stock.

    1. Name and identity.
    2. Consideration for shares.
    3. Number and class of shares.
    4. Percentage owned of outstanding stock.

E. If any of the shareholders listed in D are not members of the company's management, describe their motivation for becoming shareholders.

F. If individuals or entities who might be considered founders, promoters, or insiders under any law are no longer shareholders, describe the reason for their withdrawal from the business.

G. Provide a chronological list of sales of stock, stating prices, terms, number of buyers, and their names.

H. Describe any other transactions involving the principal shareholders and the company—such as those involving real estate, equipment leases or sales, loans to or from shareholders, and voting trusts.

Capitalization: Debt

A. Principal bank. Name of officer handling account.

B. List the following for each long term debt obligation.
1. Lender and contact.
2. Total amount.
3. Initial date.
4. Length of term.
5. Sinking fund.
6. Date of maturity.
7. Security or collateral.

C. Are seasonal loans required? What was the largest amount borrowed in each of the past two years? Minimum?

D. Amounts of current lines of credit, and with whom.

E. Describe all contingent liabilities.

F. Debt to equity ratio: for company; for industry.

G. What guarantees are currently required by lenders?

SOURCES OF INFORMATION ON PREPARING A BUSINESS PLAN

1. Small Business Reporter, P.O. Box 37000, Bank of America, San Francisco, CA, 94120 (Tel: 415-622-2491). $2.00 per copy. The "Business Operations" series is helpful for general information on running a business. Titles include: *Operating Your Own Business, Small Business Success, How to Buy or Sell a Business, Financing Small Business, Personnel for the Small Business, Steps to Starting a Business.* Other series are "Business Profiles," which cover specific small businesses, and "Professional Management," for doctors, dentists, veterinarians.

2. One of the finest pieces of information for understanding financial statements is offered free of charge by the world's largest securities firm, Merrill Lynch Pierce Fenner & Smith. This 24 page red book, entitled "Understanding Financial Statements," is so good it is often used as a free handout in graduate level college finance courses. It offers an understanding of the three basic financial tools.

1. Balance Sheet.
2. Cash Flow Statement.
3. Profit & Loss Statement.

May I suggest that you call your local Merrill Lynch office, which can be found in your local telephone directory.

3. Several excellent articles on developing a business plan are contained within the books offered by the most professional source of venture capital information, Capital Publishing Company. These books provide some of the articles on the business plan that are truly excellent and tips are practical and worthwhile.
Write:

The Center for Entrepreneurial Management, Inc.
180 Varick Street
New York, N. Y. 10014
212-633-0060

4. The Small Business Administration offers several excellent pamphlets on writing a business plan. These are very inexpensive and surprisingly good. They even offer further information on where to obtain further information on writing a business plan. I'd suggest your local SBA field office for current information.

    a. Small Marketeer Aid #153
       Business Plan for the Small Service Firm
       24 pages
    b. Small Marketeer Aid #150
       Business Plan for Retailer
       24 pages
    c. Management Aid for Small Manufactures #218
       Business Plan for Small Manufacturers
       22 pages

A new center was established in February 1978 to speed up the delivery process of SBA pamphlets. All requests to this high speed center should be on SBA Form 115A, which is a list of available SBA publications. Form 115A can be requested from the center. Write:

The Small Business Administration (SBA)
Box 15434
Fort Worth, Texas 76119
1–800–368–5855

The telephone recording service is available 24 hours per day, seven days per week.
    5. Business Plan Preparation

904 – HOW TO PREPARE AND PRESENT A BUSINESS PLAN/Joseph Mancuso, 300 pages. Brand new and already a best seller. Contains what you need to know to make your plan perfect. Includes three actual plans. $20.00 (hard)

905 – HOW TO WRITE A BUSINESS PLAN THAT RATES AN 11 (on a Scale of 1 to 10)/Four one-hour cassettes recorded live at one of Joseph Mancuso's recent live seminars on the subject. A complement to the business plan books, the tapes include questions from the audience. $65.00. The same material is available in a four hour VHS ½″ video series. Price–$100, includes workbook.

0482 – BUSINESS PLANNING GUIDE/Osgood & Bangs. 107 pages/1980 How to prepare and present a business plan in workbook format. A very popular book in 8½″ x 11″ format. $20.00

These are available from:

THE CENTER FOR ENTREPRENEURIAL MANAGEMENT
180 VARICK STREET
NEW YORK, N.Y. 10014
212–633–0060

6

Raising
New Money

THE ISSUES

After the decision to raise new money is made and a business plan is completed, several significant incremental decisions must be made. First and foremost, the fundamental decision must be made as to the basic form of the new funds—debt or equity. Straight debt financing must be paid back and it may not help the cash flow of the future business. On the other hand, although equity financing does not need to be paid back, it may prove to be an inopportune time to sell stock. This issue is reflected in the price per share of the stock. Once the basic decision is made (and often the eventual choice is to do a little of both), between equity and debt financing; a second level decision must be made which involves how to do it. The first issue was basically "what" to do, which depends on an analysis of the cost of capital.

If the "what" to do answer is debt, the "how" to do it question can become public or private, short or long term. If the "what" to do answer is equity, the "how" to do it question can become public or private, common or preferred. Naturally, various combinations of all of the above are also possible; and it is no wonder an entrepreneur is often frustrated in the area of finance just because of the vast number of possible alternatives.

After the "what" and "how" issues are decided, the next issue is "who." In other words, "who" will be the underwriter if the "what" choice was equity and the "how" choice was public. Or, if the "what" choice was debt, and the "how" choice was private long term, the "who" question becomes who will be the long term debtors of this business. Banks, insurance companies, and private individuals are potential candidates for this "who" answer.

Finally, and not least important, the question becomes "when." This is probably the most important question of all. The proper timing of a financing can make all the difference between a successful or unsuccessful issue.

Hence, the basic questions to be answered about raising new money are: What? How? Who? and When?

Of the above choices, one holds a long-lasting and undying appeal for an entrepreneur: the choice of going public. It is of such special importance that I shall deal with it in some detail.

NEW YORK STOCK EXCHANGE REQUIREMENTS[1]

A company making a public offering is expected to meet certain qualifications; and it must have a willingness to keep the investing public informed on the progress of its affairs. The company must be a going concern. In determining eligibility for going public, particular attention is given to such qualifications as: 1) The degree of national interest in the company; 2) its relative position and stability in the industry; and 3) whether it is engaged in an expanding industry with prospects of at least maintaining its relative position.

Although each case is decided on its own merits, the New York Stock Exchange generally requires the following minimums for Initial Listing:

1. Demonstrated earning power under competitive conditions of $2.5 million before Income Taxes for the most recent year and $2 million pre-tax for each of the two preceding years.
2. Net tangible assets of $16 million. Greater emphasis will be placed on the aggregate market value of the common stock.
3. A total of $16 million in market value of publicly held common stock.
4. A total of one million common shares publicly held.
5. Two thousand holders of 100 shares or more of common stock.

As any entrepreneur can see, the minimums of the New York Stock Exchange are often maximums for most small entrepreneurial ventures. However, having these goals in mind prior to deciding the issues of "what," "how," "who," and "when" can make the eventual choice a better one. In line with preceding description of the popular Regulation D, a discussion of the pros and cons of a public stock offer for a smaller company is presented below. As with so many issues in a small business, there is no single best answer: It just seems to depend on the goals of the firm and the current state of the financial markets.

ADVANTAGES OF PUBLIC OFFERING

For a small but expanding corporation, there are various advantages of having publicly held stocks. A few of them are listed below.

---

[1] These requirements are periodically tightened and made more restrictive. Please check with the New York Stock Exchange for latest requirements.

Additional Capital

Many small corporations find themselves in a position where retained earnings and short term loans do not meet their capital needs. Short term loan repayment dates often fall at disadvantageous times in the cash flow cycle. Permanent (equity) capital is often the best answer to long term expansion. Debt capital does not really strengthen a balance sheet, and the cost of capital is less for equity than for debt, at least under certain conditions.

Acquisition

Acquiring other companies in an expansion and diversification program becomes easier when the acquiring company's stock is publicly traded. Very often a company cannot be acquired or merged because the buying corporation does not have sufficient cash or because the selling corporation will not accept stock in a private, closely held corporation. However, if the buyer's stock is publicly held, the seller usually looks more favorably on marketable stocks. Some tax free transactions are also possible, but this is complicated and clearly requires legal counsel.

Repayment of Loans

Publicly held companies can sometimes more favorably renegotiate their debt structure if their equity structure is sound. This can happen if a public stock offering is extremely successful. For instance, if the after market price is significantly above the initial offering price, the issue is thought to be successful.

Valuation

Having a publicly traded stock eases a lot of valuation problems for "net-worth" calculations and estate tax purposes. The market value is known on a day to day basis.

Bank Loans

Equity financing creates a more favorable atmosphere for future borrowing, if the securities are publicly held and quoted daily in the "over the counter" market or on a regional stock exchange. A banker can better judge the firm's potential for further loans. The other alternative is to make assumptions or "guestimates" of the value of the business, neither of which is as significant as a value placed within a free market.

Visibility

If publicly held, the company receives better visibility, both for its stocks and its product. Publicly held companies are simply better known to the public.

Attracting Outside Management

The publicly held corporation has a very substantial advantage in attracting good second echelon management. The opportunity of offering these people stock option plans with the advantage of capital gains taxation can be a significant factor in hiring people. The public corporation will have outside directors: Some of these will be nominees of the underwriters, others nominees of the stockholders. If properly used, these directors can give the business new outlooks and guide it to new heights.

DISADVANTAGES OF GOING PUBLIC

Making a public stock offering is not a bed full of roses. There are also the thorns, which are demonstrated in this example. A glass company in Pittsburg was owned by Mr. X. He had been successful in business for several years, and his firm had shown a reasonable growth in both sales and profits. Mr. X and a broker arranged for a public offering of $300,000 of new stocks—representing 40% interest in the company—placing a total value of $750,000 on the company. The company received $245,000 after paying expenses for the sale of 40% of the company. Mr. X's company was originally worth $750,000 in total, but after the public sale, Mr. X's personal worth was only $367,500 on paper. This is based on the fact that Mr. X owned 60% of a company actually only worth $622,500, not $750,000. Soon after the public offering, public pressure to diversify and to raise the stock price increased drastically. Mr. X entered the boat manufacturing business, but soon found no market for the boats he built. Within a year, Mr. X had gone into Chapter XI bankruptcy and his stock was worth the same as the investors' stock—nothing. Chapter XI is a special form of bankruptcy designed to help small business, and it is explained in further detail in the last chapter of this book. The pressure to increase financial performance is a two-edged sword.

Following are a few of the disadvantages of going public.

Management of Your Company

As a publicly held corporation, you must adhere to the rules of the game—carefully and with exactness. There is no denying that you undergo a drastic change in your corporate activities as a result of a public offering. Your stockholders must be considered in every major decision. The written by-laws will have to be followed to the letter, and SEC laws will enter into the company decisions. You will lose a good deal of informal control over your company after a public stock offering, which, in essence, you've swapped for cash.

Employee Relations

Employees will now have access to financial information and may demand greater salaries. They are also prone to become stockholders, and their morale may follow the stock price.

Openness

The public corporation must operate totally in the open. Its contracts, if they are of major importance, will have to be revealed in the SEC prospectus. Payments to officers and directors must be totally open.

External Pressure

There will be considerable external pressure to continue growth. Suddenly every financial report you publish and every utterance you make will take on extreme importance. If it is not better or more optimistic than the previous one, you are in for problems, regardless of the reasons. You will be under constant pressure from stockholders—for the initiation of dividends or increased dividends, for listing the stocks, and for a host of nuisance variables.

As the owner or major stockholder of a private corporation, an entrepreneur must think long and hard about going public. You should carefully weigh the possible advantages and disadvantages of doing so. It is a different ball game when you are operating in a strange, open arena, under unfamiliar ground rules. It is not easy and it is not always the best thing to do.

PRICING THE ISSUE AND THE COST OF GOING PUBLIC

The price for which your stock will sell in the public market is a very important consideration. This price is dependent on the investment banker's or underwriter's evaluation of the company. In performing this evaluation, the underwriter obtains the following statistics about companies similar to the one being considered for underwriting. If one or some of them have recently gone public, then this firm will be studied very closely in establishing your price and valuation. The points of interest on similar companies are:

1. Number of outstanding shares
2. Where traded, and on what exchange
3. Market price on a given date
4. Dividend (current)
5. Yield (current)
6. Earnings per Share (last two years)
7. Earnings per Share (five year average, ten year average)
8. Price to Earnings (P.E.) Ratio (last two years)
9. Price to Earnings (P.E.) Ratio (five year average, ten year average)
10. Current Balance Sheet
11. Net assets per share
12. Net assets per share as percent of market price
13. Sales (current, five year average growth rate per year)
14. Percent long term debt to total debt
15. Percent preferred stock to common stock

The above data on similar companies allow the underwriter to compare and to forecast the future earnings per share, the yield values, and possibly even the book value of your business. When attempting comparisons, it is common to judge your company to be unique and to claim that it is impossible to find similar sized firms in the same industry. In that case, other companies that are comparable in size and type, even though they are not the same kind of business, may be used for these comparisons.

Other important factors in determining the valuation of the business are as follows.

Use of Proceeds

The company's intended use of the proceeds from a new stock issue is an important consideration. If the new capital is to be used for new construction or for a new product, the underwriter gains more confidence in the company's future earnings potential and will adjust the price/earnings ratio level upward, based on the expected earnings. If the intended use of proceeds is just to increase working capital or to pay off old debt, and if the firm anticipates maintaining the existing volume of sales, these applications of proceeds are unexciting to the underwriter, who subsequently reduces the valuation.

Earnings Adjustment

The underwriter will carefully examine the firm's balance sheet and income statement. For example, if the owner has been using $200,000 a year for personal expenses (perhaps for an airplane), whereas his stated salary is only $50,000, then the underwriter makes appropriate adjustments to the earnings figures and also makes subsequent valuations to adjust for these considerations.

Intangibles

After completing the comparison of similar companies, the underwriter will determine a price to earnings range of say between ten and twenty times earnings. How then, does the investment banker or underwriter decide whether to go to the top or the bottom of the range? In making this decision, they often examine the intangibles:

1. Competence of management to run an expanding and competitive business.
2. The owner-manager's plans for informing and impressing the outside financial community.
3. The quality and availability of labor.
4. The prestige the company holds within the community.
5. The prestige of the company's products with its customers.
6. The appearance and adequacy of the company facilities.
7. Acquisition or expansion policy of the company.

Size of the Issue

The total size of the stock issue can be an important variable which also affects the pricing. Some investment bankers believe that the issue must be of sufficient size in both number of shares and dollar value to generate an adequate after market. In contrast, some new issues have been richly priced as a result of the scarcity factor—that is, the relatively small number of shares in the offering. It is obviously easier to sell $1,000 of a new stock than it is to sell $100,000 of the same new stock. Simply said, fewer investors are needed to become stockholders for small issues. However, the shallow or small after market may result in wider fluctuations in the per share price of the stock.

Danger of Overpricing

The danger for a somewhat less glamorous company, if the first offering is overpriced, is that the reputation, confidence, and charisma surrounding the company can be destroyed. Once an underwriting fails to take off, it becomes increasingly difficult to stimulate market interest, and a downward propensity sets in. It is generally preferable to price an issue to yield a 10% to 15% premium in the after market for the initial investors. Keep in mind that most initial offerings of stock do not allow the founders to sell their stock at the initial offering price. This is commonly known as a bailout, and it makes the financial community nervous to discover that the proceeds of the offering are going into the founders' pockets and not into the company. Hence, the vast majority of the time, a founder will not sell his personal stock until a secondary public offering is made. Consequently, it is of significant interest for an entrepreneur/founder to maintain a healthy and growing after market for the stock.

ALTERNATIVE SOURCES OF CAPITAL

Frequently, a closely held company which needs financing will decide it is not ready to go public. Therefore, as a way of raising capital, making a new security offering may actually be the poorest choice of more than a dozen options which might be used. Until the company is absolutely ready for a public offering, here are some of the alternatives available to your firm.

Private Placement

This is an increasingly more popular method of financing. It does not require registration with the SEC if there are less than thirty-five investors who will agree to hold stocks for more than two years. This method saves a good part of the fees paid to brokerage houses, auditors, legal firms, and printers. In practice, this method almost always precedes a public stock offering.

The main disadvantage is that the private placement notes, debentures, or shares are often sold at a lower price to the private investor than the price at which the public offering might be made, thereby resulting in a greater dilution of the company stock. This, however, is also a function of the market for new issues, and the risks of this method should be examined individually, as the situation can vary greatly.

Banks and Lending Institutions

Banks can be useful in introducing corporations to other sources of capital, and they are usually the most common source of capital for inventories, short term financing, and so on. Some banks have small business investment corporations (SBIC) for equity financing, together with their banking service. Moreover, the Small Business Administration (SBA) most commonly works through banks in co-signing bank borrowing for the small businessman.

Finance Companies

These organizations provide continuing financing to business and they often supply good counsel. The disadvantage is that the cost of their money is usually higher than at banks.

Private Debt

Start-up operations are often financed by well-to-do friends and relatives of the founder. Remember that although mom and dad are not the preferred source of financial help, most of the time they are the actual source of seed money. This seed money may help to obtain further bank loans.

Family Corporations

High tax bracket families may be willing to invest money in high risk situations for their loss after taxes will be less due to the tax write-offs of 1244 stock. This is explained in more detail in Chapter 9.

Life Insurance Companies

These institutions are legally restricted to certain investments, depending on the states in which they operate. They generally do not assume a high degree of risk, but confine their investments to high quality issues and specialize in medium to long term credit. However, some insurance companies do purchase convertible debenture issues of small businesses. They may take warrants to buy common stock in order to make a long term debt package attractive.

Franchising Rights or Foreign Rights

Selling franchising rights is often another method of raising capital. The chief disadvantage is controlling and managing the franchises.

Patents or well thought out ideas may be sold to foreign countries or licensed to them as a way to raise funds for domestic operations. The disadvantage may be the loss of a significant potential sales volume. However, in many cases, the trade-off may be worth considering.

Trade Credit

Receiving inventory without paying for it immediately, or receiving prepayments for undelivered goods, are also short term sources of funds. Most of the time, in practice, these kinds of trade credit are the most common source of short term funds.

Mergers

A larger company with more available capital may merge with your firm or help out during a capital shortage. However, in such a case the founders may lose control and be dependent on the parent company for important decisions.

THE UNDERWRITER

For a small company seeking new funds, locating an appropriate underwriter may appear to be a staggering problem. Usually, most large underwriters have established minimum underwriting requirements of at least $5,000,000. Therefore, your task is to select the best interested underwriter to handle your issue. There are also those underwriters who specialize in small issues and who have experience in handling them. However, locating them is usually difficult, and it is an area where most small businessmen choose to seek assistance. An elite group of financial consultants, many located in New York, derive the major part of their livelihood from bringing together underwriters and investment bankers with small growing businesses in need of money. They are called finders or deal-makers.

Finders are normally financial or management consultants who operate on a percentage fee basis. The finder's job is to put your firm together with an underwriter, usually he will also help formulate the proposal.

Typically, a good finder will know which underwriter is interested in your type of business. The issuer pays the finder—either directly or through expenses passed on by the underwriter. Finder's fees usually range from 3 to 15% of the underwriter's compensation or between 0.5% and 1.5% of the total offering, depending upon the difficulty of placing the issue. Actually each finder has a group of underwriters with whom he prefers doing business for each type of business. Thus the selection of the finder often is the selection of the underwriter.

I suggest selecting an underwriter with an excellent business reputation—one with a reputation of handling issues similar to your own. The relationship with the underwriter does not end after the initial sale of your stock. As a matter of fact, the most important time in the offering is that period immediately following the initial offering. Typically, up to 20% of the shares purchased during the initial offerings is sold within a matter of weeks. If it appears that the market may not be sufficiently broad or strong enough to absorb such selling pressures at or above the issue price, responsible underwriters will attempt to establish a "short" position on the offering. For example, if the offering consists of 400,000 shares, the underwriter may attempt to sell 420,000 shares with a view to buy back 20,000 shares in the after market. The managing underwriter should also keep the financial community and investing public informed of a company's progress through research reports and press releases. A well-managed underwriting does not allow the per share price to fall below the issue price in the immediate after market.

During registration, your firm will be working closely with the underwriter, and you will have discussions with him on a daily basis. Because of this need for close communications, it is ideal if you can select an underwriter who has an office in your city.

In a small and primarily local stock offering, it is better to work with an underwriter who is familiar with the types of business in your industry. Of course, your prospective underwriter should have a broad experience in equity financing as well as a good retail organization so that, in the event his selling group develops an unexpected weakness, his own organization can take up the slack and sell the issues. If he has placed your stock with his own customers, the underwriter has more of an interest in sponsoring the after market of the stock.

A word of caution: Do not shop around or attempt to over-bargain for the best deal! The word will spread that you are shopping, and the prospective underwriter may not be anxious to spend the necessary time and effort to investigate and evaluate your proposal. After making a proposal to your first choice, wait until they render a decision; then move on to your second choice, and so on.

THE UNDERWRITING PROPOSAL

The specific underwriting proposal is all-important. You must put your best foot forward. Be forthright and candid, but don't hesitate to stress the positive points in your business. If you have an exclusive or exciting product, mention it. These are the ingredients which will set you apart from others and make your proposal interesting to the underwriter. Your proposal to an underwriter should include complete information on the history of your company, your current financial situation, and the future prospects for the corporation. Following is an outline of typical underwriting proposal.

I. The Company
   A. Description of the company with:
      1. Date of incorporation
      2. State of incorporation
      3. Principal stockholders
      4. Capital structure
      5. Location—area
      6. Customer description and category

II. The People
   A. Brief resume of the principal stockholders, officers, and key executives with:
      1. Age
      2. Education
      3. Previous employment experience
      4. Employment contracts and compensation
      5. Membership of other organizations, both business and social

III. The Product
   A. Description of the product line, excluding sales volume per category, major contracts, and expected future markets for existing and new products.

IV. The Future
   A. Competition
   B. Market penetration
   C. Growth and profit potential
   D. Diversification potential

V. The Proposal for a Public Issue
   A. Number and type of shares to be sold
   B. Proposed price per share and price justification
   C. Type of underwriting desired

THE UNDERWRITER'S AGREEMENT

There are many variances in underwriting contracts, depending on the nature of the purchase commitment. Because these agreements represent the essence of a deal between a business and an underwriter, they are crucial to your business. Below are some of the customary clauses that will appear in the underwriting or purchase agreement.

Purchase commitment. Under this agreement, the seller agrees to sell, and each underwriter agrees to purchase, a designated number of shares at the agreed price per share. The spread or commission deducted by the underwriter is clearly set forth in the agreement.

A "best efforts" arrangement is a denial of a purchase commitment by an underwriter. A best efforts offering usually means that the underwriter will use his or her best efforts to sell all of the stock at the agreed upon price. The underwriter does not make up the difference if the underwriting falls short. Simultaneously, some of the Regulation A best efforts underwritings do not even guarantee that a certain percentage of the stock will be sold. Be careful to determine precisely what happens if all of the stock is not sold within the specified time period. There are two basic choices when this happens: 1) The funds are returned to the new stockholders and the stock offering is either postponed or aborted; or 2) the funds are given to the company for the stock which is actually sold, and the remaining stock is sold at a lower price or returned to the firm as treasury stock.

Method of offering. The company authorizes the managing underwriter, as representative of the several underwriters, to manage the underwriting and the public offering of the shares. This authorization permits the underwriter to take any action that he deems advisable, including the determination of the time of the initial public offering of the shares, the initial public offering price, and the making of any change in the public offering price.

Trading in the shares. The company authorizes the principal or managing underwriter to make purchases and sales of the company's stock in the over the counter market at such prices as the managing underwriter may determine.

Delivery and payment. Provision is made for the payment of the full purchase price of the shares which the underwriter is obligated to purchase from the sellers.

Representations and warranties. The sellers make certain representations and warranties as to ownership of stock, marketable title, and so forth.

Statements. Certified and audited financial statements should be provided to the underwriters.

Expenses. Some contracts provide for a maximum dollar amount to be paid for this service.

In some contracts where the underwriting is on a "best efforts" basis, the company agrees to pay a fixed amount to cover the underwriter's expenses. Best efforts generally means that an underwriter will try his best to sell all of the securities at the price stated. However, if the underwriter falls short on this basis, the underwriter is not liable to make up the difference to the company, and the fees are still due and payable.

Indemnification of the underwriter. The agreement generally provides that the issuer and the selling stockholders agree, under the Securities Act of 1933, to indemnify the underwriters against liabilities which may arise as a result of misleading or untrue statements or through the omission of a material fact which should have been in the registration statement or the prospectus.

Raising new money is clearly the leadership task of the entrepreneur. No other activity is so clearly identified with the entrepreneur and, consequently, the degree of expertise used to accomplish this action is a direct reflection on one's entrepreneurial skills. Beginning with the all important business plan, the enterprise and the entrepreneur are submitted to the financial world in written form to be scrutinized and evaluated. The fundamental choices are debt or equity and public or private. Which combination and in which order will then dictate the financial ties and affiliations for the growing business. These early financial decisions are often precedent setting when the struggling new business matures. These early friends of the business will be old friends the next time the business sets out to raise new money.

MANAGING A SMALL BUSINESS

7

Managing The Small Enterprise

MANAGING THE SMALL ENTERPRISE

Over the course of the entrepreneurial life cycle, all entrepreneurs face an average of about two major and ten minor problems a day. They have to choose between alternatives, develop criteria, and guess a lot. However you look at it, it's quite a load. Whether they make their decision from a gut reaction, with eyes closed and teeth clenched, or whether they decide on the basis of solid research, there is a way to optimize success.

When given the choice of doing 80 percent of the job with 100 percent effectiveness or 100 percent of the job with 80 percent effectiveness, choose the latter. You don't have to do everything to perfection, just do everything! Leave no area uncovered. Neglect no detail. That's what I call balance. It helps minimize failure by inaction, which is a cardinal sin of entrepreneurship.

One of the most useful and enlightening books you can read has nothing to do with business. It was written by Vince Lombardi, the late, great coach of the Green Bay Packers football team. Called *Run for Daylight*, the book details his philosophy of winning in professional football. His record speaks for itself.

Lombardi was a master of strategy. While the other coaches were concentrating on super-duper, razzle-dazzle plays, he was working with the fundamentals over and over again. He ignored popular strategies—such as multiple offenses and defenses, flea-flickers, or excessive reddogging—that other coaches counted on to outfox—although they seldom did—the competition. Instead of learning fancy plays, the Packers were drilled in blocking and tackling. Lombardi's philosophy was that the team that could block and tackle best would win the game. It was primitively simple, but it worked.

Entrepreneurs who concentrate on executing the fundamentals well will increase their chances of winning manyfold—and winning's the name of the game when you are starting, financing, and managing a small business enterprise.

It's so easy to make broad generalizations when expressing a philosophy of managing a small business, that the preceding statements about execution may appear superficial. Yet, so often, the ball is dropped in expanding a small business because the owner-manager developed a plan which was too fancy for the company. Keeping the plan simple helps to smooth its execution. Don't compromise the need for simplicity in your plan, for it will make your business stumble-proof. There are many areas of small business management which must not be compromised—and simplicty of execution is one. Compromise is mandatory in politics, valuable in negotiating military conflicts, and helpful in solving legal disputes, but it can be dangerous for the struggling small business. The temptation to compromise in order to solve a current crisis exists for every entrepreneur. As the problems and decisions become more complex, such as in making the business plan just a little more complex, the temptation grows stronger.

Entrepreneurs seem to possess great intuitive powers, and it's generally best to trust your intuition for those tough decisions. Entrepreneurs are leaders, and leaders are made or destroyed on the issues they compromise or refuse to compromise. Napoleon Bonaparte said, "I'd rather have an army of rabbits led by a lion than an army of lions led by a rabbit." You are the one everyone has bet upon. They aren't so dumb; they know a good bet when they see it. Think through alternatives, weigh the criteria and then, once you've given the decision careful consideration—be a lion!

Managing a small business is fun. The tasks and responsibilities are a day-to-day joy and it's even more fun when you are able to poke fun at your down-to-earth serious work. A nose kept only to the grindstone often leads to a blurry eyed manager.

Managing a business is one thing, but running it successfully is something else altogether. All it takes to get a business going is a customer. To keep it going and to make it grow require a whole new set of expertise and skills—balance, simplicity, intuition, and an uncompromising execution of the fundamentals. And don't forget luck.

Businesspersons, unlike other professionals, require an enormous breadth of experience in order to be successful. In law, medicine, science, and engineering, the trend is toward specialization, and the person who succeeds in one of those fields has usually attained a high degree of skill in a narrow segment of it. They are *heart* surgeon, or a *criminal* lawyer, or a *microwave* engineer, or a *nuclear* physicist.

When it comes to running a large business, however, the best professional manager is a generalist—a person with a broad range of experience and knowlege which can be drawn upon to solve any problem from manufacturing to marketing. For most entrepreneurs, this transition from specialist to generalist is impossible. They often can't make the switch from doer to thinker and planner. The skills needed in a good manager don't fit the entrepreneurial personality—either they realize this soon or they fail. The strengths of the originator are in creating. The following quotation captures this message in an even more captivating way.

> An engineer is a man who knows a great deal about very little and who goes along learning more and more about less and less until, finally, he knows practically everything about nothing. A salesman is a man who knows very little about many things and keeps learning less and less about more and more until he knows practically nothing about everything.
>
> A purchasing agent starts out knowing everything about everything but, due to his association with engineers and salesmen, he ends up knowing nothing about nothing.
>
> (Source unknown)

The notion expressed in this quotation goes to the heart of the question of who is best equipped to head up a profit-seeking enterprise. Surely it's not a person with only one area of expertise. The leader must direct all areas of the business, not just a few areas.

The problems don't stop once an entrepreneur has managed to start a venture, put together a financing package, and build an organization. If anything, they increase in number and complexity. But they're different kinds of problems, more related to internal goings-on, and often they are more difficult to solve. With the money in the bank and the production line rolling, or customers rolling in, real growth requires real planning. That's how little businesses blossom into big ones.

PLANNING

For most small companies, long-range planning means thinking at breakfast about what to do after lunch. Stay alive in the short run, the practice goes, and the long run will take care of itself. On the other hand, academic theory contends that if you don't know where you're going, any road will take you there. In other words, the company that carefully plans for the future optimizes its chances for success.

No doubt academic theory is right; but for an entrepreneur, choosing between survival tactics and long-range planning is no choice at all—and here lies one of the fundamental differences between large established businesses and small businesses. The large company has advisors and staff assistants whose major function is to plan their company's every move. Small businessmen can't afford janitors, never mind planning staffs. The entrepreneur can only guess at a course or action and then try to stay flexible enough to consider another course at a moment's notice. It's a choice between thinking and doing. Big companies think; the entrepreneur does.

One of the least used but most helpful planning tools takes the simple form of an organization chart, which graphically depicts the relationships between the various functional business areas of a company. By defining the levels of authority, it minimizes confusion and optimizes efficiency.

A small company with management trouble seldom has a formal, publicized organization chart. An organization chart is effective only as long as the company's structure remains unchanged; and in a small growing company, the structure changes weekly, sometimes daily. Trying to update the organization chart would be like charting traffic at O'Hare Airport. But that doesn't mean that small companies neglect organization charts. Not at all. They just like to keep them secret. Tucked in the back of the center drawer of every entrepreneur's desk is a penciled sketch (usually on the back of an envelope) drawn for someone who inquired about his organization. It's usually covered with dotted lines and erasures, and a few names appear magically in more than one box. The entrepreneur always knows what the company would look like on an organization chart. After all, the organization chart is really the master plan designed to conquer the competition. The most meaningful allocation of a business's greatest asset, its human resources, is graphically depicted in an organization chart. Allocating resources is a central task for managers of all kinds but entrepreneurs/managers, who do it well, often keep it secret. Entrepreneurs would avoid a lot of confusion, improve communications, and stop a lot of internal politicking if they let their people in on it, too.

Beside the organization chart, another critical planning tool is the method of introducing new products. Because a small company can only have one or two significantly new products, their success or failure actually determines the success or failure of the firm.

NEW PRODUCTS

Launching new products has not usually been a champagne-bottle busting affair. A new product's success is often measured against a previous sales forecast. Sales predictions are the nerve center of the business plan. The sales forecast determines such items as how much you build or buy, for instance. Of course, new products have no sales history, and forecasting is difficult at best—but a forecast is the foundation for the vital business plan.

There are two basic approaches to predicting sales for new products. The first technique is called bottoms-up. The bottoms-up technique requires a build-up of sales by identifying potential customers and then summing up the customer requirements. Probabilities of buying are acceptable as long as you can pinpoint the customer and the application. Here, it is more important to know that the customer *will* buy than it is to know how much he will buy. Differences wash out if your customer base is above twenty-five companies.

The second technique, and it is by far the more common of the two, is known as tops-down. The tops-down technique requires that you estimate the total market and then predict your firm's expected market penetration. This technique has two dangerous weaknesses. First, errors abound in estimating the total market. Second, and more important, accurate penetration predictions are nonexistent. Typical of this technique are business plans for the new products introduced annually in the automotive industry. The sales forecast usually states: "In the U.S.A., nine million new cars are manufactured annually. We anticipate selling our product to 1¼ percent of these new car owners. Thus our first year sales will be 112,500 units." This sort of forecast is disastrous.

Forecasting new product sales by the bottoms-up method is the silent secret to happiness and success. Few follow it, and, as a result, turmoil reigns. Remember the entrepreneurial Golden Rule—Bottoms-Up. Beside the sales forecast, the other area of frequent concern for a new product is the price. Having an inaccurate sales forecast and the wrong price are a one-two punch that will knock out a small business.

Even with a bottoms-up forecast, the skill which most directly affects profits in small business is the ability to price your product properly. A great failing of many collapsing small businesses is not that they don't sell enough products but that the product that they do sell is priced too low. I have witnessed a situation where the weatherman on the local radio station also owned a small business making and selling weather instruments. The business grew and prospered, but eventually fell into hard times. The weatherman responded by using his good name as a weatherman to sell more weather instruments to a larger number of retail stores. For some reason, every year he seemed to be losing more and more money. Whenever he discovered he was losing more and more money, his solution was to sell more weather instruments to more stores. As he became more and more concerned, he sold more and more weather instruments. However, in the final analysis, the cause of the problem was really that he lost money on each unit he sold because his product was underpriced. Hence, his medicine for his problem was actually a cause for more of the disease. Pricing in a small business is a crucial issue which is seldom done very scientifically. There are three basic methods of pricing a product.

Pricing based on cost. This is probably the most common method of pricing. It involves calculating the precise material, labor, and overhead charges for a product and then adding a fixed percentage to those numbers to include profit. For instance, if the material cost is $10, and the direct labor is 2 hours at $10 per hour (or $20), and the overhead is charged at a 100% of direct labor dollars, the total cost of the product will be $10 for material, $20 for labor, and $20 for overhead for a cost of $50. Given a normal 15% profit, then under this method the product will be priced at $57.50 to the first level of distribution. Then the product would be marked up further until it reached its final retail or end user price. This method is known as pricing by cost; and it is in very common use by job shops and retail stores.

Competitive pricing. Pricing by what the competitor charges is a second popular method. In other words, when a product's actual cost data is difficult to determine, or if there is a great difficulty in selling at any price other than the market price, many companies simply choose to follow the price of the leading competitor. It is a very common pricing policy in commodities such as oil, steel, bread, and so forth.

What the market will bear. This method of pricing is by far the most difficult and is the least used. This method of pricing not only considers both a product's cost and its competitive situation but additionally factors in the third and most important variable: "What will the customer pay for your product?" This analysis deals not only with the product's individual features—comparing feature A of your product against feature A of the competitor's product—but also with the specific benefits your product provides the customer. For instance, if your product is presently selling for $100, and if by adding a new whistle or valve which costs only $1.00, it could then do twice as much as it does now, it does not make sense under this pricing technique of "what the market will bear" to price the product at only $101.00. Rather, it might make sense to price it at $110 or $120, depending upon what the customer will pay for the improved version of the product. This technique requires an appreciation of the customer's perceived benefits of your products. This is a very rare skill in a small business.

In planning a new product, an entrepreneur must not only plan for today, but even more importantly, he must prepare for tomorrow.[1] When the new product is at the early stages of its product life cycle, its entire life cycle should be planned before it occurs. This is like planning for a child's education while it's still in the womb. The value of preplanning the entire new product sequence is often the determinant for success or failure.

Good ideas for new products are plentiful, but good plans for profitable enterprises are few and far between. Profitable enterprises are all based on good ideas—in a process which roughly follows this sequence:

Idea→bread-board→prototype→product notion→first sale→repeat sale→ product profitability→profitable enterprise.

It's a long chain with many links and kinks and the danger rests in looking only at either end of the chain. The chain's weakest link is usually the product notion, not the idea. A product notion is the moment when someone sends a check for your notion. When raising venture capital, success will rest with your projections for enterprise profitability. But during the new product development, keep your eye on what actions are required to sell the first unit. And then, be sure that you receive payment for the sale. When the check is cashed, you have completed the product notion.

While your business plan may predict a going concern with $250,000 of profits within three years, that's all pie-in-the-sky when you have only an idea. The real issue

---

[1] Joseph R. Mancuso, "How to Manage Products," *Management Today*, London, England, January 1973, pp. 33–38. Joseph R. Mancuso, *Managing and Marketing Technology Products*, Artech House, Dedham, MA 1976, Vol. I and Vol. II, a handbook of readings with 48 articles on these topics.

is: "How much and how long will it take until the product notion?" That's the apple. Keep your eyes peeled for it.

Some of the above rules for product oriented businesses may seem irrelevant to service oriented businesses. This is not necessarily so. A service can be thought of as a product in its broadest sense. Hence, with certain modifications, the preceding product oriented comments can be applied to service oriented businesses. The special breed of service businesses known as retail stores, however, deserve a comment on the management issues which most directly affect their performance. This more specialized form of small business, retailing, is a favorite area for entrepreneurs.

Idea	A dream of vision
Bread-board	A crude prototype which may or may not actually do what it is supposed to do.
Prototype	A working model of what it will be like when it's done.
Product notion	When your business cashes a check for your goods or services from a bona fide customer.
Product sale	When your business actually sells your product through the normal distribution outlets to its first actual customer.
Repeat sale	When a customer buys your product or service a second time.
Product profitability	When the single initial product or service of your business becomes profitable for at least three months.
Enterprise profitability	When your business becomes profitable for at least one year.

Much speculation has been advanced as to why and how retail institutions either fail or succeed. The "natural selection" or "survival of the fittest" concept maintains that the retail institution that most effectively adapts to its environment is the one most likely to grow.

The "wheel of retailing" or life cycle concept explains the evolution of retail institutions. The basic premise, developed by Professor Emeritus Malcolm P. McNair of the Harvard Business School is that a new retail institution first appears as low-margin, low-price, and minimum-service businesses. As time passes, these establishments add more service and upgrade their facilities and offerings, which requires higher margins and higher prices. The process continues until these firms eventually become high-cost, high-price retailers at the top of the wheel that are therefore vulnerable to the next innovator who enters at the bottom of the wheel.

This wheel of retailing concept fits the empirical observations extremely well. As the fast food franchises began with a 15¢ hamburger and carry-out service, McDonald's today is difficult to distinguish from other restaurants. Discount bargain basement stores gradually move up the wheel and emerge as full service department stores. Gas stations begin as filling stations, grow to become gas stations, and then mature to service stations. The wheel continues as service station/car-wash (see appendix of book for the business plan on the B.L.T. car wash/gas station) and even service station/food outlets and service station/restaurants have emerged from the modest beginnings of filling stations.

An "accordion theory" is frequently used by retailers to explain changes in merchandise assortments. This explanation involves the historical tendency for retail business to become dominated (in an alternating pattern) by general stores, and then by specialty stores, and again by general stores. This alternating concept suggests that merchandise balance is yet another element that influences retail institutional change.

A new institution would probably begin as a specialty store because of limited capital and managerial knowledge. Gradually, as it became more successful, it would tend to expand offerings until it eventually became a general store.

BREAKEVEN ANALYSIS

A breakeven analysis is a critical calculation for every small business. Rather than calculating how much your firm would make if it obtained an estimated sales volume, a more meaningful analysis determines at which sales volume your firm will break even. The other statistic is really pie-in-the-sky, because the estimated sales volume is very questionable. Don't assume a sales volume and determine your so-called profits; do it in reverse: Determine the sales volume necessary for your firm to break even. Above the breakeven point, your firm makes money; below it, it loses money. A breakeven point, then, is a level of sales volume over some period of time, for example: "My firm broke even on $10,000 a week in sales."

The calculation of a breakeven level for every small business is one of the crucial financial pieces of information. Above the breakeven sales volume it is only a matter of how much money your business can generate, below the breakeven level of sales it's only a matter of how many days the business can operate before bankruptcy. Hence, it's a significant piece of financial data which is always changing as the business grows. A breakeven analysis might be required every few months to reflect your business growth.

A word of caution. In a small business, there is no such item as a truly fixed cost. No costs are fixed forever. Insurance can be cancelled, executives can be fired, and rent can be renegotiated. Hence, a fixed cost should be thought of as a fixed cost only over a period of time or over a finite range of production. Below is an explanation of a breakeven analysis.

Here is an example for a plant which produces only one product.
Assume the following:

A. The fixed costs are $100,000 per year. These costs include:
  —lights, power, and phones (utilities)
  —rent
  —insurance
  —administrative salaries

  These costs are fixed over 20,000 units to 40,000 units manufactured annually.

B. The variable costs over the 20,000–40,000 unit range are:
  $2.00   material
  $3.00   labor
  $1.00   overhead (50% of material)
  $6.00   per unit

C. Sales price per unit is $10.00

T.C. = V.C. + F.C.

Total costs = variable costs plus fixed costs

T.C. = Total costs, that is, all costs of operating the business over a specified time period.

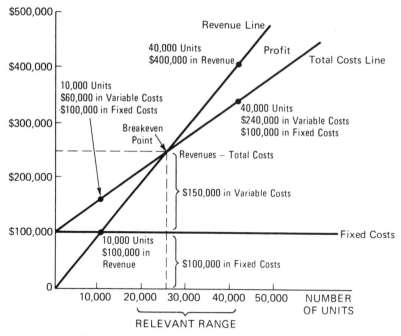

A Breakeven Chart

V.C. = Variable costs, that is, those costs which vary directly with the number of products manufactured. Sometimes called direct costs, these typically include material and labor costs plus a percentage of the overhead costs.

F.C. = Fixed costs, that is, costs which do not vary with the number of products produced. Also known as indirect costs, these costs typically include executive salaries, rent, and insurance, and are considered fixed over a relevant range of production.

B.E. = Breakeven point—that point where total costs are equal to total revenues.

The Breakeven Formula

Although the breakeven chart is probably the most useful means of visualizing breakeven analysis, we could have used the following formula:

$$\text{Breakeven} = \frac{\text{Fixed Costs}}{(\text{Revenue/Unit}-\text{Variable Costs/Units})}$$

Using the figures from our example, we have a breakdown equal to $100,000 ÷ 4 which is ($10-$6) = 25,000 units. Being able to determine the specific breakeven point is handy, but the main value of breakeven analysis comes in applying the concept to evaluate a variety of business problems.

Pricing Decisions

A common business problem is estimating the effects of raising or lowering a product's price. How many more products would we need to sell in order to maintain our profit level if we lowered our price a dollar? How many fewer would we need to sell in order to maintain that profit level if we raised our price a dollar? A rough estimate can be quickly made by drawing new revenue lines on the breakeven chart. If you do draw new revenue lines on the chart in Figure 1, you will confirm the finding that if the price is raised a dollar, the breakeven point drops from 25,000 to 20,000 units. If we lower the price a dollar, the breakeven jumps to 33,333 units. As you change the revenue line, you will also see how much the profits rise and fall with other price changes.

Breakeven is a valuable tool, but it is only one of many useful tools for analyzing your business. Breakeven oversimplifies decisions. Although the advantage is that it makes it easier to comprehend difficult small business issues, it also has some disadvantages. The assumptions behind breakeven are its disadvantages, and some of them are:

1. All fixed costs are not really fixed, even over the relevant unit range. They can and do vary.
2. A changing product mix can change the breakeven. The assumption that one plant produces one product can be misleading.
3. Costs do not vary directly with production. Material or labor costs often vary even over very narrow ranges.
4. Selling price is seldom fixed.
5. Inventory costs are seldom calculated within a breakeven, and these costs can be large.

As a final tool in *understanding* pricing decisions, the following formula can also be helpful for determining prices.

S.P. = T.C. + P.
S.P. = Selling Price = Per unit selling price
T.C. = Total Costs = Variable costs plus fixed costs per unit
P. = Profit = Profit per unit

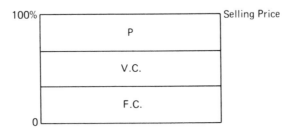

Product Price and Cost Chart

A further understanding of this breakeven calculation can be gained by comprehending a concept known as contribution analysis. Contribution is a difficult concept in practice, but it is easy in theory. Any revenue above the variable costs for a product can "contribute" to fixed costs plus profit.

Here is an example, using the formula.

S.P. = $10.00 per unit
V.C. = $6.00 per unit

$$\text{F.C.} \div 40{,}000 \text{ units} = \frac{\$100{,}000 \text{ F.C.}}{40{,}000 \text{ units}} = \$2.50 \text{ per unit.}$$

$$\text{Profit} = \text{S.P.} - \text{T.C.}$$
$$= \$10.00 - (\$6.00 + \$2.50)$$
$$\text{Profit} = \$1.50/\text{unit}$$

Hence, at 40,000 units, the firm will show a per unit profit of $1.50 per unit.

The crucial question in a contribution analysis usually occurs when the customer suddenly announces that he will pay $9.00 for your 40,0001st unit of production—take it or leave it. The classical school, which discounts the contribution type analysis, suggests that you should refuse the order. The contribution school claims that, if this is your only choice, you should take the order for the 40,001st unit at $9.00, for you will still be making 50 cents of profit [$1.50-($9.00-$8.50)].

In fact, the contribution school further argues, on this rare example, that it would be better to accept than to reject any revenue above the level of variable cost. For instance, a price of $6.01 per unit would be the lowest price where the order for the 40,001st unit should be accepted. At this level, the sale produces one cent to be contributed to profit and fixed costs. The decision, in the final analysis, will depend on other variables as well. But the purpose of this exercise is to outline the rationale of contribution analysis for use in your final decision-making.

SELECTING THE NAME AND FORM OF THE ENTERPRISE

Two of the most important tasks in starting a small business occur right at the outset of initiating the business. These are giving the corporate enterprise a name and form. This name will soon come to symbolize the entire enterprise, hence it's one of the early signs of a company's character. The form will determine how the business is to be established.

My fascination stems from the almost endless variety, the brilliant wit, and the useful information you find in the names people give their businesses. I've discovered that they all fit into one of several categories.

The most common category is ego-trippers. In this category are the people who just have to claim their little piece of immortality by putting their own names up in lights over the door. In my experience, this is often a foolish practice; and most of the time it's downright dangerous. If your business doesn't make it, having your name on it could be fatal for you (or maybe for someone else), even after the business has passed on. Beside the embarrassment of your business failing while your name is on it, just consider what might happen if it succeeds, if you then sell the business, and find that you don't like what the new owner does with your name. In both cases, the odds are strong you might change your name. I know of three cases where this happened. As I was visiting the campus of a college in Boston, I was introduced to a bright, young undergraduate named Edsel Ford. When I heard his name, I looked up and in a few mini-seconds a whole history of the Ford Motor Company's attempts to launch a fourth line of automobiles flashed before me. Before I even saw his face, I was mentally recalling one of the top half dozen business failures in the entire world. And then I saw his face and shook his hand and said, "Are you. . . ." The poor chap.

As further examples of the name problem, while not as colorful as the Edsel case, below are some of the problems of mixing your name and your business. Jim Pastoriza eventually sold his new business, Pastoriza Electronics, to a highly successful firm started by one of New England's premier entrepreneurs, Ray Stata. Pastoriza

Electronics soon became a division of Stata's business, Analog Devices, Inc. Incidentally, isn't that a great name for a business—Analog Devices? It's descriptive and thus it helps the customer seeking an analog device to find it. Anyway, Jim Pastoriza started a second company, Memodyne, and became disenfranchised with the use of his "name" on the products sold by Analog Devices. While Memodyne's products were not similar to the Pastoriza Electronics Division of Analog Devices, Inc., both companies serviced similar customers. Hence, Mr. Jim Pastoriza spent a few hours per day explaining the situation to his new group of Memodyne customers. Sounds funny, but it wasn't.

To look at another example, Royden Sanders, the founder of Sanders Associates of southern New Hampshire, had a similar experience. After selling his firm, he became so fed up with the acquiring management's so-called misuse of his name that he eventually brought a legal suit against them. He believed the company's new direction was so opposed to his chances of an optimal future, that he sought to disassociate his name from his former business. So, you can see that naming can be a problem.

Then there are those who understand the folly of putting their names on the business, but who can't quite resist it either. They use their initials (usually B.J. becomes BEE-JAY), or they combine initials or syllables to form the company name. Or they use the name of the street they happen to live on, or their children's name, to identify the business.

The best name for a company, in my opinion, is one that tells customers—especially potential customers—what the company does, makes, or sells. In fact, naming the company is the first move out of many in which you should keep the customer's needs first and foremost in mind. After all, there is only one essential ingredient for any business—a customer.

By the way, a few of my favorite names for the ego-trippers are classics.

Did you know that the first multipurpose liquid cleaner, Lestoil, was named for Jacob L. Barowsky's three children—Lenore, Edith, and Seymour. Moreover, Mr. Barowsky's business, Adell Chemical Company of Holyoke, Mass., was named for his wife, Adeline. Better yet, it's rumored that Eugene Ferkauf[2] named his world famous department/discount store E. J. Korvettes on the same basis. Although no one at Korvettes will confirm the rumor, the founders disclaim it stands for Eleven Jewish Korean War Veterans. In my home town, small businesses have been named after streets, wives' maiden names, and children, in that order. For instance, Sherman Olson named his highly successful plastics extrusion business after his daughter, Dana, and called his firm Danafirms. Howard Freeman named the Jamesbury Valve Company after his street, Jamesbury Way. Alan R. Pearlman named his firm, which is the world's leading manufacturer of electronic music synthesizers, after his initials—ARP Instruments, Inc. The same is true of Arthur I. Metzer, whose business is AIM Associates. It has been claimed that ITEK in Lexington, Massachusetts, stands for "I'll Takeover Eastman Kodak," but I could not confirm this. The list is endless.

Beside having a name, the business must also have a legal form, which will be explained in the next section. Just having a name does not establish a business: The

---

[2] Eugene Ferkauf and Joseph Blumenberg were co-founders of Korvettes Department Stores. They publicly claim that they chose the name Korvettes from a Canadian submarine chaser they were on in WWI. The "E" stands for Eugene, the "J" stands for Joseph. The "K" was changed from "C" and the "S" was added later. Incidentally, William Constantine founded and named Gurnard, Inc., in Beverly, Massachusetts, on a similar basis. He initially requested to use the name Cunard, based upon a pleasure trip he took on the famous Cunard ship line. They said no; he was disappointed; and so he named his business Gurnard.

real birth of the business occurs at the lawyer's office. Even for the smaller businesses, a single choice of legal form is necessary in order to establish records, to sign leases, to get bank accounts, and to file for taxes.

THE LEGAL FORMS OF BUSINESS

When establishing a new business, there are a number of choices for the legal form of the enterprise. Basically, the choices are as complex as one would like to make them. The eventual selection of a single form of legal enterprise for your business will depend a great deal on the goals of the business and on your individual goals. On the one hand, if you want to run a small quiet "mom and pop" type of operation, it may well be that a simple proprietorship is your best alternative. On the other hand, if you are interested in building another General Motors, it would be advantageous to structure your business for that eventuality and start a corporation with Section 1244 stock. This is explained further later on in the first section of chapter 9. The question facing all new businesses is how to organize at the beginning for the long term goals of the business. The advantage of organizing the most appropriate manner at the beginning is obvious to anyone who thinks ahead. The problem is that most businesses begin as proprietorships and after several changes eventually settle into the right niche. If, on the other hand, proper care and thought is given at the beginning of the new enterprise to the future of the business, it could begin on the right foot and not have to experience the changes necessary for expansion. This could avoid numerous changes and expensive legal fees for doing, undoing and doing again.

However, in many cases, it is not always best to start with the same form of business as you envision ten years in the future. It may make more sense to be sure that the form of business you choose will be most appropriate for your present business. The best advice in this area is to seek competent professional legal advice right at the beginning. Although I hold no bias toward do-it-yourself lawyers and do-it-yourself law books, my advice is to seek out the biggest and best lawyer in the nearest city to give advice—and then to listen to what he says. He will be most able to advise you on your selection from among the different types of businesses. Below are the fundamental forms of business that you could establish.

Partnerships

Limited partnership. A business association formed by one or more general partners or formed by one or more limited partners is known as a limited partnership. The limited partners will have liability to a definite pre-stated amount. The limited partners cannot participate in management, and that is how they protect their limited liability status.

General partners contribute both capital and management time, and are responsible for business debts. Limited partners may contribute capital without management liabilities and responsibilities. The general partners may also be responsible personally for any debts or obligations of the partnership. Hence, they may actually have more at risk than just the funds they have actually invested.

For several reasons a partnership is often chosen as the preferred legal form of a business. They are popular for real estate and for small businesses. One of their advantages is that they do not have a double taxation, as a corporation does. Hence, if your equal five-person partnership made $10,000 in one year, each partner would claim $2,000 of income on his personal income tax.

As a limited partner, an investor may deduct partnership losses from personal income. Under subchapter "S" of the Internal Revenue Service (IRS) Code, corporations with ten or fewer stockholders may elect to be taxed as a partnership. Beginning in 1977, the maximum number of stockholders in a subchapter S corporation has been increased from ten to fifteen, provided the corporation has been electing subchapter S corporation tax status for five consecutive years. This tax advantage can be substantial for high income individuals who can now combine their high personal income with the losses in the corporation for an overall lower taxable income. Without subchapter S, the losses in the corporation could only be used to shield corporate income and never pass through to shield stockholders' income. In the event the corporation never generated any positive income (some never do), this can be a truly significant advantage as without it, the corporate losses are never utilized to shield any income. They are simply wasted or unused. Hence, this tax advantage of a partnership can also be available to certain corporations.

General partnership. An association of two or more persons to act as co-owners and cofounders of a business for profit is known as a general partnership. A joint venture is more limited in scope and duration, although otherwise it is basically identical to a general partnership. For tax purposes, both are treated the same.

Proprietorships

Sole proprietorship. This is a non-corporate ownership of a business by one single individual with no partners. A sole proprietorship is actually the absence of any legal form of business organization. It does not require a lawyer to establish. It can be done with no action as a sole proprietorship is, the absence of any legal form of business.

A business or A Massachusetts trust. An unincorporated organization created for profit under a written instrument or trust arranged by trustees for the benefit of persons whose legal interests are represented by transferable certificates of participation. No filing fees or taxes are required in order to establish this form of business trust; the only expense is the legal services to draw up the declaration.

Corporations

A corporation. This is the most common form of business enterprise. A corporation is a legal entity, which is created under legal statute, and which is composed of stockholders under a common name. It has limited liability which is its greatest attraction, and thus a succession of ownership becomes possible. Under ordinary business law, a corporation is treated as though it were another individual, and it has rights and obligations similar to those of an individual.

A joint stock company. An association of individuals who join together for the purposes of making a profit in a business enterprise can be established as a joint stock company. These individuals must contribute common capital, which is represented by transferable shares held by the members. In essence, the joint stock company is a corporation whose members have unlimited liability. This varies from state to state. It is not a very popular form of business.

The above highlights two of the central chores which must occur at the birth of a business—the name and legal form of the business. The birth of a business is exciting when it is done right. A stillborn business is a tragedy. So pay close attention to the name and legal form of the enterprise in order to make the baby a healthy child.

Drawing the analogy that starting a small business is like having a baby is a common practice among writers in the field of entrepreneurship. No less care or concern should be given to the very early stages of starting a small business than to the early care given to a pregnant woman.

Once the business is named and formed, the tasks of the entrepreneur shift to managing and allocating resources. The starting process only occurs once, and it is therefore unique; the managing function continues every day, and it is continual. An entrepreneur who has created a business must begin the managing process by using external and internal resources in order to accomplish the stated mission.

Resources. There are three fundamental elements which must be mixed together to make an on-going profit-seeking enterprise. When the three elements are blended in the proper proportions at the proper time, the business enterprise will succeed. When the mix is optimal, the business can blossom beyond human expectation. The efficient use of internal resources is a most important task, and blending the 3Ms efficiently is a crucial skill. These three fundamental elements are known as the 3Ms.

1. money—finances
2. men—personnel
3. machines—the function which produces your product or service.

Triangle of Small Business

The rule to remember in an entrepreneurial venture is that some of each of the three ingredients are always necessary for an on-going profit-seeking enterprise to exist. Marketing is the fourth M, but it is hidden in the 3M triangle of small business. Marketing, or in other words, customers, is what makes the triangle churn and turn. The rule below, which should not be forgotten, describes the interrelationship among these three variables within a small business.

The men who manage men, manage the men who manage machines.
The men who manage money manage the men who manage men.

In other words, these three ingredients are ranked in this order: money, then men, and finally machines.

Along with the internal resources symbolized by the 3Ms, an entrepreneur must prudently make use of external resources in order to assist the business in meeting its objectives. External resources are usually considered those resources not fully under control of the business, and part-time employees are a good example of an external resource. These part-time outsiders often become part of the full-time team at a fraction of the cost of a full-time member. It's often a good value. Together with the 3Ms for internal resources, these external resources become the tools for fulfilling the entrepreneurial dream. See the section on the use of management consultants and outside assistance in the third chapter, "Building an Entrepreneurial Team."

A central issue in small business is the entrepreneur's effectiveness in using non-employee help. Consultants are but one example of this type of help: Bankers, lawyers, accountants, insurance agents, advertising agencies, manufacturers' representatives, boards of directors, suppliers, customers, friends, and ex-employees are additional examples. These non-payrolled friends of the small business are invaluable because they often offer more value than they cost to a small business. Not always; but many times this working relationship is an excellent exchange for both parties. Typically, this depends on the entrepreneur's individual effectiveness in dealing with these groups. An entrepreneur can derive infinite value from this non-fixed cost group of helpers.

However, there are two fundamental aspects of small business which should never be delegated or subcontracted to outsiders. It's even risky to allow insiders to make these two decisions. These two topics are so central to the success of the small business that delegating these decisions would in fact be an abdication of the responsibility for the decisions. They are: 1) The nature of what you take to the market; and 2) The price of what you take to the market. The above two decisions are at the heart of all business, small businesses included. Be careful about relinquishing this decision; and be sure to gather in everyone's opinion before you make the ultimate decision. During any planning task, the resolution of these decisions is the final achievement. When these decisions are made well, the enterprise wins; when they are flubbed, the enterprise loses. I call the first the heart of the business, and the second its brains.

AVOID MISTAKES

Starting and managing a small business is similar to two dissimilar American pastimes: motherhood and gambling. Like a mother with her child, the entrepreneur becomes emotionally attached to his business; and just as it isn't easy for a mother to untie the apron strings, the entrepreneur hates to let go of the "baby." Often this attitude prevents the enterprise from realizing its full potential. On the other hand, a business is often like a card game; and the entrepreneur who adopts the card player's attitude will be better able to cope with the inevitable separation. A cardplayer is a specialized form of gambler who bets on acquired card playing skills for fun or profit. He seldom develops a love for the cards per se, but more romance is generated for the game and even more romance is generated for the results of the game.

In a card game, the gamblers place the stakes on the table and play to win. In reality, they may win, break even, or lose. But the wise players know when to quit—when they have obtained the maximum possible leverage from their combination of capital and talent, or when they have taken enough abuse. There's no room for emotion in a card match.

So should it be in a small business. Leave emotion behind, and, at the appropriate time, get up from the table. Don't be ashamed to take your winnings; and be courageous enough to walk away from your losses. There will always be another game on another day. If this sounds too callous, and you'd prefer to continue playing—or should I say, managing—there are ways to ease some of the pain. Aspirins help, but they don't cure the sickness. There are good sources of advice which can help avoid mistakes.

Every entrepreneur needs good, competent advice from time to time. Of course, there's usually plenty around—from friends, family, and associates. And for the really deep stuff there are consultants, lawyers, accountants, and bankers. Everybody knows about them. But here are a couple of generally unknown sources of help and advice. Also, see my grouping in Appendix B entitled "Associations of Value to Small Businesses."

The Bums Club

In Boston there is an informal club of formal entrepreneurs who have successfully started, managed, and left their own small businesses. Usually they built their companies to a sizable volume, found the problems beyond their scope, and then sold the company. Typically, they've stayed on for some time as consultants, and then left for greener pastures.

They've come to be known as the BUMS (Boston Unemployed Men's Society); and they make up one of the most socially elite "clubs" around. They are mostly operating people, capable of putting together people, technology, ideas, and profits; and they often show up as consultants and friends to businesses in trouble. There are BUMS or their equivalents everywhere; and no entrepreneur should overlook this source of help. You can usually find them in the yellow pages under management consultants.

Psychologists

Bruce Patterson defines a psychologist as a man who, when a beautiful girl enters a room, watches everybody else. This could be, but when they're not watching the girl-watchers, professional industrial psychologists are playing an increasingly important role in small business. More and more, entrepreneurs use their services to help them over tough spots.

Entrepreneurs are often driven by deep-seated desires, and they experience periods of deep frustration and depression. A competent psychologist can do them a lot of good. I've known several entrepreneurs who have gained valuable insight into their own motivations and drives with psychological assistance, and have improved their own situations in the process. So, if you ever feel the need, don't be ashamed to call on a psychiatrist or a psychologist. They don't perform miracles; but in the process of getting to "know thyself" better, you can relieve some of the tension and frustration experienced by both successful and unsuccessful entrepreneurs.

These small business frustrations are honestly natural and should not be avoided. Only mistakes should be avoided; frustrations should only be controlled. One of the greatest sources of frustration occurs during sudden expansions of the business. Here, the nice and simple separation of frustration and mistakes is not as well defined. Almost universally, entrepreneurs strive to expand, and the mistakes which inevitably occur through expansion are often the source of the frustration.

Every business enterprise eventually has to choose between bigger sales or bigger profits. Most entrepreneurs will choose sales on the assumption that bigger sales equal bigger profits. This is a serious source of frustration and can be a source of mistakes.

Sales are, after all, the most visible sign of a company's success, and sales draw the most applause from spectators. Outsiders seldom know a firm's level of profitability. What outsiders know is what they see—a new and larger building, more sumptuous offices, more and more employees. The entrepreneurs must choose between nice offices and a good return on investment or a bigger net worth.

Profits are what keep a business healthy and growing. In the early stages, sales growth may attract capital; but only rarely can a company consistently have sales growth and profits. So, when the business reaches that stage where a crucial choice between sales and profits develops, the entrepreneur is often the wrong person to be making the choices: The monster he created is more than he's equipped to handle. The entrepreneur will surely opt for sales growth and blow the whole shebang.

This is a difficult issue which should be continually readdressed. There is no best answer for when the baby has outgrown the parent. It's just another of the difficult decisions facing the owner-manager of a small business. Although its importance is vital to long term success, it is just another area requiring sound entrepreneurial judgment. The successful entrepreneur makes the majority of these judgments well, and the others fail in both the judgments and the business.

In the course of every entrepreneur's career he experiences both successes and failures. Being realistic, you must admit that you can't strike out every time, but you're not going to clear the fence every time either. Even in his prime, Ted Williams walked back to the dugout with a hit six out of every ten times at bat.

For the entrepreneur, though, a .400 batting average isn't good enough; what he has to do is to get up to bat more often and thereby get more hits. Now this doesn't mean a higher batting average; but it can mean more hits. Improving the batting average is tough, but getting more hits just requires more effort.

An entrepreneur in the machine shop business had the right idea. When asked whether it was better to work hard or to work smart, he said, "I work hard and smart. You can't beat that!" Remember too, that it's not necessary that you always choose the best course of action; but that you make the course you *do* choose work—and often you can do it by getting to bat more often.

When an entrepreneur is starting his business, the last thought to enter his head is that of failure. This is as it should be; but keep in mind the wise words of Henry Ford, America's premier entrepreneur, who said that "Failure is the opportunity to begin again, more intelligently." One of the ingredients most necessary for success is failure. Entrepreneurs nearly always pass through failure on the road to success. Most don't even try to avoid it, recognizing that it may be only a necessary detour on their way. Think of failure as a resting place, and you're in the proper frame of mind to start a business.

Remember, too, that success is relative. That is, you must measure it against a previous level of accomplishment: such-and-such was more or less successful than something else. To express it another way, success (or lack of it) is what's left after you subtract your total failures from your total successes. It's the remainder that counts.

There is a fundamental law of business, commonly known as Murphy's Law, which governs success and failure. Like the law of gravity, it can't be explained—it is just accepted as a universal truth. On the basis of my experience, it is especially pertinent to the entrepreneur. When starting a business, remember Murphy's Law: "If anything can go wrong, it will." Mancuso's corollary to Murphy's law adds: "When it goes wrong for you, it'll be when you least expect it." You'll see.

I've enclosed a collection of Murphy's Laws for your enjoyment and betterment, and as a final message to help the small businessperson avoid mistakes.

A COLLECTION OF MURPHY'S LAWS

Some authorities have held that Murphy's Law was first expounded when he stated that "If anything can go wrong, it will—during the demonstration."

1. Nothing is as simple as it seems.
2. Everythings takes longer than it should.
3. The more innocuous a change appears, the further its influence will extend.
4. All warranty and guarantee clauses become void upon payment of invoice.
5. The necessity of making a major design change increases as the fabrication of the system approaches completion.
6. Firmness of delivery dates is inversely proportional to the tightness of the schedule.

7. Dimensions will always be expressed in the least usable term. Velocity, for example, will be expressed in furlongs per fortnight.

8. An important Instruction Manual or Operating Manual will have been discarded by the Receiving Department.

9. Suggestions made by the Value Analysis group will increase costs and reduce capabilities.

10. Original drawings will be mangled by the copying machine.

11. In any given miscalculation, the fault will never be placed if more than one person is involved.

12. In any given situation, the factor that is most obviously above suspicion will be the source of error.

13. Any wire cut to length will be too short.

14. Tolerances will accumulate unidirectionally toward maximum difficulty of assembly.

15. Identical units tested under identical conditions will not be identical in the field.

16. The availability of a component is inversely proportional to the need for that component.

17. If a project requires n components, there will be $n - 1$ units in stock.

18. A dropped tool will land where it can do the most damage. (This is also known as the law of selective gravitation.)

19. The probability of failure of a component, assembly, subsystem, or system is inversely proportional to the ease of repair or replacement.

20. A transistor protected by a fast-acting fuse will protect the fuse by blowing first.

21. Left to themselves things always go from bad to worse.

22. Nature always sides with the hidden flaw.

23. If everything seems to be going well, you have obviously overlooked something.

Leading
The Small
Enterprise

LEADERSHIP

Effective management of a small business requires a clear and concise answer to the question: "What business are you in?" This single question has been the most difficult to resolve for all businessmen, for small as well as large businesses. The answer is elusive, and the pace of internal or external changes in a small enterprise requires a never ending examination of this question. This question is the focus of most presidents and managers. Its answer is the zenith of intellectual achievement for any leader. All but a handful of leaders answer it ineffectively and thereby fail at this most fundamental level of conceptualization. According to Drucker, *all* companies which answer this question properly eventually succeed.[1]

"What business am I in?" is the question which establishes the mission of any organization. An effective answer requires a definite, accurate, and meaningful statement of an organization's goals, objectives, and purposes. The question is a bit circular and jelly-like, but it lies at the heart of leadership related activities in a profit-seeking business. A complete answer requires a comprehensive analysis of the strengths and weaknesses of the firm, combined with an appreciation of the firm's future needs within a changing marketplace. This issue was originally articulated by Peter Drucker in the mid-fifties in his classic book, *The Practice of Management*. It was reintroduced in the mid-sixties in an award winning *Harvard Business Review* article by Theodore Levitt, "Marketing Myopia."[2] The importance of the question and its subsequent answer is widely accepted as the pivotal survival issue for every small businessman. This question is analogous for a leader and an organization to the soul-searching question confronting

[1] Peter F. Drucker, *Practice of Management*, Harper & Row, 1954.
[2] Theodore Levitt, "Marketing Myopia," *Harvard Business Review*, 1965.

every individual: "Who am I?" "Who am I?"—for the individual; "What business am I in?"—for the organization.

The preceding parallel is not perfect, but the significance of a comprehensive answer for each question is similar. The more clearly and meaningfully these questions are answered, the more successful the individual and the organization will be.[3] When an organization is successful, so is its leader. It does not follow that because a leader is succcessful, the organization will be successful as well.

The highest managerial position in any business requires a generalist. This is the way it is in both profit and non-profit business. It is true for all competitive types of organizations. The top position in a small company also requires a generalist. A man or woman capable of broadly understanding each of the business functions is universally judged the most able administrator. A small company president is seldom expected to have obtained a high degree of proficiency at a narrow skill within a specific discipline. The single best person in finance seldom makes the best small company president. The single best engineer seldom makes the best small company president, and the single best salesman seldom makes the best small company president. Entrepreneurs have some difficulty understanding this fact of life, but it is one of the few universal truths which seems to hold from company to company. The president of a small company must have a broad experience and scope, for he or she will be responsible for *all* business functions, not for just a select few. The individual who possesses a high degree of specialized skill as well as the broad based skills required of a generalist is very rare. The degree of specialized and generalized skill of the highest positions is a fundamental difference between management and other disciplines.

LEADERSHIP TASKS

One of the central tasks for any president is to lead. A small company president who doesn't lead is seldom the best person to be allocating resources and deciding complex issues. Although this declaration may overstate the importance of a leader in small business, many entrepreneurs believe it may just be that the speed of the leader is the speed of the pack. But what is leadership within a small company? How can an entrepreneur lead?

There are three components to the answer to this question. The first element can be ascertained by determining whether or not the administration is active or reactive. Just classifying management actions in these two categories can offer insight into an organization's effectiveness. When analyzed in this manner, it's surprising how few actions can accurately be classified as active. Most actions are responses to previous actions; hence, they are reactive. Don't be confused, because in some way every action is a response to another action. Moreover, some actions are inconsequential regardless of their source. The "active" actions are originally initiated by the person who takes the action; and the consequences of these actions must be significant. In simple words, active actions are not putting out day-to-day brush fires but instead are gathering fuel to develop a crossfire for the problem.

The life blood of any organization is the changes it generates based upon the improvements it makes. These changes and new actions have a beginning somewhere—they come from someone. Nothing ever happens by itself, especially in a small business. Individuals cause things to happen.

[3] Joseph Mancuso, "How A Business Plan is Read," *Business Horizons*, August 1974, p. 33–42.

Leadership's vital function, based upon the above, is to have some balance between active and reactive actions. With such a balance, new blood, new thinking, and new ideas can be introduced in order to provide new directions. The more mundane administrative tasks—the day-to-day routines—are demanding, and they can exhaust any leader's excess available drive. The demanding nature of the leader's job barely allows time to process and decide the issues which require immediate attention. A great leader, on the other hand, accomplishes all the mundane tasks in the morning and initiates new active actions in the afternoon. That's what makes a great leader great: He is out front.

The second component of how an entrepreneur can lead is the image created by an effective small business leader—the manner or style which separates him from the follower. This style is known as charisma for great leaders, and not mentioned for the others. The only ingredient necessary to be a leader is to have followers. Without followers, a leader is not a leader.

In private conversations and in small groups, many leaders have a tendency to let their hair down—to tell it like it is. And, in so doing, they might claim, "Hell, this company is full of misfits, the whole group's below average." And most would be right on both counts. But, in turn, this private statement of the existing reality ignores the positive image a great leader must create. If the leader's aspirations drop off, how will the group view itself? The same organization of employees could be viewed as "dedicated people" or "comers," with their future ahead of them. It's the president's job to carry the torch and to lead the way. And it's a central job in managing a small business of your own.

Thirdly, a leader sets goals and allocates resources according to priorities. This is the classic management function at its best. What to do, how to do it, and whom to have do it, are the charges. Only the top person in a hierarchy can resolve conflicts. This role is the most visible and feedback on these decisions is immediately available.

The statement which has survived several thousand years—"No man can serve two masters; for either he will hate the one and love the other or else he will hold to the one and despise the other" (Matthew 6:24)—is commonly ignored in managing small businesses. It's only occasionally ignored in managing larger businesses. In either case, it should *not* be ignored, as it appears to be as true today as it was 2,000 years ago. A great leader doesn't encourage split loyalty among the followers; rather, he emphasizes the value of following a specific course of action.

A MODEL FOR THE FUTURE EXPANSION OF A SMALL BUSINESS

Below is a conceptual framework for evaluating the fundamental options available for the future expansion of a small business. The model offered is that of a baseball infield, with the small business examining the impact of moving toward any of the four bases placed around the pitcher's mound.[4]

1. Home base: suppliers
2. First base: related businesses
3. Second base: customers
4. Third base: unrelated business
5. Pitcher's mound: small business as it is today

[4] Dereck A. Newton, *Cases in Sales Force Management*, Richard D. Irwin, Richard D. Irwin, 1970, p. 7.

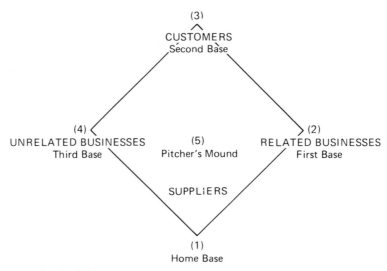

Baseball Diamond Model for Evaluation of a Small Business
Expansion Alternative

This model forces an analysis by a company president: He can systematically evaluate all the bases before eventually selecting the most appropriate future direction for an expanding enterprise.

Goal setting can be simplified by envisioning a firm as having strategic options which are modeled after the simple baseball infield diamond. Given the analogy above, with a company pictured on the pitcher's mound of a ballfield, the firm's strategic options are more comprehensible. In setting goals for any organization, this simple baseball field provides a model for a systematic planning process that can evaluate the alternative directions in which an organization could consider expansion. No organization is static, and while some are more dynamic than others, each organization's future direction is a function of its internal strengths in combination with the most promising alternatives available. Hence, judging the organizational attractiveness of moving toward first base or third base is a valuable input to be factored into the goal-setting process.

Below is an example of how to use this strategic model in evaluating the expansion of a small business.

Home Base (Suppliers)

Who are the suppliers of raw material and input products to the company? Are any of these inputs crucial elements to the company's long term survival? If these input products are made better or less expensive, do the company's products also get better or less expensive in the same proportions? For instance, one of the suppliers to a computer manufacturer are the many semiconductor manufacturers. As the semiconductors improve, so do the computers. In turn, one of the suppliers to a semiconductor manufacturer would be a silicone chemical manufacturer. As the silicone gets better or less expensive, so do the semiconductors. And, in turn, so do the computers which incorporated the semiconductors which use the better or less expensive silicone. This form of input/output analysis is a common practice in business, and it recognizes the reliance of one manufacturer on another.

The interesting issue to address in this input-output analysis is how much "better" each output becomes as a function of the improvements of the inputs. For instance, does the semiconductor become four times better when the silicone becomes twice as good? Following on, does the computer become five times "better" when the semiconductors become five times better?

To follow this exercise for a company requires identifying the suppliers to the firm. Obtaining a list of suppliers could begin by examining the products and services the company purchases. Although this is only one input (purchased goods), this point of departure often produces interesting findings and clues as to appropriate additional inputs to the company. When this input is coupled with other (purchased) inputs, a more complete list of suppliers becomes available (travel agencies). These indirectly purchased goods or services must be carefully analyzed to determine just what is being paid for, for example, a leased company automobile. From such a complete list of suppliers, a more meaningful analysis of expanding a small business toward the home base (or suppliers) can be conducted.

This same approach to evaluating meaningful corporate objectives was followed by a manufacturer of computer printers in Woburn, Massachusetts called Printer Technology, Inc. (P.T.I.). This young technical firm designed a new computer printer and subcontracted the manufacturing of the component parts to outside vendors. While examining the 800 different parts which comprised the new computer printer, PTI discovered that three basic parts accounted for over half of the purchased parts costs. As PTI sought to improve its competitive position, it examined the cost savings available from manufacturing these three components internally rather than subcontracting them externally. The decision to examine in-house manufacturing for these three components had two important considerations.

First, in-house manufacturing offered better control and availability over the most important portions of PTI's product. This type of manufacturing represented both better quality and broader control over production schedules for the new computer printer. Hence, as these three parts became slightly better, the PTI Printer became much better.

Second, PTI was eventually able to reduce the cost of the overall computer printer because in-house manufacturing allowed them to reduce the majority of the cost of the three out of 800 components which comprised the majority of the computer printer. Although three out of eight hundred components is less than 1% of the components by number, these specific three components represented more than 50% of the costs of all eight hundred components. The profit margin of the previous subcontractors became available to PTI after they reached minimal levels of in-house manufacturing.

In extending this method of analysis to a growing small business enterprise, the two fundamental questions become, "What does the firm purchase on a repeat basis?" and "What are the critical inputs to the small business?"

The strategic question for the small company located on the pitcher's mound is whether or not to integrate backwards by offering either less expensive or better control over its input products. Should a small business offer its own private labels or contract these services to an outside vendor? Does "in-house" production of these raw materials allow more quality, a reduced price, or better control? In establishing the company's goals, the implications for long run survival via backward integration toward home base should be compared to the other choices of expanding toward first base, second base, and third base alternatives.

First Base (Related Products)

The choice of expanding toward first base is one of the most popular options for an expanding profit-seeking enterprise. The computer printer manufacturer mentioned earlier (PTI) eventually decided to offer computer-related products in order to broaden its product line. The chosen additions to the product line need not have the same customers or suppliers as the existing products, as that choice might be best classified as being a home base or a second base alternative, respectively. A related or first cousin product is what is considered as a first base alternative.

An example of PTI was a video display terminal better known as a television screen. This product may have a few customers and suppliers in common with the original computer printer, but there need not be a great deal of commonality between the computer printer and the video display terminal. The technology of the two products is related but not identical. Hence, it represented a first base choice, or in other words, a related product for PTI.

Examining this question for a specific firm requires an initial determination of the business of the firm. The secondary question becomes, "What are the related businesses or products?" There are several levels to any business. For instance, the customers or suppliers can be segmented by sex, age, technology, and geography as well as by several other variables. Hence, one could define related businesses (or first base alternatives) as segments of markets.

Methods of Determining Related Business

1. New users for existing products
2. More varied uses for existing customers
3. More frequent usage among current users
4. New uses for the product

Articulated originally by Theodore Levitt[5] of the Harvard Business School, these methods represent the classic four choices available to a product manager of an industrial product or a brand manager of a consumer product.[6] Transferred into small business, these four choices can also provide a framework for examining the options of a small business to expand its products.

Just identifying the market segment or the new product area is not enough. The small firm must recognize its own resources when evaluating this alternative. The grass is not always greener in another, but related, market area. Success would require a small business to offer a superior product in a free marketplace. This may be a utopian objective which is discarded by the president during the evaluation of all the strategic options. However, in the baseball model, the alternative of expanding toward first base or related businesses requires a careful evaluation of a firm's strengths and weaknesses prior to accepting first base as the best choice. Too often, the attraction of the new area or product is not weighed against the firm's ability to satisfy this market.

[5] Theodore Levitt, "Exploit The Product Life Cycle," *Harvard Business Review*, November–December, 1965, p. 81–94.

[6] Joseph Mancuso, *Marketing and Managing Technology Products*, Artech House, Volumes I and II, 1976.

Second Base (Customers)

Expanding toward the customers or the marketplace (second base) by competing with your firm's current customers by offering other end-user oriented products is a promising but difficult undertaking. Every small company must consider the merits in its own special case of moving toward the market presently served by its customers. Typically, as any organization moves toward its customers, it must rely more and more on marketing skills. These alternatives are often not as promising after an unbiased evaluation of a small firm's marketing skill. Moreover, there is a real danger of eventually succeeding, and, in turn, alienating your existing "customers." This could discourage many of them into no longer consuming your product. This is the common danger faced by all small businessmen during any expansion toward the customer or the marketplace. However, in some cases the risk may be worth the reward.

Third Base (Unrelated Businesses)

Third base, expanding into unrelated business, is the area usually considered last when examining an entrepreneurial venture's options. No organization desires to tread unfamiliar waters: There is a natural fear of the unknown. Organizations which eventually diversify *often* choose this third base alternative by default. When the safer, surer alternatives are discarded, someone eventually suggests trying the heretofore unknown opportunities. This leads to the evaluation of other alternatives, among which merging or "acquiring" other unrelated businesses would be included.

However, in realistically examining the future of a small business, the third base alternative should not be discarded without a careful analysis. The long term future of every small business is not all positive. In some ways, the specific industry could be at the beginning of a significant downturn. Just as the railroad industry failed to respond to the changing transportation market, and the office equipment industry failed to respond to the growing importance of the newest piece of office equipment, the computer, one could support the argument that even a small business should consider diversifying into growth markets in order to survive.

Looking toward the future, one could conclude that a viable alternative might be to slowly add to the current base other activities which offer a greater growth opportunity. For instance, a small business in a mature market may be wise to expand gradually into areas such as energy or health care or any of the projected growth markets of the future. This expansion, in combination with the basic business, may offer a viable and profitable combination solution. The third base alternative may suggest that two or more small businesses with totally diverse disciplines should join forces in order to increase each other's chances of survival. A winter peaking seasonal business (snowshoes) might find an advantage of summer peaking business (swimming pools). This alternative may be the best for both, although there are only a few natural forces that will work to promote this merger. Individual decision makers in these opposite type businesses seldom travel in the same circles or view business in a similar manner. To consider a radical, but possibly beneficial, arrangement with an opposite type business requires owners with the broadest range of perspective to be found in any small business.

Adding a new and diverse business to an older, more established base is always a demanding exercise; but many times it is the only viable alternative to long run survival. Evaluating this alternative is complex, and often times it fails during the implementation, even when the basic reasons to diversify were sound. Consequently, this area of third base is not as frequent a solution in practice as it is in theory.

TASK OF A MANAGER

Most basic management texts teach that there are five fundamental responsibilities of a manager: 1) Recruiting; 2) Selecting; 3) Training; 4) Motivating; and 5) Managing. Of these five sequential responsibilities, none is more crucial or difficult in starting a small business than the first two—recruiting and selecting. Each of these functions is important—but to differing degrees at different stages of a company's growth. In a company's growth, the first is the most important when the company is born and the fifth is the least important. For mature established businesses, this order is often reversed. In the beginning, it's the raw talent of the entrepreneurial team which makes the vital difference.

A basic question which must be asked throughout the recruiting process is, "Why not hire exceptionally qualified employees as a beginning step towards improving the company?" This is actually a very popular small business strategy. In sports, the classic example of this approach is offered by George Allen, the former manager of the Washington Redskins' professional football team. Allen has built several championship football teams by ignoring draft choices (rookies) and concentrating on trading in order to acquire established veteran players. As a means of achieving the desirable objective of being a winning professional football team as fast as possible, this tactic has obvious advantages. Many small companies have followed this approach and hired senior members new from outside in order to strengthen the quality of the management. This is especially true for some small companies which grow beyond the skills of the existing management team.

Although this technique can have short term benefits, its durability does not compare to the long run process followed by the most successful small companies which eventually grew into the large U.S. businesses of today. They chose to develop a recruiting system that generates quality managers. Just as the large successful businesses in the U.S. have management development programs, successful small companies should consider the value of effective management development programs. Perennially, great football teams have highly developed scouting and farm systems and training programs. With a well-run and well-organized system of recruiting, selecting, and training future managers, there is little need to scurry about at the last second to attract established managers. However, the latter choice, scurrying, remains the most common practice.

Given the five tasks of a manager, each task builds on the next. If good people are recruited and selected, then it becomes demonstrably easy to motivate or manage these good people. Unfortunately, the process of starting a business is so hurried and hit-or-miss that selecting high quality people is almost impossible when you are often so relieved just to have anybody else do the job so that you can do other things. The tragedy here is so strong that an outsider would undoubtedly wonder how some small companies can have such a preponderance of low talent employees. I've even heard it said, "Even if I purposely tried, I couldn't assemble a sorrier cast of characters than this." While this may seem funny on the surface, it's often like a ball and chain around the owner-manager's leg.

The above might lead a person considering small business as a lifelong career to decide once and for all to get a job in the service of the government. The chances are too bleak in small business. If anything can go wrong, it will.Why buck the odds by working for a small business? If the company is composed of misfits and low level second choice help, should I sacrifice my carefully planned career for this?

Such questions can only be answered by each individual. Moreover, many of the answers are often wrong. To counterbalance the point of how ineffectively the entrepreneur/manager usually performs on tasks one and two of a manager—recruiting and selecting—the small business has some important inherent strengths. These natural advantages often offset the disadvantages, and the overall situation can be positive.

One of the advantages of managing a small business is that the business size can be used as an advantage when facing the tougher and larger competition. Small businesses often characterize themselves as being faster to react to change because they possess less red tape than the larger company. Consequently, they are often first to innovate, to find new ways of doing things. For instance, many more significant new product advances have occurred within small companies than within their larger competitors. A surprising number of new products have emerged from within small businesses, as compared to larger companies—despite their sizable new product staffs.[7]

In Massachusetts, the classic example of a small company that succeeded with a new product is Adell Chemicals of Holyoke, the pioneers of Lestoil all-purpose liquid cleaner. This small business was the first company to introduce a liquid multipurpose heavy duty cleaner in the 1950s. The new product proved successful, and the company attained more than thirty million dollars in annual sales in a few years. Their competitors, the large U.S. soap manufacturers, eventually entered the market and offered difficult, if not impossible, competition. The temporary advantage gained by Lestoil in being first was eroded over time by the overall strength of the larger competitors, until finally Lestoil merged with one of the competitors.

A similar pattern developed in the stainless steel razor blade business in the nineteen sixties, Wilkinson, an English manufacturer, captured a large share of the U.S. shaving market when it surprised the larger Gillette by aggressively marketing a new stainless steel razor blade. Eventually Gillette was able to muster its overpowering resources and recapture the bulk of the stainless steel razor blade market. But this did not happen until a smaller company had pioneered a new product and generated a good deal of profit. In both cases, the smaller company identified a consumer need and was quicker to the market with a new product. In both cases, the larger companies eventually regained their original market share, and the smaller company failed to continue pioneering new and different products.

In the case of Polaroid versus Kodak, the ending was not the same. As a small company in the early 1950s, Polaroid was not only first in the instant photography market but it also managed to discourage the larger competitors until the mid-1970s. The same holds for ARP Instruments and Roland Piano. ARP, founded by Alan R. Pearlman, is the leading manufacturer of electronic music synthesizers in the world. Why didn't Steinway or Roland or Baldwin pioneer this new product? Why did a small company and an entrepreneur have the vision, while the larger firms had all the natural advantages?

The advantage of being small allows some small companies to succeed by pioneering new products. This advantage is often voided when the larger company finally enters the market with all its resources (Wilkinson vs. Gillette Blades). The advantage held by a small business is not simply a function of its size, but rather of its relative flexibility and of its ability to make decisions quickly.

Neither Ward Baking nor National Biscuit nor Bond Bread, the big three of the baking industry, created the frozen cake revolution. The credit for this belongs to a female entrepreneur, Sara Lee, whose new company soon grew beyond its modest beginnings. Furthermore, two other new small businesses, Pepperidge Farms and Arnold's, created the revolution in quality white packaged bread. Again, new small businesses surprised the larger competition.

[7]Joseph R. Mancuso, *The Academic Entrepreneur*, Boston University, School of Education, 1975, p. 67–69.

Swanson—not the giants such as General Foods, Pillsbury, or Campbell Soups—created the convenience food revolution. And Swanson was an entirely new company at the time it did so.

A new upstart in the semiconductor business, located in Texas and known as Texas Instruments, upstaged both General Electric and RCA by pioneering the transistor. In turn, a small new company known as Intel of California has surprised the hundreds of semiconductor firms with its newest form of large scale integration (LSI) known as the micro-computer. Armstrong Cork and Congoleum-Nairn did not create the vinyl tile revolution in floor care. It was a totally unknown company, Delaware Floor Products.

Metro-Goldwyn Mayer and Paramount did not create the feature television series which made television an entertainment success. It was entirely new companies like Four Star, Revue, and Desilu, which pioneered in the field. None of these companies created the newest half hour situation comedy begun originally by the show, "All in the Family." It was an independent entrepreneur named Norman Lear, who has since created another dozen or so programs—while the older and larger businesses watched with envy.

The sequences of these revolutions are more common than the infrequent instances where larger companies are first to the marketplace. For instance, RCA (a large business) was first with color television and Raytheon (a large business) was first with the microwave oven. Amana is now a wholly owned subsidiary of Raytheon and Amana markets and manufactures the microwave oven. The ratio of new companies beating old companies to a new growth market is not all one-sided. It's only out of line with the resources available to small and large firms. The smaller firms seem to be first in new marketplaces with new products—in disproportion to their strength or size. There are big advantages to being small, one of which is pioneering new products in new growth markets.[8]

These advantages must be balanced against the disadvantages of a small business for a fair assessment of a company's future promise. A leader's task, especially in small businesses where there are no staffs and where the entrepreneur is nakedly visible, is to lead. And leading is a tough task, one filled with frustrations. On the other hand, business in the other half of the world is not conducted under this sort of stress. In the communist and social systems, there is no small business. There is no way to independence. The government owns it all. The incentive is minimal. There would certainly be an unwillingness to sacrifice under a system which claimed: "To each according to his needs, from each according to his abilities." The capitalistic system has sort of evolved, with Adam Smith occasionally given credit as its chief father. In 1776, Adam Smith wrote his classic book *The Wealth of Nations*, in which he first eluded to the invisible hand of free enterprise guiding all transactions in a laissez-faire economy. Karl Marx wrote his classic book a century later than Adam Smith and entitled it, *Das Kapital*, which translates into *Capital*. The communist system was born out of the writings of Karl Marx. Each system operates and competes in the world and each has some extremely positive points.

The difference between the two fundamental economic systems is dramatic. While I'm tempted to claim that the entrepreneur will be the vital factor in tipping the scales clearly towards the capitalistic system, that would be an emotional claim, not one based on research. In either case, the small business system in the U.S. must be conducted within the rules and laws established by the federal government. These rules

[8] Arnold C. Cooper, "Small Companies Can Pioneer New Products," *Harvard Business Review*, Sept./Oct. 1966.

are the outer boundaries of the capitalistic system, and they are vital to the small businessperson.

GOVERNMENT LEGISLATION AFFECTING SMALL BUSINESS

Too often, the entrepreneur ignores the reality that government officials in Washington, D.C. set policies which affect his firm. Because he is in a small business, an entrepreneur commonly believes that the large complex political scene in Washington is beyond his control or influence. Yet this is hardly the case. One of the most active and popular lobbies in Washington is the small business lobby. In fact, the small business lobby has a unique appeal to the American free enterprise system, and the voices of the little guys are often better received than those of the well-organized national lobbies for large business. Ignoring the opportunity to influence legislation in Washington is naive, although it runs contrary to conventional wisdom. In the past few years, small businesses have received more favorable tax treatment than in the past twenty years.

From the 1930s until 1974, taxes on small busines income were based on the following formula: The first $25,000 of income was taxed at a 22% level, and any income beyond $25,000 was taxed at the normal corporate tax rate of 48%.

Because of the efforts of small business groups and unpaid entrepreneurs who gave of their time, the government changed that taxing system in 1974 to the following basis. The tax base for small business now is 20% of the first $25,000 of earned income and 22% on the second $25,000 of earned income. On profits above $50,000, the tax rate reverts to the normal corporate rate of 48%. This is a savings in excess of $7,000 in taxes to a small business earning $50,000 annually. These types of preferential treatment are often initiated at the grass roots level by small businessmen who invest time and energy with their local political representatives, their congressmen, and their senators. Current pending legislation will help small business by altering the inheritance tax for family businesses. Listed below are several of the important laws with which you, as a small businessman, should be familiar.

The Sherman Anti-Trust Act of 1890

The Sherman Anti-Trust Act prohibits restraint of trade and monopoly in business.[9] The two main sections of the Act read as follows:

Section 1: Every contract combination or form of trust or otherwise, or conspiracy in restraint of trade or commerce among the several states or the four nations, is hereby declared to be illegal.

Section 2. Every person that shall monopolize or attempt to monopolize or combine or conspire with other persons to monopolize any part of the trade or commerce among the several states or the four nations shall be deemed guilty of misdemeanor.

Typically, the restraint of trade section of the Sherman Anti-Trust has been applied to price fixing arrangements between firms. Several large firms have been cited for this act, and many examples are well documented in the legal profession. The case of several large manufacturers in the electrical industry in the 1960s was a landmark in

[9] U.S. Code, Title 15, sec. 1–8.

price fixing. It should be noted that this was the first time in history that American business executives were actually sent to prison for violations of this act. Hence, it may be wise to understand this act very carefully. The Sherman Anti-Trust Act is administered by the Department of Justice, and it can be prosecuted under either the civil or criminal codes. Under criminal prosecutions, persons may be subject to fines not to exceed $50,000 or imprisonment of no more than one year. Civil injunctions involve asking the courts to issue a decree correcting the violation of the Sherman Act. In addition, business people may institute civil proceedings to cover up to three times the amount of damages proved, plus attorney fees from persons or firms guilty of violations of the Act.

The Clayton Act of 1914

The Clayton Act was intended to strengthen action by the federal government in the anti-trust suits. Basically, it was a clarification of and a more specific legislation than the Sherman Act. The Clayton Act prohibits four practices of business:

1. Exclusive and tying contracts
2. Price discrimination
3. Interlocking directorship in competing corporations
4. Corporate stockholding, leasing, corporate stockholders lessening competition

The Federal Trade Commission Act of 1914

When the courts interpreted the Sherman Anti-Trust Act, they condemned unfair competition but declared that the act did not make it illegal. In response to public and small business pressure, the Federal Trade Commission Act was established by Congress to contain the following basic provisions:

1. The Federal Trade Commission was empowered to collect information about business and its conduct which was made available to the President, the public, and the Congress.
2. Any unfair methods of competition were declared illegal.

Hence, the F.T.C. has two programs of particular interest to the small businessperson: 1) To interpret laws for each industry; and 2) to investigate unfair practices.

The Robinson-Patman Act

An amendment to the Clayton Act declared personal price discrimination to be illegal. Basically, this act was put into law in order to protect small businesses from price discrimination. Unless a price difference can be justified in terms of costs of selling, handling, or manufacturing, similar products must be made available to different buyers at equal prices. However, a manufacturer may lower prices in certain geographic regions in order to meet competition. This is a law that is difficult to interpret, and it is often wise to seek legal advice if an issue of concern arises. The original objective of not allowing price discrimination to harm the small businessman who might be paying more for the same merchandise than the larger competitor has been somewhat lost in the application of the law.

The Bankruptcy Act

When a court of law declares a person or a business to be unable to pay debts, this person or business is legally declared bankrupt. The assets are sold, and then awarded on a pro rata basis to the creditors. The Chapter XI form of bankruptcy is of particular interest to the small businessperson because it allows an extension of the act of selling assets to recover some funds to retire debts. This form of bankruptcy is discussed in more detail in Chapter 9 of this book.

The Small Business Act

The Small Business Administration was created in 1953 to further the cause of the small businessperson. This government agency employs 4,000 people in the U.S., and is managed by a presidentially appointed administrator in Washington, D.C. The scope of this agency is large and meaningful. This text will offer more details on the services offered by the SBA in the next few pages.

National Labor Relations Act (Wagner Act)

In 1935, the first important law, known as the Wagner Act, established the National Labor Relations Board to administer labor disputes. According to the act, numerous practices by employees were considered to be unfair. This act allowed employees to organize, and, further, to have a great deal of power in negotiating with employers.

By 1947, unions in the U.S. had grown to such strength that employers were hand-tied in negotiating fair contracts. The Taft-Hartley Act was passed in 1947 to hold both employers and employees responsible for unfair labor practices. In 1959 the Landrum-Griffin Act was passed to protect employees from autocratic use of union power. In addition, the unfair labor practices provisions of the Taft-Hartley Act were strengthened.

These laws and their interpretations are extremely complex. Hence, good legal advice for a small businessperson is a vital necessity in this area.

Probably the most vital government legislation for small business was the creation of the Small Business Administration. This government agency was specifically created in order to promote the interests of the millions of small businesspersons in the U.S. Any effective leader of a small business would be extremely foolish if he or she failed to acquaint himself with the functions of the Small Business Administration (SBA). A visit to a local office can be extremely helpful. Moreover, they can also assist in unraveling some of the issues raised about the impact of pending government legislation affecting small business.

THE SMALL BUSINESS ADMINISTRATION (SBA)

Small business is represented on many fronts in its overall dealings with the federal government. The SBA is a government agency operated by an appointed administrator headquartered in Washington, D.C. The White House Committee on Small Business works closely with Congress to offer positive programs for small business. The third week in May is National Small Business Week during which the Small Business Person of the Year is selected.

The Senate voted in mid-1976 to transfer legislative jurisdiction over the Small

Business Administration (which was created in 1953) from the Senate Banking, Housing and Urban Affairs Committee to the Senate Small Business Committee. The Small Business Committee will have authority to bring legislation to the Senate floor for the first time in its twenty-six year old history. Previously, the committee's function had been to investigate, through hearings and other methods, problems affecting small business. The legislation it recommended was referred to other committees.

America's small businesses constitute 97% of the business community. They provide 52% of all private employment, 43% of U.S. business output, and one-third the gross national product. Their problems and needs are quite different from those of big business, and it has been the function of the Small Business Committee for more than a quarter-century to study and understand these problems and needs.

If only 2% of all American firms have more than fifty employees, isn't every business a small business, and therefore eligible for SBA assistance? Not according to the SBA's definition of what constitutes a small business. The SBA uses the following criteria to determine whether or not a specific business qualifies for the prefix "small."

1. Number of employees
2. Dollar sales volume
3. Type of business
4. Nature of business within the industry.

A manufacturing enterprise is small if it employs less than 250 people. This guideline varies dramatically within specific industries. American Motors, the fourth largest United States automobile manufacturer, employs close to 25,000 people, yet it has been classified as a small business because its market share has been less than 5%. A steel rolling mill can be classified as small if it employs less than 2,500 people, and a household appliance manufacturer can be classified as small if it employs less than 500 people.

The measure of what is or isn't small in the non-manufacturing industries is annual sales volume measured in dollars. Retail and service businesses are small when the annual volume is between $2,000,000 and $7,500,000, depending upon the industry. A firm whose primary business is wholesaling qualifies for the "small" label if it has annual sales between $9,000,000 and $22,000,000, depending upon the industry. Manufacturing firms employing between 250 and 1,500 workers, and construction firms grossing under $9,500,000, can qualify as small, depending upon the industry. The quantitative measures are not cast in granite, as they are occasionally adjusted to reflect inflation and changing business situations.

The SBA offers three basic services to small companies. These services are:

1. Financial assistance
2. Procurement assistance
3. Management and technical assistance.

Around the country, the SBA is organized into ten major districts and into many smaller regions. For instance, New England is counted as a single district, and the headquarters for the New England district is in Boston. Simultaneously, Boston is also one of the sub-districts (known as a region), and this is one of several regions within the New England district. By visiting the SBA at their district or regional locations, a small business person will find numerous pamphlets and brochures that may, all by themselves, make the trip worthwhile. In addition, you can become acquainted with a number of the different individuals in the government agency which is charged specifically with helping the entrepreneur in his day-to-day business. A good place to begin is with management assistance. Very few entrepreneurs actually take the time and effort to deal with the SBA; rather, they view the SBA only as a source of capital. This is often a significant oversight, because there are literally 4,000 employees in the SBA—all dedicated to serving the needs of the small business person. Although it can be a bit frustrating trying to find your way through the SBA maze, it does make sense to make an effort. Usually a telephone call, followed by a personal visit, is the most fruitful contact. Below are the three areas of assistance offered by the SBA.

1. The SBA offers services in the area of procurement assistance. A special division of the Small Business Administration assists small companies in securing government "set-asides" on major defense contracts. In other words, specific percentages of each large government contract must be competitively bid by small firms in order to help stimulate the small business economy. These portions of large contracts must be let to small firms. Under a special program within the procurement assistance division, a joint determination program allows more than one small firm to team up for larger contracts.

The government set-aside program is specifically designed to assist small businesses in capturing segments of contracts. In addition, the procurement assistance within the SBA helps to provide lists of government installations, such as air force, army, and navy bases, that may well be consumers for your product or service. The SBA will also mail statements to these people, telling them that you are now an approved vendor for certain items. In addition, some of the procurement assistance offices have sales people who will represent your product or service to government agencies. Each small company which is able to solicit some of these sales persons' effort can have an expanded sales effort for its products or services. Although these individuals receive no commission or direct compensation from your firm, they can make a difference in your procurement assistance with government agencies. This is especially true for minority small businesses which are helped by the Minority Business Opportunity Committee (MBOC) and the Office of Minority Business Enterprise (OMBE), which was established in 1966 in the Department of Commerce.

It generally makes sense to become listed with the Small Business Administration as a qualified source even if you don't consider yourself a typical defense contractor or related small business.

2. The SBA employs a group of individuals who are basically concerned with helping small businesses through management and technical assistance. These individuals are small business consultants. Within this category are a number of services. Below is a listing of the kinds of services offered by the SBA.

A. ACE—Active Core of Executives—is a group of executives interested specifically in small business who volunteer their time to the SBA to help small companies. Contact with these individuals can be made through the management assistance department at your local SBA office. These individuals will often be busy at their full time jobs but will work for no pay to help a small enterprise.

B. SCORE—the Service Core of Retired Executives. Just as the ACE program offers assistance to small business, the SCORE program is designed to offer management and technical assistance from retired executives. This program has been more active than the ACE program because typically the individuals have more available time to donate. There are just about 3,500 SCORE volunteers around the country, which is about the same as the total number of full-time SBA employees. However, the SCORE volunteers receive no compensation— other than out-of-pocket expenses—for their assistance. But many enjoy the work so much that they even pay their own expenses personally. Traditionally,

SCORE chapters are organized on a local basis, and they can be contacted through the local SBA office. The same holds true for ACE volunteers.

C. The Small Business Institute—SBI. This is a relatively new program within the Small Business Administration. It involves college students working at no cost for small businesses under the guidance of faculty members of nearby universities. These student teams will take on projects and activities as co-agreed by the faculty member and the entrepreneur. Often these student teams provide valued assistance beyond just simple advice to small business. In addition, the management assistance officers (MAOs) of the local Small Business Administration office are available to help your business. All of these sources of help are available at no charge by contacting the nearest SBA office. As this book goes to print, another program—known as University Business Development Centers (UBDCs)—is being launched to coordinate college students and faculty with Small Business.

3. Financial Assistance

A. Debt financing
B. Equity financing

A. *Debt financing.* To a very limited degree, the Small Business Administration participates in direct loans of SBA money to small businesses. Rather than use the limited amount of capital allocated by Congress for small businesses, the SBA more typically cosigns bank debts for small businesses. Hence, an entrepreneur who is interested in borrowing money and who has been turned down by several banks may find it possible to approach these same banks again, and with the SBA as a co-signatory on a bank note, a loan may become bankable. This is the most common method of financial assistance offered by the SBA to small businessmen. The bank loans the money directly to the small company, while the SBA guarantees to pay somewhere between 50% and 90% of the loan in the event of a default. This is a very popular program, and one used very effectively by a number of small enterprises.

SBA LOAN VEHICLES

The federally funded SBA either makes direct loans or guarantees bank loans through three distinct programs: the 7A term loan, the Economic Opportunity Loan (EOL), and the Operation Business Mainstream (OBM) loan. Direct loans (except in the EOL program) are currently made for up to $100,000; but they are only available after the SBA's guarantee has been rejected by two banks, and when the SBA has enough funds. Thus, 90% of the SBA's transactions are guarantees.

The 7A Term Loan Guarantee

The *7A term loan guarantee* is made for up to $350,000, or 80% of the bank loan, whichever is less. A borrower is required to put up about 50% of the project's cost. Fixed assets, real estate, or inventory are taken as security. The loan may be extended for up to six years for working capital financing, up to ten years for purchasing fixed assets, and up to fifteen years for construction.

The OBM Program

The *OBM program* operates with the same loan ceiling and maturities as the 7A loan; but it allows economically or socially disadvantaged minority group members to borrow up to 80% of their business needs. Although these applicants must pledge all available collateral, they cannot be rejected for insufficient security.

The EOL Program

The *EOL program* also assists would-be business owners who can only contribute 20% of their capital needs. However, EOL loans are extended to economically disadvantaged borrowers regardless of race, including Vietnam era veterans and the physically handicapped. The EOL program extends working capital loans for up to ten years; but both direct loans and guarantees are limited to $50,000.

Line of Credit Guarantees

Line of credit guarantees are also made for $350,000, or 90% of the bank line, whichever is less. The line is secured by the firm's specific contracts for construction, goods, or services—which are assigned to the bank. The loan funds may be used only to pay for materials or labor on these assigned contracts. The line of credit is granted for one year, but it may be extended for periods up to an additional year.

Because the SBA caters to businesses that are not bankable without its guarantee, its clients are obviously intermediate risks. They may be undercapitalized, lack sufficient collateral, or have a minimal track record or an imperfect operating history. In order to curb these risks, the SBA sets modest loan ceilings, and provides its clients with free management assistance. But regardless of its risks, the SBA is committed to public service, not profit. Interest rates on its guaranteed bank loans cannot exceed current maximums set by the SBA. The interest on hard-to-get direct loans is normally several points below comparable bank rates.

Applications for SBA loan guarantees are first reviewed by the bank and then passed to the SBA. Like the banks, the SBA must first be convinced that a business can repay the loan from profits. Consequently, the SBA is interested in profitability ratios and business projections. But, unlike commercial lenders, the SBA will sometimes ignore a losing track record if the business shows signs of improvement leading to a healthy future. The Small Business Administration will also stretch loans for longer than bank terms, and it will accept borrowers whose collateral does not support the full value of the loan.

Equity Financing

The SBA does not involve itself as directly with equity or long term debt financing for new ventures as it does with co-signing bank debt. The Small Business Investment Corporation (SBIC)[10] is the arm charged with overseeing equity and long term debt

---

[10] The licensing of SBICs, which are funded and regulated by the SBA, was made possible by the Small Business Investment Act of 1958.

investments in small companies. These SBICs, about 300 across the country, are typically affiliated with another financial institution such as a bank. Their basic task is to act as venture capitalists in order to stimulate small business. They compete in the open market with traditional financial sources for an affiliation with desirable small companies. The unusual feature of an SBIC is that it receives substantial financial assistance via long term subordinated debentures from the government (SBA) to support its activity. Hence, the SBA itself does not make equity investments; but rather, it makes loans on favorable terms to an SBIC–which supports the formation and growth of small business. Through 1989, SBICs have disbursed over $5 billion by making over 100,000 loans and investments.

In November of 1969, the SBA and the Department of Commerce instituted a Minority Enterprise Small Business Investment Company (MESBIC) program in order to provide financing and assistance to minority-owned business. The MESBIC application to the SBA is more specialized than a standard SBIC license.

Both MESBICs and SBICs have a good deal of associated paper work and red tape. Most of it is necessary, however, in order to prevent misuse of funds. For instance, an SBIC may only invest up to 20% of its capital in a single firm. It must have a minimum capital base of $1,000,000 in order to qualify for the $4,000,000 (3:1) long term subordinated low interest debentures. This ratio of initial equity of the SBIC to long term subordinated low interest debentures. This ratio of initial equity of the SBIC to long term subordinated low interest SBA debt (the equity/debt ratio) will increase from 1:3 to 1:4 when the initial equity is above $1,000,000. In practice, the SBA discourages SBICs from beginning with only the minimum initial equity of $1,000,000.

The above is a brief sketch of the nature and purpose of the SBA. Many entrepreneurs have felt alone in their businesses, and have claimed that their government did more to hinder their success than to help them. They often become sore or mad at the government, and the SBA is often the agency they criticize.

In my first book, I, too, shared and expressed this feeling. But in the last few years I have begun to appreciate the value of the services of these government agencies, especially the SBA. However, I only began to understand them about five years ago, and my appreciation was fully realized only about two years ago. This was after about thirty-five years of little involvement. My own case is not an untypical example; and I wish that I had learned more about the function of these government agencies sooner. They can and do help.

9

Preparing
For Failure

REASONS FOR FAILURE

Most small businesses that fail do so because they are undercapitalized. Their working capital is inadequate and they go broke before they can get off the ground.

You can minimize this problem by using the building block concept of planning each action sequentially so that the profits from the first action form a base for the next action. For instance, your firm can employ manufacturers' representatives to generate sales and profits until you can eventually employ direct salesmen. Manufacturers' agents operate solely on a commission basis and represent almost no fixed costs. To sequence these actions the other way would drain limited capital, and it could jeopardize further operations.

It's easy for a young business to become overwhelmed by the sudden infusion of large amounts of capital, as, for example, after a successful placement. Some entrepreneurs and small companies judge that this excess capital will let them skip certain building blocks, and they want to spend it. They hire direct salesmen, for instance, or they buy an expensive piece of equipment which provides a capacity that won't be needed for a year. Lately, a more popular choice has been either to buy a computer or to build a new plant. Then, suddenly, the money is gone and so is the business. Removing the cautionary controls on spending, even for a brief period, can unleash many dollars in sound long term investments for the business. A good many of these insurmountable opportunities may be premature, and they can create an insurmountable cash drain to service the new short term debt.

The skip-a-step concept is suicide. The building block concept builds a strong foundation for your company, impresses the financial community, and increases your chances for success dramatically.

Most entrepreneurs have the vision needed to see beyond the present requirements of the company; but the financial community, suppliers, employees, and customers don't have that foresight. They are more interested in nice neat building blocks. They subscribe to the brick of the month club philosophy. The secret to a successful business lies in execution, not in speed. Perform each step in sequence better than the competitors and better than your previous step. Whatever you do, don't try to make some of your decisions in a logical building block manner and the rest in a short, spurting manner. Having a little bit of the building block concept is as impossible as being a little bit pregnant.

At the other extreme are the owner-managers who seem to plod along, going nowhere. Because of their fear of failure, this type of entrepreneur often decides not to grow. He chooses to avoid even the possibility of trouble, and operates his little business at a reduced scale of activity. He has been said to hibernate. A sizable number of entrepreneurs relish the idea of keeping their businesses small, manageable, and uncomplicated. They believe that if their companies grow too much, all of the fun and romance will be lost. They don't want the baby to get too big. They prepare for failure every day, by avoiding any or all situations which may create any anxiety.

To a certain extent, their uneasiness is justified, and there are advantages to being small when it comes to attracting people, introducing new products, instituting new production techniques, and simply keeping tabs on everything that goes on. The one big disadvantage of being small is that you can't make too many mistakes, and the ones you do make had better be little ones. Big companies have a higher tolerance for mistakes. They can write off losses, lay off employees, and get back on the track. The small company, however, doesn't have a cushion to fall back on. Its mistakes can wipe out just as finally as anything. Ford managed to survive Edsel, RCA the computer, General Dynamics the Convair. Your firm couldn't. Keep your mistakes small, few, and far between. Give this notion some consideration as you try to keep the baby in diapers too long.

If a small company fails, the entrepreneur can still offer his stockholders one benefit—provided that his lawyer was on the ball in the beginning and used Section 1244 of the Internal Revenue Code. This section, established to encourage investments in small business, gives stockholders, the right to write off against ordinary income up to $100,000 on a joint return ($50,000 on a single return) of any loss due to the failure of such a company during any tax year. By contrast, if no Section 1244 plan has been adopted, only $3,000 of a net capital loss can be offset against ordinary income.[1] In the years to come, these laws will change; but capital losses of only a few thousand dollars will most likely be the new maximum.

It's only a small point, but if your company goes under, 1244 stock could be a big "small point" for everyone. It could also make facing your stockholders again easier for you. Ask your lawyer about 1244 stock. The small points can all add up to a big point someday.

YOUR FIRM AND THE INTERNAL REVENUE SERVICE (IRS)

As an employer, you are charged by the federal government to collect a portion of each employee's Income and Social Security (FICA) Taxes. In addition, there may be local and state taxes that are deducted from an employee's paycheck and must be remitted periodically to the Internal Revenue Service or other collecting agencies, such as a bank. There is also the unemployment tax, which must be paid to the state.

[1] This law was changed in 1976 to allow $2,000 in 1977 and $3,000 thereafter.

Because of these rulings, the money withheld from the employee's paycheck may remain in the company's checking account for from several weeks to several months, creating an inflated checkbook balance. The danger lies in forgetting that this isn't your money and in drawing on it "temporarily" to solve some current financial need. You can get into a mess of trouble: First, there are penalties for late payment of withholding taxes—and we all know the tax burden is heavy enough without adding penalties to it. Second, you—as the president, officer, or board member—can be held personally liable for those taxes. If you're ever tempted to tap that source for a little extra cash, take a cold shower and then try to find the money somewhere else. Before you borrow from your employees, there are other more suitable alternatives to consider, such as Chapter XI form of bankruptcy.

Chapter Eleven is a legal state that can do wonders for small companies in financial troubles. It's a form of bankruptcy, not a chapter of some book. You have probably always thought that bankruptcy was bad. Not necessarily.

As I discussed earlier, the name of the game in small business is raising the venture capital. Successful companies raise the right amounts of money at the right times. This capital, among other things, helps cover up problems and hide mistakes. The company that's unsuccessful in raising capital leaves all its mistakes hanging out for the whole world to see.

Many small businesses fail because a planned financing collapses, a public stock offering doesn't come off, or someone backs out of a private placement. If the company has been spending freely, anticipating the new capital, it may find itself deep in the hole. That's when they should seek cover behind the skirts of Chapter Eleven. It gives them time to work things out and have another go at it.

Bankruptcy can be voluntary or involuntary. Chapter Eleven requires that if 51 percent of the creditors, by dollar and by number, agree to settle for a portion of what the company owes them, then other creditors must accept the deal made by the majority. Since not all creditors think alike, this task may not be as easy as it sounds. The small ones tend to be aggravations; the big ones worry. They all want their money.

But Chapter Eleven and a new financial plan can salvage the company and provide a chance for it to continue in business. Someday, it may make amends to its creditors, rehire its employees, and, eventually, make a profit for its stockholders. Alternatively, you can try to operate with insufficient capital and continue to pile up debts until forced into bankruptcy; at such time, the company, its creditors, employees, and stockholders are all wiped out.

Unfortunately, most entrepreneurs don't consider Chapter Eleven bankruptcy as a viable alternative; but in fiscal 1988, about 2,000 Chapter Eleven petitions were filed in the United States. Could anything that popular be all bad?

In line with the preceding discussion, you should be aware of the pecking order of creditors in the event that your business declares bankruptcy.

1. The lawyers and court costs come first. The legal fees alone are quite large; and consequently more and more small businesses in trouble are opting to go bankrupt out of court. They can't afford the legal umbrella of protection provided by a court.

2. The Internal Revenue Service gets the next cut. Any taxes owed them must be paid, and they always get what's owed to them. If they can't get it out of the company, they can go after the principals. So don't take your responsibility as president, treasurer, or board member too lightly.

3. Creditors with a secured interest on the company's assets, inventory, or accounts receivable (e.g., the bank that loaned you that $10,000 to tide you over a period of slow collections) are licking at the heels of the IRS. They usually win the collateral

they hold. One small point of interest on the issue of which debt is secured and which isn't: This is always a judgmental issue, and one which is commonly debated. The law reads that it takes four months to perfect a security agreement.

Hence, an asset which is pledged prior to four months of bankruptcy may not be allowed as a secured asset; and, in turn, it may actually remain the property of the unsecured creditors.

4. Unsecured creditors get a cut only after the lawyers, the IRS, and the secured creditors have sliced away as much as they can. These include most of your suppliers who hounded you to pay those invoices or to suffer the consequences. Now they suffer, too, and soon come to realize they shouldn't have pushed quite so hard.

5. The last to be paid in a bankruptcy are the stockholders. Poor chaps. You can imagine what's left for them, and that may be the cruelest cut of all for you. But then, they knew the risk involved.

Another interesting fact you should know about a bankruptcy is the law regarding credit cards. If you issue company credit cards to your employees and they lose one, you and the company are liable for $50.00 of unauthorized charges as long as you notify the credit card company within the specified period. However, if you declare bankruptcy, and the credit card company doesn't get its money out of the business, they can go after the employee to whom a card was issued for the amount due. This is a serious area, for the little items such as credit cards are often overlooked. This is not a frequent problem, as most credit cards are only secured by the company's credit, not by personal credit. But, then again, most small businesses don't go bankrupt, either. The ones that do often must countersign personally for credit cards. Consider that before you get too generous with those little plastic cards.

Your lawyer can provide you with all of the gory details, and you should know them. Forewarned is forearmed.

BANKRUPTCY

Bankruptcy: A process created by law to solve, in a fair way, the interests both the creditor who is owed money and the debtor who is not able to pay his debts.

Early bankruptcy laws stated that if the total assets of the debtor fell short of the total debt to creditors, the debtor would be responsible for paying the remaining balance. If he was not able to pay the total amount, the debtor would end up in jail. Unable to earn any money in jail to pay his debts, he would remain there. Today, however, the laws have changed, and the debtor can be relieved, with a few exceptions, of his remaining liabilities after the bankruptcy. The debtor can be discharged from his debts totally or partially, according to the amount and case.

Congress enacted and instituted three different early bankruptcy laws (1800-1803, 1841-1843, and 1867-1878). These laws were passed in order to respond to economic crises. Prior to these laws, the practices varied greatly across the United States. Some state laws tended to treat out of state debtors and creditors unfairly. No set of courts was directly responsible for bankruptcy filings, which added to the confusion. Another law was passed in 1898, which has continued, with some modifications, to rule until today. This law repealed all of the states' bankruptcy laws and established the federal system of bankruptcy. The most important changes to the Bankruptcy Act of 1898 came with the acceptance of the Chandler Act of 1938.

Today, the Bankruptcy Act consists of fourteen chapters. The first seven chapters build the foundations and structure of the system. The Act establishes the federal district courts responsible for bankruptcy cases and gives them jurisdiction; it also defines and specifies the rights and obligations of both creditors and debtors. In addition, the law defines the rigorous procedure to be followed in the courts of bankruptcy, creates the offices of trustees and arbitrators, and defines the process by which the estate of the debtor is to be administered and distributed. The first seven chapters rule and guide the bankruptcy procedure. Chapter Eight deals with the reorganization procedures, through bankruptcy, for farmers. The size and complexity of these corporations makes it a very complicated procedure. Chapter Nine explains the procedure for reorganization, through bankruptcy, of some public authorities. The fact that public authorities are essential to the society underlines the importance of this chapter. Both Chapters Eight and Nine were created to help the ailing railroad and public authority corporations, which often have financial troubles. By the government saving these businesses through the bankruptcy acts, the society will still obtain the needed services from these corporations.

Chapter Twelve was brought to life by Congress during the depression of the 1930s as a hybrid relief bill to aid financially strapped Chicago homeowners. Although it helped to stall off their mortgage foreclosures, its use since then has been extremely infrequent. However, in the past few years, the Chapter Twelve filings have increased dramatically; it is now used to adjudicate large real estate deals. Below is the current information on the increasing use of Chapter Twleve and, if the trend continues, this could be a central issue in the near future.

	Number of *Chapter Twelve Filings*
Fiscal year 1976	527
Fiscal year 1975	280
Fiscal year 1974	172

Although Chapter Twelve was initially tailored for homeowners in financial difficulty, it has been most recently used by large real estate operators with debt secured by property which has improvements on it. The individual homeowner is more likely to be a candidate for Chapter Thirteen's wage earner plan, which is cheaper and quicker. Below is a synopsis of the traditional users of the bankruptcy laws:

Chapter 1–7	Personal failures
Chapter 8	Farmers
Chapter 9	Municipalities
Chapter 10	Companies in serious trouble (liquidation)
Chapter 11	Companies in trouble (stay of execution)
Chapter 12	Big real estate partnership
Chapter 13	Wage earners overburdened with debt.

There are two types of bankruptcies. The first is a private or personal bankruptcy, in which the personal property of the debtor is liquidated, or arrangements are made to pay the creditors. In the second, the corporate bankruptcy, the assets of the business are frozen or liquidated, or arrangements are made for paying the debts. The difference between them is that one deals with an individual's capital, and the other with corporate assets. Bankruptcies can be reached by voluntary disposition of the debtor or by involuntary decree of the court.

In order to bring forth an involuntary bankruptcy charge to a debtor, three signatures or petitions are required by the court if there are more than ten creditors; or two signatures if the creditors number less than ten. Today, the number of involuntary filings is less than five percent. Hence, most debtors choose bankruptcy as a preferred choice.

A straight bankruptcy is a process by which the debtor is declared insolvent, his assets are sold, and the proceeds are used to pay his creditors. This type of case could apply to both personal and corporate bankruptcies; it is the simplest and most commonly used process.

In a bankruptcy case, the assets of the debtor are liquidated, producing certain funds. These funds are used first to pay for administrative and legal fees of the case and the remaining amount is used to pay the creditors. Because, in 28% of the cases filed in 1985, the creditors did not receive a single penny, the bankruptcy law had created mixed attitudes in the minds of both creditors and debtors. When a debtor cannot pay his bills, most creditors will apply pressure in order to get their own bills paid—thus creating a worse situation for the debtor. With the creation of the Chandler Act in 1938 and under the provisions of Chapter Thirteen, a debtor is now allowed to reorganize his debts. The creditors, fearing that in a straight bankruptcy court they will receive nothing, will tend to settle for less than they would have otherwise. Also, besides reducing the total owed amount, they might increase the allowed time for payment. Under certain circumstances, the court provides, under Chapter Thirteen, for payments under the court's supervision. In such cases, a referee, who is named by the court, meets with both creditors and debtor to decide on a plan for repaying debts. Here again, the debtor can suggest an extension of time for payment, a partial payoff, or a combination of both.

The success of any repayment plan often depends on the creditors. For a corporate bankruptcy, the repayment plan has to be approved by more than one half of the creditors—in both numbers and in total dollars. In personal bankruptcies, since the amount of assets involved is usually small, the success of the plan depends upon secured creditors. A secured creditor holds property that secures the fulfillment of the debtor's obligation. Secured creditors also approve partial payoff plans because of this preferred position as creditors. They are the first creditors to be paid after the liquidation of the debtor's assets.

Chapters Ten and Eleven were also created by the Chandler Act of 1938. The former is a petition for a re-organization and the latter is a petition for an arrangement.

In Chapter Eleven, the bankrupt party is called the "debtor," thus removing some of the negative connotations of the term "bankruptcy." This term tends to save face for the people involved in the proceedings. Chapter Eleven is designed to help the business survive and operate without the constant harassment of creditors. The moment a corporation files under Chapter Eleven, all lawsuits, creditor harassment, and problems stop—the filing action freezes all the debts and creates a new corporation called "debtor in possession." By stopping the creditors, the corporation can continue to buy supplies and merchandise, and can continue to operate. Any new creditors stand first in line for getting paid; and very often the supplies have to be paid for on a cash on delivery basis.

While the old creditors are restrained from collecting past debts, the corporation can attempt to solve the problems that caused the economic situation. Chapter Eleven should be used only in cases where there is a good possibility of future survival for the corporation. Even through the use of this chapter, a good percentage of the filings end up in total bankruptcies or liquidations. Under Chapter Eleven, the corporation is forced to propose an arrangement or plan—to be approved by creditors and the court—with the object of eliminating the past debts. Again, the plan could be a combination of time extension and partial payment.

Chapter Ten is designed to handle big corporate reorganizations. The differences between Chapter Ten and Chapter Eleven are in procedure rather than in content.

It is possible for the larger corporations to accomplish significant changes in corporate and stockholder's structure under the provisions of Chapter Eleven. The Securities and Exchange Commission is one of the biggest obstacles in the proceedings under a Chapter Eleven Bankruptcy. The S.E.C. is a guardian for the public interest with wide powers, and it is able to force a corporation from a Chapter Eleven to a Chapter Ten proceeding. It is the S.E.C.'s responsibility to see that all stockholders and bondholders are treated fairly in any kind of bankruptcy case. Obviously, the S.E.C. would have jurisdiction only in the case of bankruptcy for publicly owned businesses. Otherwise, it would not be involved in the bankruptcy proceedings.

Among the biggest reasons for a corporation to be forced to file under Chapter Ten is the total amount of legal and administrative fees involved in the bankruptcy proceedings. A Chapter Ten proceeding has scores of legal advisors, lawyers, and accountants, because anyone who makes a contribution to the final settlement is entitled to a fee for his services. In a Chapter Ten case, the court appoints a trustee to manage and operate the corporation while the proceedings last. Even if the trustee retains the management of the corporation, the management has no real power, and the trustee is the one who makes the final and important decisions. The trustee serves as a bridge between the corporation and the court supervising the case.

Since all the corporations that file under Chapter Ten or Chapter Eleven are in financial difficulties, it is reasonable to claim that in Chapter Eleven it is possible to preserve some stockholders' hope for equity; but in Chapter Ten, the stockholders have no hope. Once the court determines the insolvency of the corporation, the stock has no real value, and the assets are used to pay creditors and fees. The stockholders would receive any remainder, but this is extremely rare.

Bankruptcy cases have many effects on the United States economy. In 1987 over 10 billion dollars were discharged in bankruptcy courts. Two-thirds of this figure is attributed to business bankruptcies and the remainder to personal bankruptcies.

Many parties lose in a bankruptcy. The customers, workers, investors, and suppliers: All lose in different ways. Often, it is to their advantage to keep a business or person from going bankrupt. The customers cannot acquire any more of the product, and thus cannot receive the value of the product to be used in their business. The workers cannot get their wages, and they cannot receive benefits from the business. The investors lose their capital investment in the bankrupt business; and the suppliers can no longer sell their product to the bankrupt business, thus creating a loss of profit. Most of the time, lawyers and legal advisors in the bankruptcy courts are the only individuals to profit from the bankruptcy.

Assets are often converted to cash at distress values just before a bankruptcy is filed. One of the most commonly used methods of extracting funds illegally from a dying corporation is by selling inventory at distressed prices or by misusing travel and expense accounts. It is not uncommon for a corporation going into bankruptcy to sell the inventory below the cost in order to create a source of cash for private use, or to favor certain select creditors. Such procedures are difficult for the courts to detect and prove. The penalties for those who are convicted of such devious practices are severe.

The Security and Exchange Commission oversees bankruptcy cases to assure that such practices are not used, and to see that all creditors are treated fairly by public companies.

Today's bankruptcy courts leave much to be desired. The system is generally inefficient and very slow. It handles more than 200,000 cases per year, creating enormous amounts of paper work. Routine cases occupy the precious time of the courts. There is not an established system for speeding up or optimizing simple cases. The judges no longer have the time to act as "administrators" of the assets, and with the increased number of cases, their competency decreases.

These bankruptcy laws were altered again in 1982 and 1986, and I'd suggest checking with a good bankruptcy lawyer because they'll probably be changed again before you complete this book.

SELLING A SMALL BUSINESS

Beside going out the back door through a bankruptcy, there are more attractive alternatives of going out the side doors. Neither is as attractive, naturally, as an exit through the front door. But, then again, the last chapter of this book is more for those small business persons who disregarded the other eight chapters.

There are a number of ways of selling a business—almost as many as there are buyers and sellers. Most purchasers of small businesses are straightforward. However, it is not at all uncommon for a small business to be purchased "out of bankruptcy." In other words, the new buyer may not want to assume the financial responsibility for the old debts of the old management. The new buyer may, therefore, require the business to go into a Chapter Eleven bankruptcy in order to wipe away the old unsecured debts before the new buyer takes over. This is extremely common.

Another alternative is not to sell the business per se, but to sell the assets or products of the business. This is a less common practice. However, it is often preferred to a straight liquidation. In such cases, the new owner doesn't buy the corporate stock in the failing business but chooses to leave this worthless stock with the current stockholders. The new owner may choose to buy only the so-called good part of the business—certain of its assets. These dealings must be conducted openly and fairly, and they are subject to the approval of the creditors and stockholders. It is illegal to sell off assets in certain cases and to leave the creditors and stockholders with only the liabilities. This is more than just a case of getting caught holding the bag; it can be a criminal case of fraud. Hence, superior legal counsel is needed for those cases where selling a business is one of the more attractive alternatives.

Eventually, every entrepreneur, successful and unsuccessful, reaches the point where he wants to buy or sell a company. During the last decade, this sport has challenged baseball as the national pastime; and it has become so important that numerous publications, monthly bulletins, and books discuss the subject. I'll tell you what these sources tell you: Get outside assistance, including legal counsel.

In order to sell a business, begin by exploring the logical avenues for prospective buyers or sellers—your largest supplier, your customers, or your smallest competitor. Then talk to a broker. Business brokers make their living in the marketplace, and if anyone knows who's buying or selling, they do. Remember, too, that they make their commission only if they're successful in finding a buyer or seller, so the bad ones don't last too long.

Here, in order of importance, is a list of business broker sources for you:

1. Management consultants
2. Venture capitalists

3. Stock brokers

4. Bankers

5. Certified public accountants

6. Legal firms

7. Financial/business editors

8. Publishers of trade periodicals

9. Advertisements in the *Wall Street Journal* and in your local newspaper

10. Manufacturer's representatives

11. Insurance agents

12. Advertising agencies

13. College professors in departments of business or management

14. Local business directories

15. Telephone book

CONCLUDING COMMENTS

Although this final chapter has addressed the failure issue, the focus should never be on the negative possibilities of the start of a business process. This book is about entrepreneurs who create an ongoing business from nothing. There are just less than 15 million businesses in the United States, of which about 14 million are so-called small businesses. These small businesses produce 43% of the U.S. business output, one-third of the GNP, and more than half of all private employment. A special category of small businesspersons, the entrepreneur, has given the American economy its direction and thrust since the Civil War. To start, finance, and manage a small business of your own from nothing, and to succeed at it, requires motivation and perseverance bordering on obsession. Besides all that, it takes a good deal of plain old luck, too. It's an uphill battle at which more people fail than succeed. Other countries believe individuals willing to risk so much against these odds (some studies claim eight out of ten new businesses fail) should be classified as crazy but the American capitalistic system labels them rags-to-riches folk heroes.

Consider what entrepreneurs can and have created. Men like Edwin Land (Polaroid), Kenneth Olson (Digital Equipment Corporation), and William Hewlett and David Packard (Hewlett-Packard) are the current version of the past greats such as John Rockefeller (oil), Andrew Carnegie (steel), and Henry Ford (automobiles). In Massachusetts alone, three firms which came into being in the late 1950's and the late 1960's now have the following employment data:

Entrepreneurs	Year of Formation	Company	Number of Employees Jan. 1, 1977	Estimated Number of Employees Jan. 1, 1984
Kenneth Olson	1958	Digital Equipment Corp.	27,000	75,000
Ray Stata	1965	Analog Devices, Inc.	1,200	4,000
Edison DeCastro	1968	Data General, Inc.	5,000	25,000

Moreover, Polaroid, Xerox, Texas Instruments and Digital Equipment Corporation, firms which were all founded by entrepreneurs about 20 years ago, employed over 200,000 persons in 1985. All these businesses were created to deliver a better product to a willing base of satisfied customers. They are one of the reasons America has been characterized as the land of opportunity. None of the other countries which are suffering from unemployment and inflation, especially in Western Europe, have been able to continually foster entrepreneurism. Because of the inadequacy of launching new enterprises, many of these foreign countries are experiencing financial sickness (England, Italy). These diseases can spread to America, too, if the entrepreneur continues to be an endangered species.

The American capitalistic process of starting your own business wins for three distinct groups when it is allowed to function. First, the American consumers win because they are able to choose a better product in a free marketplace. Second, the stockholders win because the business generates capital appreciation for their investment. The beauty of the entire capitalistic process is that everyone wins (even suppliers to the new firm) when a new company succeeds in a free marketplace.

These three distinct groups of so-called winners are the most effective method of fighting the combined problem of unemployment and inflation. Here's how they counteract unemployment and inflation.

1. Customers win: Superior products with some relative advantage over existing products become available in a free marketplace. Prices will fall (calculators, minicomputers), and the tasks these superior products perform will be available on a more cost-effective basis to a wider base of users.

2. Employees win: More jobs that add value to the GNP (not public sector jobs) are made available. These jobs seldom depend on continuing government subsidies to exist.

3. Stockholders win: American capital appreciates and, in turn, this capital becomes the investment in other businesses.

Besides the three basic categories of direct winners above, other associated winners emerge as well. Suppliers to the new firm experience an expansion of business, new superior products made in the USA are now available for export and the balance of payments and the strength of the U.S. dollar all improve.

The central message to this argument, that entrepreneurs are America's best hope for economic growth, is best supported with examples. Besides the preceding logical argument about how the capitalistic system works, a few examples of how it has worked in practice will reinforce the American dream of starting, financing, and managing a small business of your own.

The once mighty railroad companies have given way to the better mousetrap of the Wright Brothers, and now a person can travel from New York to California in five hours versus five days. It wasn't the large railroad firms that spawned the airline industry. It was a whole host of new businesses started by entrepreneurs. Competition from small automobile exports eventually forced American manufacturers in Detroit to produce compact cars. Left alone, the larger U.S. manufacturers had little impetus to change. Competition in the capitalistic system forced these changes and the U.S. consumer is now better off.

Development of office business machines in the early 1950s did not come from the existing business machine manufacturers. In fact, typewriters were the prominent business machine of that era, and today all the major typewriter manufacturers are no longer independent businesses. Royal Typewriter is now a division of Litton Industries; Underwood Typewriter merged with Olivetti Typewriter (Italy); and three smaller firms joined forces to become Smith Corona and Merchant (SCM). The new business that pioneered the new product area (known as business machines) was an international business machine company that became known as IBM, the International Business

Machine Company. IBM grew and prospered and it employs several hundred thousand people today. It, too, left opportunities for the little fellows. Digital Equipment Corporation, DEC, pioneered the minicomputer, not IBM. Although the computer giant (sales of $40,000,000,000) pioneered the office machine known as the computer, it failed to recognize the need for small computers. The pattern repeats itself, time and again.

The two newest innovations, digital watches and hand-held calculators, were not pioneered by either the existing watch or the calculator companies. The electronic industry provided the push to launch both these products. Eastman Kodak, a giant well-established business, was not the pioneer of instant photography. Instead, an entrepreneur, Edwin Land of Polaroid, proved that an instant picture was a product of value to consumers. Moreover, Kodak rejected the development of the instant copy process, which allowed a fledgling company to be born and eventually prosper—Xerox. These smaller firms did not initially possess the manufacturing expertise or the financial muscle to dominate a market against such large, established competitors. But they did. It was not RCA or General Electric, the two established electronic component suppliers, who created the mass market for the transitor. It was a remote and tiny company in the geophysical business, founded by Pat Haggerty in Texas, now known as Texas Instruments, Inc.[2] In all these cases, the energy of the entrepreneur made the vital difference, not the initial resources of the existing businesses.

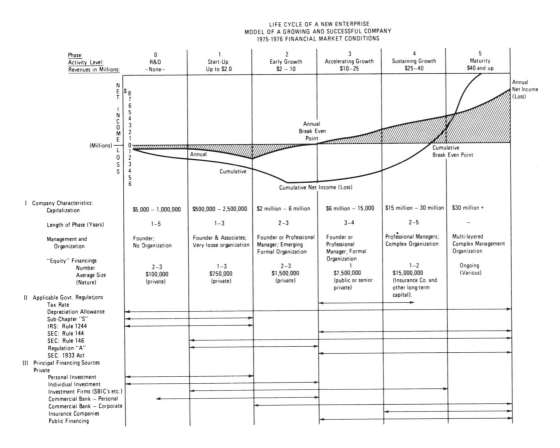

LIFE CYCLE OF A NEW ENTERPRISE
MODEL OF A GROWING AND SUCCESSFUL COMPANY
1975-1976 FINANCIAL MARKET CONDITIONS

[2] Theodore Leavitt, *Marketing for Business Growth*, McGraw-Hill, p. 123, 1974.

Even in non-high-technology businesses, the pattern repeats. Federated Department Stores and Allied Stores did not develop the mass merchandising, one-floor, suburban shopping revolution known as "the discount house." It was people who never before were in the retailing business, such as Two Guys of Harrison. Neither Ward Baking nor National Biscuit Company nor Bond Bread created the frozen cake revolution. It was a small local baker in Chicago, Sara Lee. These same large well-established baking businesses failed to innovate in the revolution toward quality in white, packaged bread. This was accomplished and pioneered by two tiny companies absolutely new to the baking business, Pepperidge Farms and Arnolds. Moreover, a novice in kitchen appliances, Raytheon, pioneered the newest miracle appliance, the microwave oven. Along with its newly acquired subsidiary, Amana, they caught the large stove manufacturer sleeping when the market finally blossomed. Last year several million microwave ovens were sold, and Amana has the largest share of this exploding market.

The above is only a partial list; no mention has been made of so many other examples. The reason this list seems long is that the actual experience based on history is heavily on the side of the entrepreneur. Not always (RCA did pioneer the color T.V.), but the new business headed by an entrepreneur seems to be how the American capitalistic system works best.

APPENDIXES

A

Information Questionnaire

TO BE USED AS BACKGROUND FOR THE
DEVELOPMENT OF A BUSINESS PLAN

1. What is the present name of the company?

2. Is the company a corporation, partnership, or sole proprietorship?

3. If the company is a corporation, please set forth the date and the state of incorporation.

4. Please furnish the names of the persons who caused the company to be formed.

5. Was the company originally organized as a corporation, partnership or sole proprietorship?

6. Please furnish the names of the initial shareholders and/or providers of funds (debt and equity) of the company. Supply dates of each sale of securities, number of shares issued, and the consideration received for the shares. If no cash consideration was received, indicate the dollar value ascribed to such consideration.

7. Please describe the nature of the company's business. Has the nature of the company's business changed or evolved since its inception? Is it intended to place future emphasis on different areas?

8. Does the company conduct business under names other than its own? If so, please set forth the names and places where they are used.

9. Does the company utilize any trademarks or tradenames? If so, submit copies.

10. What geographical areas does the company serve? Are there any limitations on what markets can be reached, e.g., freight, duties, service, maintenance, patent

*Reprinted with permission of a law firm that prepares business plans for clients, Pollock, O'Connor, and Jacobs, Waltham, Massachusetts.

licenses, tariffs, government regulation, etc? Does the company intend to enlarge its present areas of distribution or service?

11. Please describe the major products or services of the company.

12. In which states and/or countries other than its state of incorporation is the company licensed or qualified to do business?

13. Please furnish a listing plus a physical description of all offices, plants, laboratories, warehouses, stores, outlets, studios or other facilities (include size of plot, square footage of enclosed space, etc.).

14. Please describe the method or methods of distribution and sales. If any contractual arrangements are involved, please describe and/or furnish copies.

15. Please list and describe to the degree relevant, all patents, technical information, trademarks, franchises, copyrights, patent and technical information, licenses owned and/or used.

16. Please furnish a detailed five year breakdown of sales, earnings, income or losses of the company's major divisions, departments, and product categories. Give percentage of total income or loss attributed to each.

17. Please furnish a detailed breakdown of major suppliers of raw materials, goods, etc. Give their names, addresses, and volume of purchases. Are other sources readily available or is the company dependent to any degree on any one supplier? What would result if the product or products of said supplier or suppliers were no longer readily procurable? Does the company have any long term contracts with its suppliers?

18. If the company utilizes the services of subcontractor and/or processors of its products or components or subassemblies, please describe the work done and the availability of other subcontractors or processors. Does the company have any long term contracts with such persons?

19. Furnish a 3-year record of names, addresses, and volume of purchases of major customers or outlets for the company's products or services. The prospectus or offering circular will list names of customers who account for more than 10% of the company's business. Could this in any way be deleterious to the company?

20. Please furnish names of the company's major competitors; describe the nature and area of their competition—is it direct or indirect? What is the company's approximate rank in the industry? Are there numerous competitors? What is the degree of competition? Can new companies readily enter the field? Do the company's competitors possess greater financial resources? Are they longer established and better recognized?

21. Please furnish a complete list of all officers and/or directors plus the following data:

    (a)   Age.
    (b)   Education.
    (c)   Title and function—responsibilities.
    (d)   Length of service with company.
    (e)   Posts held and functions performed for company prior to present post.
    (f)   Compensation.
    (g)   Past business associations and posts held.
    (h)   Special distinctions.
    (i)   Other directorates or present business affiliations.

22. Please furnish a copy of all Stock Option Plans.

23. Please furnish a copy of or describe any bonus and profit sharing plans.

24. Please furnish copies of or describe any other employee fringe benefits.

25. Please furnish copies of any pension plan.

26. Please state the total number of employees, full and part time, the major categories of employees and member within each. If the company is to any degree dependent on technology or other expertise, please give details, e.g., number of Ph.D.s, M.A.s, engineers, technicians, medical personnel, etc.

27. Are your employees represented by one or more unions? Please list each union by name or number. Please furnish copies of the union contracts.

28. Please furnish a general description of labor relations, past strikes, handling of grievances, etc. Has the company experienced any difficulties in obtaining qualified personnel? Has company had any problems with respect to personnel turnover?

29. Please describe all acquisitions of other companies, assets, personnel, etc., made by the company, or any intended acquisitions. Please furnish copies of all acquisitions agreements.

30. Please describe any major dispositions of subsidiaries, divisions, assets, equipment, plants, etc., made by the company.

31. Has any officer, director or major shareholder ever (a) had any difficulties of any nature with the Securities and Exchange Commission, the National Association of Securities Dealers, or any state securities commission or agency, (b) been convicted of a felony, or (c) been under indictment, investigation or threatened by the SEC, NASD, a state commission, or public agency with prosecution for violation of a state or federal statute? Has any such person ever been adjudicated a bankrupt?

    If the answer to any of the questions is in the affirmative, please describe the circumstances in detail.

32. Has the company made (a) any private placements or its equity of debt securities, or (b) any public sale of its equity or debt securities? If so, please furnish complete details including copies of documents used in the placement and/or sale.

33. Furnish a specimen copy of all outstanding and authorized equity and debt securities.

34. Furnish the following data regarding the distribution of the company's voting stock:
    (a) classes of stock and number of shares of each outstanding;
    (b) total number of shareholders plus list of shareholders;
    (c) names, residence addresses and shareholdings of ten largest shareholders of each class;
    (d) relationships of major shareholders to each other or to the officers and directors of the company; and
    (e) details of any voting trust agreements, shareholders agreements or other arrangements to vote stock jointly.

35. Are there any options to purchase stock or other securities or warrants outstanding other than employees' stock option plans? If so, please furnish copies or describe such plan.

36. Does the company have any long term or short term debt, secured or unsecured, or has the company guaranteed such debt on behalf of others? Please furnish copies of the documents creating the debt or guarantee, or describe the debt or guarantee.

37. Please furnish detailed audited statements for the last five years if available.

38. Please furnish interim statements covering the period subsequent to the last audited financial statement.

39. Please furnish comparative figures of earning and net worth for five years.

40. Please furnish an explanation of any and all abnormal, non-recurring or unusual items in earnings statements or balance sheets.

41. Please furnish a statement of cash flow if materially different from statement of net earnings.

42. Please furnish a statement as to any contingent or possible liabilities not shown on balance sheet. Please include guarantees, warranties, litigation, etc.

43. With respect to the company's inventories, please state (a) major categories, (b) method used in valuation, LIFO, FIFO, other, and (c) control systems. If your "inventories" are distinctive in any fashion, e.g., film libraries, promotional displays, etc., please state how they are handled on your books.

44. What is the company's policy regarding depreciation, depletion and amortization? Which items are capitalized and which expensed? Are there any deferred write-offs?

45. Are your company's methods of accounting similar to the rest of the industry? If not, please describe the differences and the reason for such differences.

46. Please state the status of federal and state tax examinations. When was your last examination, and are there any open questions?

47. Please describe all bank relationships and credit lines. Are factors involved?

48. Please describe any pending or threatened claims and litigation, by identifying the parties, the amount involved, the names of involved and please furnish copies of all documents with respect thereto.

49. Please describe all insurance coverages, e.g., plant, equipment, properties, work interruption, key employees, other.

50. Please describe your company's projection of sales and earnings for the next three years, including explanations with respect to any increase or decrease.

51. Please furnish lists of all real estate owned by the Company, including, without limitation, the following: (a) the improvements on the property, (b) the assessed valuation and amount of current real estate taxes, (c) any mortgages, including amount, rate of interest and due date, (d) any liens or encumbrances, and (e) the estimated present value.

52. Please furnish a list of all real estate leased by the company, including without limitation the following: (a) the amount of space, (b) the rent-fixed and contingent, (c) the term of lease, (d) the renewal options, (e) the purchase options, (f) the minimum annual gross rentals, and (g) the minimum total gross rental obligation to expiration of all leases in force.

53. Please list all equipment leased by the company if aggregate annual rentals exceed $5,000 or if the company is dependent on the equipment. If any other property is leased at a sizable aggregate annual rental, please furnish details of the lease, including without limitation the terms, options to renew and/or purchase, etc.

54. Please describe all depreciable property owned by the company including without limitation the following: (a) the original cost to company, (b) the depreciation to date, in addition to a statement as to the method employed, (c) the remaining cost, and (d) the aging of items listed (remaining depreciable life).

55. Please furnish copies of all brochures, catalogues, mailers, publicity releases, newspaper or magazine articles, literature and the like distributed by the company or concerning the company, its products, personnel or services.

56. Please describe the company's research and development activities.

57. Please give us a complete description of any unusual contracts relating to the company, its business, products or services.

58. Please describe exactly how the net proceeds (after underwriting commission and all expenses) are to be used by the company.

59. Please describe the company's plans for expansion or growth.

60. Please set forth any information not previously disclosed in your answers that an investor would use in making a decision as to whether he should invest in the company.

61. Please furnish copies of the following:
    (a) Certificate of Incorporation and all amendments.
    (b) By-laws and all amendments.
    (c) Employment agreements, if any.
    (d) Instruments creating any long term or short term indebtedness.
    (e) Material contracts.
    (f) Leases—real property, equipment, other.
    (g) Stock Option Plan and option agreements.
    (h) Union contracts.
    (i) Licenses or franchises.
    (j) Stockholders agreements, voting trust agreements, and any other voting agreements.
    (k) Major sales contracts.
    (l) Major supply contracts.
    (m) Specimen stock and debt certificates.
    (n) Government permits.

B

Associations
Of Value
To Small Business

A. AIRPORT LOUNGES*

If you wait between planes at an airport, have a delayed takeoff, or arrive early to relax or complete paperwork before departure, airline lounges provide quiet comfort, reading materials, complimentary coffee or soft drinks, TV, and cocktail service. Lounges can be found at most airports.

You can join one or more clubs by writing for a membership application to one of the following:

The Admirals Club: American Airlines; $45 per year or $450 lifetime membership. Write:

P.O. Box 61616
Dallas Ft. Worth Airport
Dallas, Texas 75261
Phone: (214) 267-1151

The Council Club: Braniff International; $35 per year, $90 for 3 years, or $300 for lifetime membership. Write:

P.O. Box 61747
Dallas Ft. Worth Airport
Dallas, Texas 75261
Phone: (214) 357-9511

The Presidents Club: Continental Airlines $65 first year membership, $35 each consecutive year thereafter. Lifetime membership is $300. Write:

Continental Airlines
c/o Karen Lemons
7300 World Way West
Los Angeles, Ca. 90009
Phone: (213) 772-6000

The Ionosphere Club: Eastern Airlines; $40 per year, $160 for five years, or $400 for lifetime. Write:

Miami International Airport
Miami, Fl. 33148
Phone: (305) 873-3000

*Spouses and/or guests may also enjoy the convenience and comfort offered by these airline lounges. If you travel frequently for business or pleasure, you may enjoy the benefits of a private airline club.

The Clipper Club: Pan American World Airways; $50 annually, $135 for three years, $500 for a lifetime. Senior Citizens lifetime membership $300. Write:

Pan Am Building
New York, N.Y. 10017
Phone: (212) 752-3151

The Ambassador Club: Trans World Airlines, Inc.; $35 annual membership or $500 for lifetime. Write:

605 Third Avenue
New York, N.Y. 10016
Phone: (212) 290-2121

The Red Carpet Club: United Air Lines, Inc.; rates are $35 annually or $525 for lifetime. Spouse's card is $10 or $150 lifetime. Initiation fee is $50. Write:

P.O. Box 2247
Boston, Ma. 02107
Phone: (617) 482-7900

The Horizon Club: Western Air Lines, Inc.; $40 annual, $10 for spouse card. Write:

Box 92005
Los Angeles, Ca. 90009
Phone: (213) 776-2311

B. BEST-SELLING BOOKS

Below is a list of the all-time best selling self-development books and the authors. These books are readily available in any library and are listed under both author and title. They are all great, not good, because they have stood the test of success in a free marketplace. They have been "noted" as the best because more people have bought or read them.

All-Time Best-Selling Self-Development Books

- *Think and Grow Rich* by Napoleon Hill.
- *Laws of Success* by Napoleon Hill.
- *Psycho-Cybernetics* by Maxwell Maltz, M.D.
- *Success Through a Positive Mental Attitude* by Napoleon Hill and W. Clement Stone.
- *The Success System that Never Fails* by W. Clement Stone.
- *The Power of Positive Thinking* by Dr. Norman Vincent Peale.
- *The Greatest Salesman in the World* by Og Mandino.
- *How To Win Friends and Influence People* by Dale Carnegie.
- *Your Greatest Power* by J. Martin Kohn.
- *How I Raised Myself from Failure to Success in Selling* by Frank Bettger.

C. BUSINESS PLANS

A document written to articulate the directions of a growing business enterprise is a business plan. These road maps are often written to raise new money for an expanding business. Internal and external entrepreneurs write them to show the obvious strengths of their business. Below are discussed several sources to help in the preparation of these plans.

One of the finest pieces of information for understanding financial statements is offered free of charge by the world's largest securities firm, Merrill Lynch, Pierce Fenner & Smith. This 24-page book entitlted *Understanding Financial Statements* is so good it is often used as a free handout in graduate-level college finance courses. It offers an understanding of three basic financial tools: Balance Sheet, Cash Flow Statement, and Profit and Loss Statement.

You can call your local Merrill Lynch office, which can be found in your local directory, and ask for a copy.

Several excellent articles on developing a business plan are contained within the books offered by the most professional source of venture capital information, Capital Publishing Company. Although these books are a bit expensive, some articles on the business plan are truly excellent because the tips are practical and worthwhile. Write:

Stanley Pratt
Capital Publishing
2 Laurel Street
Wellesley Hills, Ma.
(617) 235-5405

How to Prepare and Present a Business Plan is a comprehensive guide to the development of a business plan. It includes three complete business plans and synopses for five more. Call or write:

The Center for Entrepreneurial
    Management, Inc.
83 Spring Street
New York, N.Y. 10012
(212) 925-7304

The Small Business Administration offers several excellent pamphlets on writing a business plan. They are surprisingly good. They even offer further information on where to obtain information on writing a business plan.

- Business Plan for Small Manufacturers #MA–2007
- Business Plan for a Small Construction Firm #MA–2008
- Business Plan for a Retailer #MA–2020
- Business Plan for a Service Firm #MA–2022

To receive these pamphlets and an index of all SBA material contact your local field office, or write:

Small Business Administration
Box 15434
Fort Worth, Tx. 76119

If you have a high-tech firm, you might want to look at Stephen Burrill's "Outline for a New High Technology Business Plan," available free from Arthur Young & Company. Call, toll-free: (800) 344-8324; in California, call (415) 393-2731.

Another source of information on business plan's development is a two-part document. Part I is a five-page approach to developing a business plan, and Part II describes how to prepare a business plan.

Institute for New Enterprise Development
385 Concord Avenue
Belmont, Ma. 02178
(617) 489-3950

D. ENTREPRENEURIAL EDUCATION

A small but fascinating school for entrepreneurs is housed in a quaint inn in the beautiful village of Londonderry, Vermont. It's headed by two men:

1. Brian Smith, head of the business department at Franklin Pierce College, founder of a New England-based electronic medical instruments company, and a former IBMer.
2. James S. Howard, founder of the Country Business Brokers in Brattleboro, Vermont, and a former public relations executive on Madison Avenue.

The seminar program they offer is couple-oriented, with small classes appropriate to the charming setting. The fee is $260 per couple for a weekend. Couples are recruited primarily through newspaper advertisements, and the operations of the inn are often cited as an example of those of a small business of your own. For more information write to:

The Country Business Brokers
12 Linden Street
Brattleboro, Vt. 05301
(802) 254-4504

The School for Entrepreneurs
Tarrytown, NY

About four years ago, Mr. Robert Schwartz, the owner of the twenty-six acre magnificent estate known as the Tarrytown Conference Center in Tarrytown, New York, was interviewed by an aggressive reporter on behalf of a small magazine based in Boston, Massachusetts known as *New Age Journal*. The interview resulted in a cover story for this magazine (circulation of about 30,000 to a somewhat avant-garde readership), where Schwartz expounded upon the values of entrepreneurship as a way of life. The new generation had traditionally been turned off to business and turned on to new and greater sets of social values. The notion proposed by Schwartz was that, through the entrepreneurial role of starting your own business, new expressions can take place in society. The new generation can make its greatest impact as change agents not as renegades, claimed this unusual innkeeper.

The message was so powerful in this journal that Schwartz received thousands of telephone calls and letters, and this article moved him to consider starting a school for entrepreneurs.

Being the owner of a conference center twenty miles north of New York City, he concluded that two weekend sessions, back-to-back, to sharpen their entrepreneurial skills would have the most immediate appeal. After counseling with academicians, entrepreneurs, and a host of others, he introduced the first school for entrepreneurs in 1976. Since that time, approximately 500 people have graduated from his school, including myself. The school has been written up in *Psychology Today*, TWA's *Ambassador Magazine*, and a host of other prominent magazines and journals. The reason for the school's success to date is Robert Schwartz, the colorful founder of The School of Entrepreneurs. An entrepreneur himself, he sees the school as a vehicle for expressing a number of his innovative ideas. While some of the more traditional entrepreneurial courses in universities look to The School of Entrepreneurs as something close to "touchy-feely," in fact, it is really a combination of EST and entrepreneurship—what I call "entrepreneurism." Schwartz not only imparts how to make money values and the importance of a business plan, but he also imparts a significant message about how to get your life together. A bit of an inspirational thinker and a philosopher, Schwartz is the main star in the revolving cast at the school.

The school is composed of games, tests, and the development of a business plan. It is highlighted by the presentation of a specific business plan to Alan Patricoff, a venture capitalist in New York City. That is followed by an exciting party which centers around Bob, his life, and the people who surround him. It is an interesting school, worthy of note.

The man who has earned the right to talk about entrepreneurship, Robert Schwartz, is a businessman who has a knack for putting together ventures that are not only profitable, but also exciting. According to an article in TWA's *Ambassador* in-flight magazine, ' his ideas are tacked up on the bulletin boards of "Fortune 500" companies as well as in Vermont communes. He synthesizes the value systems of people who would not normally talk to each other, and he is respected in both camps."

As a businessman, Bob Schwartz is the sole owner of the multi-million dollar Tarrytown House Executive Conference Center. As a writer and publishing executive, he has been a national magazine journalist on the staff of *Harper's*. He has served as the New York Bureau Chief of *Time*, was "entrepreneur-in-residence" and assistant to the publisher of *Life*, and has been a part owner of *New York Magazine.*

As a humanitarian, he is a former board member of the Association for Humanistic Psychology and the Humanistic Psychology Institute. As a concerned citizen, he has been on boards ranging from Amnesty International to the National Commission on Resources for Youth. As a speaker, he has addressed international audiences including Swedish industrialists, the Direct Mail Marketing Association, and the World Affairs Conference at the University of Colorado. As an orchestrator of social change, he is President of The Tarrytown Group, a forum for high-level dialogue about emerging planetary concerns, which was originally conceived by the late Margaret Mead.

As an entrepreneur, he has built unlikely hostelries like the Japanese-designed "Motel on the Mountain" and America's first executive conference center at a hilltop estate in Tarrytown, New York, which has played host to seminars and training sessions of over 2,000 corporations.

Interested? Write?

Bob Schwartz
The School for Entrepreneurs
Tarrytown House
East Sunnyside Lane
Tarrytown, N.Y. 10591
(212) WE 3-1232
(914) LY 1-8200

SBA Business Management Courses

Business management courses in planning, organization, and control of a business are co-sponsored by the Small Business Association in cooperation with educational institutions, chambers of commerce, and trade associations. Courses are usually held in the evenings and last between six and eight weeks. In addition, conferences covering subjects such as working capital, business forecasting, and marketing are being held on a regular basis.

The SBA also conducts Pre-Business Workshops dealing with finance, marketing assistance, business site selection, and types of business organizations for prospective business owners. Clinics focus on particular problems of small firms in specific industrial categories and are held on an as 1-1 needed basis.

Small Business Goes to College: College and University Courses in Small Business and Entrepreneurship is a booklet that traces the development of small business management as a college subject and provides samples of courses offered by some 200 colleges and universities. It is available for $3.25 from:

The Superintendent of Documents
Government Printing Office
Washington, D.C. 20402
(202) 783-3238

For additional information on SBA Business Management Courses, contact:

The Office of Management Information
    and Training
Management Assistance, Small Business
    Administration
1522 K Street, N.W.
Room 636
Washington, D.C. 20416
(202) 724-1703

Another school of entrepreneurs is headed by William J. McCrea, the chairman of the Entrepreneurship Institute. This school moves from city to city and offers weekend training seminars entitled "How to Create and Manage Your Own Business." For a schedule, call or write to:

Jan William Zapnizk
The Entrepreneurship Institute
3592 Corporate Drive
Suite 100
Columbus, Oh. 43229
(614) 894-1153

Dr. Leon Danco of the University Services Institute in Cleveland, Ohio offers a host of interesting family-oriented business seminars. Dr. Danco is one of the finest authorities on the father–son team and on issues of families within small business.

University Services Institute
5862 Mayfield Road
Box 24197
Cleveland, Oh. 44124
(216) 442-0800

If you have ever felt that penetrating the U.S. government was like kicking a two-hundred-foot sponge, help is now available. The Small Business Administration (SBA) appointed an exceptionally qualified individual to its newly created post of Small Business Advocacy. This means that his taxpayer-funded job is to champion entrepreneurial causes. He will tell you where the SBA is offering seminars in your area. Do you need help of any kind or do you have positive suggestions to offer? Write:

Chief of Advocacy
Small Business Administration
1441 L Street, N.W.
Washington, D.C. 20416

Help From Colleges for Small Business

University Business Development Centers (UBDCs) were originated in 1973 under the auspices of the National Science Foundation (NSF) and are affiliated with local universities. The purpose of these centers is to (1) conduct research on the innovation process, (2) develop curricula on technological entrepreneurship, innovation, and product and new venture development, and (3) provide technical and management assistance to new and emerging technology-oriented businesses. However, budgetary cuts have forced these centers to seek alternate sources of funding as of 1984. Presently, it is estimated that six of these centers have a good chance of receiving alternate support and continuing operations through 1985 and that the other three centers have a fair chance.

The nine centers are as follows:

Product Development

Dr. David Jansson, Director
MIT Innovation Center
Room W–91–209
Cambridge, Ma. 02139
(617) 253-6946

Dr. Arthur Gerstenfeld, Director
UBDC
Department of Management
Worcester Polytechnic Institute
Worcester, Ma. 01609
(617) 793-5000

Dr. James J. Conti, Director
UBDC
Polytechnic Institute of New York
Broad Hollow Road
Farmingdale, N.Y. 11735
(516) 454-5100

Dr. Don S. Ousterhour, Director
Research and Sponsored Programs
University of Arkansas
120 Ozark Hall
Fayetteville, Ar. 72710
(501) 575-3754

New Venture Development

Dr. Raymond Radosevich, Director
New Mexico Technological Innovation
    Center
University of New Mexico
Albuquerque, N.M. 97191
(505) 277-2009

Dr. Wayne Brown, Director
Utah Innovation Center, Inc.
1730 Arlington Drive
Salt Lake City, Ut. 84103
(801) 581-3433 or (801) 581-6441

Mr. Paul Cartledge, Director
Industrial Technology Research &
    Development Foundation (ITRAD)
P.O. Box 1335
Durant, Ok. 74701
(405) 924-5094

Dr. Narinder Kapany, Director
UBDC
University of California/Santa Cruz
Class Room Building
Santa Cruz, Ca. 95064
(408) 429-2506

Dr. Dwight Baumann, Director
Carnegie-Mellon University Innovation
    Center
Schenley Park
Scaife Hall
Pittsburgh, Pa. 15213
(412) 621-0700 or (412) 578-2490

Small Business Development Centers

The Small Business Development Center (SBDC) Program is sponsored by the Small Business Administration and is a cooperative effort by the Federal, state and local governments, with universities and the private sector, to provide management techniques and technical assistance to the small business community. It is meant that this program will expand the services already available from the current local SBA offices. Each SBDC has a full-time director and staff.

The pilot program was inaugurated at the end of 1976, and there are now 23 SBDCs in operation, in 22 states and the District of Columbia. This year the SBDCs are making special efforts to reach more women, minorities, and veterans. Also, emphasis is being directed to those small companies that are interested in exporting their goods.

SBDC assistance is available to anyone interested in entrepreneurship. Below are listed the directors and addresses of the 23 SBDC centers. We've alphabetized the states, to make it easier to find yours.

Dr. Fred Myrick, SBDC Director
School of Business
University of Alabama
1000 S. Twelfth Street, Suite F
Birmingham, Al. 35294
(205) 934-7260

Dr. Roy Robbins, SBDC Director
New Business Building
University of Arkansas
33rd & University Avenue
Little Rock, Ar. 72204
(501) 371-5381

Mr. Everett R. Shaw, SBDC Director
School of Business Administration
University of Connecticut
Box U-41D
Storrs, Ct. 06268
(203) 486-4135

Mr. Charles G. Maass, SBDC Director
College of Business and Economics
University of Delaware
005 Purnell Hall
Newark, De. 19711
(302) 738-8401

Mr. Warren Van Hook, SBDC Director
Howard University
2361 Sherman Avenue, N.W.
Washington, D.C. 20059
(202) 636-7187

Mr. Gregory Higgins, SBDC Director
University of West Florida
137 Hospital Drive, Suite H
Ft. Walton Beach, Fl. 32548
(904) 243-7624

Mr. Adolph Sanders, Acting SBDC
  Director
University of Georgia
Brooks Hall, Room 348
Athens, Ga. 30602
(404) 542-5760

Mr. Lloyd E. Anderson, SBDC Director
Center for Industrial Research & Services
Engineering Annex, Room 205
Iowa State University
Ames, Ia. 50011
(515) 294-3420

Mr. Jerry Owens, SBDC Director
College of Business and Economics
University of Kentucky
Commerce Building, Room 415
Lexington, Ky. 40506
(606) 257-1751

Mr. Warren Purdy, SBDC Director
Small Business Development Center
University of Southern Maine
246 Deering Avenue
Portland, Me. 04102
(207) 780-4423

Mr. John Ciccarelli, SBDC Director
School of Business Administration
University of Massachusetts
Amherst, Ma. 01003
(413) 549-4930, ext 304

Mr. Tim Donahue, SBDC Director
St. Thomas College
2115 Summit Avenue
St. Paul, Mn. 55105
(612) 647-5840

Mr. Bob Wilkinson, Acting SBDC
  Director
School of Business
University of Mississippi
660 Lakeland East Drive
Jackson, Ms. 39208
(601) 939-0001

Mr. Felipe Garcia-Otero, Acting SBDC
  Director
St. Louis University
Tegeler Hall/3rd Floor
3550 Lindell Boulevard
St. Louis, Mo. 63103
(314) 534-7232

Mr. Robert Bernier, SBDC Director
Peter Kiewit Center
University of Nebraska
Omaha, Ne. 68182
(402) 554-2521

Ms. Adele Kaplan, SBDC Director
Rutgers University
Ackerson Hall/3rd Floor
180 University Street
Newark, N.J. 07102
(201) 648-5627

Ms. Susan Garber, SBDC Director
The Wharton School
University of Pennsylvania
3201 Steinberg Hall-Dietrich Hall/CC
Philadelphia, Pa. 19104
(215) 898-1219

Mr. Thomas Sullivan, SBDC Director
Bryant College
Smithfield, R.I. 92917
(401) 231-1200

Mr. W. F. Littlejohn, SBDC Director
College of Business Administration
University of South Carolina
Columbia, S.C. 29208
(803) 777-5118

Mr. Richard Haglund, SBDC Director
Graduate School of Business
University of Utah
Salt Lake City, Ut. 84112
(801) 581-7905

Mr. Ed V. Owens, SBDC Director
College of Business and Economics
Washington State University
Pullman, Wa. 99164
(509) 335-1576

Dr. Richard T. Adams, SBDC Director
University of Charleston
2300 MacCorkle Avenue, S.E.
Charleston, W.V. 25304
(304) 346-9471

Dr. Robert Pricer, SBDC Director
University of Wisconsin
One South Park Street
Madison, Wi. 53706
(608) 263-7794

E. THE ENTREPRENEURS HALL OF FAME

While college enrollment in general has been on the decline, enrollment pertaining to entrepreneurship and small business has been on the rise. One of the many schools with established chairs and programs in entrepreneurship is the Babson Institute in Wellesley, Massachusetts. Babson College instituted the Entrepreneurial Hall of Fame in 1978.

Recipients for 1978

Kenneth H. Olsen is the president of Digital Equipment Corporation, which was founded in 1957. It was a new idea to start a company, at this time of recession, when a number of new companies were in trouble. With only $70,000 to work with, every dollar was carefully watched, and most of the work, from cleaning the floors to making their own tools, was done by Olsen and his associates. He started with the idea of no government funding for their research, and they sought to make a profit from day one.

Berry Gordy, the president and chairman of Motown Industries, Inc., loved writing and creating songs. His first record store in Detroit was opened in 1953, and in 1955 he was bankrupt. After not being able to collect from a publisher who owed him $1,000, he decided to start a company for young writers. He was told that he could not do it. That was all he needed to hear, and Motown was born. He believes that you must first consider happiness before success so that success does not destroy you later.

Royal Little is the former chairman of Textron, Inc. He used his textile business to expand into more diversified areas of industry. He believed that if one business is not perfomring, get out—sell it—and then buy another one. His idea worked, and this started the conglomerate trend in the United States.

Ray Kroc, chairman of the McDonald Corporation, started out with the Lily Cup Company and sold paper cups for about 17 years. As a salesman for a multiple milkshake mixer, the Multi-Mixer, he heard of an operation in California run by the McDonald brothers. Their stand was using eight of these mixers, making up to 40 milkshakes at one time. After his association with the McDonalds, Kroc felt that he was growing faster than they were, and in 1954 he opened his first "McDonald's." In 1960 he bought the business for $1.5 million. His theory is that "part of being an entrepreneur is knowing what to give and when to give it."

Soichiro Honda founded the Honda Motor Company 30 years ago. He first brought motorcycles to the United States 20 years ago and thus created a new product. His first task was to sell the United States on motorcycling; then he had to sell Honda.

He is not sure that he is an entrepreneur, only that he is a man with imagination, creativity, and desire behind him.

1979 Recipients

John Eric Jonsson, 77, is the founder and former chairman of Texas Instruments. After graduating from Renssalaer Polytechnic Institute in 1922, he became interested in Texas Instruments, then Geophysical Services, Inc., in Newark, New Jersey. The outfit moved to Texas in 1934, and Jonsson and Eugene McDermott bought out what is now a billion-dollar concern.

Diane Von Furstenburg, president of DVF, Inc., came to the United States in 1969 and saw a great need in the fashion industry. She designed a basic dress in a basic material called jersey. Her claim to success is that you can be a woman and mother and be in business, too, if you are willing to work, plan, and discipline yourself.

John H. Johnson is the founder of *Ebony* magazine. Poverty motivated him to work harder in high school, which earned him a scholarship to the University of Chicago. In his junior year, he worked on a company magazine, which gave him the idea to publish a *Negro Digest* similar to the *Reader's Digest*. The profits he received from the magazine enabled him to start *Ebony* magazine.

Thomas Mello Evans is the chairman of Crane Company, which manufactures everything from steel to antipollution gear. He took over Crane Company in 1959 and, more recently, purchased 7.3% of the outstanding common stock of MacMilan, Inc., the broadly based purchaser. He has always shown a profit, and companies usually succeed under his management.

Byung Chull Lee, chairman of Samsung Group, started a rice cleaning plant in South Korea in 1935. After deciding that his country could prosper only through trade, he established the Samsung (Three-Star) export-import company in 1952. Today, as Korea's richest man, his fortune is over $500 million, and Samsung has become a 24-company conglomerate with sales of $2 billion per year.

1980 Recipients

1. Mary Wells Lawrence of Wells, Rich, Greene and Company.
2. Lewis E. Lehrman of the Rite-Aid and Lehrman Institute.
3. Mary Hudson of the Hudson Oil Company.
4. Peter Grace of W. R. Grace and Company.

Recipients for 1981

The 1981 inductees into the Babson College Academy of Distinguished Entrepreneurs represent four continents. All, men of managerial enterprise, were honored on April 15, 1981.

Frank Perdue started raising chickens and selling eggs when he was ten years old. In 1952 he took over control of Perdue Farms Inc. from his father and began marketing chickens along the eastern seaboard. His television marketing strategy, which includes a money-back guarantee, is one of the factors making the Perdue organization one of the five largest privately owned companies in the country.

Perdue interviewed over 40 advertising agencies before choosing one to represent his firm. At the agency's insistence, he appeared in his own ads. The slogan, "It takes a tough man to make a tender chicken," helped his name recognition jump to over 50% within a few months.

Frank Perdue is most concerned with all aspects of his business and is known to make frequent spotchecks of his 5 plants from Maryland to North Carolina. Perdue is now opening a chain of restaurants in the New Jersey area but is not ready for expansion into other chicken products.

The first Babson College alumnus to be named to the Babson College Academy of Distinguished Entrepreneurs, Gustavo Cisneros (Class of '68) is president of a Latin American conglomerate that is involved in banking, food, retailing, communications, and manufacturing.

The Organization Diego Cisneros (ODC) has extensive holdings in Venezuela and elsewhere in Latin America; its operations were recently expanded into Florida. ODC sales were close to $2 billion in 1980. The business employs more than 12,000 people.

ODC's major holdings include Venevision, one of two commercial TV networks in Venezuela; Circuito Nacional Radio-vision, a 13-station radio network which encompasses 80% of the country; C. A. Distribuidora de Alimentos, the largest supermarket chain in Venezuela; Pepsi-Cola and Hit De Venezuela, C. A., a soft drink corporation consisting of 24 bottling plants and 12 warehouses and holder of the Pepsi franchise for Venezuela, the largest independent bottler in the world; and most recently, the Burger-King franchise for Venezuela. ODC has started renovating 30 of the soda fountain style restaurants within its supermarket chain.

Married, with three children, Cisneros is a director of many organizations and corporations. He is presently president of the Simon Bolivar Foundation of New York. Among his many awards, Mr. Cisneros holds the Order of Isabel la Catolica from the King of Spain.

Wang Labs was started by An Wang in 1951 in the Lowell-Tewksbury section of Massachusetts. By its 25th anniversary in 1976, Wang Labs showed a compounded sales growth of about 40% . . . in 1980 it posted a 66% growth rate. According to *Financial World's* tabluation of high-growth companies, Wang ranks fifth in earnings per share growth.

A leader in the microcomputer and word processing field, Wang employs 14,000 people. They are in direct competition with IBM and Burroughs in selling directly to customers. Wang stock is traded on the AMEX because Dr. Wang feels that NYSE requirements are too cumbersone.

Dr. Wang came from Shanghai, China after World War II to study at Harvard. In 1954 he became a naturalized citizen. While a staff-member of the Harvard Computation Laboratory, Wang developed the patent for the memory core and sold it to IBM. He has worked closely with Lowell in its renewal efforts and is now rehabilitating a Boston building. His plans are to open a new plant in Chinatown to employ Chinese-Americans in the computer industry. Dr. Wang is married and has three children.

Dr. Marcus Wallenberg, of Sweden, is the prime mover behind a $13 billion business empire that includes Scandinavian Airlines Systems (SAS). The Wallenberg dynasty has had complete or partial control of eight of the country's top industrial companies, a leading bank, and numerous smaller concerns, totaling 33% of Sweden's economy.

Dr. Wallenberg made the family bank, founded by his sea captain grandfather, into the brain and nerve center, as well as the financial guide and advisor, of the best in modern Swedish business—what has been called the Wallenberg Group. His directorships on company boards as the bank's representative has enabled him to influence and hand-pick managers who are considered among the best in Europe.

Through stock control of a few companies that have controlling interest in other firms, Marcus was able to build an empire that includes SKF, the world's largest ball-bearing manufacturers; L. M. Ericcson, a telephone equipment supplier that is the only substantial competition to ITT; Electrolux; SAAB-Scania car; ASEA, a truck and aircraft maker; and the Swedish answer to General Electric.

Dr. Wallenberg has managed to retain control of the $13 billion sales empire through accepting the heavily-socialized Swedish government and labor unions as partners in the complex Swedish system. Wallenberg found time for various public activities including service to the domestic and international business communities. Retired from his position as Chairman of the Board of SAS in 1976, Wallenberg previously served in capacities such as President of the International Chamber of Commerce and as a member of the board of the Nobel Foundation.

"I've got a love affair with chocolate chip cookies," says "Famous" *Wally Amos*, "that borders on being fanatical." Today Amos is chairman of the board of the Famous Amos Chocolate Chip Cookie Corporation, which grosses over 5 million dollars a year. The company has retail outlets in Hollywood and Santa Monica, several in Hawaii, plus wholesale and baking facilities in Van Nuys, California and Nutley, New Jersey, where they bake six tons every week.

Like many successful entrepreneurs, Amos did not finish high school. He dropped out of school in Harlem in 1957 to be a stock clerk at Saks Fifth Avenue. Hired for the Christmas holidays, he was asked to stay on, promoted to supply manager, and sent to New York University to study retailing and merchandising on a part-time basis. When his request for a raise was denied, Amos left Saks to become a trainee with the William Morris Agency.

Before long he was a talent agent, booking the Temptations, the Supremes, Marvin Gaye, and Bobby Goldsboro and signing the then unknown team of Paul Simon and Art Garfunkel. Amos founded his own talent agency on the west coast in 1967, and on his daily rounds, he passed out chocolate chip cookies baked from his Aunt Della's recipe. He soon became known as the "chocolate chip cookie man," and friends urged him to open his own retail store.

Amos did open a store, on Sunset Boulevard in 1975, with backing from United Artists' Artie Mogull, and Marvin Gaye, Helen Reddy, and her husband, Jeff Wald. Working 18-hour days and doing everything from giving interviews to mixing the dough, Amos soon turned himself and his cookies into celebrities. His costume, a Hawaiian print shirt with a straw hat, is in the Smithsonian Institute.

His cookies sell in stores like Macy's, Neiman-Marcus, and Bloomingdale's at $4 a pound, although supermarkets are now introducing a 7-ounce package for two dollars.

Since 1979 Amos has been the national spokesman for the Literacy Volunteers of America, which helps to educate the 23 million American adults who have been identified as functionally illiterate. As he puts it, "To support the community is to support yourself, because the community is your customer."

Armand Hammer was a medical student at Columbia University when he made his first million, turning around the fortunes of his family's drug business.

Journeying to Russia in 1921 to collect a $150,000 debt owed the family business and to assist the victims of a typhoid epidemic, Hammer discovered that the real problem was not typhus but starvation. He initiated the first trading between the United States and the Soviet Union, negotiating U.S. grain in exchange for Russian hides and furs. At the suggestion of Lenin, Hammer became a Russian concessionaire and at one point represented 38 American manufacturers, including Ford and U.S. Rubber.

Following Lenin's death, Hammer sold his Russian interests. "I couldn't do business with Stalin," he says. He took with him an extensive art collection and proceeded to market it throughout the world, calling it "the Romanov Treasure." With his brother Victor, he owns the Hammer Galleries in New York.

Hammer has been in and out of the cattle business and the whiskey business and bought (and then sold) the Mutual Broadcasting System. In 1956 he became involved in a small west coast oil company, Occidental Petroleum. The company was drilling two sites and had a net worth of $100,000. Hammer invested $50,000 into the ailing firm. The two wells paid off and Oxy, as it has become known, was launched on its way to its present status as the 20th largest industrial corporation in the U.S. It has assets of over six-billion dollars.

Today Hammer is concentrating his efforts on rescuing the Hooker Chemical Company from the financial morass resulting from lawsuits by residents of the Niagara Falls area regarding the chemicals in the Love Canal. He is also developing gold and silver mines in Nevada, uranium prospects in Canada, and shale oil stakes in Colorado. Recently Oxy has completed a merger agreement with Iowa Beef Processors Campany, the nation's largest beef producer. Another recent investment is in a gigantic ammonia plant in Odessa, USSR, for the chemicals needed for fertilizer in this country.

As chairman of the President's Cancer Panel, Hammer jolted the medical world in December by announcing a two-million dollar donation from his foundation, to be used for cancer research. One-million dollars have been set aside for the first scientist to come up with a cure, while smaller awards will go to the individual making the most progress each year toward this goal.

He is also chairman of the board of trustees of the Salk Institute, to which he gave five-million dollars in 1969 to establish a center for cancer biology research. In 1977 he created a five-million dollar endowment for a health science center at his alma mater, Columbia.

Born and raised on a Nebraska farm, *William C. Norris* attended the University of Nebraska, graduating in 1932 with a degree in electrical engineering. In 1957 he founded Control Data Corporation, and today he serves as chairman and chief executive officer of that three-billion dollar company.

Norris began his career as a sales engineer for Westinghouse Electric. This was followed by five years of service in the navy during World War II when he became interested in electronic equipment through work on a project which helped to break the German code.

After the war he co-founded Engineering Research Associates, Inc. in St. Paul, Minnesota. ERA made substantial contributions to the development of digital computer technology and later merged with Sperry Rand Corporation, Norris headed the Univac Division of Sperry Rand for two years before leaving to found Control Data.

Norris financed his start-up company by selling 615,000 shares in the new venture for one dollar each. According to an article in *Time* on February 15, 1982, these original shares are now worth $324 apiece.

Today Control Data is actually two operations: the original scientific computer business, greatly expanded and diversified to include computer services, systems, and peripheral products such as disc memory products; and Commercial Credit, a financial and insurance service company.

As head of CDC, Norris has led the movement among American corporate leaders to locate plants in rundown urban areas, thus aiding in the economic turnaround of decaying cities. Part of his philosophy is that business must work with government and technology to solve society's major problems. This has led to business ventures in seven economically depressed areas, under the aegis of City Venture Corporation. In another aspect of his program of corporate responsibility, Norris established a sister consortium to City Venture, called Rural Venture, to upgrade poverty-stricken rural areas by bringing in industry.

A frequent writer and lecturer on social and economic problems, Norris is the author of a series of booklets describing the use of technology to solve society's ills.

Although he heads a large corporation, Norris encourages small business, chiefly through providing business and technology centers for budding entrepreneurs. These centers offer space and facilities to fledgling business owners and advice on finances and management of new ventures. In addition, CDC operates Control Data Institute, a combination of 22 national and 14 international centers to train, in nine months, computer programmers and engineers.

Physics and cooking might seem to have few common ingredients but *Carl C. Sontheimer*, a retired MIT-trained physicist and accomplished cook, has combined his two loves to carve a permanent niche in the annals of the small appliance industry.

In 1971 Sontheimer and his wife, Shirley, founded Cuisinarts, Inc. He originally intended it to be a part-time activity, importing an exclusive line of quality stainless steel cookware, utilizing his knowledge of France, where he spent his teens. Today the name "Cuisinarts" is synonymous with "food processor," and the Sontheimers' market not only cookware and food processors, but cutlery, ovens, and a host of extras such as croissant-cutters and rolling pins.

Following his graduation from college, Sontheimer worked for RCA, invented 47 patented gadgets, founded three electronics companies, and sent some of his inventions to the moon in the form of components of a radio-microwave system—all before his 53rd birthday. Then he retired from the world of electronics, taking up a career as a newspaper writer, specializing in his lifelong avocation, cooking. Restless in retirement, he then founded Cuisinarts Inc. with his wife.

At a French housewares show they had been intrigued by a commercial food preparation machine marketed to restuarants. "That machine gave me the horrors," Sontheimer recalls, "it was totally unsafe . . . ." He spent the next 18 months perfecting the prototype of a home version of the food preparation machine. His final product minimized the time needed to cut, chop, slice, grate, and grind and combined the functions of many existing machines into one machine with attachments.

The Sontheimers are sole owners of the firm, which did 100 million dollars worth of business in 1980. Cuisinarts employs 150 people in its home office in Greenwich, Connecticut, its distribution center in Norwich, and its branch offices in Boston, San Francisco, and Allentown, Pennsylvania.

In 1978 Sontheimer began publishing *The Pleasures of Cooking*, a bimonthly magazine designed to provide cooking enthusiasts with thoroughly tested recipes. The magazine is an outgrowth of customer requests for recipes and averages fifty advertising-free pages each issue.

What does Sontheimer see happening in American kitchens in the years ahead? "The population will grow; land will not," he says. "There will be less living space and kitchens will be smaller. There will be less storage space and less energy available per person. All ovens will be convection; food processors will become more capable." Following his own advice, Sontheimer recently introduced a convection oven with a glass bubble cover.

Recipients for 1983

Nolan K. Bushnell. Nolan Bushnell has done it all, from "Pong" to pizza to personal robots—and he's done it before the age of 40!

Bushnell's entrepreneurial career started in 1971 when he invented the first successful coin-operated video game, *Pong*. The following year he and a partner put up $500 each to start an electronic game and home computer company with the name *Atari*—it is the word equivalent to "check" in the Japanese game of *Go*. Bushnell ultimately developed and manufactured 35 types of video games before selling the company to Warner Communications in 1976. He served as chairman of the board of Atari until 1979. Later this year he will launch another video game enterprise which will compete with Atari, that will have the name *Sente*, the word in *Go* for "checkmate!"

In 1976 Bushnell founded his second successful company, Pizza Time Theatre, a new concept in family entertainment combining a pizza restaurant with electronic games and amusements, plus musical entertainment provided by the "Pizza Time Players," computer-controlled robot characters, including an eight-foot robot rat, Chuck E. Cheese.

Most recently, Bushnell has been heavily involved with a company he founded in 1982, Catalyst Technologies, whose purpose is to sponsor small companies with a view to creating whole new industries. Catalyst conceives, finances, staffs, and guides an enterprise from the beginning. Each fledgling company is headquartered in the Catalyst Building (Sunnyvale, Ca.), where it receives the expertise of the company's brain trust. This is done to prevent the new companies from making typical start-up mistakes and to bring them to quicker profitability.

One of these incubating companies Androbot is about to graduate and move into its new quarters, the seed work having been done and the manufacturing process begun. Androbot will produce personal robots programmed to do their owners' bidding. As Bushnell himself puts it: "Can anyone really envision the year 2000 without robots running around the home?"

Bushnell has been called a revolutionary. As one publisher has written: "When you are with Nolan Bushnell, you see the future . . . and you know it will work."

Frederic C. Hamilton. Fred Hamilton graduated from Babson College in the late forties. Instead of going into the family natural gas business, he joined the army and afterward took a job with a Texas oil company as an ordinary "roughneck" on an oil-drilling crew.

In 1950, with his brother, Ferris, he went into business for himself. They bought a broken down 6,000-foot drilling rig for $5,000, and it carried a $45,000 note.

From that one-rig drilling company, there has grown a group of 12 affiliated natural resource companies (based in Denver) that had combined revenues in 1982 of over 226.8 million dollars.

Hamilton has described his philosophy of oil and gas exploration: "It takes just as much time to find the little fields as the big ones, so why not spend the time looking for the big ones?"

This reasoning paid off in 1956, Hamilton's first major *coup*, when he figured that underneath Texas's famous Hugoton gas field there were even larger untapped wells. Where the deepest wells were 3,000 feet, Hamilton went to 6 and 8,000—and struck a subterranean mammoth worth millions of dollars.

In 1962 Hamilton took aim at the Edson field in Canada and uncovered gas reserves of two trillion cubic feet, the second largest in Canada. In 1964, again in Canada, he discovered the Nipisi oil field, with reserves of more than 400 million barrels.

Still on the lookout for giant fields, Hamilton had the foresight to begin seismic surveys (in 1964) of the British North Sea. "It was totally virgin," he recalls, "but I had a simple theory: If there's gas on one side of the North Sea and oil and gas on the other, somewhere underneath that water, there's going to be oil."

As everyone now knows, he was right, and in 1969 Hamilton Brothers was the first company to find oil in the Argyll Field.

Since then the company has made major oil and gas discoveries in Oklahoma, the Gulf of Mexico, South America, and the East China Sea. In conjunction with expanding operations, Hamilton Brothers Petroleum Corporation, a public company, has been formed. Fred Hamilton serves as chairman of the board and CEO. The operations are continuing to grow, and the company now employs over 1,250 people in seven countries.

Sidney R. Rabb. He is called "Mr. Sidney." His business acumen, over a period of more than half a century, has built the Stop & Shop Companies into New England's largest and most innovative supermarket chain.

Sidney Rabb began working as assistant to the general manager of Economy Grocery Stores, in 1918, while attending Harvard College. Within six months, at the age of 19, Rabb himself was general manager.

"It didn't take a genius to be in the right place at the right time," Rabb states. However, the Economy chain was in financial trouble and young Rabb, using his summer experience as manager of one of its stores, with the skills learned at Harvard plus his own innate marketing brilliance, soon had Economy turning a profit. By the age of 30 he was chairman of the board.

During the Depression Rabb decided that large "warehouse" type grocery stores were what people wanted—a radical experiment for those difficult times. In 1937 the first of these new stores opened—the concept of the supermarket was launched. The store did more business in four days than 35 of Economy's other stores did in a week.

Today, the Stop & Shop Companies include 120 supermarkets and 106 Bradlees discount department stores stretched along the East Coast from Maine to Virginia. Three other chains round out the company's merchandising efforts: Medi-Mart (50 drug, health, and beauty stores); C. B. Perkins (53 tobacco stores); and Off the Rax (72 women's clothing stores).

Rabb's dedication to building a successful business chain has been matched by his commitment to help others. There are few charitable, cultural, and educational institutions in Massachusetts that do not list him on their boards of directors and fewer still that have not benefitted from his philanthropy. "When I made a statement one day that a corporation has to have a soul, I meant it."

Today, at age 82, "Mr. Sidney" still puts in a full week's work as chairman of the board of Stop & Shop. And he also finds time to devote to the charities with which he has worked for years. "After all," he says with a smile, "shrouds have no pockets."

Frederick W. Smith. In 1981 *Dun's Business Month* named Federal Express Corporation one of the nation's five best-managed companies. In fiscal 1982 the company's revenues were over $800 million. Quite a turn-around for an organization that lost $29 million in its first 26 months of operation and whose company payroll once had to be met with the founder's winnings at blackjack.

The story of Federal Express is the story of one man, founder Fred Smith. As a Yale undergraduate, Smith submitted an overdue economics paper that proposed a revolutionary "hub-and-spokes" overnight package delivery service. "To cut cost and time," he wrote, "packages from all over the country would be flown to a central point, there to be distributed and flown out again to their destination." His professor was unimpressed and gave Smith the acceptable "Gentleman's C" for his effort.

Following his graduation in 1966, Smith went to Vietnam as a Marine platoon leader, was wounded twice, and ended up as company commander. He enrolled in flight school, thinking that his next tour of duty would be in Hawaii or Japan.

Instead he was sent right back to Vietnam, where he flew more than 200 ground-support missions, receiving the Bronze and Silver Stars and a dozen Air Medals.

He also learned about people. "A lot of people in my platoon had an influence on my life," he says. "The one who made the strongest impression was my platoon sergeant, Jack Jackson, a black guy who had been in the Marines about 14 years and was not very well educated. He lost his life in Vietnam later. Sgt. Jack was probably the wisest man I ever met."

Smith left Vietnam weary of destruction and eager to do something. At age 28 he put together a venture capital package that totalled nearly $80 million, reputed at the time to be the largest sum ever raised for a new company. Federal Express was born.

Federal has grown from a handful of packages and aircraft on its first day of operation in 1973 to more than 140,000 shipments daily and an operating fleet of more than 60 aircraft. The company also operates over 4,500 radio-equipped vans that pick up and deliver the shipments; it has a work force of more than 12,000 men and women.

All this is a far cry from the day, many years ago, when student Fred Smith received his "Gentleman's C" from a skeptical economics professor. It hasn't always been easy, but his revolutionary package service is flying high.

F. GRANTS

In 1979 over 26,000 United States foundations gave away close to $3 billion in grants. The federal government, mostly the Department of Health, Education and Welfare, gave away over $60 billion. Very few of these grants were awarded to small businesses. Although it is true that 95% of the grant proposals submitted are rejected, it is also true that small businesses seldom seek or receive financial grants.

A special exemption is needed to give a grant to a profit-seeking business, but it is not uncommon for a grant to be awarded to a nonprofit organization (such as a college or university) for a project and that an entrepreneur will be a subcontractor on the project. It may be very much in your interest, therefore, to support the efforts of local nonprofit institutions to obtain funds. Information on organizations that give grants can be obtained by consulting the following sources.

1. The Foundation Center, an information clearing house that maintains national libraries in Chicago, New York City, and Washington, D.C., as well as regional libraries in 48 states, Mexico, and Puerto Rico. These libraries are open to the public at no charge.

2. The *Foundation Directory*, a reference work which lists 2,800 foundations that awarded $1.8 billion in grants in 1976. The directory gives the following data on the foundations it lists: names and addresses (by state); founders' names; total assets; officials' names; purposes and activities; and the number and dollar amounts of grants awarded during the year. This directory is available at any large library.

3. The *Foundation Grants Index*, which lists grants of more than $5,000 made by the 300 major foundations. It lists the names of the recipients, the purposes of the grants, and the dollar amounts awarded. A separate "Key Word & Phrase" index is especially useful in determining the current real interests of each foundation. This book is also available in most large libraries.

4. The *Catalog of Federal Domestic Assistance and the Annual Register of Grant Support*. This is the single best starting point for research on grants. For information on obtaining a copy write:

Marquis Who's Who
4300 West 62nd Street
Indianapolis, In. 46206

The Register lists procedures for requesting grants; programs; names of agency officers; and the total number of applications received and awarded by programs each year.

G. INFORMATION ABOUT PREMIUM AND INCENTIVE BUYING

Many products can be sold to companies or organizations that will use them as premiums or giveaways or in incentive buying programs. Perhaps your product(s) can be used in this way. For a list of such buyers, there are several sources you can contact:

The Salesmen's Guide
1140 Broadway
New York, N.Y. 10001
(212) 689-2985

Premium/Incentive Business
1515 Broadway
New York, N.Y. 10036
(212) 869-1300
Circulation: about 24,000

Incentive Marketing
633 Third Avenue
New York, N.Y. 10017
(212) 986-4800
Circulation: about 35,000

NPSE Newsletter
1600 Route 22
Union, N.J. 07083
(201) 687-3832
Circulation: about 2,000

H. MANUFACTURER'S REPRESENTATIVES

How to select the proper manufacturer's representative for your product line? is one of the most difficult questions facing an entrepreneurial venture. The following sources offer services and information that can help find competent sales representatives for small businesses.

Albee-Campbell
806 Penn Avenue
Box 2087
Sinking Springs, Pa. 19608

Sysmark
Box 636, Riverdale Station
Riverdale, N.Y. 10471
(914) 576-2187

United Association of Manufacturers'
Representatives
808 Broadway
Kansas City, Mo. 64105
(816) 842-8130

Rep World is a quarterly publication that focuses on manufacturers' representatives.

Rep World
578 Penn Avenue
Sinking Spring, Pa. 19608

I. PATENTS, INVENTIONS, TRADEMARKS, AND LABORATORIES

How to Get a Patent is about America's patent law. For a copy of the booklet, write:

Consumer Information Center
Department 126E
Pueblo, Co. 81009

The Inventors News, published by the Inventors Club of America, offers information on protection before patent, marketing and manufacturing, and development. The Inventors Club of America is a non-profit organization established to help inventors who are willing to help themselves. They show you ways to develop and market your ideas yourself. Write:

Inventors News
Box 3799
Springfield, Ma. 01101
(413) 737-0670

New Products and Processes Newsletter, a publication of *Newsweek Magazine, Inc.*, is a source for the most comprehensive, timely, and usable new product information available anywhere. Each issue contains reviews of 75 to 100 new products and processes, including complete product descriptions, many with illustrations, availability for manufacturing, and sales of licensing arrangements. Write:

New Products and Processes
Newsweek International
444 Madison Avenue
New York, N.Y. 10022

The United States Trademark Association is a nonprofit organization dedicated to the protection, development, and promotion of the trademark concept. USTA is the only organization in the United States totally devoted to trademarks, protecting the rights of trademark owners as well as communicating with business educators, the press, and the public to foster understanding and appreciation of the role of trademarks. The services offered by USTA concern all aspects of the trademark field: federal, state, and foreign legislation; education, promotion advertising, and merchandising; publicity and use by the press; proper handling of trademarks by corporate personnel, sales staff, dealers; and more. An important caveat: The services of USTA do not purport to substitute for or duplicate in any way the advice of legal counsel. To obtain information about ordering any of their publications, write:

The United States Trademark Association
6 East 45th Street
New York, N.Y. 10017
(212) 986-5880

Where to Get Help on Patents and Licensing

Have a good idea? Is it patentable? Where can you turn for help? Here is a comprehensive listing of help available.

Inventors associations. Arrange meetings with inventors to educate them in aspects of the patenting process and the seeking of licenses:

Inventors Assistance League, Inc.
345 W. Cypress Street
Glendale, Ca. 91204
(213) 246-6540

Inventors Club of America
121 Chestnut Street
Springfield, Ma. 01103
(413) 737-0670

Publications. Several specialized publications seek to match products offered for license with licensors:

American Bulletin of International
 Technology Transfer
International Advancement
5455 Wilshire Boulevard
Suite 1009
Los Angeles, Ca. 90036
(213) 931-7481

International New Product Newsletter
Box 191
390 Stuart Street
Boston, Ma. 02117
(617) 631-3225

New Products and Processes
Newsweek International
444 Madison Avenue
New York, N.Y. 10022
(212) 350-2000

Technology Mart
Thomas Publishing Co.
One Penn Plaza
New York, N.Y. 10001
(212) 695-0500

Technology Transfer Times
Benwill Publishers
167 Corey Road
Brookline, Ma. 02146
(617) 212-5470

One publisher produces two excellent newsletters on patents and inventions that may prove of interest to you:

1. *Invention Management.* An informational and educational journal for individuals and companies concerned with intellectual property. This is published monthly and costs $60.00 annually. It is excellent in the area of patents, technology transfer, and inventions.

2. *Copyright Management.* This is also published monthly. It deals with copyrights, licensing, and trademarks.

If you are interested in either monthly newsletter, write:

Richard A. Onanian
Institute for Invention & Innovation, Inc.
85 Irving Street
Arlington, Ma. 02174
(617) 646-0093

The Federal Laboratory Consortium (FLC) consists of the 180 federal research and development laboratories. In each there is a person with the title "technical transfer representative," whose job is to respond to questions from businesses. The good news is that there is no charge. A directory is available from:

FLC Headquarters
Federal Laboratory Program Manager
National Science Foundation ISPT
Washington, D.C. 20050
(202) 634-7996

J. PUBLICITY

Free Publicity

Rather than launching a marketing program with a series of paid-for advertisements, consider the advantages of a publicity release program. Your firm may be eligible for news releases or product releases or literature releases, all of which are free. Doesn't it make sense to have all initial effort directed toward the free material? Entrepreneurial managers obtain all the available free products releases before they succumb to paid-for advertisements.

The procedure for contacting the various trade journals varies from industry to industry. Some journals require black-and-white photographs, others require color photographs, and others accept no photographs. To obtain specific information on how to obtain publicity and to obtain a list of relevant trade journals, these four publishers offer you directories and publicity release programs.

Ayer's Directory of Newspapers and
  Periodicals
1 Bala Avenue
Bala Cynwyd, Pa. 19064
(215) 664-6203

Bacon's Publicity Checker
322 South Michigan Avenue
Chicago, Il. 60604
(800) 621-0561
(312) 922-2400

Ayer's and Bacon's are comprehensive sources of newspaper information. For an excellent overall list of periodicals, use the *Standard Periodical Directory*, available in most libraries or from:

Oxbridge Communications
150 Fifth Avenue
New York, N.Y. 10011
(212) 741-0231

Another excellent source is *Ulrich's Directory of Periodicals*, also available in most libraries or from:

R. R. Bowker Company
1180 Avenue of the Americas
New York, N.Y. 10036
(212) 754-5100

Clipping Services

Below is a partial list of services that will clip newspaper and magazine articles about your company or about a product area. This can be a valuable service to keep you posted on the advertising and public relations efforts of your competitors, as well as your own company's programs. *Note:* This list is only a partial list because no organization keeps this information on a national basis. We suggest that you inspect your local Yellow Pages to determine if such an organization exists in your geographical areas.

Allen's Press Clipping Bureau
657 Mission Street
San Francisco, Ca. 94105

Bacon's Clipping Bureau
332 South Michigan Avenue
Chicago, Il. 60604
(312) 621-0561

Florida Clipping Service
Box 10278
Tampa. Fl. 33679
(813) 831-0962

Luce Press Clipping Service
912 Kansas Avenue
Topeka, Ks. 66612
(913) 232-0201

New England Newsclip Service
5 Auburn Street
Framingham, Ma. 01701
(617) 879-4460

Marketing Sources

The National Research Bureau is a subsidiary of the Automated Marketing Systems, Inc. It offers the *Gebbie House Magazine Directory*, which lists company house organs, newsletters, and internal company information. It is an often overlooked source of publicity. This directory is a part of the *Working Press of Nations*, a five-volume set of invaluable aids to over 100,000 prime media contacts, available from:

National Research Bureau
310 South Michigan Avenue
Chicago, Il. 60604
(312) 663-5580

Trade Shows

Conventions and trade show listings are compiled and offered by:

The Hendrickson Publishing Company
79 Washington Avenue
Hempstead, N.Y. 11550
(516) 483-6883

Sales Meetings Magazines
633 Third Avenue
New York, N.Y. 10017
(212) 986-4800

K. RESOURCE ORGANIZATIONS SERVING SMALL BUSINESS

National Federation of Independent
    Business
490 L'Enfant Plaza East, S.W.
Washington, D.C. 20006
(202) 554-9000

National Small Business Association
1604 K Street, N.W.
Washington, D.C. 20006
(202) 293-8830

Center for Small Business
Chamber of Commerce of the United
    States
1615 H Street, N.W.
Washington, D.C. 20062
(202) 659-6000

COSIBA

The Council of Small and Independent Business Associations (COSIBA) is a federation of eight regional small business associations. They are identified below:

Council of Smaller Enterprises of the
  Greater Cleveland Growth Association
690 Union Commerce Building
Cleveland, Oh. 44115
(216) 621-3300

Independent Business Association of
  Wisconsin
415 East Washington Avenue
Madison, Wi. 53703
(608) 251-5546

National Association of Small Business
  Investment Companies
512 Washington Building
Washington, D.C. 20005
(202) 638-3411

National Business League
4324 Georgia Avenue, N.W.
Washington, D.C. 20011
(202) 824-5900

National Federation of Independent
  Businesses
150 West 20th Avenue
San Mateo, Ca. 94402
(415) 341-7441

National Small Business Association
1225 19th Street, N.W.
Washington, D.C. 20036
(202) 293-8830

Smaller Business Association of New
  England
69 Hickory Drive
Waltham, Ma. 02154
(617) 840-9070

Smaller Manufacturer's Council
339 Boulevard of Allies
Pittsburgh, Pa. 15222
(412) 391-1622

House and Senate Small Business Committees

You might like to know who's on the Small Business Committees in Congress, especially if he happens to be from your state or district:

In the Senate:

Republicans.

- Lowell Weicker, Ct./Chairman
- Rudy Boschwitz, Mn.
- Warren Rudman, N.H.
- Alfonse D'Amato, N.Y.
- Don Nickles, Ok.
- Bob Packwood, Or.
- Larry Pressler, S.D.
- Orrin Hatch, Ut.
- Slade Gorton, Wa.
- Robert Kasten, Wi.

Democrats.

- Dale Bumpers, Ar.
- Sam Nunn, Ga.
- Alan Dixon, Il.

- Walter Huddleston, Ky.
- Paul Tsongas, Ma.
- Carl Levin, Mi.
- Max Baucus, Mt.
- David Boren, Ok.
- Jim Sasser, Tn.

In the House:

Democrats.

- Esteban Torres, Ca.
- Andy Ireland, Fl.
- Charles Hatcher, Ga.
- Richard Ray, Ga.
- Berkley Bedell, Ia.
- Neal Smith, Ia.
- Frank McCloskey, In.
- Gus Savage, Il.
- John Fary, Il.
- Romano Mazzoli, Ky.
- Buddy Roemer, La.
- Nicholas Mavroules, Ma.
- Parren Mitchell, Md./Chairman
- Ike Skelton, Mo.
- C. Robin Britt, N.C.
- Joseph Addabbo, N.Y.
- John LaFalce, N.Y.
- Henry Nowak, N.Y.
- Dennis Eckart, Oh.
- Thomas Luken, Oh.
- Ron Wyden, Or.
- Jim Cooper, Tn.
- Henry Gonzalez, Tx.
- Charles Stenholm, Tx.
- Tom Vandergriff, Tx.
- James Olin, Va.
- Norman Sisisky, Va.

Republicans.

- Gene Chappie, Ca.
- David Drier, Ca.
- Michael Bilirakis, Fl.
- John Hiler, In.
- Silvio Conte, Ma.

170

- William Broomfield, Mi.
- Vin Weber, Mn.
- Hal Daub, Ne.
- Christopher Smith, N.J.
- Guy Molinari, N.Y.
- Sherwood Boehlert, N.Y.
- Lyle Williams, Oh.
- Joseph McDade, Pa.
- Dan Marriott, Ut.
- Toby Roth, Wi.

It is never a waste of time to write to your congressman, especially on a specific subject (small business, for example). They *do* pay attention to their mail. They have to.

Helpful Phone Numbers at the Small Business Administration

Active Corps of Executives (ACE)
(202) 653-6768

Office of Business Loans
(202) 653-6574

Office of Economic Research
(202) 634-4885

Office of Financing
(202) 653-6570

Office of International Trade
(202) 653-6544

SBA Library
(202) 653-6570

Office of Management Information
and Training
(202) 724-1703

Minority Small Business and Capital
Ownership Development
(202) 653-6407

Prime Contracts Division—Procurement
Assistance
(202) 653-6826

Procurement Assistance
(202) 653-6635

Publications Hotlines
(202) 653-6365
(800) 433-7212
(800) 792-8901 (in Texas)

Office of Public Affairs
(202) 653-6832

Service Corps of Retired Executives
(SCORE)
(202) 653-6725

Office of Small Business Development
Centers
(202) 653-6519

Technology Assistance Division
(202) 653-6938

Office of Women's Business Enterprise
(202) 653-8000

Washington Information Sources

The Division of Information Services has data available on employment, living conditions, prices, productivity, and occupational safety and health.

Bureau of Labor Statistics
441 G Street, N.W., Room 2106
Washington, D.C. 20212
(202) 523-1913

The Bill Status Office will provide you with the current status of any legislation or tell you if legislation has been introduced on a topic.

Senate
Capital
Washington, D.C. 20510
(202) 224-3121

or

House of Representatives
Capital
Washington, D.C. 20515
(202) 224-3121

The National Referral Center will find an organization willing to provide information on any topic free of charge.

Research Services
Library of Congress
10 First Street, S.E.
Washington, D.C. 20540
(202) 426-5670

The Federal Information Center will locate an expert in the federal government to tell you how the federal government can help you.

Office of Consumer Affairs
General Services Administration
18th and F Streets, Room 6034
Washington, D.C. 20405
(202) 566-1937

Reference Section, Science and Technology Division offers both free and fee reference on bibliographic services.

Research Services
Library of Congress
110 2nd Street, S.E., Room 5008
Washington, D.C. 20540
(202) 287-5639

Data Users Services Division will identify census data on your topic.

Bureau of the Census
U.S. Department of Commerce
Washington, D.C. 20230
(301) 763-2400

Bureau of Domestic Business Development. Industry analysts can provide or guide you to information on a company or industry.

Office of Public Affairs/Economic Development Administration
U.S. Department of Commerce, Room 7019
Washington, D.C. 20230
(303) 377-5113

Information Central will identify an association that can help with your problem, if you cannot find help in Gale's *Encyclopedia of Associations.*

American Society of Association Executives
1101 16th Street, N.W.
Washington, D.C. 20036
(202) 659-3333

Energy information sources are:

National Energy Information Center
Energy Information Administration
Department of Energy
1000 Independence Avenue, S.W.
MS 1F048
Washington, D.C. 20585
(202) 252-8800

Technical Information Center
U.S. Department of Energy
P.O. Box 62
Oak Ridge, Tn. 37830
(615) 576-1301

National Solar Heating and Cooling
   Information Center
P.O. Box 1607
Rockville, Md. 20850
(800) 523-2929
(800) 468-4983–Penn;
(800) 523-4700–Alaska and Hawaii

U.S. Civil Service Commission, Bureau of Manpower Information Systems has this material available: Civil Service employment, payroll information, and paydays (particularly useful in scheduling campaigns for consumer goods in Washington).

Manpower Statistics Division
1900 E Street, N.W.
Washington, D.C. 20415
(202) 655-4000

Useful Non-Government Data

Materials that can be very beneficial to you are published by all the Nader groups. A wide variety of reports and publications is available. To obtain copies of the following free citizen action materials send a self-addressed, stamped envelope to P.O. Box 19404, Washington, D.C. 20036 (unless another address is indicated).

1. Public Citizen, Reports and Publications. A complete list of all reports and publications by Ralph Nader and other well-known consumer advocates.

2. Public Citizen Action Projects. A list of many citizen action projects that can be undertaken by any interested group.

3. Public Citizen Health Research Group's list of reports and publications includes information in the areas of food and drugs, occupational safety and health, pesticides, product safety, health care delivery, and how to get a copy of your health records.

4. Toll-free hotline numbers. A complete guide to all federal agencies designed to help and inform consumers.

5. Airline Passenger Rights. Information on your rights as an airline passenger, including how to deal with an airline-related problem. Write to ACAP (Aviation Consumer Action Project), P.O. Box 19029, Washington, D.C. 20036.

6. Freedom of Information. Pamphlet on the Freedom of Information Act and how to use it. Send SASE (self-addressed stamped envelope) to Freedom of Information Clearinghouse, P.O. Box 19367, Washington, D.C. 20036. Pension Rights. Information on the rights of employees, retirees, and spouses under the new private pension reform law. Send SASE to the Pension Rights Center, 1346 Connecticut Avenue, N.W., Room 1019, Washington, D.C. 20036.

7. Human Rights and the Elderly. Information on programs involved with agism and other special projects. Send a first-class stamp to the Grey Panthers, 3700 Chestnut Street, Philadelphia, Pa. 19104.

8. *People and Taxes.* Monthly newspaper of the Public Citizen's Tax Reform Group. Include a first-class stamp.

9. *Critical Mass.* Newspaper covering nuclear power information and activity. Write to *Critical Mass*, P.O. Box 1538, Washington, D.C. 20013. Please include a first-class stamp.

10. *People and Energy, CPSI Quarterly, The Nutrition Newsletter*, and publications list. Newsletter from the Center for Science in the Public Interest. Send SASE to Center for Science in the Public Interest, 1757 S. Street, N.W., Washington, D.C. 20009.

In addition to the aforementioned publications, the following are some other helpful publications:

A monthly newsletter, *Cose Update*, is offered by:

Council of Smaller Enterprise of the Greater
   Cleveland Growth Association
690 Union Commerce Building
Cleveland, Oh. 44115
(216) 621-3300

The Family Business Forum is the newsletter of the National Family Business Council. As the "voice of family business," this publication discusses important issues that affect the small business owner/managers. It also keeps its membership informed of the happenings within the organization on a local and national level. Write:

National Family Business Council
3916 Detroit Boulevard
W. Bloomfield, Mi. 48033

National Memo is a monthly newsletter that provides timely information on economic and business issues and events. *The Corporate Guide to Minority Vendors* is a resource manual for use by corporate executives and minority entrepreneurs to strengthen the communications network between the two sectors. The NBL also maintains a file of minority vendors and a comprehensive list of corporate procurement and purchasing agents for constituents. Write:

National Business League
4324 Georgia Avenue, N.W.
Washington, D.C. 20011
(202) 829-5900

The Voice of Small Business is a monthly newsletter for small business owners/managers in all industries, trades, or professions. It deals generally with news of interest to small business relating to legislative and governmental activities in Washington. It is the membership newsletter of the National Small Business Association, a nonprofit and nonpartisan organization dedicated to the preservation and expansion of the small business sector of the economy. Write:

Voice of Small Business
1605 K Street, N.W.
Washington, D.C. 20006
(202) 296-7400

The newsletter of the Chamber of Commerce of the United States is called the *Washington Report*. Most of its subscribers are business people, and the majority of its articles are geared to information about federal policies and programs that can affect their firms and the economy. Write:

Washington Report
Chamber of Commerce of the United States
1615 H Street, N.W.
Washington, D.C. 20062

Your local chamber of commerce can also be a source of valuable assistance, including information about plant or storage locations and financing. It is most quickly located via the local telephone directory.

L. SMALL BUSINESS AIDS

Improvement to SBA Guaranteed Loans

The Bank Certification Program hands the financial decision-making for Small Business Administration Guaranteed Loans over to professional lenders. Processing time for these loans will be cut to between two and four weeks and when the loan is obtained from a certified lending institution. The SBA has authorized some large nationwide financial service organizations to provide and prepare guaranteed loans, in addition to many banks. Credit Financial Corporation, a subsidiary of Control Data Corporation, was incorporated for lending under the SBA Guaranteed Loan Program. Their loans are being made via Control Data Business Centers and Satellite Centers.

Control Data Business Centers are rapidly expanding around the country, offering data processing services, business planning and marketing assistance, a full range of lending services, and more. For more information, contact Control Data's Minneapolis office (see below) or one of the following Control Data Business Centers.

Commercial Credit Services Corp. Business Centers*

Location	Telephone Number
BALTIMORE, MD. P.O. Box 549 Suite C-152 22 West Padonia Road Timonium, Md. 21093	(301) 561-1800
ATLANTA, GA. 300 Embassy Row 6600 Peachtree-Dunwoody Road Atlanta, Ga. 30328	(404) 399-2170
CHARLOTTE, N.C. P.O. Box 34189 3726 Latrobe Drive, Suite 101 Charlotte, N.C. 28234	(704) 365-1420
CHICAGO, IL. Business Center 2001 Midwest Road Suite 105 Oak Brook, Il. 60521	(312) 629-7991
CLEVELAND, OH. Business Center Western Reserve Building 1468 W. 9th Street, Suite 100 Cleveland, Oh. 44113	(216) 523-1510
DALLAS, TX. Control Data Building 14801 Quorum Drive, Suite 200 Dallas, Tx. 75240	(214) 385-5750
DENVER, CO. 7100 East Belleview Avenue Suite 200 Englewood, Co. 80111	(303) 779-2900
KANSAS CITY, KS. Executive Hills Office Park 11011 Antioch Overland Park, Ks. 66210	(913) 648-1422
LOS ANGELES, CA. 18831 Von Karman Avenue Suite 300 Irvine, Ca. 92715	(714) 851-5620
LOUISVILLE, KY. Triad East, Suite 150 10200 Linn Station Road Louisville, Ky. 40223	(502) 423-1660
MINNEAPOLIS, MN. 5241 Viking Drive Bloomington, Mn. 55435	(612) 893-4200

Location	Telephone Number
NEW YORK, N.Y. 1350 Avenue of the Americas New York, N.Y. 10019	(212) 887-1010
SAN FRANCISCO, CA. One Bay Plaza, Suite 330 1350 Old Bayshore Highway Burlingame, Ca. 94010	(415) 342-7622
TAMPA, FL. Business Center Suite 285 4511 N. Himes Avenue Tampa, Fl. 33614	(813) 877-5523

*Information about Control Data Business Centers is also available from Commercial Credit Services Corporation, 300 St. Paul Place, Baltimore, Md. 21202/(301) 332-3000.

Sources: Other SBA Non-Bank Lenders

1. Money Store Investment Corporation, Springfield, N.J., (201) 467-9000. Offers SBA Guaranteed Loans in branch locations in 12 states.

2. Merrill Lynch Small Business Lending Company, New York City, (212) 637-7455. Loan program will function nation-wide later this year.

3. Allied Lending Corporation, Washington, D.C., (202) 331-1112. SBA Guaranteed Loans for the Washington area.

4. NIS Capital Funding Corporation, White Plains, N.Y., (914) 428-8600. Provides SBA Guaranteed Loans locally.

5. Independence Mortgage Company, Inc., Odessa, Texas, (915) 333-5814. SBA Guaranteed Loans for the Odessa area.

6. The First Commercial Credit Corporation, Los Angeles, California, (213) 937-0860. Provides SBA loans in Los Angeles.

M. SOURCES OF CAPITAL

How to raise capital for growing enterprise is a fundamental question. The very nature of the venture capital industry has changed dramatically with the advent of Small Business Investment Companies (SBICs) launched by the Small Business Administration (SBA).

Locating sources of available venture capital can be both time consuming and frustrating if you don't know where to go or whom to contact. We have compiled the following comprehensive list of venture capital sources to aid you in your search.

Small Business Administration (SBA)

SBA. The United States Small Business Administration is an independent federal agency that was created by Congress in 1953 to assist, counsel, and champion American small businesses. The agency provides prospective, new, and established members of the small business community with financial assistance, management training and counseling, and help in getting a fair share of government contracts through over 100 offices throughout the nation.

SBIC. Small Business Investment Corporations are licensed, regulated, and in certain cases, financed by the SBA. They supply venture capital and long-term financing to small businesses for expansion, modernization, and sound financing for their organizations.

MESBIC. Minority Enterprise Small Business Investment Corporations have been incorporated into SBICs. They exist only to assist small business concerns owned and managed by socially or economically disadvantaged persons.

For more information about the services that the SBA provides consult the Yellow Pages for the office nearest you or write:

SBA
1441 L Street, N.W.
Washington, D.C. 20005

SBIC Division
SBA
1441 L Street, N.W.
Washington, D.C. 20005

A Small Business Investment Company (SBIC) is a licensee of the federal government charged with making investments in small entrepreneurial ventures. A MESBIC is an SBIC that does the same thing for businesses with strong minority group interests. The way it works is simple. A pool of money is established (currently a minimum of $500,000 for an SBIC, $300,000 for a MESBIC), and then the manager of the pool of money applies to the SBIC division of the Small Business Administration (SBA) for an SBIC license. Once the pool of money qualifies for an SBIC license, you can accomplish the following:

1. A loan of between 3:1 and 4:1 times the amount in the pool of equity funds, you can leverage the equity by 3 or 4 times with an SBA loan.
2. The loan will be subordinated to bank debt. Consequently, with the total capital you should be able to borrow several million dollars on a short term basis from the banks.
3. The loan will be unsecured and all investors will have limited liabilities.
4. The loan will be a balloon payment loan with interest only payable.
5. The interest rate is currently three points under prime rate.

These features are a few of the incentives to reach the minimum targets of paid investment capital. There are some disadvantages to an SBIC and it is not a panacea, but the advantages often outweigh the disadvantages. One disadvantage is that any investment is limited to 20 percent of the paid-in capital ($500,000). Hence you could invest only up to $100,000 on any single deal. A second disadvantage is the paperwork that the SBA creates to prevent fraud in distribution of their funds.

Approximately 60 percent of the SBIC financing by number (and a little higher by dollars) are first or initial financings. This has been a fairly constant pattern for SBICs over the years. About half of the SBIC dollar financing is in the form of straight debt versus straight equity. The average interest on the debt in 1979 was just under 13 percent annually. The SBICs have an interest ceiling of 15 percent and, rather than charge excessive interest, they are motivated to opt for equity in the form of warrants along with a debt financing.

The United States Small Business Administration (SBA) publishes on a quarterly basis a complete listing of SBICs as well as minority enterprise small business investment companies (MESBICs), listing name, address, and size category. Write:

SBA Investment Divisions
1441 L Street, N.W.
Washington, D.C. 20416

American Association of MESBICs
1413 K Street, N.W., 13th Floor
Washington, D.C. 20005
(202) 347-8600

The AAMESBIC newsletter is sent monthly to about 1,000 subscribers.

Banks

Foreign-owned banks. The rapid expansion of foreign-owned banks in the United States is due primarily to the devaluation of the United States dollar and their ability to avoid United States banking regulations. They are allowed to open branches outside of their countries (United States banks are not), and they are not required to tie up funds in the Federal Reserve system. These foreign-owned banks fall under state banking regulations. The banks are most often found in metropolitan areas. Suggested banks to contact are Britain's Barclay Bank, the Bank of Montreal, or the Japanese, Swiss, or French banks. We suggest you consult your local Yellow Pages for the foreign-owned bank nearest you.

Two-tier lending. A major change in commercial bank lending was triggered by the heroes of small business at the Mellon National Bank in Pittsburgh, Pennsylvania. They began offering small businesses a borrowing rate below the prime rate. They did this in times of money shortages (now) to help entrepreneurs, and they deserve pioneering recognition! For an up-to-date list of banks that offer a two-tier lending rate that is revised monthly write:

Chief Counsel for Advocacy
SBA
1441 L Street, N.W.
Washington, D.C. 20005

T.H.E. Insurance Company. The role of T.H.E. Insurance Company is to write an insurance policy to protect a lender against bankruptcy. They essentially appraise the collateral asset and insure to repossess it from a lender at the assessed rates. The value of T.H.E. policy allows more capital to be secured from existing lenders. It often happens that an asset or inventory can be borrowed against although it was given zero valuation by a bank because of T.H.E. insurance.

Lending institutions prefer to loan money against collateral because they maintain the option of liquidating the collateral to repay the loan. The table below is the rule of thumb for what can be loaned against different forms of collateral from the balance sheet of an entrepreneurial venture.

	Percentage to be Loaned Against
Accounts Receivable	75%–80% under 90 days
Inventory	10%–20%
Fixed Assets	70%–80% market values

In practice, the actual ratios are even more pronounced. In other words, banks prefer not to lend against inventory as contrasted to lending against receivables.

In turn, easily liquidated, fixed assets are the most attractive type of collateral (automobiles), and they usually command both a high percentage of their lendable market value as well as a subsequently lower interest rate.

A lender is basically unsure of an inventory's value until it is converted to cash by being sold. That's the underlying reason that lenders shy away from accepting inventory of certain types of fixed assets as collateral for a loan. Thus, the role of T.H.E. Insurance Company is to write an insurance policy to protect a lender against bankruptcy. They essentially appraise the collateral asset and insure to repossess it from a lender at the assessed rates. Rather than paying off the insurance policy on a death, the policy is paid upon default in the loan. Here's how it works:

1. T.H.E. appraises the assets to be pledged, including both inventory and fixed assets.

2. T.H.E. will then issue an insurance policy for the amount of their appraisal.

3. The company hands this policy over to the lender and then borrows 100 percent of the value of the policy in a loan.

4. If the company defaults, T.H.E. takes title to the collateral and sells it. The lender is paid in full using T.H.E.'s credit and capital to be reimbursed.

What does all this insurance protection cost?

1. Appraisal fee: minimum amount: $1,000. This is for the appraisal and it is one percent of the appraised value of the collateral plus out-of-pocket (travel) expenses.

2. A two percent add-on interest rate on the outstanding loan balance, not on the full appraisal of the collateral. The premium interest rate of two percent is charged only on what's borrowed or what is at risk.

The value of T.H.E. policy allows more capital to be secured from existing lenders. On the one hand, a lender will typically allow only ten percent of inventory value to be used as loan collateral; with a policy, the inventory allowed as collateral might be above 50 percent of its value, depending upon T.H.E.'s assessment. This often allows a two or three times greater amount to be loaned against an asset.

An asset or inventory can often be borrowed against when it was given zero valuation by a bank because of the T.H.E. formula. On a theoretical basis, the lending interest rate can be reduced if you can convince the lender of the merits and security of the guarantee. In effect, given the policy, the lender should advance funds on T.H.E.'s credit, not the credit of your entrepreneurial venture.

In practice, you are seldom ever able to negotiate the bank interest rate lower by securing a T.H.E. guarantee, and in total, you are paying five to six percent above prime rate for this type of lending. If your entrepreneurial venture can service debt write:

T.H.E. Insurance Company
180 Bent Street
Cambridge, Ma. 02141
(617) 494-5300

Farmers Home Loan

The SBA is supposedly the government agency charged with helping the entrepreneur, but in practice, other federal agencies also provide a great deal of help. The FmHa is the loan program of the Farmers Home Administration that offers guaranteed loans to growing businesses. Unlike the SBA's program with a $500,000 ceiling, the FmHa loan program has no ceiling. In fact, loans have ranged from $7,000 to $33 million with an average of about $900,000.

The FmHa loan gives preference to distressed areas and rural communities of less than 25,000 inhabitants. It will loan money for any worthwhile business purpose. The minimum equity requirement is ten percent and, if your venture can be shown to be job-creating, your loan has a greater chance of approval. Unlike the SBA, you do not have to prove to be an unbankable company to secure an FmHa loan. The loans are for fairly long terms—30 years for construction, 15 years for equipment, and 7 years for working capital. The interest rate is about the same as can be negotiated with a bank, but the FmHa has a one-time fee that is calculated by multiplying one percent of the principal loan amount by the percentage of the guarantee. Even give the one-time fee, the good standing of the U.S. government stands behind the guaranteed portions of the loan, and the interest rate eventually negotiated often effects these favorable considerations.

Why not write the Farmers Home Administration, United States Department of Agriculture, Washington, D.C. 20250, or check your telephone book (under U.S. Government–Agriculture) for one of the 1,800 county offices.

EDA Funds

If your company needs funds to expand or strengthen an existing business, you may be eligible for federal funds without knowing it. The federal government has designated two-thirds of all counties in the U.S. as "economically depressed." If you're located in one of these areas, you may apply for a loan under the special program of the Economic Development Administration. To qualify for such a loan, a company must show that it has been unable to borrow under similar terms and conditions from other sources. There is no limit on the amount that may be requested. Most of the loans are under $1 million, or $10,000 per job created or saved.

On direct loans for fixed assets, or where there is mortgagable collateral, the interest rate is currently under ten percent. EDA would provide up to 65 percent of the total funds, but the applicant has to put up at least 15 percent of his own and get five percent from his state or a nongovernmental community organization, such as Community Development Corporation. The repayment time is usually the useful life of the fixed assets. The interest rate on a direct loan for working capital or for less mortgagable assets is usually on a ¼ percent higher than fixed assets.

A list of economically depressed areas, the loan application form, and other details of the loan program can be obtained from any of EDA's six regional offices. For the address of the office nearest you, write or call:

Office of Business Development
Economic Development Administration
Room 7876
14th / Constitution Avenue, N.W.
Washington, D.C. 20230
(202) 377-2000

N. SMALL BUSINESS PUBLICATIONS

Frequency	Magazine	Advertising Accepted	Publisher
Monthly	The Business Owner 50 Jericho Turnpike Jericho, N.Y. 11753	No	Thomas J. Martin

The Business Owner is getting better editorially since the recent repurchase of the magazine by Tom Martin from the Transamerican Media Corporation, in Riverton, Ct. Martin is now investing more editorial time to produce quality work and doing a good job on his monthly magazine.

| Monthly | Venture Magazine 35 W. 45th Street New York, N.Y. 10037 | Yes | Joe Giarraputo |

Venture Magazine is geared toward the individual who is starting his or her own business, and it best serves the zero to one million dollar business. Editorially it is excellent.

Frequency	Magazine	Advertising Accepted	Publisher
Monthly	*Inc. Magazine* 38 Commerce Wharf Boston, Ma. 02110	Yes	Bernard Goldhirsh

The focus of *Inc. Magazine* is directed to the market of managers of small businesses in the range of $1 million to $25 million. In my opinion, it is a serious competitor to *Business Week*.

Monthly	*Entrepreneur* 631 Wilshire Boulevard Santa Monica, Ca. 90401	Yes	Chase Revel

Entrepreneur is an opportunity magazine focusing on retailing and the retail trades. To receive it you must be a member of the International Entrepreneurial Association (IEA).

Monthly	*Small Business Report* 550 Hartnell Street Monterey, Ca. 93940	No	Gene E. Mattauch

Small Business Report is a pleasant, helpful, and non-controversial magazine with an orientation to the people side of business.

Monthly	*The Professional Report* 118 Brook Street Scarsdale, N.Y. 10503	No	John L. Springer

The Professional Report is basically a tax and management newsletter of well-established quality. It has been around much longer than any of the newsletters, and it is an excellent value.

Bimonthly	*In Business* 18 South 7th Street Emmaus, Pa. 18049	Yes	Jerome Goldstein

In Business is a new magazine with a combination of nature and small business, somewhat of an entrepreneur's "mother earth catalog."

Monthly	*The Entrepreneurial Manager* 83 Spring Street New York, N.Y. 10012	No	Joseph Mancuso

The Entrepreneurial Manager is the newsletter of the Center for Entrepreneurial Management. It provides up-to-date source material and management insight for small business presidents and entrepreneurs.

O. SOURCES OF HELP

Have You Considered Incorporating?

From a legal standpoint, incorporation is a tax advantage for smaller businesses. For businesses with an income exceeding $100,000, going the corporate route provides attractive tax incentives after allowing for a reasonable salary.

1. Income left in the corporation is taxable on each $25,000 level, beginning at 17 percent and increasing to 46 percent. See table below.

Corporate Income Tax Rate

The corporate income tax rate structure is as follows:

Taxable Income	Rates effective January 1, 1979
$0　　　$25,000	17%
$25,000– $50,000	20%
$50,000– $75,000	30%
$75,000–$100,000	40%
Over　　$100,000	46%

The alternative tax rate on corporate capital gains has been reduced from 30 percent to 28 percent. However, a portion of capital gains may continue to be a tax preference item for purposes of the minimum tax.

This means a corporation with taxable income of:

- $50,000 pays $9,250 in taxes for an effective rate of 18½%
- $75,000 pays $16,750 in taxes for an effective rate of 22-1/3%
- $100,000 pays $26,750 in taxes for an effective rate of 26¾%

Hence, only about one-quarter of profits up to $100,000 are taxes, and retained earnings can now be the preferred method of financing growth.

2. The Keogh plan contribution for an individual owner or partner is limited to $7,500 with the exception of large partnership. The limit is much higher for a corporate employee. The allowable contribution can be several times the Keogh limit. All money put in the Keogh plan or corporate pension plan is tax sheltered until paid out, and the unpaid balance at death can avoid estate taxes.

For more details on capital gains tax check with your personal accountant and/or investment advisor. This can alter the method of buying or selling assets.

Lost in the Mail

At one time or another, everyone seems to experience something missing or lost in the mail. Before panic takes over call the U.S. Postal Service for help in locating your mail. The Postal Service's Transportation Management Office is responsible for monitoring mail as it moves across the country. If you have a problem try contacting the regional office. Your local post office can direct you to the correct regional office for help in locating missing mail. Listed below are some helpful numbers to aid the process.

Northeast Region:
- Boston, (617) 223-1160
- New York City, (212) 660-5630

Western Region:
- Denver, (303) 327-4471
- Los Angeles, (213) 793-9610
- Salt Lake City, (801) 588-4516
- San Francisco, (415) 467-9234

Southern Region:
- Atlanta, (404) 214-3180
- Jacksonville, (904) 346-1386
- Memphis, (901) 222-4547

Central Region:
- Chicago, (312) 353-2101
- Detroit, (313) 226-4700
- St. Louis, (314) 279-7209

Eastern Region:
- Philadelphia, (215) 481-7054
- Washington, D.C., (202) 763-6215

P. TRIBUTE TO ROYAL LITTLE

Best known as the founder of Textron, Royal Little has also founded Narragansett Capital Corporation and Amtel Inc. and co-founded Indian Head, Inc., American Television and Communications Corporation, and All American Beverages. He has established a special endowment at the Harvard University Graduate School of Business Administration, where the Royal Little Chair of Business Administration was named in his honor, and has lent financial assistance to the governments of East Africa for creating national parks in Tanzania and Kenya. A member of the Business Hall of Fame and the Babson Academy of Distinguished Entrepreneurs, Royal Little is well known throughout the business community, where his extraordinary talents and business philosophy make him a sought-after speaker to business groups and financial editors—invariably to advise his audience on how not to follow his example.

How to Lose $100,000,000 and Other Valuable Advice*

Dedication. To the future entrepreneurs of America whose courage to risk, whose ability to create, and whose determination to achieve will assure the survival of the free enterprise in this country.

"No businessman in the past has ever written such a book possibly because no one else has compiled such an impressive record of errors," entrepreneur Royal Little writes in the introduction to *How to Lose $100,000,000 and Other Valuable Advice.* In this candid, tongue-in-cheek business memoir, Wall Street's famed "father of conglomerates" recalls how he became involved in dozens of disastrous business ventures during nearly sixty years in the business community.

It all began in 1923 when Little took out a loan for $10,000 to start the first synthetic-yarn processing plant in New England. The tiny plant eventually led to the formation of Textron and, thirty years after its inception, revolutionized the concept of a conglomerate with Little's theory of "unrelated diversification." Textron today boasts such top names in their fields as Gorham silverware, Bostitch staplers, Homelite chainsaws, Fafner bearings, and Talon zippers.

As the director of some thirty businesses and charitable organizations over the subsequent three decades, the intrepid entrepreneur gambled on enterprises dealing in woolens, hardware, helicopters, cement, cable television, outboard motors, fiberglass, and pharmaceuticals, as well as in ventures with printers, booksellers, and promoters of golf courses. His more unlikely, and unprofitable, risks included a Nebraska cattle ranch, bowling alleys in suburban Rhode Island, and a resort development in the Bahamas.

The dizzying number and variety of things that can go wrong—and did in Little's distinguished association with finance—prompt his droll conclusion, "It isn't necessary to have an MBA from Harvard to lose $100 million!"

Shoestring financing. This country must encourage its entrepreneurs. We must find ways to help the creative people who wish to develop their new ideas, processes, and products. There are not too many sources of capital for start-up situations available today. The reason this is so important is that we must plant the seeds of our future important businesses today to reap the benefits of their expansion and growth in the future.

Most readers may feel it unusual that Textron could have built up a $3 billion business from its humble beginning in 1923 with a $10,000 bank loan and no equity capital—not even a shoestring. People do not realize that practically every large corporation in the country was originally started by some entrepreneur with very limited capital. Many of our large corporations today resulted from mergers during the 1920s when the stock market was booming, but if one could go back to the origins of these companies we would find that some entrepreneur started with very limited capital to create the original business. The replies I have received to my inquiries from these companies indicate how frequently this has occurred. It's true, however, that one could not start a railroad, a public utility, or a steel mill on a shoestring.

Since no one has yet published a summarized list of who started many of today's billion dollar corporations and how they were financed, I would like to. I have received some most interesting information from sixty-one companies that were started on a shoestring, each with current sales in excess of $1 billion. However, because of space limitations, I am limiting the story to 16.

Avon. David H. McConnell started Avon in 1886 with a $500 loan from a friend. In 1977, sales were $1,648,000,000 with profits of $191,000,000. The total market value of the company as of August 15, 1978 was $3,486,000,000.

Campbell Soup. Campbell Soup was founded in 1869 in Camden, New Jersey, as a partnership of Joseph Campbell and Abraham Anderson, with no specified capital. In 1977, sales were $1,769,000,000 and earnings were $107,000,000. The market value as of August 15, 1978 was $1,213,000,000.

Coca-Cola. An Atlanta druggist, Dr. John Pemberton, produced the first Coca-Cola syrup in 1886, and he had earnings that year of $50. In 1977, sales were $3,560,000,000, and profits were $326,000,000. The market value as of August 15, 1978 was $5,510,000,000.

Digital Equipment. Kenneth H. Olsen, his brother Stanley, and Harlan E. Anderson started Digital Equipment when American Research and Development Company purchased 70 percent of the stock for $70,000 in August 1957. In 1977, sales were $1,059,000,000, and profits were $108,000,000. The market value as of August 15, 1978 was $1,941,000,000.

Du Pont. Eleuthere Irenee du Pont organized the company in 1802 with eighteen shareholders providing $36,000 equity. In 1977, sales were $9,435,000,000, and profits were $545,000,000. The market value of the comapny as of August 15, 1978 was $6,152,000,000.

Eastman Kodak. Eastman Kodak was founded by George Eastman a few days before Thanksgiving in 1880 with a $3,000 investment. In 1977, sales were $5,967,000,000, and profits were $643,000,000. The market value of the company as of August 15, 1978 was $10,625,000,000.

Ford Motor. Henry Ford and eleven associates filed incorporation papers for Ford Motor on June 16, 1903 with only $28,000 in cash invested. I was amazed to learn that on October 26, 1909 General Motors offered to purchase Ford Motor Company for $8,000,000 with $2,000,000 down and the balance in the future. Henry Ford held out for all cash, and since William Durant was unable to raise the money, that acquisition fell through. In 1977, sales were $37,842,000,000, and profits were $1,673,000,000. The market value of the company as of August 15, 1978 was $5,513,000,000.

Gillette. On September 28, 1901, King Camp Gillette founded Gillette with $5,000 of equity. In 1977, sales were $1,587,000,000, and profits were $80,000,000. The market value of the company as of August 15, 1978 was $896,000,000.

Goodyear. Frank Seiberling started the Goodyear Tire and Rubber Company on August 29, 1898 with $13,500 of borrowed money. Sales in 1977 were $6,628,000,000, and profits were $206,000,000. The market value of the company as of August 15, 1978 was $1,277,000,000.

Hewlett-Packard. In 1939, William R. Hewlett and David Packard invested their personal savings of $538 in Hewlett-Packard. In 1977, sales were $1,360,000,000, and profits were $122,000,000. The market value of the company as of August 15, 1978 was $2,486,000,000.

McDonald's. In 1954, Ray Kroc obtained the exclusive franchise rights from the McDonald brothers to start hamburger drive-ins, using their name, throughout the country. Since then, Kroc has built McDonald's into the leading fast-food business in the country. In 1977, sales were $1,406,000,000, and profits were $137,000,000. The market value of the company as of August 15, 1978 was $2,366,000,000.

Pepsico. Caleb Bradham originally incorporated Pepsi Cola in North Carolina in 1902 and produced the first drink in his drugstore. He had no equity capital. In 1977, sales were $3,546,000,000, and profits were $187,000,000. The market value of the company as of August 15, 1978 was $2,779,000,000.

Proctor and Gamble. William Proctor and James Gamble organized the company on October 31, 1837, in Cincinnati, with equity capital of $7,192. In 1977, sales were $7,284,000,000, and profits were $461,000,000. The market value of the company as of August 15, 1978 was $7,311,000,000.

Sears, Roebuck. Richard Warren Sears started the company in the fall of 1886 at North Redwood, Minnesota, to sell watches. In 1977, sales were $17,224,000,000, and profits were $838,000,000. The market value of the company as of August 15, 1978 was $7,846,000,000.

Singer. Isaac Merrit Singer, with $40 in borrowed capital, invented the first practical sewing machine in 1850. In 1977, sales were $2,285,000,000, and profits were $78,000,000. Market value of the company's shares on August 15, 1978 was $327,000,000.

Xerox. Xerox Corporation was founded in 1906 in Rochester, New York, by Joseph C. Wilson, Sr. and three other businessmen under the Haloid name. In 1977, sales were $5,077,000,000, and profits were $407,000,000. The market value of its shares on August 15, 1978 was $4,931,000,000.

Advice. After reading about all these shoestring-financed companies don't say, "That all happened in the past. It can't be done again." Under our free enterprise system, it will continue to be possible for entrepreneurs to duplicate in the future what has been done in the past; but it will just be more difficult to do so. It's up to the younger people of this country to have the vision and determination to accomplish it. More power to them—they'll need it!

Q. VENTURE CAPITAL RESOURCE PUBLICATIONS

The Capital Publishing Company was originally started by the late Stanley Rubell in 1961 and has since been acquired by Stanley Pratt. It has been the single clearinghouse for most industry-wide information on venture capital. They offer several publications, including a monthly newsletter entitled *Venture Capital Journal. The Guide to Venture Capital Sources, 9th edition*, is the single most valuable source on venture capital ever published. It offers over two dozen informative articles by venture capitalists, focussing on all phases of funding. And its geographically indexed directory features the principals of each firm, the type of firm, its project preferences, geographical preferences, industry preferences, and more.

For more information on these publications call or write:

Capital Publishing Corporation
2 Laurel Avenue
Box 348
Wellesley Hills, Ma. 02181
(617) 235-5405

The National Venture Capital Association offers its membership directory free with a written or telephone request.

National Venture Capital Association
1730 North Lynn Street
Suite 400
Arlington, Va. 22209
(703) 528-4370

The National Association of Small Business Investment Companies (NASBIC) offers a twice-monthly newsletter from Washington, D.C. *NASBIC News* is one of the better sources of what is happening within the venture capital industry. The NASBIC membership directory is also available for a one dollar handling fee. Requests should be in writing only.

National Association of Small Business
   Investment Companies (NASBIC)
618 Washington Building
Washington, D.C. 20005
(202) 638-3411

A Handbook of Business Finance and Capital Sources is a 460-page reference book on more than 1,000 capital sources. It contains information on financing techniques and instruments for both private and government sources of capital. It is a strongly detailed and well presented reference book that will be useful to anyone who is raising capital. The author/editor is Dileep Rao, Ph.D., who is both an entrepreneur (by way of this self-published book) and India's former number-one ranked table tennis player. Call or write:

Dileep Rao
InterFinance Corporation
305 Foshay Tower
Minneapolis, Mn. 55402
(612) 338-8185

Sources of Corporate Venture Capital

Kenneth W. Rind, the principle in the Xerox Development Corporation, states that there has been a resurgence in corporate venture capital. The following list contains the industrial firms that have been most active in this resurgence:

Textron	Johnson & Johnson
Xerox	3M
Gould	Corning
Time	Dun & Bradstreet
Innoven-Monsanto/Emerson	Fairchild Camera
Exxon	CTS
Standard Oil of Indiana	Control Data
General Electric	Burroughs
Syntex	NCR
Motorola	TRW
Bolt Beranek & Newman, Inc.	National City Lines
Arthur D. Little	Telescience
Inco	

Foreign-based companies are also active in venture capital. They include:

Northern Telecom	Fujitsu
Siemens	Robert Bosch
Nippon Electric	Lucas Industries
Seiko	Jaegar
Oki	VDO
Mitsui	

R. WOMEN ENTREPRENEURS

One of the great changes in the 1980s has been the emergence of the woman entrepreneur. The Women's Liberation Movement has brought women out of the home and into the work force. Now women understand the value and the importance of the start-your-own-business process, and they are beginning to become entrepreneurs at a much faster rate. A recent study indicated that ten percent of all businesses were owned by women. However, more than half of the United States wealth is in the hands of females. Sources of help for women entrepreneurs are listed here; however, don't disregard the other sources of information that are equally valuable.

Women have specialized needs to help combat some of the natural forces that work against them in business. These sources of information are offered to help women combat these problems.

American Women's Economic
  Development Corporation
250 Broadway
New York, N.Y. 10007

The Businesswoman's Letter
P.O. Box 337
Wall Street Station
New York, N.Y. 10005

Organizations

The National Association for Female Executives, Inc. seeks out opportunities, provides information, arranges special offers, and offers information on extending your money power. Write:

NAFE Executive Office
32 East 39th Street
New York, N.Y. 10016

NAFE Administrative Office
31 Jeremys Way
Annapolis, Md. 21403
(301) 267-0630

National Association of Women Business Owners
200 P Street, N.W.
Suite 511
Washington, D.C. 20036
(202) 338-8966

More and more women are becoming entrepreneurs. Other sources of help are available.

New England Women Business Owners
c/o SBANE
69 Hickory Drive
Waltham, Ma. 02154
(617) 890-9070

New York Association of Women Business Owners/Enterprising Women
525 West End Avenue
New York, N.Y. 10024
(A monthly newsletter is offered to subscribers.)

Savvy magazine's February 1984 issue lists the Savvy Sixty, a ranking of the top U.S. businesses run by women.

Savvy Magazine
111 Eighth Avenue
New York, N.Y. 10011
(212) 255-0990

S. S.B.I.R.

The Small Business Innovation Research Act directs that small firms receive at least a fixed minimum percentage of research and development awards made by Federal agencies with sizable R & D budgets.
    The act was signed into law by President Reagan on July 22, 1982. The Small Business Administration (SBA) estimates that $47 million will be awarded in Fiscal Year 1983. *That amount is expected to increase tenfold by Fiscal Year 1987.* Each participating agency will make awards to small firms on a competitive basis. Selection criteria will be included in each solicitation.

Background

In 1977, the National Science Foundation (NSF) pioneered seed-money grants to entrepreneurial companies. Since then, NSF has provided roughly $20 million in funding through the SBIR program, with follow-up funding expected to exceed $47 million. Firms completing the second phase of funding have received $41 million to date. *Nearly 40% of all awards have been to firms with ten or fewer employees.* The same ratio holds true for the Department of Defense, which became involved in seed-money funding two years ago. Of the 1,103 proposals received by DOD thus far, just over 100 awards have been made.

There have been five NSF solicitations since 1977 and one DOD solicitation. Each year there has been a consistent ratio of about one winner for every eight proposals submitted. Last year, NSF received 764 proposals, and 154 of these were recommended for Phase I awards; however, only 108 were actually funded.

The real attraction of the SBIR programs is not so much the initial seed money ($30,000 to $50,000) but the fact that approximately 40% of all first round winners go on to receive second round funding ($200,000 to $500,000) within 12 months. *And as the odds for receiving funding go up, so do the odds of finding outside financial investors particularly venture capital firms.* Endorsement from the SBIR is not taken lightly by the private sector in Phase III.

Present and Future

If none of the foregoing information provides you with the incentive to go after this seed money, the future of the Small Business Innovation Act should. This legislation, which is being phased in over a five year period, will eventually provide as much as $450 million in grant money. Therefore, those of you making the initial effort to win these grants will be in on the ground floor. It is estimated that as many as 2,000 Phase I proposals and 1,000 Phase II proposals will be funded in the final 12 months of this program.

Specifically, the SBIR program requires Federal agencies with R & D budgets of over $100 million to eventually devote 1.25% of their research funds to establish Small Business Innovation Research programs within the respective agencies. As we said, the program will be phased in gradually, beginning this year, and continuing through 1987. This total expenditure will go from about $50 million in 1983 to about $470 in 1987–88.

SBIR Proposals as of August 1, 1983

Agency	Number of Proposals Received	Estimated Number of Awards
Department of Energy	c, 1700	100
Environmental Protection Agency	214	10
Department of Health and Human Services	727	100
Department of Transportation	372	8–10
Department of Defense	c, 2900	c, 200
Department of the Interior	105	6
Nuclear Regulatory Commission	172	7–8
NASA	978	c, 100
Department of Agriculture	268	8–10
Totals	7,436	544

The word from the respective government agencies is that the quality of the SBIR proposals being received is in general high, with more good proposals than can be funded, so that careful and difficult choices must be made. This is, of course, good for the SBIR program. If the situation were reversed, it would justify the sniping the established big research centers have been directing at the program since its inception (let alone trying to keep the SBIR act from passing in the first place). The latest and quite subtle attempt to undermine the program has come from Representative John Dingle of Michigan, who buried three seemingly innocuous amendments in the appropriations bill of the Department of Health and Human Services, which, if passed, would make it possible to reject SBIR proposals on the basis of quality and return the unused monies to the Department's general research fund. Mr. Dingle was acting on behalf of the powerful medical research community. This attempt at subversion was spotted, and it is expected that the amendments will be removed before the bill's passage. However, there will probably be further attempts of this kind, at least until the SBIR funded projects start to prove themselves. It is therefore doubly important that the quality of the proposals remain high.

Agency SBIR Program Representatives

Department of Agriculture

Ms. A. Holiday Schauer
Office of Grants and Program Systems
Department of Agriculture
1300 Rosslyn Commonwealth Building
Suite 103
Arlington, Va. 22209
(703) 235-2628

Department of Defense
Mr. Horace Crouch
Director, Small Business and Economic
 Utilization
Office of Secretary of Defense
Room 2A340, Pentagon
Washington, D.C. 20301
(202) 697-9383

Department of Education
Dr. Edward Esty
SBIR Program Coordinator
Office of Educational Research and
 Improvement
Department of Education
Mail Stop 40
Washington, D.C. 20208

Department of Energy
Mr. Mark Kurzius
c/o SBIR Program Manager
U.S. Department of Energy
Washington, D.C. 20545

Department of Health and Human Services
Mr. Richard Clinkscales
Director, Office of Small and
 Disadvantaged Business Utilization
Department of Health and Human Services
200 Independence Avenue, S.W.
Room 513D
Washington, D.C. 20201

Department of Interior
Dr. Thomas Henrie
Chief Scientist
Bureau of Mines
U.S. Department of the Interior
2401 E Street, N.W.
Washington, D.C. 20241
(202) 634-1305

Department of Transportation

Dr. James Costantino
Director, Transportation System Center
Department of Transportation
Kendall Square
Cambridge, Ma. 02142
(617) 494-2222

Environmental Protection Agency

Mr. Walter Preston
Office of Research Grants and Centers—
 (RD 675)
Office of Research and Development
Environmental Protection Agency
401 M Street, S.W.
Washington, D.C. 20460
(202) 382-5744

National Aeronautics and Space
 Administration

Mr. Carl Schwenk
National Aeronautics and Space
 Administration
SBIR Office—Code R
600 Independence Avenue, S.W.
Washington, D.C. 20546
(202) 755-2450

National Science Foundation

Ritchie Coryell
Roland Tibbetts
SBIR Program Managers
National Science Foundation
1800 G. Street, N.W.
Washington, D.C. 20550

Nuclear Regulatory Commission

Mr. Francis Gillespie
Director, Administration and Resource
 Staff
Office of Nuclear Regulatory Research
Nuclear Regulation Commission
Washington, D.C. 20460

Projected SBIR Funding by Agency

This chart is a projection of the funding for the SBIR program through 1987 based on current budget levels. In illustrating the effect of annual percentage increase against agency budgets, the chart assumes zero inflation and zero expansion. All dollar figures are in thousands.

Agency					Projected Funding					
	%	1983	%	1984	%	1985	%	1986	%	1987
Department of Defense	.1	$16,340	.3	$ 49,020	.6	$ 98,040	1.0	$163,400	1.25	$204,250
NASA	.2	5,500	.6	16,500	1.0	27,500	1.25	34,375	1.25	34,375
Department of Energy	.2	4,161	.6	12,483	1.0	20,805	1.25	26,006	1.25	26,006
Department of Health and Human Services	.2	6,476	.6	19,428	1.0	32,380	1.25	40,475	1.25	40,475
National Science Foundation	.2	5,500	.6	6,000	1.0	9,700	1.25	12,125	1.25	12,125
Department of Agriculture	.2	579	.6	1,737	1.0	2,895	1.25	3,619	1.25	3,619
Department of Transportation	.2	491	.6	1,473	1.0	2,450	1.25	3,062	1.25	3,062
Nuclear Regulatory Commission	.2	391	.6	1,173	1.0	1,955	1.25	2,444	1.25	2,444
Environmental Protection Agency	.2	288	.6	864	1.0	1,440	1.25	1,800	1.25	1,800
Department of the Interior	.2	231	.6	693	1.0	1,155	1.25	1,444	1.25	1,444
		$39,957		$109,371		$198,320		$288,750		$329,600

C

Sample Business Plans

These business plans are included not as examples of either effective or ineffective business plans, but rather to acquaint the reader with several actual business plans. These were chosen more for their representation of various types of plans. They are all actual plans, disguised where needed, especially as relates to geographic location, financial information, and individual's identities, which may account for their unusual collection of inconsistencies, errors, and omissions.

BRIOX TECHNOLOGY, INC.

This is an interesting story—one with a good ending. It began when my brother, John Anthony Mancuso, acting as a salesman for a valve company, called in upstate New York on Briox Technologies. He mentioned my interest in small business to the Briox entrepreneur, David Gessner. As can be observed from the résumés in the business plan, Gessner was the holder of a technical master's degree, and, as such, he elected to attend an interesting three-day workshop sponsored by the Institute for New Enterprise Development (INED) in Belmont, Massachusetts. This agency specializes in helping new entrepreneurs get started. For a small fee, Gessner attended a weekend "how to write a business plan" seminar which was held in Salt Lake City, Utah. Hence, Gessner was fairly well versed in the construction of a business plan. Moreover, as will be evident in a moment, he possessed a deep and burning desire to start, finance, and manage a small business of his own. John Mancuso suggested that he show the business plan to me.

Gessner and I met; I was impressed with him and his business, and I introduced him to a Minority Enterprise Small Business Investment Company (MESBIC). Gessner cleverly restructured the business plan to highlight the minority employment aspect of his business. The plan, as attached, was financed by several friends and relatives (angels) and by the Worcester Cooperation Council, Inc. (WCCI). The business moved to Worcester, and Gessner began to operate the medical oxygen company.

This is where the story becomes interesting. It took only a few months to use up all of the original investment. During that time the company was unable to perfect the oxygenerator which was to make oxygen from water. The idea was good—even great—but the technology was only fair—maybe poor. Within six months of the private placement, the business was bust, Al Stubman was fired, and Gessner was all alone with no money, no sales, and no product. A more sensible man would have known when to quit, and would have gone in search of a job. Instead, he sought part-time employment, did some consulting (he assisted in a small business course at WPI), and collected unemployment. The last of these actions—collecting unemployment—was the most emotional and most rewarding experience of all. Gessner collected for over one year, and these funds provided the main sustenance for his family.

With the addition of hindsight, these unemployment checks were a vital motivation to keep him going: They supplied the nourishment for the next year or so. If a person who contemplates going into a small business has never collected an unemployment check, may I recommend that he visit his unemployment office. The sign over the door will read "Employment Office" but everyone calls it the "Unemployment Office." It's a very dehumanizing process. Go see for yourself, if you haven't already.

During these never-ending months of product development, Gessner continued to improve his radical new invention, the oxygenerator. Finally, after two years of trying, he decided to shift horses.

Just as Ed Land of Polaroid was initially interested in building a business around polarized glass (supposedly for the windshields and headlights of automobiles), Dave Gessner began his business with the wrong initial product. Gessner soon improved upon the existing and proven technology pioneered by the competitors—making oxygen by filtering air. He developed a brochure, attracted new investors, acquired a new partner/investor, and began again. In the past few months, after 2½ years, he is beginning to show modest profits.

I said, in the third paragraph at the beginning of this book, that starting a business and succeeding at it requires perseverance and motivation—sometimes bordering on obsession. Gessner proves my point. Moreover, his wife, Lea, who is never mentioned in this business plan, is the real star. She helped, and helped, and helped.

AMERICAN LASER, INC.

This is not an untypical story. In fact, it's recurring quite frequently. Although this story is disguised, it is true. These two fellows bought a business when their employer decided to go out of the business. And, best of all, they succeeded. I would guess that this will become an even more common practice in the future.

In fact, the largest employer in the entire state of Vermont, an asbestos mine, experienced a similar transaction. After years of poor financial performance, the parent company announced plans to close its doors. The people were going to lose their jobs, and it was a statewide concern. The good news is what happened. The employees banded together, obtained financing from the State, and bought the companies. Naturally, as with many of these stories, the elected president was the former foreman of the maintenance division. After one year under employee ownership, all the stockholders were able to have their entire initial investment returned. In the subsequent years, the business has demonstrated excellent profitability.

The same is true in the case of American Laser. As a division of the larger parent company it consistently lost in excess of $1,000,000 per year. This is devastating, given the size of the sales of the division. When these two people took over the company, they had only marginal management experience. The business plan was written in module form. This allowed the entrepreneurs to package the appropriate modules in order to maximize the appeal. The plan is a good one. However, in fact, the list of customers in the plan failed to materialize in the first year. In other words, *none* of the customers listed in the report bought products during the first year the firm was in business.

The plan failed to raise venture money. However, it did *not* fail to launch the business. Moreover, the business is extremely successful; and in the third year after the start of this business, the firm has produced $100,000 of profits.

After discussing the appeal of this new business with several venture sources, the founders were extremely dejected. They found the terms and conditions of any new money to be terribly limiting. Subsequently, they walked into a bank and pleaded their case with an unusual, creative, and friendly banker. Within a half an hour, the banker advanced them a personal, unsecured loan to launch their business. I was there and I saw it happen—an unusual event if I ever saw one. Earlier in this manuscript I said, "Pick a banker, not a bank." Later on the same page, I said, "A good banker can be a venture capitalist in disguise." This one was more than that: He became an admired friend. He received all of the loan back and kept the new growing company in town. An interesting story.

PERSPECTIVES, INC.

This is an excellent business plan. It is well written; the entrepreneur is successful; the idea is superior. However, the plan never raised any money: It was a failure.

It was shown to many investors, probably more than it should have been, but it was always a bridesmaid. One of the common criticisms of the plan was the inability to test the idea on a small scale. One of the investors claimed that the plan was too large an investment prior to any measurable level of success being obtainable. There was considerable negotiating about the viability of a regional publication for the senior citizens, say, in Florida. But on a regional scale, it was much less appealing financially. So the idea died.

However, as with most good ideas, it only died for this entrepreneur. Publishing, like many industries, is a special and private business, and John O'Mara had very little publishing experience. But another entrepreneur with a different business plan, totally unrelated to this venture, launched a very similar product. The data obtained by the grapevine claims that the business is now a solid financial success.

John O'Mara gained a great deal of experience in developing this business plan—so much so, in fact, that he wrote another one. Soon, he left the secure arms of his large company employer in order to launch a new business called the Computer Security Institute. This venture provided newsletters, information, and seminars for larger firms interested in protecting confidential information stored in computers. I'm told that the venture is extremely successful because as the initial membership fee alone, from my outside vantage point, certainly must help cover some overhead. The advantage of having customers send money in advance (membership fees) is an interesting method of advancing the product notion.

IN-LINE TECHNOLOGY

The attached plan is a shortened version of the actual document used to finance In-Line Technology. The actual document was about four times longer. It contained numerous photos and product descriptions. The financing was successful. The firm was able to raise the funds stated in the prospectus. The funds were supplied by friends and relatives, and the final $50,000 was provided by an extremely successful and well-known New York venture capitalist. The venture capitalist, because of his reputation, was able to negotiate an extra bonus for investing in this young but promising business. The two founders were extremely reluctant to give extra compensation to the venture sources, but they finally decided to go along.

The new money transfusion helped, and the firm began to grow. The venture source forced the additional services of a paid-for management consultant to work several days per month at In-Line Technology. This was not part of the private placement but the verbal persuasion was sufficient. In other words, the original private placement legal document did not specifically require In-Line to accept outside consulting advice. The legal agreement for private placements of this type and size are usually secondary to verbal agreements. In fact, the business improved based on this consulting advice.

In-Line never made money. Occasionally, it had a few months of profits but never any sustained or significant profits. It always seemed to almost make a profit in the following few years, but it never became very successful. Finally, the venture capitalist grew restless and introduced In-Line Technology to a larger firm on the West Coast—Applied Materials, Inc. The firms were merged in January of 1976, and the investors in this business plan realized a 3:1 gain. Hence, the firm raised money and performed at an average level, yet the investors and stockholders still made a profit. This is seldom the case, and without the assistance of the New York venture capitalist, the firm would still be struggling. The venture placement was determined at a breakfast meeting in New York. This was the only meeting the venture source had with the firm. He never visited the plant.

About nine months after the merger, one of the two founders was fired and the other was made a consultant. In other words, they were both eased out of the business. This partnership of Gene St. Onge and Hank Bok works well and they have just launched a new business. Based upon the funds gained from the sale of In-Line Technology, the two men have started another small business, Hydro-tech. This firm is entering the interesting area of hydrophonics, which is a form of scientific farming. This business calls for year around growing of tomatoes, cucumbers, and lettuce in greenhouses. The success of this newest business is still undetermined. It's interesting to recall some of the early comments that the likelihood of starting a small business is increased if you have previous experience in starting businesses. Many entrepreneurs will start five to six businesses in a lifetime.

B.L.T.

The reader of this business plan must be careful not to let recent events such as the energy crisis cloud the proper reading of the document. This plan was written in 1969. It followed very closely on the heels of a successful public stock offering for Robo-Wash, a competitor. The plan was written by three extremely talented men who spent most of their careers on Wall Street in New York. While none of the three founders had any experience in either the gas station or car wash fields, they knew their way around Wall Street. They were experts at raising money.

The business plan is extremely simple. It is not terribly exciting to read. The strongest point is the level of management achievement of the three principals. This was enough for this start-up business to raise in excess of $1,000,000 from a handful of venture capitalists. The money was raised over several placements, and the firm experienced continual delays and postponements in building and operating the gas station/car wash combination. The business began in fine style with a prototype gas station/car wash operating profitably in southern Connecticut. However, this was the only profitable business enterprise with B.L.T. The business as a whole never made money. The firm lost the $1,000,000 of investment plus a good deal of bank debt. The reasons for failures were manyfold. However, the business plan, as simple as it was, was sufficient just as it was, to raise over $1,000,000.

BRIOX TECHNOLOGIES
Medical Oxygen Generator

MEDICAL OXYGEN GENERATOR

FOR HOMECARE PATIENTS

BUSINESS PLAN

SEPTEMBER, 1974

Briox Technologies, Inc.
65 Tainter Street
Worcester, Massachusetts 01610
617/757-7474

CONTENTS

Summary

The Company and Its Business   I

The Product   II

The Market   III

The Marketing Plan   IV

The Production Plan   V

The Management Team   VI

The Financial Plan   VII

Potential Risks and Problems   VIII

APPENDIX   IX

A. Management Resumes

    David M. Gessner
    Albert B. Stubbmann
    Jeanne E. Gutmann

B. Financial Statements

    Balance Sheet - August 31, 1974
    Income Statement - Year-to-Date August 31, 1974
    pro forma Cash Flow
    pro forma Income Statement
    pro forma Balance Sheet
    Stockholder Breakdown

C. News Releases

SUMMARY

   Briox Technologies, Inc. is a company in the Biomedical Equipment
field which is responding to the needs of homecare service businesses
and hospitals. The company was founded in September 1973 by David M.
Gessner with the commitment of his personal funds. WCCI Capital Corporation of Worcester, Massachusetts, and several individuals have provided
additional seed financing.

The Product

   The first product is a home oxygen generating system, the OXY-
GENERATOR, to replace expensive-to-deliver high pressure cylinders currently in use for the treatment of Chronic Obstructive Pulmonary Disease (COPD). The company has completed a full-scale prototype which was
complete and operating on April 9, 1974.

Field Evaluation

   Five demonstrator OXY-GENERATORS are being built for laboratory and
field evaluation. At the recent national meeting of the American Tho-
racic Society in Cincinnati six board certified pulmonary specialists
expressed interest in conducting field evaluations with their patients.

The Market

   The total market size for home oxygen generating systems is 66,000
and is growing at an annual compounded rate of $7\frac{1}{2}\%$. The company will
capture at least 6% of this market by 1978 with annual sales of 5,000
units @ $2100 yielding revenues of $10.5 million with a net profit
greater than 15% of sales.

Production

   OXY-GENERATORS will be produced by assembly of commercial components and subcontracted subassemblies. The primary subassembly will be
provided under exclusive license by TELEDYNE ISOTOPES. As the company
grows the investment in manufacturing facilities will be increased in
order to reduce costs and to increase capability and flexibility.

Distribution

   OXY-GENERATORS will be sold to existing Respiratory Therapy Equipment Dealers who will rent them to COPD patients for use in the home.
Dealer reaction to the product is positive. The company will trade exclusive distributorships within a territory for firm order commitments.

Financing Required

   The company needs $100,000 to fund the development and implemen-
tation of a manufacturing plan to produce 20 units/month. Management
proposes to issue an additional 25,000 shares which will bring the
total issued to 85,000. Twenty thousand shares will be sold in private
placement at $5.00 per share. Financial arrangements should be complete
by October 31, 1974.

I. THE COMPANY AND ITS BUSINESS

The Company

Briox Technologies, Inc. (Briox) was founded last year in order to take advantage of market opportunities arising from the recent marked increase in chronically ill persons who are living and being cared for at home. These unfortunate individuals must rely for treatment and therapy upon a mixed lot of professional and volunteer homecare service organizations who are often equipped with inappropriate hospital service hardware.

Briox will serve this market by providing innovative products for use in the home by the chronically ill. The company will use existing marketing channels at the outset, but will foster the development of integrated homecare service companies, possibly on a franchise basis.

Briox is monitoring the homecare market and will introduce new products to meet its specific needs. The general strategy of Briox will be to take advantage of existing technology and product opportunities and to avoid investment in basic research and development.

The First Product

An electrolytic oxygen generator, the OXY-GENERATOR, to be used in homes and long term nursing homes for the regular treatment of low blood oxygen content (hypoxemia) associated with Chronic Obstructive Pulmonary Disease (COPD). This device is not intended for life support or emergency.

The Primary Customer

The primary customer will be qualified Respiratory Therapy (RT) dealers who will rent or lease the generator to private patients under a doctor's prescription for oxygen. Sales to nursing homes will also be through the RT dealers. There are 600 RT dealers nationwide who provide oxygen therapy, inhalation therapy equipment, homecare and general sickroom needs for COPD and cardiac patients. RT dealers are to be distinguished from less sophisticated welding gas suppliers who also serve the medical oxygen market. In the United States today, there are approximately 100,000 COPD patients who could benefit from the OXY-GENERATOR.

The Customer's Application for the Product

The RT dealer will rent or lease the product to the end user who is a patient with severe COPD and who will use the OXY-GENERATOR to generate oxygen for inhalation treatment of hypoxemia. These patients must presently use stored oxygen from cylinders. Because of the expense, many patients who need oxygen do not receive this life extending therapy. These patients also use other inhalation therapy equipment such as positive pressure breathing machines (IPPB) and nebulizers, which are supplied and serviced by RT dealers.

Customer Reactions

Bill Leombrumo, President of Medical Oxygen Service, Burlington, Massachusetts, a company which serves 700 home oxygen therapy patients in Eastern New England, wants exclusive distribution rights for the OXY-GENERATOR in his territory. He is convinced that this type of device will dominate the home oxygen market in 10-15 years.

Chuck Vastbinder, President of Home Therapy Equipment, Inc. in Clifton Park, New York, initially will use the OXY-GENERATOR to serve his most distant patients who live as far as 25 miles from his office. He wants to charge 10% of the purchase price per month in order to pay off the machine in a year. He feels that $1800 is an acceptable selling price. Most of his patients have prescriptions for 2 liters/minute or less.

Stan Rowland, President of Med-Mark, Inc. in Salt Lake City, Utah, corroborated the need for an improved method for delivery of home oxygen therapy. He contracts for most of his home oxygen deliveries.

Gerry Conoscenti of the Inhalation Therapy Company in Clifton, New Jersey, will use OXY-GENERATORS in a Cystic Fibrosis research program as well as in his regular business.

Gary Vick, Vice-President - Sales at United States Welding in Denver, Colorado, feels he could put 500 machines to work in Denver and Salt Lake City. This assumes a selling price of $1500 to $2000.

Stan Berman, who runs six RT dealerships in Connecticut, New York, and New Jersey, is not satisfied with three OXY-GENERATORS offered to him. Stan claims that it will take 50 units to make an impact on his business.

Physician Reactions

Dr. Ralph L. Kendall of St. Vincent Hospital, Worcester, Massachusetts, is uncomfortable prescribing cylinder oxygen for his patients because of the hazard inherent in handling high pressure oxygen. Dr. Kendall has offered to evaluate the OXY-GENERATOR in the hospital setting.

Dr. Thomas L. Petty, Head, Division of Pulmonary Medicine at the University of Colorado Medical Center in Denver, Colorado, and the leading expert in COPD and oxygen therapy stated, "Your device will be appealing if it is safe, reliable and reduces cost....Increased activity within the home and the relief of pulmonary hyper-tension will be valuable....The vast majority of patients require 1 to 2 liters at rest and very few more than 4 liters." Dr. Petty participated in the development of the Linde Walker system which is in use by 5,000 patients nationwide.

The customer will be motivated to buy OXY-GENERATORS by the following advantages:

To the RT dealer

- Up to 60% lower total cost to deliver equivalent oxygen therapy thereby increasing profits. Patients' charges could be reduced in order to extend the oxygen therapy market.

- Staff reduction possible. If the dealer uses OXY-GENERATORS to replace cylinders in all applications, he will no longer need deliverymen. If the dealer uses only OXY-GENERATORS to serve his most distant (and least profitable) patients, he can use his remaining deliverymen more efficiently.

- Off-hour deliveries eliminated. The RT dealer cannot charge a premium for this service.

- Another source of supply. Many RT dealers are in competition with their oxygen suppliers, the welding gas distributor. Due to Teamsters Union restrictions the RT dealer will often find it economical to contract with the welding supplier for domestic oxygen delivery service. Oxygen generators will reduce this restriction on the RT dealer's business.

To the COPD patient

- Dependence upon oxygen deliveries eliminated. Fears of delayed delivery or of supplies running out in the night will be allayed.

- Up to 35% reduced cost to the patient for therapy, especially when there is no third-party reimbursement such as Medicare.

- Increased safety. Oxygen cylinders have been known to topple over causing injuries and, in rare cases, to explode. The U.S. Navy uses electrolytic oxygen generators to provide breathing oxygen in advanced nuclear submarines where safety requirements are critical.

To the physician

- The OXY-GENERATOR can be installed such that the patient's prescription is set electronically and the patient cannot over-treat himself.

- The OXY-GENERATOR's instrumentation will record the patient's exact monthly oxygen usage. The RT dealer will report this information to the physician.

To the third-party insurer

- As much as 35% lower cost for equivalent therapy.

- The possibility of a fixed relationship between the parameters of the doctor's prescription for oxygen and the monthly charge for oxygen therapy.

BRIOX' HISTORY

1973

August	–David M. Gessner participates in Entrepreneurial Talent Assessment Workshop sponsored in Salt Lake City by the Institute for New Enterprise Development. –Decision made to start medical products company.
September	–D. M. Gessner Enterprises, Inc. formed. Office opened in Scotia, N.Y. Market development activities for Home Oxygen Generation System (OXY-GENERATOR) began. –Teledyne Isotopes of Timonium, Maryland, is approached for technological assistance.
November	–Informal understanding entered into with Teledyne Isotopes' general management. Technology transfer begins with shipment of Teledyne Isotopes' industrial hardware to Scotia.
December	–Two Community Development Corporations (CDC) in Massachusetts are approached and presented with business plans and pro forma statements.

1974

January	–Hardware development begins on prototype oxygen generator. –Albert B. Stubbmann joins management team.
March	–Massachusetts CDC's offer commitments for seed financing.
April	–Assembly of prototype OXY-GENERATOR completed. System operates unattended.
May	–Gessner and Stubbmann attend American Thoracic Society meeting in Cincinnati with mock-up OXY-GENERATOR. Physician response is positive. –WCCI Capital Corporation (CDC) advances the company $5000.
June	–Company name changed to Briox Technologies, Inc. Company relocates to Worcester, Massachusetts, and closes Scotia office. –Full time staff doubles. –Three agreements signed with Teledyne Isotopes.
July	–Subassemblies for demonstrator unit arrive from Teledyne Isotopes.
August	–WCCI Capital Corporation investment agreement closed with the payment of $20,000 additional equity financing. –Prototype OXY-GENERATOR, in modified form, surpasses 500 hours of operation.

II. THE PRODUCT

Description of the OXY-GENERATOR

The OXY-GENERATOR is an electrolysis oxygen generator which operates on a normal household circuit. It produces up to two liters/minute of ultra-pure (99.999%) oxygen, humidified to 50% relative humidity for inhalation treatment of hypoxemia due to Chronic Obstructive Pulmonary Disease (COPD). The OXY-GENERATOR will operate continuously at full output or as needed to satisfy the physician's prescsiption for oxygen. The electrolysis process ensures that the generator is self-sterilizing in operation.

The OXY-GENERATOR will be about the size of a typical floor standing hi-fi speaker and will be styled so as to be unobtrusive in the home. It will be noiseless in operation (less than 35 dba) and will dispense oxygen immediately upon the turn of a switch.

The OXY-GENERATOR will incorporate safety features which will disconnect the generator from the household circuit should there be any deviation from normal operation.

OXY-GENERATOR Development

The development of this product represents the successful transfer of technologies developed for aerospace and military applications to the medical sector. Briox formulated the product specifications according to expressed medical and market needs. Teledyne Isotopes agreed that their existing proprietary electrolysis hardware could be adapted to meet the needs of the proposed product application.

Teledyne Isotopes Relationship

In November of 1973 a joint development program was started. Teledyne Isotopes was given the responsibility for providing an electrolysis subassembly suitable for the application. Briox developed the associated power supply, safety control circuit, feed water subsystem, cabinet and user software. This program produced a full-scale prototype OXY-GENERATOR on April 9, 1974. This prototype underwent testing for one month at Teledyne Isotopes' Maryland facility where it accumulated over 150 operating hours. It is presently undergoing refinement and additional testing at Briox' offices.

On June 21, 1974 three agreements were closed with Teledyne Isotopes providing for:

- Sales of electrolysis subassemblies by Teledyne Isotopes to Briox at a fixed but periodically renegotiable price.

- Transfer of technical information by Teledyne Isotopes to Briox. Five electrolysis subassemblies for use as field demonstrators are being supplied free to Briox by Teledyne Isotopes.

- Briox has given Teledyne Isotopes a $1,000 face value, three year, 4% balloon payment convertible debenture. The debenture is convertible into 20% of the issued and outstanding shares of Briox anytime during the three year period. It is the expectation of the parties that Teledyne Isotopes will exercise their conversion rights.

Briox' Product Development Program

In order to be acceptable to the market, the OXY-GENERATOR must demonstrate the following:

- Continuous reliable performance on a 4 month maintenance cycle, regardless of user attention.

- Ready installation in typical lower socioeconomic class housing without modification of existing house wiring.

The most significant Briox development is a passive current-controlled power supply which isolates the electrolysis cell from variations in household line voltage (brownouts) and from the effects of changes in room temperature. This is an improvement over the basic industrial system (HG) developed by Teledyne Isotopes.

The second area of development is the continual refinement of the system, using the prototype as a test bed, to reduce cost of components and increase reliability.

The third area of development, initiated in August, is the redesign of the OXY-GENERATOR to enable manufacture by final assembly of sub-assemblies made up of interchangeable parts.

Finally, software development is proceeding to meet the needs of the Marketing program.

Status

- The prototype unit continues to serve as a test bed for new components and as a life test unit.

- Five field demonstrators are undergoing final assembly. The first demonstrator OXY-GENERATOR will be ready to be placed in a hospital test program by October 1.

- The final production design will be frozen on December 1.

ANALYSIS of PRODUCT CONCEPT

The factors set out below will place the OXY-GENERATOR concept in perspective.

Patents and Trade Secrets

- Teledyne Isotopes has a patent covering the overall design of the electrolysis cell and electrolyte system.

- The overall design of the product will be patented by Briox Technologies, Inc.

- Briox Technologies, Inc., has a growing body of marketing information that would be expensive to duplicate by a competitor.

Design Features

vs. Current pressurized or cryogenic stored oxygen supplies presently used in the home:

- Because of its small size the OXY-GENERATOR can be installed in a convenient location near the patients. Full size oxygen cylinders are prohibited above the first floor by fire codes in many communities.

- Patient anxiety over oxygen delivery is eliminated.

- Oxygen is generated only as needed and is not stored in the system so as to be a hazard.

- Oxygen is dispensed in humidified form; no need for separate oxygen humidifiers, which are a source of microbiological hazard. Disposable humidifiers also represent an expense of $5 - $10 per month that will be eliminated.

vs. Potential electromechanical (membrane or sieve process) home oxygen generators:

- The OXY-GENERATOR does not have a noisy, vibrating (70 dba) air compressor.

- The OXY-GENERATOR does not have any rotating or wearing parts. Service requirements will consist of a quarterly electrolyte change and renewal of the demineralizer cartridge.

- This product will be technologically advanced. There are no other advanced methods of oxygen generation known to Briox that are not mentioned herein.

Weaknesses

- The OXY-GENERATOR produces hydrogen, and although the hydrogen and oxygen are carefully separated throughout the system, the provision will be made to insure that the hydrogen is safely disposed of, concern over this issue will probably persist.

- It needs water to produce oxygen. Water will be added to the generator daily by the user. Provision could also be made for the use of semi-permanent plumbing connections in suitable installations.

- The house circuit should be inspected and serviced at installation in order to insure reliable operation.

It could reduce dealer per patient revenues due to lower operating cost for equivalent oxygen therapy. To maximize profit the dealer should establish pricing based on a fixed monthly charge plus an hourly usage rate.

Extension of the Product Concept

Eventually the OXY-GENERATOR could be only one component of a complete, portable home Inhalation Therapy console, which will include aerosol nebulization of medication and IPPB. Other medical applications for OXY-GENERATORS will be explored in 1975.

III. THE MARKET

The total annual United States market for medical oxygen is
estimated at $125 - 200 million. This includes hospitals (bulk
systems and cylinders) and 2 - 3 million individuals in private homes
and nursing homes who use medical oxygen. Of the home patients, all
but 50 - 75,000 use oxygen sparingly (less than 2 cylinders per month).
The high users (greater than 3 cylinders per month) use as much oxygen
as all the rest of the home medical oxygen users in the United States.

Due to the cut-back of the Federal Hill-Burton Act funding new
hospital construction, and the increased pressure for hospital bed
space by acute patients, fewer chronic patients are being treated in
the hospital. Nursing homes have not been able to keep up with the
increased patient load, primarily because of the imposition, in recent
years, of stricter state requirements for accreditation. The result
is that patients with chronic diseases are being treated at home to
an increasingly greater extent. Because of the lower cost of home
care versus hospital care, insurers are beginning to recognize home
care by para-medicals as a reimbursable medical expense. Qualified
service businesses are emerging to participate in this growing market,
respiratory therapy dealers being the most apparent.

The demand for oxygen generators is derived from the number of
patients with advanced COPD.

TABLE III - 1

TOTAL U.S. MARKET FOR HOME OXYGEN SYSTEMS

Potential Sales	1974	1975	1976	1977	1978	1979
Units (x 1000)	66.1	71.0	76.3	82.1	88.5	95.3
Dollars x 1,000,000	139	149	160	172	186	200

COPD patients need regular daily oxygen therapy during the last
year of life. The oxygen generator will be primarily applicable
to their needs. Mortality data are taken from Systems Analysis
Study for Respiratory Devices, #PB 210 560, prepared for Medical
Devices Application Program of the National Institutes of Health
by TECNA Corporation.

Market size is equal to the projected annual mortality due to
COPD for all ages and both sexes.

The above is a conservative estimate of the total market size for
the following reasons:

1. The data do not consider patients dying by other causes who
    may also have advanced COPD.

2. The data do not consider patients needing domestic oxygen for
    a variety of other reasons including Cystic Fibrosis, Cardiac
    Insufficiency, Angina Pectoris.

3. Properly administered oxygen therapy may significantly extend the lives of severe COPD patients beyond the one-year average currently observed.

Competition

The competition in the market for supplying oxygen for treatment of COPD and other conditions requiring low-flow oxygen therapy comes from three sources:

1. Oxygen cylinders, in a variety of sizes, are currently the most widely used source. They are distributed by a variety of dealers who are either respiratory therapy equipment dealers, expanded medical supply houses, or welding gas suppliers. Dealers make several deliveries of oxygen cylinders per week to patients and charge a per/cylinder rate, plus rental, for regulators. Their source of oxygen can be either their own plant or an oxygen manufacturing firm, such as Linde Gas Products.

2. Cryogenic liquid oxygen is transferred to tanks at the dealership; the tanks in the patients' homes are filled from the tank delivery trucks. Linde Gas Products, a Division of Union Carbide, is marketing a home cryogenic system that permits the patient to fill a small, portable tank. This system also requires deliveries several times per week using specialized vehicles.

3. Electro-mechanical devices which boost the oxygen concentration of room air do not deliver the equivalent of the first two sources since they do not produce pure oxygen. Bendix Corporation is producing a product in this category. Their device uses a molecular sieve process to remove nitrogen from air, which increases the volumetric concentration of oxygen. Bendix has a number of units in the field. General Electric Company, experiencing many technical and production problems, is currently in the process of re-evaluating their product.

The Briox OXY-GENERATOR produces humidified oxygen, purer than cylinder oxygen, while the mechanical air-enrichers do not.

TABLE III - 2

COST COMPARISONS FOR OXYGEN SOURCES

This table has been prepared using the following assumptions:

1. Patient using 2 liters/min (or equivalent) of pure oxygen

2. Usage is 18 hrs/day, 30 days/mon

3. "Other Costs" include any accessory equipment necessary to dispense 2 liters/min and humidify

4. Visits by therapist required by all (cost not included)

Source	Unit Cost (or rental rate)	# Units per Month	Cost per Month	Other Costs	Total
Oxygen Cylinders	$15 to $25/cyl	15 to 18/cyl*	$225 to $450	$15 to $50**	$240 to $500
Linde Walker Cryogenic	$80/mon $10-20/del	8 to 12	$160 to $320	$20	$180 to $340
Bendix $1500/unit	$80/mon $30/hr	540 hrs	$240	$20	$260
General Electric $1800/unit	$100/mon $35/hr	540 hrs	$290	$20	$310
Briox $2100/unit	$120/mon $40/hr	540 hrs	$335	-0-	$335

*64,800 liters
**Includes rental of regulators and humidifier

IV. MARKETING PLAN

Sales Objectives

The OXY-GENERATOR sales objectives were developed after consideration of both the expected market penetration rate and the internal
needs of Briox. A rapid acceptance of the OXY-GENERATOR is expected
based on:

- Increasing emphasis on respiratory therapy for chronic pulmonary
  disease

- Current lack of innovations in equipment for home health care

- Dissatisfaction on the part of many physicians with the safety
  of oxygen cylinders for use in the home

At the same time, it would not be advisable to accelerate production
too rapidly and not benefit from early production and field experience.
Briox will be learning from both factory and marketplace and will
adapt when necessary.

TABLE IV - 1

Sales Objectives for Oxygen Generators*

	1975	1976	1977	1978
Target Sales				
Units	300	1,000	3,000	5,000
$000	610	2,100	6,300	10,500
Maximum Reasonable Sales				
Units	500	2,500	5,000	8,000
$000	1,050	5,250	10,500	16,800
Break-even Sales				
Units	250	300	300	300
$000	525	610	610	610

*Sales for 1975 will be in the northeast only. From 1976 and after
the sales region will grow continually to become nationwide.

Marketing Strategy

While COPD patients will use the OXY-GENERATOR, Briox' customers
are RT dealers. The RT dealers will rent and service the OXY-GENERATOR
to patients on advice of physician. The market strategy will be to
gain acceptance of both RT dealers and Pulmonary Disease Physicians.
Of the two, the physicians are more critical, since they must prescribe
or at least approve the use of an OXY-GENERATOR by the patient. The
RT dealer will be quick to utilize OXY-GENERATOR if area physicians
are recommending them to their patients. At the same time, rapid dealer
acceptance will help speed up physician acceptance. It will be necessary to provide patient literature as well, although, in most circumstances, the patients will accept advice of physician and dealer.

In order to efficiently market the OXY-GENERATOR, Briox will focus on the northeast - New York, New Jersey, Pennsylvania, Massachusetts, Connecticut, and Rhode Island - during 1975. In this area, there are a minumum of 20,000 advanced COPD patients concentrated in just 3.2% of the United States land area.

Medical Evaluation & Endorsement

Medical evaluation is the first and most significant part of the early marketing plan. Its objectives are:

- Impartial outside evaluation of the OXY-GENERATOR.

- Establishing medical history and endorsement through actual experience under controlled and uncontrolled conditions.

- Gaining experience with the OXY-GENERATOR to detect and correct any idiosyncrasies or weaknesses not detected in prototype and laboratory testing.

The medical evaluation phase will include both hospital and supervised home operation and will continue indefinitely. This will be the base for Briox' involvement with the medical community and will be the first step when the OXY-GENERATOR is introduced into a new geographical area.

Marketing Tactics

The tactics to be used in product introduction will be to approach the RT dealers, Pulmonary Disease Physicians and Major Hospital Respiratory Disease Departments simultaneously and get all three groups involved in and educated from evaluations and utilization of the OXY-GENERATOR. Five demonstrator units will be used to introduce the product to the market. The plan is to use the hospital evaluation programs as attention-getting devices in the local medical communities. It is important that the RT dealers are involved at this stage as well. In many communities Visiting Nurse Associations will also be approached, since they are active in providing home health care.

Product literature development will be completed during this period and will include

- Patient-oriented brochure giving explanations of the OXY-GENERATOR and a brief description of its applications and operation.

- A physician's prescription guide, giving detailed specifications and operating instructions.

- An operator's instruction manual (user-oriented).

- A dealer's operating manual including set-up preparations and routine maintenance guide.

- A trouble shooting guide and repair manual giving schematic diagrams and parts specifications.

- A direct mail piece and trade show brochure which will be designed for both medical and commercial audiences.

Marketing Timetable

The first orders for the OXY-GENERATOR will be taken during October. These orders will be solicited from 4 or 5 key RT dealers displaying strong interest in the product. Later orders will be from an expanded dealer list.

Current plans are to grant exclusive territories to RT dealers who have well established reputations for service and the resources to meet these commitments. The exclusivity will be on a trial basis and continuation will be contingent on observed performance with OXY-GENERATOR. Since the product does not require weekly or semi-weekly deliveries, the RT dealers can actually expand beyond current territories limited by regular oxygen cylinder deliveries.

Pricing Strategy

The pricing strategy for the OXY-GENERATOR will be designed to encourage quantity purchases rather than single unit orders. A quantity order may be scheduled with deliveries staggered over time and this lightens the RT dealer's economic burden and aids Briox' production scheduling. The pricing schedule will be:

$2,600	1 unit	per order
2,500	2-4 units	per order
2,400	5-10 units	per order
2,300	11-15 units	per order
2,200	16-20 units	per order
2,150	21-25 units	per order
2,100	26 & above units	per order

If a dealer orders additional units for delivery during a calendar year, the discount provided will be given for the total units ordered for delivery during that year. At least two months in advance of delivery will be required on orders.

V. THE PRODUCTION PLAN

Production will begin when a six month backlog of orders is booked. OXY-GENERATORS will be produced at a fixed monthly rate. Material for each month's production will be inventoried during the previous month. Production rate will be increased as is warranted by the production backlog.

OXY-GENERATORS will be produced by final assembly of conventional fluid handling and electrical hardware and patented electrolysis cells in a custom enclosure. Initially these components will be OEM parts and outside-contract subassemblies.

In 1975, management will determine where the in-house manufacturing capability should be extended in order to:

-   Reduce manufacturing costs.

-   Increase the "value added" and uniqueness of the product.

-   Gain manufacturing expertise which can be applied to new products.

Production Time Cycle

Final assembly of components - less than one workday/unit.

Quality assurance testing - less than one workday/unit.

Subassembly procurement and preparation for assembly - indeterminate as of this writing.

Basic Manufacturing Needs

A manufacturing facility has been leased on 65 Tainter Street, Worcester, Massachusetts. It has access to motor, rail and air shipping as well as manufacturing services nearby, such as machining shops. Plant operations will require 3000 square feet until after 1975. The Tainter Street site allows for at least threefold expansion. Normal sanitary, power, heat and telephone services are provided.

Issues

-   Production raw material - Due to current business conditions, suppliers' inventories are at low levels resulting in delivery times as long as six months for specific materials.

-   Production engineering - Reduce the manufacturing cost of the present design through effective engineering.

-   Mixed labor requirements - Because there will be need for intercraft cooperation in assembly, there is a potential for trade union friction.

-   Rapidly growing production volume will require frequent changes in manufacturing procedures.

Manufacturing Cost Savings

-   The product will contain the latest technological advances in
    methods and materials.

-   The venture will benefit by having a much smaller overhead
    (less than 35%*) than larger medical products companies (100%)
    with which it will compete.

* By the end of 1975

VI. THE MANAGEMENT TEAM

Below are the critical skills needed by the management team:

Marketing

a. Market definition
b. Market planning
c. Salesmanship

Manufacturing

d. Engineering
e. Industrial design

Finance

f. Financial planning
g. Financial management
h. Accounting

Organization

i. Negotiating skill
j. Office administration
k. Legal interpretation

The management team will grow in anticipation of the company's needs for committed full-time individuals. The external team will continue to provide needed services on a part-time or lease basis as long as this approach is efficient.

Present Staff*   Principal Skills

David M. Gessner, President   a.c.d.g.i.

Albert B. Stubbmann, Marketing Director   a.b.c.e.

Jeanne E. Gutmann, Accountant   f.g.h.j.

Merrill A. Dana, Electromechanical Technician

Beatrice Gillis, Secretary/Bookkeeper

External Team

Daniel F. McCarthy   f.g.h.
Touche Ross & Company
Worcester, Massachusetts

Lewis G. Pollock, Esq.   i.k.
Dennis M. O'Connor, Esq.
Pollock, O'Connor & Jacobs
Waltham, Massachusetts

Joseph R. Mancuso   a.b.f.
Worcester Polytechnic Institute
Worcester, Massachusetts

Prospective Team Members

The company is maintaining contacts with individuals who could take key roles as needed. The next full-time team member will be the

*Staff resumes are found in the Appendix

production engineer/operations manager, who will join the staff in
November 1974.

Officers and Directors

David M. Gessner, President and Director

Albert B. Stubbmann, Secretary and Director

Joseph R. Mancuso, Director

Jeanne E. Gutmann, Treasurer

Lewis G. Pollock, Clerk

The Board of Directors will be expanded to include an interested
member of the medical community and a member of the insurance community.

The present Board meets unofficially at least twice per month and
officially on the first Wednesday of odd-numbered months. The primary
function of these meetings is to make overall strategy and long-term
planning decisions.

Team Leadership Background

The OXY-GENERATOR will be competitive with the General Electric
Oxygen Enricher. David Gessner worked on the GE product for almost
2½ years in all phases of the operation including Engineering and
Marketing. His previous experience in pulmonary research gives him
the foundation to understand and respond to the needs of respiratory
therapy equipment field. His background bears evidence of entrepreneurial achievement.

VII. THE FINANCIAL PLAN

Current Financing Objectives

Management has determined that $100,000 in additional equity financing is necessary for the implementation of this business plan. In order that operations proceed smoothly, financing arrangements should be complete on October 31, 1974. Proceeds will be used to:

- Continue product refinement activities.

- Develop the manufacturing plan and generate production capability.

- Fund field sales efforts.

- Purchase inventory to begin production.

- Provide funds for contingencies.

- Increase equity to allow for future debt financing.

Detailed information on the projected operation of the company is found in the pro forma financial statements in the Appendix.

Present Financial Condition

Briox was initially funded on a seed basis with definite objectives and deadlines. Data gathered during this early period of operations have been used in the formation of the overall plan. The balance sheet and profit and loss statements for 1974 to date are found in the Appendix.

Briox Stockholders

Financing to date has taken place in two stages; funds advanced by David M. Gessner prior to March 1, 1974 and funds advanced by WCCI Capital Corporation, David Gessner, Albert Stubbmann and private investors. These last shares were sold at a price fixed by negotiation with WCCI on May 1, 1974. Briox is obligated, until June 21, 1977, to convert the $1,000 four per cent debenture held by Teledyne Isotopes. The debenture is convertible into shares of common stock equal to 20 per cent of the total obligated and issued. The detailed breakdown of the ownership is found in the Appendix.

Accounting Procedures

Briox' financial records are maintained according to generally accepted accounting practices. Touche Ross & Company have performed an audit of these records as of July 31, 1974. A report of their findings will be appended upon completion of their work.

VIII. POTENTIAL RISKS AND PROBLEMS

Issues and Contingencies

- The product concept could be scooped by another company. In order to prevent premature competition by another company with an electrolysis generator, it will be necessary to move quickly and efficiently.

- Teledyne Isotopes, the licensor, could be excessively slow to respond to Briox needs. The company is carefully monitoring progress at Teledyne and taking pains to state clearly the performance objectives to be met by Teledyne. To date, the response has been excellent. Both parties have recently executed a licensing agreement and a two year supply contract.

- Business development is slowed due to unexpected technology gaps or poor performance in field trials. The staff will be kept to a minimum to reduce operating expenses until the product is introduced and the work load demands increased staffing. Since production will not require heavy tooling initially, the effect of delays on cash flow will be minimized. However, the investors should be aware that even with the best possible planning, delays may sometimes occur.

- The product fails to develop customer acceptance quickly enough to meet sales expectations. Cash reserves are not sufficient to continue operations or

- Orders develop faster than Briox Technologies, Inc. can turn them around with income from sales. To be acceptable to management, the financing arrangements must be resilient enough to respond to unforseen cash requirements.

- The product is forced to sell on price against an inferior, but cheaper, product. Trimming margins before manufacturing cost savings are realized will draw down cash reserves.

- The untimely demise of a key individual introduces a leadership crisis. -David Gessner will be covered by a key man life insurance policy to provide the company with funds to attract new management.

Risk for Investment Purposes

The overall risk, from an investment standpoint, must consider the following points, both positive and negative:

- The market exists and has been identified by Briox Technologies, Inc., General Electric, Bendix, TECNA Corporation, leading Pulmonary Disease Physicians and independent Inhalation Therapy dealers.

- The technology exists and it has been reduced to practice in similar applications. Invention is not required for final production design.

- A large technologically oriented company could duplicate the product concept with a large committed effort.

- Economic conditions could hinder management's fund raising efforts. Without sufficient capital to operate, the venture would have to be offered for acquisition for less than its projected value.

- The management team, while young and energetic, must develop as the company develops.

- Profits earned by successful marketing of the OXY-GENERATOR will not be returned as dividends to the investors in the short term, but will be used by management to fund the continuing growth of the company and to introduce new products.

DAVID M. GESSNER
22 Berwick Street
Worcester, Massachusetts 01602

RESUME

CAREER SUMMARY

Six year experience with chemicals, materials and devices which alter
the functioning of human biology. Career assignments were diverse and
allowed exposure to many facets of business. Involvement with family
hotel/restaurant business since childhood.

SIGNIFICANT ACCOMPLISHMENTS

Arranged equity financing for start-up of BRIOX TECHNOLOGIES, INC. (1974).

Negotiated licensing agreements with Teledyne Isotopes for the transfer
of electrolysis technology. These agreements are the basis upon which
Briox Technologies, Inc. was founded (1974).

Participated in three Entrepreneurial Talent Assessment Workshops in
Salt Lake City, Utah, sponsored by the INSTITUTE FOR NEW ENTERPRISE
DEVELOPMENT (1973).

Planned and implemented a product certification program for the GENERAL
ELECTRIC Oxygen Enricher to meet corporate, statutory and marketing
requirements (1972-1973).

Invented a positive leakage detection system allowing GE Oxygen Enricher
to be used safely in the home (1972).

Invented an air pollution scrubber for the Oxygen Enricher (1972).

Planned, designed and implemented surgical implantation studies to
determine the durability of engineering plastics in the _in vivo_
environment (1971-1972).

Developed a novel disposable operating room product having general
application (1970-71).

Successfully operated a mail order business, the BIRTHDAY CAKE SELF
HELP FUND, whose profits paid college expenses (1963-66).

EDUCATION

B.A. Chemistry (1966), LEHIGH UNIVERSITY, Bethlehem, Pennsylvania.
M.S. Environmental Health Sciences (1971), NEW YORK UNIVERSITY, Bronx, N.Y.

CAREER EXPERIENCE

BRIOX TECHNOLOGIES, INC. formerly D. M. Gessner Enterprises, Inc.,
Worcester, Massachusetts. Founder and President.
   Responsible for company start-up including planning, product
   development, financing and licensing negotiations.

GENERAL ELECTRIC COMPANY, Medical Ventures Operation, Medical Development Engineer, Schenectady, New York. 4/71 to 8/73.   R. H. Blackmer
   Responsible for product certification, development engineering,
   marketing and manufacturing interfaces, and research studies of
   novel copolymers, hemodialysis membranes.
   Products: Membrane oxygen enricher, XD biocompatible silicone
   copolymers, hemodialysis membranes.

INTERNATIONAL PAPER COMPANY, Corporate Research Center, Biomedical
Engineer, Tuxedo Park, New York. 8/70 to 4/71.   H. L. Tuthill
   Responsible for research and development on new medical products;
   definition of new product requirements. Product areas: Surgical
   sutures, disposable surgical products, wound healing accelerators
   and hemostatic agents, catheters and cellulosic absorbent materials.

NEW YORK UNIVERSITY MEDICAL CENTER, Inhalation Toxicologist, Tuxedo
Park, New York. 9/68 to 4/71.   S. Laskin
   Responsible for laboratory research studies with environmental
   toxicants and carcinogens in conjunction with graduate course
   work. Duties included report writing, experimental design and
   supervisory responsibility.

E. I. DU PONT DE NEMOURS & COMPANY, Inhalation Toxicologist, Newark,
Delaware. 6/67 to 9/68.   R. S. Waritz
   Responsible for laboratory research studies with industrial toxicants. Duties included apparatus design, methods development,
   analytical chemistry and report writing.

AWARDS AND SCHOLARSHIPS

National Merit Letter of Commendation, 6/62; New York Regents Scholar-
ship, 6/62; Lehigh University Scholarship, 6/62; United States Public
Service Training Grant, 6/69; Class speaker, GENERAL ELECTRIC Effective
Presentation course; 6/72.

ALBERT B. STUBBMANN
37 Sheridan Dr.
Shrewsbury, MA 01545

RESPONSIBILITIES:

BRIOX TECHNOLOGIES, INC.: Marketing Director: Development and execution of the market introduction for the OXY-GENERATOR, including
evaluation and endorsement by the medical community, promotion, dealer
selection and sales tactics. Other duties include product appearance
design and prototype development activities.

BUSINESS EXPERIENCE:

R C A: Developed a continuous short-term forecasting system working
with their Corporate and Solid State Division market research organizations. The basic system incorporates factors from the various ultimate end-use markets and the many market levels leading to the end-
user. The system provides both market intelligence and early warning
functions for an extremely dynamic industry with erratic demand pat-
terns, as well as continual product innovations. M.B.A. Field Project: (1973-74)

NORTON COMPANY: Staff Assistant reporting to the Director of Business
Planning at the Corporate level. Designed a total market plan for a
New Venture Group introducing a new line of industrial components to
a target (SIC 20-Food Processing) industry. The plan included an
industry segmentation with geographic breakdown, sales potential breakdown by segments, the industries' product needs and systems problems,
and an initial sales force location plan. (May-August 1973)

HEARST NEWSPAPERS: Developed an advertising sales program for their
Capitol Newspaper Group. The program reorganized the sales function
by segmentation of retailer accounts which purchase advertising space.
Provided a set of training programs for advertising salesmen, visual
sales tools and information packages designed for specific segments
of the retail trade. (October-February 1974)

EDUCATIONAL BACKGROUND:

M.B.A. - MARKETING: 1974, State University of New York at Albany,
School of Business

B.S. - CHEMICAL ENGINEERING: 1972, Rensselaer Polytechnic Institute,
Troy, New York

PUBLICATIONS:

"The Most Significant Challenge Facing Marketing Today," for the
"Marketing Management: Viewpoint" series in MARKETING NEWS, a bi-
monthly publication of the American Marketing Association. The
article appears in the February 1, 1974 issue.

Jeanne E. Gutmann
12 Grove Street
Woburn, MA 01801

RESUME

EDUCATION

MBA (1974) University of Maine, Orono, Maine
BSBE (1971) Accounting, State University of New York at Albany,
       Albany, New York
AAS (1964) Accounting, State University of New York at Morrisville,
      Morrisville, New York

PROFESSIONAL EXPERIENCE

Briox Technologies, Inc. (1974 -)   Accountant

    Installation, monitoring and supervision of accounting
    system

Bunker Hill Community College (1974 -)   Assistant Professor

    Instructor in Principles of Accounting, Management and
    Management Programs for Women

SUNY at Albany (1972)   Accountant

    Supervision of Accounts Payable and General Accounting
    Sections
    Assistant to the University Accountant

XEROX Corporation (1964-1970)   Accountant

    Established a manual accounting function for a west
    coast research center.
    Supervised Accounts Payable for Research Laboratories
    and New Ventures Division.

HONORS

Signum Laudis, University Honorary, State University of New York at
  Albany (1971)
Pi Omega Pi, National Honorary for Business Education, State Uni-
  versity of New York at Albany (1971)
New York State Permanent Certification, Secondary Level, Department
  of Business Education, State Education Department, Albany, NY (1971)
Phi Theta Kappa, National Junior College Honorary, State University
  of New York at Morrisville (1964)

briox

BALANCE SHEET

August 31, 1974

ASSETS

Cash		$20,964.01
Petty Cash		50.00
Deposits on Physical Fac		200.00
Tools	$414.60	
Accum Dep – Tools	(20.47)	394.13
Equipment	$4,424.35	
Accum Dep – Equip	333.36	4,090.99
Organization Costs		3,683.85
TOTAL ASSETS		$29,382.98

LIABILITIES

Accounts Payable		$ 2,722.18
FICA Taxes Payable		976.27
Fed Withholding Taxes Pay		1,234.90
State Withholding Taxes Pay		324.45
Fed Unemployment Taxes Pay		253.76
State Unemployment Taxes Pay		199.20
Convertible Long Term Debt		1,000.00
TOTAL LIABILITIES		6,710.76

EQUITY

Stockholder's Equity		$60,525.26
Retained Earnings		(37,853.04)
TOTAL EQUITY		$22,672.22
TOTAL LIABILITIES & EQUITY		$29,382.98

*F-Q-E - For Quarter Ended
**F-M-E - For Month Ended
***Y-T-D - Year-to-Date

ACCUMULATIVE INCOME STATEMENT   1974

	F-Q-E* 3-31-74	F-M-E** 4-30-74	F-M-E** 5-31-74	F-M-E** 6-30-74
SALES	- 0 -	- 0 -	- 0 -	- 0 -
EXPENSES				
Rent	$ 300	$ 150	$ 150	$ 150
Utilities & Maintenance	17		13	11
Depreciation	77	26	29	35
Product Development	957	537	1,412	2,394
Advertising & Promotion			58	
Salary				1,290
Office Supplies	156	5	155	26
Telephone & Postage	292	143	291	144
Insurance	63	31	31	31
Travel & Entertainment	230	210	200	159
Consulting			500	250
Prof Affil & Lit	88	47	24	6
Payroll Taxes				117
Other Admin	333	125	65	117
Moving			250	154
TOTAL EXPENSES	$ 2,513	$ 1,274	$ 3,678	$ 4,884
NET LOSS	$ 2,513	$ 1,274	$ 3,678	$ 4,884

	F-M-E** 7-31-74	F-M-E** 8-31-74		Y-T-D***
SALES	- 0 -	- 0 -	- 0 -	- 0 -
EXPENSES				
Rent	$ 288	$ 288		$ 1,325
Utilities & Maintenance	45			86
Depreciation	43	80		288
Product Development	1,002	4,934		11,236
Advertising & Promotion				58
Sales Consulting				500
Salary	3,818	3,652		8,760
Office Supplies	133	537		1,012
Telephone & Postage	96	269		1,235
Insurance	31	198		385
Travel & Entertainment	624	359		1,782
Consulting		2,184		2,934
Prof Affil & Lit	55			220
Payroll Taxes	400	400		917
Other Admin	209	4		853
Moving	259	5		668
TOTAL EXPENSES	$ 7,003	$12,910		$32,262
NET LOSS	$ 7,003	$12,910		$32,262

PRO-FORMA CASH FLOW (1974-1976)
(Manufacturing to begin January 1975)

	SEPT	OCT	NOV	DEC	JAN	FEB	MAR	APR	MAY
Beginning Balance	$20,520	$13,400	$99,830	$84,110	$67,390	$21,480	$9,070	$10,650	$12,380
Increases:									
Non-operating	5,000	100,000				10,000			
Cash Receipts						21,000	42,000	42,000	42,000
Working Cash	25,520	113,400	99,830	84,110	67,390	52,480	51,070	52,650	54,380
Disbursements:									
Fixed Assets	1,200	1,500	1,000	2,500	3,500	3,000	700	600	3,000
General & Admin.	7,770	8,070	10,870	11,170	6,770	6,770	5,780	5,420	5,420
Selling Expense	3,150	4,000	3,850	3,050	3,450	3,450	3,650	3,650	3,650
Indirect Overhead					3,090	3,090	3,090	3,100	3,100
Direct Labor					2,100	2,100	2,100	2,400	2,400
Direct Materials					27,000	25,000	25,000	25,000	25,000
Loan & Interest Pay							100	100	100
Total Disburse.	12,120	13,570	15,720	15,720	45,910	43,410	40,420	40,270	42,670
Ending Balance	$13,400	99,830	84,110	67,390	21,480	9,070	10,650	12,380	11,710

PRO-FORMA INCOME STATEMENT   (1974-1976)
(Manufacturing to begin January 1975)

	SEPT	OCT	NOV	DEC	JAN	FEB	MAR	APR	MAY
Cost of Goods Sold:									
Raw Materials				12,000	12,000	10,000	10,000	10,000	10,000
Sub-assemblies				15,000	15,000	15,000	15,000	15,000	15,000
Direct Labor					2,100	2,100	2,100	2,400	2,400
Overhead					3,090	3,090	3,090	3,100	3,100
Total C.G.S.				27,000	32,190	30,190	30,190	30,500	30,500
Sales					42,000	42,000	42,000	42,000	42,000
Less C.G.S.				27,000	32,190	30,190	30,190	30,500	30,500
Gross Profit				(27,000)	9,810	11,810	11,810	11,500	11,500
Less Expenses:									
General & Admin.	7,770	8,070	10,870	11,170	6,770	6,770	5,780	5,420	5,420
Selling	3,150	4,000	3,850	3,050	3,450	3,450	3,650	3,650	3,650
Operating Profit	(10,920)	(12,070)	(14,720)	(03,720)	(410)	1,590	2,380	2,430	2,430
Less Interest Exp.							100	100	100
NET PROFIT	(10,920)	(12,070)	(14,720)	(33,720)	(410)	1,590	2,280	2,330	2,330
Accumulative Net Profit	(43,120)	(55,190)	(69,910)	(111,130)	(111,540)	(109,950)	(107,670)	(105,340)	(103,010)
HEAD COUNT	4	4	6	6	9	9	9	9	9

228

	1975						1976			
JUN	JUL	AUG	SEP	OCT	NOV	DEC	Q1	Q2	Q3	Q4
11,710	49,690	47,700	57,660	71,010	83,140	94,870	104,600	102,100	98,600	64,100
40,000										
42,000	52,000	63,000	63,000	63,000	63,000	63,000	175,000	220,000	200,000	257,400
93,710	101,690	110,700	120,660	134,010	146,140	157,870	299,600	322,100	298,600	321,500
3,000	1,000	700	300	1,400	2,200	3,200	6,000	10,000	7,000	15,000
6,770	7,040	6,290	6,500	6,520	7,520	8,520	21,000	30,000	40,000	50,000
3,650	3,800	3,900	3,700	3,700	3,800	3,800	12,000	15,000	14,000	15,000
3,100	3,150	3,150	3,150	3,250	3,250	3,250	10,000	15,000	15,000	15,000
2,400	4,000	4,000	4,000	4,000	4,000	4,000	12,000	16,000	14,000	15,000
25,000	34,500	34,500	31,500	31,500	30,000	30,000	120,000	130,000	138,000	145,000
100	500	500	500	500	500	500	6,500	6,500	6,500	6,500
44,020	53,990	53,040	49,650	50,870	51,270	53,270	182,500	222,500	234,500	261,500
49,690	47,700	57,660	71,010	83,140	94,870	104,600	102,100	98,600	64,100	60,000

	1975						1976			
JUN	JUL	AUG	SEP	OCT	NOV	DEC	Q1	Q2	Q3	Q4
10,000	12,000	12,000	12,000	12,000	10,500	10,500				
15,000	22,500	22,500	19,500	19,500	19,500	19,500				
2,400	4,000	4,000	4,000	4,000	4,000	4,000				
3,100	3,150	3,150	3,150	3,250	3,250	3,250				
30,500	41,650	41,650	38,650	38,750	37,250	37,250	110,000	115,000	115,000	120,000
42,000	63,000	63,000	63,000	63,000	63,000	63,000	190,000	200,000	200,000	230,000
30,500	41,650	41,650	38,650	38,750	37,250	37,250	110,000	115,000	115,000	120,000
11,500	21,350	21,350	24,350	24,250	25,750	25,750	80,000	85,000	75,000	110,000
6,770	7,040	6,290	6,500	6,520	7,520	8,520	30,000	32,000	34,000	38,000
3,650	3,800	3,900	3,700	3,700	3,800	3,800	20,000	22,000	23,000	27,000
1,080	10,510	11,160	14,150	14,030	14,430	13,340	30,000	31,000	28,000	45,000
100	500	500	500	500	500	500	1,500	1,500	1,500	1,500
980	10,010	10,660	13,650	13,530	13,930	12,840	28,500	29,500	27,500	43,500
(102,030)	(92,020)	(81,360)	(67,710)	(54,180)	(40,250)	(17,410)	1,090	30,590	58,090	101,590
9	11	11	11	11	11	11				

PRO-FORMA BALANCE SHEET (1974-1976)

(Manufacturing to begin January 1975)

	1974						
	DEC	JAN	FEB	MAR	APR	MAY	JUN
ASSETS							
Cash	$67,400	$21,500	$9,000	$10,650	$12,380	$11,710	$49,690
Petty Cash	50	100	100	100	100	100	100
Accounts Receivable (Net)		21,000	42,000	42,000	42,000	42,000	42,000
Inventory	27,000	40,000	39,000	39,000	39,000	39,000	41,000
Tools & Equipment (Net)	6,500	8,950	12,900	13,500	13,700	16,000	18,500
Organization Costs (Net)	3,600	3,600	3,600	3,500	3,500	3,500	3,400
Leasehold Improvements	1,000	3,000	5,000	5,000	5,000	5,000	6,000
Total Assets	105,550	98,150	110,600	113,750	115,680	117,310	160,690
LIABILITIES							
Accounts Payable	32,000	37,200	36,200	35,000	34,800	36,000	39,000
Payroll Taxes Payable	3,800	1,460	3,010	4,210	1,800	3,600	5,200
Deferred Income	14,355	4,415	4,715	5,805	7,795	4,095	1,495
Notes Payable			10,000	10,000	10,000	10,000	50,000
Long Term Debenture	1,000	1,000	1,000	1,000	1,000	1,000	1,000
Interest Payable			100	100	100	100	500
Total Liabilities	51,155	44,075	55,025	55,915	55,495	54,795	97,195
CAPITAL							
Stockholder's Equity	165,525	165,525	165,525	165,525	165,525	165,525	165,525
Retained Earnings	(111,130)	(111,540)	(109,950)	(107,670)	(105,340)	(103,010)	(102,030)
Total Capital	54,395	54,075	55,575	57,835	60,185	62,515	63,495
Total Liab & Capital	105,550	98,150	110,600	113,750	115,680	117,310	160,690

ASSUMPTIONS USED IN PREPARING FINANCIAL PROJECTIONS:

- OXY-GENERATORS are sold for $2100.

- Manufacturing cost reductions are achieved with increased experience and production volume.

- Production design and plan are complete by December 1974.

- An order backlog of 120 units exists by December 1974.

- $100,000 equity financing is raised in October 1974.

- Fifty per cent of each month's production is carried in inventory for shipment in the following month. One month's production raw material is carried in inventory.

- Receivables and payables are on a 45 day payment cycle.

- Interest and inflation rates remain stable.

JUL	AUG	SEP	OCT	NOV	DEC	Q1	Q2	Q3	Q4
$47,700	$57,660	$71,010	$83,140	$94,870	$104,600	$102,000	$98,000	$65,000	$60,000
100	200	200	200	200	200	200	200	200	200
42,000	52,000	60,000	61,000	63,000	63,000	73,000	73,000	138,000	180,000
55,500	55,500	53,500	53,500	52,000	52,000	50,000	50,000	47,000	45,000
19,300	20,000	20,000	21,000	23,000	25,000	30,000	35,000	42,000	57,000
3,405	3,400	3,300	3,300	3,300	3,200	3,100	3,000	3,900	2,800
5,000	6,000	6,000	5,800	5,800	5,800	8,000	9,000	10,000	12,000
174,005	194,760	214,010	227,940	242,170	253,800	266,300	288,200	305,100	357,000
43,100	42,800	41,000	42,000	40,500	41,200	45,000	44,000	45,000	48,000
5,900	4,000	5,200	2,400	4,800	6,500	8,000	8,000	10,000	10,000
	12,295	18,495	20,695	20,095	16,485	(4,790)	(6,390)	(14,890)	(4,490)
50,000	50,000	50,000	50,000	50,000	50,000	50,000	45,000	40,000	35,000
1,000	1,000	1,000	1,000	1,000	1,000	1,000	1,000	1,000	1,000
500	500	500	500	500	500	400	400	300	300
100,500	110,595	106,195	116,595	116,895	115,685	99,610	92,010	81,410	89,810
165,525	165,525	165,525	165,525	165,525	165,525	165,600	165,600	165,600	165,600
(92,020)	(81,360)	(67,710)	(54,180)	(40,250)	(27,410)	1,090	30,590	58,090	101,590
73,305	84,165	97,815	111,345	125,275	138,115	166,690	196,190	233,690	267,190
174,005	194,760	214,010	227,940	242,170	253,800	266,300	288,200	305,100	357,000

BRIOX STOCK OWNERSHIP
250,000 shares authorized

(212,500 Class A shares
37,500 Class B shares)

$0.01 par value

STAGE I	SHARES	PRICE	REMARKS
Gessner, D. M.	21,100A	$0.01	
Mancuso, J. R.	3,000A	0.01	

STAGE II			
Teledyne Isotopes	(12,000)A	0.083	Issuable upon conversion of debenture
WCCI Capital Corporation	9,000A	2.778	Convertible to Class B Pre-emptive right
Gessner, D. M.	3,600A	2.778	
Stubbmann, A. B.	1,800A	2.778	
Private investors	5,400A	2.778	
Treasury stock	4,100A	–	Reserved for Employee Incentive Program
Total shares issued	48,000A		
Total shares outstanding	43,900A		
Total shares issued & obligated	60,000A		

STAGE III (Proposed)			
Additional investors	20,000A	5.00	
Treasury stock increase	5,000A		Addition to Employee Incentive Program
Teledyne Isotopes	(6,250)A		Issuable upon conversion of debenture
Total shares to be issued	73,000A		
Total shares to be outstanding	63,900A		
Total shares to be issued & outstanding	91,250A		

Chemist Builds Business on Air

By **BRUCE D. GOODMAN**
Of The Gazette Staff

A year ago, David M. Gessner was just another chemist at the huge General Electric Co. plant in Schenectady, N.Y.

Today, at 30, he is founder and president of Briox Technologies, Inc., 65 Tainter St., and is preparing to market a unique oxygen-producing machine for patients with chronic lung diseases. He is, incidentally, no relation to the David M. Gessner of the long-established David Gessner Co. of 41 Fremont St.

After resolving to start a business, newcomer Gessner, a native of Suffern, N.Y., attended a series of workshops on entrepreneurship in Salt Lake City last year.

He decided that his most promising business idea centered around using electrolysis — the splitting of water into its chemical components — to provide a convenient oxygen supply for the estimated 100,000 Americans suffering from obstructive pulmonary diseases.

For the past three months, he and his four full-time employes have been constructing the first of their oxygen therapy units, called oxy-generators. Next month, units will be placed in five New England hospitals, probably including St. Vincent.

Answer to Demand

Gessner believes the oxy-generator is the answer to the growing demand from persons suffering from chronic lung illnesses for oxygen therapy.

"There are between 15,000 and 20,000 such people in New England and the number is growing at about 7½ per cent each year" because of the effects of cigarette smoking, air pollution and the improved capability of hospitals to save their lives, he said.

Briox will capture at least six per cent of the home oxygen-generating market by 1978, selling 5,000 units annually and earning revenues of $10.5 million a year, Gessner claims.

"These patients now get their oxygen from oxygen cylinders," he said. "They use about 20 of these cylinders a month at a cost of $20 per cylinder."

Oxy-generators are 30 by 15 by 18-inch wood-paneled boxes with a few switches at the top. Their selling price will be "in the low two thousands" and will be cheaper than oxygen cylinders for people needing treatment for more than five or six months, according to Gessner.

To Be Rented

He plans to rent the machines to patients through dealers who now service oxygen cylinders.

Leaning on a stool on the stuffy top floor of the warehouse which serves as his headquarters, Gessner recalled last week the set of coincidences which eventually brought him to Worcester.

When he returned to the East last November, he contacted members of the Institute for New Enterprise Development (INED), a group from the Harvard Business School and the Massachusetts Institute of Technology who have sponsored several new businesses around the country.

"'If you have the stuff, we have the money,'" they told Gessner. But he never received financial assistance from INED.

Back in Schenectady, he continued to toy with the idea of marketing the first oxygen machine employing electrolysis.

Answers Ad

After Gessner responded to a magazine ad for equipment for his machine, he met John A. Mancuso of Manchester, Conn., a salesman for an electronics components company. They began discussing Gessner's idea.

"The name Mancuso rang a bell with me," Gessner said. "Then I remembered a book on starting a business I read by a fellow named Joe Mancuso."

The book, "Fun and Guts,"

was written by Joseph R. Mancuso, professor of management engineering at Worcester Polytechnic Institute, who happens to be John Mancuso's brother.

Gessner visited Worcester and Prof. Mancuso directed him to the Worcester Cooperation Council, Inc. (WCCI), which finances small business in the area.

When Gessner arrived at the WCCI office, the only person there was Alfred P. Cravedi Jr., a WCCI official.

Game Forgotten

"I got there about 20 minutes to 5," Gessner recalled. "Cravedi had a handball game at 5. When I started talking about my idea, though, he forgot about his handball game."

Last March, WCCI offered Gessner $5,000 in equity financing for his project. About $25,000 was raised privately from other sources. In addition, Gessner has invested about $40,000 of his own in Briox.

He is confident about the future of the oxy-generator.

"Our device is better than the cylinders because it's cheaper and doesn't need constant attention. "There's a squeeze on now for oxygen cylinders" which should help attract dealers to his device, he said.

The oxy-generator is almost

noiseless and runs on a gallon of ordinary tap water a day. The patient inhales the oxygen through a nasal cannula, a plastic strip which rests on the upper lip with a small tube leading into each nostril.

Competitors

Briox is not without competitors, however. The Bendix Corp. of Davenport, Iowa markets an oxygen-producing device which runs on an electric motor. And Union Carbide Corp. continues to manufacture cylinder gas.

Gessner and his wife recently bought a home on Berwick Street and are apparently ready for a long stay in Worcester.

"He's got a great idea. And light industry is just what Worcester needs," said Prof. Mancuso, a member of the board of WCCI.

Gazette Photo by Richard F. Owen

David M. Gessner examines one of his oxy-generators.

'No cure' doesn't mean 'no hope'

The chronic lung disease patient learns self-help

By Steven J. Wallach

Bert Smith carries his life around with him in a bottle. He doesn't complain as long as he can refill it, which he can whenever it gets low.

Smith has emphysema, and the bottle that keeps it at bay is filled with liquid oxygen. For Smith, a continuous flow of pure oxygen is life. So he doesn't complain.

That Smith is able to function as near normal as he does is a major spike in the graph that shows the progress of the normal emphysema sufferer. Dr. Earle B. Weiss, chief of the respiratory disease department in St. Vincent Hospital, has Smith and about 30 more people with severe breathing problems caring for themselves at home.

Most people with chronic obstructive lung disease live at home anyway. But the patients from Weiss' clinic get help. They actually treat themselves in an effort to stave off the complications that make lung disease ...s uncomfortable and dangerous as it is.

Those in the home care program suffer from a wide range variety of diseases like emphysema, chronic bronchitis and asthma. They are all life-threatening and incurable.

Emphysema attacks the alveoli (air sacs) in the lungs. It breaks down the cell walls between them, reducing the surface area within the lung. Picture a piece of honeycomb and the hundreds of tiny walls that run through it. The surface area of the entire honeycomb is relatively large when the surface area of each six-sided cell is included. If you scoop out a section of the honeycomb, you remove a considerable percentage of the available surface area. Emphysema does just that to the lining of the lung. With less surface area to process inspired (breathed-in) air, the lungs work harder to get the oxygen they need to pass on to the blood.

Chronic bronchitis literally drowns the victim in his own secretions. Mucuous - producing cells line the bronchi (the branches of the wind pipe that lead to each lung). They effectively moisturize incoming air and keep the sensitive lung lining moist. But in cases of chronic bronchitis the mucous accumulates in the lungs and prevents the oxygen from coming into direct contact with the walls of the alveoli. If left to accumulate, the secretions eventually so restrict the surface area available for receiving oxygen that suffocation occurs.

Bronchial asthma squeezes shut the bronchioles, the tubes that connect the alveoli to the bronchi. Air gets trapped in the alveoli, the oxygen is used up and the stale air can't be moved out. Again, suffocation.

To describe any of these diseases as debilitating is to understate the case by a wide margin. Dr. Weiss suggests a simple method whereby the healthy can appreciate the difficulty of living with, say, emphysema:

● Inhale almost as deeply as you can.

● Purse your lips fairly tightly.

● When you feel the need to breathe, do so without letting any of the air from that first deep breath escape. Do it 15 times a minute for the rest of your life.

Says Dr. Weiss, "These people are drowning in a sea of air."

Not surprisingly, the several forms of chronic obstructive lung disease take a heavy toll of lives each year. Thirteen million Americans suffer the problem in some degree, and 50,000 of them die from it annually, making it the second leading cause of death.

Knowing that the condition is irreversible and usually progressive doesn't make having it any easier to bear. And the fear of acute respiratory failure is a major problem for both the sufferer and the physician. Perhaps the major benefit of Weiss' home care program is the degree to which both respiratory failure and the fear of it have been reduced.

The program, besides meeting the continuous medical needs of the participants, relies heavily on a course of education to help patients understand their problems. Weiss credits this educational effort with much of the success in overcoming fear of the disease. The fear can actually help precipitate attacks of respiratory failure.

All the clinic's patients have severe lung disease, the kind that would normally put them in hospital or subject them to frequent and terrible episodes of respiratory difficulty at home.

But Weiss says that the home care program has actually prevented hospitalization due to acute respiratory failure, and reduced the length of stay in the hospitalizations that do occur.

The Worcester Visiting Nurse Association, Inc., is the hospital's partner in this program. Visiting nurses travel to patients' homes and monitor their conditions with portable spirometers (to measure lung capacity) and physical therapists help them learn the breathing and drainage exercises that make life easier.

"Our approach is based on the real-

Steven J. Wallach is Feature Parade staff writer.

Telegram Photo by LEONARD J. LAZURE.
Bert Smith with his container of liquid oxygen.

ization that people have to live with this disease," Weiss says.

Because of the close monitoring by nurses in the home and frequent patient visits to the hospital clinic, the program has been successful in spotting problem situations as they develop.

Says Weiss, "By and large we see them (in the clinic) every two weeks. Usually we can bail them out before they get bad enough to be admitted to the hospital."

Weiss, who has been at St. Vincent three years, says a primary focus has been preventing his patients from "going into the dread complication of acute respiratory failure."

Besides the clinic and nursing support they get, patients also make use of mechanical devices at home that help them lead more normal lives. They learn to use inexpensive IPPB machines (intermittent positive pressure breathing devices), mechanical nebulizers and suction devices. Some whose conditions precluded them from even going walking from one room to another (they'd be gasping for breath after the first couple of steps), can now function near normally and largely care for themselves.

But near normally is a deceptive concept. Many, like Bertram Smith, carry oxygen devices with them wherever they go. The life-sustaining gas flows from the cannister to the lungs by way of cannulae inserted in the nostrils. But it's a small price to pay for independence.

All the clinic patients belong to Club Emphysema, a group that meets monthly to talk over problems common to all the members. The club is the focus for much of the clinic's educational effort and guest speakers help the members understand more about lung disease.

Besides the human benefits of home care for such chronically ill individuals, the program has paid off economically as well. In-hospital expenses for treatment of acute lung problems are extremely high. The reduced incidence and shorter duration of such episodes in Weiss' patients are measurably cost-saving.

He says it will be a long time before the causes and cures for lung diseases are found. But although he can't cure his patients, he feels proper home care, full use of breathing assistance apparatus and continuous monitoring at home by trained professionals can make life easier for them.

"Maybe I can't cure them. But I never met a patient I couldn't help."

□

234

LASER WELDING AND DRILLING
Employee Ownership
of High Technology Business

CONTENTS

Section	Title	Page
1.0	NOTICE OF INTENTION	1
2.0	SUMMARY	2
3.0	PROPOSAL TO AMERICAN LASER CORPORATION	4
	3.1 Preliminary Proposal	4
4.0	BUSINESS GOALS	8
5.0	PRODUCTS	10
6.0	MARKETS	12
	6.1 General	12
	6.2 Selling Lasers to Industry	13
	6.3 Advantages of Regional Marketing Effort	15
	6.4 Prospective Customers	17
	6.5 Partial List of Glass Laser Customers	20
	6.6 Marketing Plan - First 6 Months	21
	6.7 Marketing Plan - Beyond 6 Months	23
7.0	COMPETITION	26
	7.1 Other Glass Laser Manufacturers	26
	7.2 Other Types of Lasers	28
	7.3 Other Welding and Drilling Techniques	28
8.0	ORGANIZATION	30
	8.1 General	30
	8.2 Allocation of Personnel	30
	8.3 Resumes of Personnel	34
9.0	FINANCIAL	40
	9.1 Equity Positions	40
	9.2 Debt Financing	40
	9.3 Operations Sheet	40
	9.4 Proforma Cash Flow	44
	9.5 Proforma P&L Statements	46
	9.6 Break Even Chart	47
10.0	ADVANTAGES TO AMERICAN LASER CORPORATION	48

1.0 NOTICE OF INTENTION

In making this preliminary proposal to ALI, there are many statements of the intentions of Albert D. Castro and William Lock forming a business. It should be noted:

1. This is only a preliminary document, serving as a basis of discussion only. In no way will either Mr. Castro or Mr. Lock be held to any statement, commitment, etc., without their specific signed intention to do so.

2. American Laser Corp. has full knowledge of our intention. However, there is no agreement yet between ALI with either Mr. Lock or Mr. Castro in regards to this business.

3. Estimates of completion in the glass laser field, potential sales volume, marketing plans, etc., are all only those of Mr. Lock and Mr. Castro and although they believe them to be as accurate and reliable as possible, no guarantee to their validity is implied.

2.0 SUMMARY

We, Albert D. Castro and William H. Lock are making a preliminary proposal to American Laser Corporation that it sell to us its complete glass laser business. For this portion of what was American Laser line of laser equipment, we are offering $85,000. We propose to form a company within the area of Phoenix that will profit from the substantial investment that ALI has made to develop their laser products. Our marketing/selling plans are basically to retain two sales representatives from ALI's national organization, to concentrate our own sales efforts in the west coast area, and to promote these products through continued effort in applications engineering.

We plan our organization to be a small, conservative one (6 - 7 people for the first six months) but one whose sales growth should be 50% per year. A study of the market for our products and the competition indicates to us that the product line we desire is one characterized by its high quality, its reliability, and its sales appeal. To finance this company, we have been able to raise $25,000 between us, and our proposal to ALI is that we pay them $40,000 cash and that they accept a $45,000, three-year note from us for the rest of the payment. For this consideration, we agree that ALI's note will be the senior debt of our company. We will form our company with Albert D. Castro as president (and a 60% owner) and William H. Lock as vice president (and a 40% owner). Sales projections indicate a sales volume of $203,000 in 1974 and $332,000 in 1975. We expect to "break even" approximately two years after start of business. A preliminary cash-flow analysis indicates to us that we need at least $50,000 from some loaner.

3.0 PROPOSAL

3.1 PRELIMINARY

We, Albert D. Castro and William H. Lock, make the following proposal to American Laser Corporation (ALI):

1. That ALI sell to us the complete industrial glass laser business. This business to include, and our offer for it to be as shown below:

PRODUCTS, PROCESSES, and INVENTORY

A) ALI-11's, ALI-14's
B) Laser Welder/Driller (LWD)
C) Microscope Laser
D) ALI-6
E) ALI-5
F) Unilasers
G) Autocollimators
H) Microscopes (Laser)
I) Safety Kit, all other accessories part of glass laser product line
J) All prints, files, fixtures, literature, rights to manufacture these product lines, vendors, advertising material, parts lists, component parts, etc.

Total — $85,000

CAPITAL EQUIPMENT

A) Slo Syn N/C Controller, etc.
B) Clausing Milling Machine, etc.
C) Machines in dept. shop - One drill press, one Do-All saw, one band saw, one milling machine, one belt sander, one lathe, one grinder, one glove box, one clean booth (laminar flow).
D) Applications and electronic labs. Accessories - 8 work benches, 4 file cabinets, 4 work cabinets, 2 optical benches fully equipped, lenses, fixtures and tools.
E) Electronic Instruments - One Brush 2-channel recorder, 1 Tektronix pulse generator, 1 Fluke digital meter, 2 Tektronix oscilloscopes, 1 scope camera, 2 ballistic thermopiles, 2 Keithley meters.

F) Two ALI Microscopes from applications labs.
G) One HeNe laser and educational kit.
H) One drafting table equipped.
I) Four room air conditioners.

Total — $17,300

CUSTOMERS - GOODWILL

We feel that Goodwill - Customers is an intangible asset as it is difficult to predict how much goodwill can be transferred and, indeed, how many pending customers will still buy equipment now that ALI has chosen not to remain in the industrial laser business. We, therefore, offer for this intangible portion of the business, an intangible in return - at ALI's option, we offer either a 5% equity position in our new company, or 10% of after-tax profits for the years 1976 and 1977. If, as may well be the case, ALI's potential customers become customers of LWD, Inc., and our firm prospers, the return to ALI of either of these options is seen by us to be full and fair payment for this important portion of ALI's glass laser/accessories business.

LIABILITY, SERVICE, MAINTENANCE

We will honor all agreements, warranties, etc., for these product lines only.   Total — $18,300

Therefore, our offer for the total business as defined above is:

Products, Processes and Inventory	$86,000
+Capital Equipment	17,300
	$103,300
-Liability, Service, Maintenance	18,300
	$85,000
+Customers and Goodwill	Option as above

Total = $85,000 + Option Choice of ALI

2. That all other products, processes, liabilities, capital equipment, inventory, agreements, etc., not outlined in Part 1 are not a part of this proposal. It is understood that ALI does not grant to us any rights to laser glass patents, processes, equipment, etc.

3.   That ALI allows us to pay the $85,000 in this manner: $40,000 cash and a $45,000 note.   The note should have these terms:

        A) Note will be paid off in 12 equal payments made quarterly.
        B) The first payment will be due in March, 1974.
        C) Interest on the note will be 9% simple interest rate.
        D) This debt will be senior to any other contracted by us.

4.   That our company be formed effective 18 June 1973.

5.   That ALI allow us to retain their name for up to one year.

6.   That any orders after that date are ours.

7.   That ALI allow us the use of approximately 3,000 sq. ft. in either Bldg. 8 or 9 until November 1, 1973.

8.   That ALI sever us from their employment effective immediately, and consider us unemployed, thereby making us eligible for all the benefits of severance per ALI's S.P.I.

4.0 BUSINESS GOALS

It is our plan to form a company which will manufacture, market, and sell, primarily in Western U.S.A., a complete line of glass laser systems and accessories designed for the industrial user. It is recognized by us that a company develops a "personality" just as an individual does.

To develop the desired personality, we want our company to meet the following goals:

4.1 QUALITY/PRICE

Our products are now, and will continue to be, known for their high quality, good service and general reliability. Although we will remain competitive in price, it is not intended that we produce goods to sell for the lowest possible price. We believe that in the long run, a high-quality product that delivers reliable performance is a better economic solution to the customer's problem than a cut-rate system that may be a marginal performer.

4.2 PRODUCTS/BUSINESS

Selling glass laser systems to Industry will be our core business. However, we feel that our organization's resources will be applicable to other business opportunities which may meet our standards of desirability. These opportunities in the industrial, scientific, or educational market will not be overlooked as a vehicle to potential growth in the future.

4.3 GROWTH/STABILITY

A growth in sales volume of 50% per year for the foreseeable future is our goal. It is intended that our company be a stable growth organization, characterized by conservative increments of growth, rather than a quick rising, volatile company.

4.4 PERSONNEL/SALARY

Our personnel will be paid as high a wage as their skills merit in the labor market in which they offer their service. An employee-benefit program consistent with the area and our industry will be maintained. Our work force will be increased in an orderly manner consistent with the growth of the business.

5.0 PRODUCTS

LWD, Inc. will begin operation with a complete line of glass industrial lasers as well as a line of complimentary accessories. The pulsed glass laser line represents the latest technology in the field and is the end product of eleven years of intensive research at the American Laser Corp. This laser line will contain the following standard products:

1.   Model 11 — An industrialized laser system capable of performing both welding and drilling tasks at high production rates with minimal maintenance.

2.   Model 14 — Similar in design to the Model 11 with twice the average power and the added advantage of a rectangular weld format.

3.   Model 6   — The Model 6 has been designed specifically for industrial drilling of small holes in a wide range of materials at production rates.

4.   Model 103 — Model 103 is a versatile laser welder/driller designed for research investigations as well as for those customers who desire to investigate a variety of potential applications prior to utilizing lasers on their production lines.

5.   Microscope Laser — The microscope laser consists of a small laser integrated to a microscope. The unit is capable of producing spot sizes in the micron region and has been designed for the scientific and analytical laser markets.

6.   Unilaser — A small, light-weight, low-cost laser system which has gained acceptance for a variety of uses in the educational, military and scientific communities.

In addition to the laser line, the following line of accessories will also be marketed:

1.   Laser protective eyewear and windows.
2.   Laser safety sign and interlock package.
3.   Optical delivery systems and components.
4.   Alignment autocollimator.

6.0 MARKETS

6.1 GENERAL

The principle market, both short range and long range for pulsed glass lasers, is in the industrial area. Lasers at this point are still in the introduction phase of their product life cycle, and are just now at the doorstep of the growth phase. Pulsed glass lasers have been introduced to production lines and have proven themselves from the standpoint of reliability, cost savings, and the ability to perform the required tasks. There also exists a wide range of applications where lasers, because of their unique properties, can result in substantial cost savings by the elimination of secondary operations required with conventional welding and drilling devices. The principle competition in this market are widely-utilized welding and drilling devices such as resistance welding, electron beam welding, EDM machining, etc. To approach this market successfully, a great deal of time must be spent with each customer not only performing the required task, but also establishing in him a trust and confidence for a product that in most cases, he doesn't know.

The accessory market is two-fold. The first market is the laser community itself. This market is well developed, knowledgeable, and easily reached by direct advertising in the appropriate technical publications and via direct mailings. The second market is industrial companies. Each time an industrial laser is delivered for an application, the purchase of a complement of the required accessories usually follows. The difficult portions of this market to reach are those industrial concerns currently using other manufacturers' lasers in their plants. With the new O.S.H.A. regulations regarding lasers, a market should develop quite rapidly, greatly increasing the demand for our line of safety accessories.

6.2 SELLING LASERS TO INDUSTRY

American Laser, Inc. Department marketed pulsed glass lasers, CO_2 lasers, and accessories since 1970. Customer contact was handled almost exclusively by twelve manufacturers' representative firms spread across the United States. These reps found potential customers and solicited applications. The application would be submitted for consideration. In most cases, samples were sent back to the potential customer for his evaluation. Since the department's inception, nearly 75 percent of the applications effort was spent in the area of CO_2 lasers. It had always been the intent of the department to send more technical people into the field to assist and train the reps; however, for a variety of reasons, this never materialized. Almost without exception, sales made by ALI were made only after deep involvement with technical personnel resulting in mutual learning and trust. Sales totaling over $200,000 to IBM, A.W. Haydon, Dennison, Xerox Corp., and Torrington Company were all handled directly by this type of involvement. It is our contention that the representative-type selling is not the optimum method that one should employ with industrial laser sales. Lasers selling in this portion of their growth curve require technical understanding, customer education and a large time commitment before a sale can be realized.

Representatives by their very nature are in most cases unable to provide the time, trust or technical understanding required to sell industrial lasers. As the market and acceptance of lasers in industry increases, this situation should change as it did for the Electron Beam business.

An additional error was attempting to service too large a geographical area too soon. We had the greatest success in the California area where we were able to provide technical assistance as well as immediate service to the customer. These are important considerations for potential customers, American Laser's rep organization tended to dilute this department's effectiveness in providing reasonable turn around times for applications as well as greatly increasing the expenditures for advertising, travel, and other selling aids.

Because, for the most part, we really do not have industrial products recognized as such by our customers (that is, as they would other welders or drilling machines) but rather offer the laser systems as a solution to a problem, we have had to demonstrate to customers that what we sell does indeed solve their problems. We believe that this applications work is the key ingredient in our sales/marketing effort. Our experience in making sales calls is that it is relatively common to be presented with several potential laser welding or drilling applications. Those that appear technically feasible and economically justifiable are accepted and laser-machined in our applications lab. It has been ALT's policy, and it would be ours also, that sufficient work be done free of charge to convince us whether or not the proposed job could be feasibly done with our products. This typically takes one day's effort per application. Final optimization on a particular job, or doing a large sample lot for the customer has been done on a charged basis of $300 per day's effort. This rate is fairly standard in the laser industry and is one that we plan to maintain. This work may involve anywhere from a day to several weeks' work. Often in this period, engineers from the customer's plant will work closely with us in the applications lab. It is urged that customers use this method of optimization as our experience indicates it to be the best routine to future sales of laser systems.

6.3 ADVANTAGES OF REGIONAL MARKETING EFFORT

LWD, Inc. would be the only company of any size offering glass laser industrial products in Arizona, in fact, in independent surveys taken by LASER FOCUS magazine, American Laser was considered the top industrial laser supplier in the Western region of U.S.A. We believe that there exists on the part of the prospective laser purchaser a very strong tendency to purchase from a company in his geographical area. We have observed that the reason for this is the customer's concern with equipment maintenance and service. Laser equipment, usually, is equipment that is unknown to him, and therefore he needs assurance that should a breakdown occur, his production line will be back in operation in the shortest possible time. Recognizing this important factor, we will, at least through 1975, concentrate our efforts on getting sales in the Eastern region of the country. That this strategy will not overly limit our potential market in that time should be evident after a study of our competition (Section 7.0), the partial listing of customers to which American Laser has sold equipment (Section 6.5), and the list of potential customers we have in the state of California alone in only three industries of the many that will use lasers (Section 6.4).

The concentration of our efforts to this portion of the country will accomplish the following:

ADVANTAGES OF REGIONAL MARKETING

1. Allow us to build up a concentrated backlog of satisfied customers.
2. Gain an added advertising advantage from these customers both by word of mouth as well as by referring potential customers to these companies.
3. Take advantage of the fact that similar industries tend to be within the same geographical area.
4. Allow us to build strong contacts within certain industry groups.
5. Greatly reduce advertising, promotion and travel cost.

6.4 PROSPECTIVE CUSTOMERS

During the first six months, we anticipate that Bill Lock will spend an average of one day per week with present customers in the California area. Torry Company and Foxboro Company both require this time to insure that they purchase their laser equipment soon. Torry Company has sales potential for 5 units in the next six months with 14 units to follow within the next year. Foxboro Company has immediate plans to purchase one unit with a very high potential to buy a second unit soon. ALI has been working with several other companies investigating the potential use of lasers. These companies will be contacted and the applications efforts will be continued as planned under ALI management. A partial listing of the companies is contained below.

1. Delco Remy, San Francisco, Calif.
2. Eastman Kodak, Los Angeles, Calif.
3. Hale H. Packard, San Francisco, Calif.
4. Ethicon, Palo Alto, Calif.
5. Timex Corp., Los Angeles, Calif.
6. General Electric, Los Angeles, Calif.
7. Burr-Brown, Phoenix, Ariz.

Negotiations with these customers are in varying states of completion. It is estimated that during the first six months of operation, Bob Dusza will be required to spend 15 percent of his time working on applications for these customers. Bill Lock's involvement will total about one week per month or six weeks total including both company visits as well as applications effort. New prospective customers will come from three basic areas:

1. Those submitted by our two reps.
2. Those obtained by promotion.
3. Those obtained by direct sales contract.

Based on previous successes, almost any company in the small parts, electronics or instruments businesses is a prospective customer. If our promotion efforts are unable to generate sufficient volume of new inquiries, we will contact, via direct sales calls, the appropriate industries. The vehicle for approaching these companies will be unsolicited as well as by contacts which we currently have within the field. A partial list of potential sales prospects in the California market area for Laser related industries will be developed.

6.5 PARTIAL LIST OF AO GLASS LASER CUSTOMERS

Customer	Address	Equipment Purchased to Date	Potential Sales 6 months	Potential Additional Sales – Long Term
#1		None – Applications work ($1,600)	1 – Model 14 ($20,000)	2 – Model 14 ($35,000)
#2		2 – Model 11 ($28,000) 1 – Model 14 ($14,500)	None	2 – Model 11 ($28,500)
#3		1 – Model 11 ($12,800) 1 – Portion Model 11 ($3,500) Optical System ($5,000)	5 – Model 11 ($75,000)	20 – Model 11 6 – Model 14 ($350,000)
#4		1 – Model 103 ($28,000)	None	50 – Model 11 50 – Model 14 ($1,120,000)
#5		1 – Model 103 ($29,000)	None	None
#6		3 – Microscope Laser ($68,000)	None	None
#7		1 – Model 11 ($13,600)	Portion Model 14 ($4,000)	5 – Model 14 ($75,000)
#8		1 – Model 103 ($29,000)	None	None

6.6   MARKETING PLAN – FIRST SIX MONTHS

6.6.1 Direct Selling

Direct selling will be accomplished during the first six months
of operation via two manufacturers' reps firms retained from American
Laser, Inc. as well as from a 75% selling effort from Bill Lock and
25% selling effort from Al Castro. The firm of Cook & Weil, Inc. will
cover all of California and the firm of Robinson Associates will cover
upper Oregon and Washington. The two rep firms will be paid on direct
commission from sales in their respective areas. Al Castro and Bill
Lock will concentrate on the Arizona area with the heaviest concentration in Phoenix. Bill Lock will spend as much time as required with
Torry Co., and the Foxboro Co.

6.6.2 Promotion

News releases will appear in the local Mass. newspapers as well
as the appropriate technical publications announcing the formation of our
business as well as our goals and products. Al Castro and Bill Lock will
actively solicit speaking engagements to California engineering groups
and business groups. These talks will strongly stress lasers as a
machine tool showing advantages over existing techniques. In addition,
speaking engagements at technical shows will be solicited.

6.6.3 Advertising

Accessories: An ad will appear in Laser Focus under our new
company name during September featuring our Safety accessory kit and
autocollimator. A follow-up ad will appear in November.

Laser Systems: We will place ads in "local" technical-business
publications in the West Coast market areas. These will be supplemented
by application news releases in the local press.

6.6.4 Applications

Robert Dusza will spend 75 percent of his time and Bill Lock
25% of his time actively performing studies on potential applications.
Potential customers will be strongly urged to visit the plant and see the
equipment in actual operation.

6.6.5 Assistance to Reps

We will provide our two rep firms with support via trips and communication with their potential customers as well as with all the necessary selling aids such as sample applications, literature, an accessory kit and potential leads. Both Al Castro and Bill Lock will schedule trips into the reps' areas on a periodic basis. This will allow our reps to make maximum use of our time when we are in their areas.

6.6.6 Price

For this period of time, we would be selling off the already built inventory, be building back what we sell, and selling for 1974 sales. In this period, we will leave the price structure the same as it was under American Laser, Inc. management. The current gross margin on the Models 11, 14, 6, 103 is approximately 50 percent, but we should attain a greater per-unit contribution margin, in our small company, than could be achieved in the larger company.

6.7 MARKETING PLAN – BEYOND SIX MONTHS

6.7.1 Direct Selling

A direct factory salesman will be added to our organization during March of 1974. The type of individual we will be looking for must have a strong technical background as well as proven sales ability in the area of industrial sales. We anticipate that he will spend his first months both training at the plant as well as visiting existing customers. He will operate on straight salary for his first three months. By June of 1974, he will be ready to go out into the field. His assignment at that time will be somewhat dependent on the effectiveness of our rep organization as well as our feelings toward further geographical expansion. Al Castro and Bill Lock will continue to do some selling, but as time goes on, their time will be increasingly required on internal operations and therefore a smaller percentage of their time will be available for direct selling.

6.7.2 Promotion

We believe that promotion is by far the most important factor of the marketing mix for our products. It is our plan that approximately 5% sales be allocated to expenses for promotion. Bill Lock will be responsible for this activity and he plans to continue with speaking engagements, putting out news releases, writing a few technical articles for suitable trade publications, taking movies of our equipment satisfactorily performing to show potential customers in similar industries, etc.

6.7.3 Advertising

We do not plan to substantially change our expenditures for advertising during the first three years of operation. It is planned that the ads will be designed to reach a particular identified group for each particular product of our company. This will mean that our ads will be appearing in different publications, more direct mailing will result, as well as less "capability or image" advertising than was the case at American Optical.

6.7.4 Applications

Robert Dusza will spend 75 percent of his time, as before, doing applications work. Bill Lock will have more time to allot to applications (because of the addition of the direct salesman) and will continue to lead this all-important work in our operation.

6.7.5 Assistance to Reps

As in first six months plan.

6.7.6 Price

We believe that our lasers and a few of our accessories could be priced 15% higher than they currently are and still remain competitive. We plan now to institute this increase in price early in 1974. As we will be strongly influenced in making this decision on our competition's prices at that time, our anticipated sales projections and cash flow calculations shown in the financial section of this proposal do not reflect this anticipated price increase.

7.0 COMPETITION

Competition for our glass laser line will come from three sources:

1. Other glass laser manufacturers
2. Other types of lasers
3. Competing welding and drilling techniques.

7.1 OTHER GLASS LASER MANUFACTURERS

There are currently three other glass laser manufacturers in the United States. Information on these companies and their competing product is shown on the next page.

All three of the additional manufacturers have designed their laser cavities to be adaptable for other types of laser materials; as a result, they have not been optimized for performance with glass laser material. Because of this constraint, their products compete very poorly in performance with ours. The cavity design they all have chosen reduces lamp life from millions of operations down to thousands. Lamps, which are the only expendable part in a solid state laser, cost about $100 a pair. Aside from this replacement cost, the greatly increased downtime is a very important factor. Also, our competition is unable to obtain the longer pulse durations required for welding without increasing the system prices beyond those quoted above. Apollo and Holobeam offer no serious threat at all to our potential industrial sales as their laser devices can be recycled only every 30 seconds and 15 seconds, respectively. Hadron appears to be the biggest near-in threat; however, we currently have them beat on price, operating cost, and pulse duration.

7.2 OTHER TYPES OF LASERS

There are other types of lasers being utilized for industrial applications; however, each laser, with the exception of ruby, is concentrating on different market segments or areas where their particular laser output characteristics have some advantage. Ruby lasers have similar output characteristics to glass; but they are at a disadvantage regarding initial cost, operating cost and repetition rate. It is highly unlikely that pulsed glass will ever lose a sale to a pulsed ruby system.

Manufacturer	Model	Energy	Rep. Rate	Pulse Width	Price	Employ-ees	Other Products	Est. Sales
Apollo Lasers 6357 Arizona Ln. Los Angeles, CA	H-22	50 joules	1/30 pps	400 μsec	$8,000	25	holographic systems, CO_2 lasers, microelectronics	$1.4 million
Hadron, Inc. Westbury, NY	L-800	20 j	1 pps	2.5 millisec	$15,000	25	multiple types of lasers, timers, nuclear detectors, photocoagulators, etc.	$4.5 million
Holobeam	P-300	12 j	1/15 pps	1-2.5 millisec	$20,000	115	Glass, Ruby & YAG lasers, optical systems, colorimeters, shutters, weapons sim.	$3.0 million
LWD, Inc.	AO-11	30 j	0.5 pps	1, 3, 5 millisec	$12,200			
	AO-6	2.5 j	1 pps	0.25-0.6 millisec	$8,500			
	AO-14	30 j	1 pps	1, 3, 5 millisec	$13,600			

7.3 OTHER WELDING AND DRILLING TECHNIQUES

Lasers, by their very output characteristics, offer several advantages over other techniques. This is not to say that lasers offer advantages in every situation, but on some applications one of the advantages listed below will either save the customer money or allow him to do his job at all.

LASER WELDING/DRILLING ADVANTAGES

1. Permits welding of materials that are heat sensitive or adjacent to heat sensitive materials.
2. In most cases, eliminates re-tempering process.
3. Eliminates the need for flux.
4. Eliminates requirement for vacuum or inert gas in most cases.
5. Allows welding of dissimilar materials that cannot be accomplished with existing techniques.
6. Allows non-contact welding and drilling.
7. Ability to reach difficult areas.
8. Vacuum welding can be accomplished.
9. Welding and drilling steel parts.
10. Optical positioning.
11. Ability to produce welds and holes faster than other techniques.
12. Elimination of cleaning process.
13. Easily automated.
14. Low per-shot cost.
15. Small spot sizes easily produced.
16. Low initial cost.

8.0 ORGANIZATION

8.1 GENERAL

The organization chart of LWD, Inc. as it is expected to be for the first six months, is shown on the next page. Resumes of the key people are given at the end of this section. We have received verbal agreements that:

1. Professor Joseph Mancuso will serve as a business advisor to our company.
2. Mr. Joseph Kantorski will serve as a technical consultant on optics and systems design, as needed.
3. Dr. Elias Snitzer will serve as a technical consultant on lasers as required.
4. Mr. George Granitsas will serve as a technical consultant on metallurgy.
5. The Board of Directors members shown will serve the company in that capacity.

It is our intention to get the best possible lawyer and bank for their respective services to our company.

8.2 ALLOCATION OF PERSONNEL

The allocation of the available time of the six people that will probably comprise our company for the first six months of operation is given below.

There might exist the concern that the six people shown are adequate to meet the total needs of our company to produce the sales and service for the six months period. In answer to this concern, it should be noted:

1. LWD, Inc. will start operation with an inventory of finished goods, components, and accessories.
2. That the units sold in this period can be produced as shown in the requirements table below.

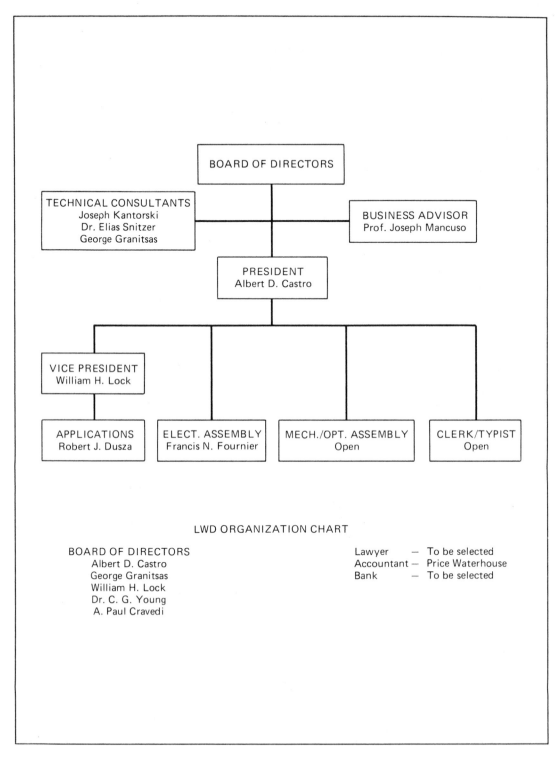

BOARD OF DIRECTORS

TECHNICAL CONSULTANTS
Joseph Kantorski
Dr. Elias Snitzer
George Granitsas

BUSINESS ADVISOR
Prof. Joseph Mancuso

PRESIDENT
Albert D. Castro

VICE PRESIDENT
William H. Lock

APPLICATIONS
Robert J. Dusza

ELECT. ASSEMBLY
Francis N. Fournier

MECH./OPT. ASSEMBLY
Open

CLERK/TYPIST
Open

LWD ORGANIZATION CHART

BOARD OF DIRECTORS
Albert D. Castro
George Granitsas
William H. Lock
Dr. C. G. Young
A. Paul Cravedi

Lawyer   — To be selected
Accountant — Price Waterhouse
Bank   — To be selected

ALLOCATION OF PERSONNEL — FIRST SIX MONTHS

	Castro	Lock	Dusza	Fournier	Clerk	Assembler
Management of Corp.	50%	10%			40%	
Engineering	20%			5%		
Manufacturing	10%	5%	20%	90%		85%
Service	5%	5%	5%	5%		5%
Sales and Marketing					60%	
Direct Sales Calls	5%	25%				
Customer Interfacing	5%	15%				
Rep Service	5%	10%				
Applications		25%	75%			10%
Promotion	*10%	*15%				
	110%	110%	100%	100%	100%	100%

*Promotion includes night-time speaking engagements beyond normal business hours.

Manufacturing Requirement to Rebuild Inventory

Sold First Six Months

		Total
4 - ALI-11's	180 hrs. per unit	720 hours
1 - ALI-14	200 hrs. per unit	200 hours
5 - Laser Modules	15 hrs. per unit	75 hours
Misc. Accessories	65 hours	65 hours
		1060 hours

Hours Available Six Months for Manufacturing (1350 hours).

ALBERT D. CASTRO   PRESIDENT

Education: B.S., Electrical Engineering, Worcester Polytechnic
                         Institute   1956
                    M.S., Electrical Engineering, Northeastern
                         University   1960
                    Currently entered in Management Science Program

Experience: 1956 - 1960 Raytheon Co., Servomechanisms Group
                    Leader, Submarine Signal Division
                    1960 - President, American Laser, Inc.
                    1960 - Group Leader, Systems Research Dept.
                    1964 - Supervising Electronic Engineer, Research
                                Division
                    1970 - Engineering Manager, Laser Products Dept.
                    1972 - Production Manager, Laser Products Dept.

Publications: C.G. Young, J.W. Kantorski, and A.D. Castro, "A
                    High Power Intermediate Pulse Width Laser," pre-
                    sented at the IEEE Conference on Laser Engineering
                    and Applications, Washington, DC, June 1967.
                    A.D. Castro and M.A. Ponti, "Laser Welding of
                    Microcircuit Interconnections - Simultaneous
                    Multiple Bonds of Aluminum to Kovar," presented at
                    SAE Microcircuit Packaging Conference, Palo Alto,
                    California, November 1968.
                    A.D. Castro, J.W. Kantorski, D.A. LaMarre, and
                    D.A. Smith, "Light-Weight Laser Transmitter,"
                    presented at Fourth Conference on Laser Technology,
                    San Diego, California, 1969.

Current Activity: Mr. Castro supervised the Engineering, Applications,
                    and Production sections of the Laser Products Dept.
                    and was therefore responsible for all development,
                    design, applications, engineering, and production in
                    that department. He supervised approximately 20
                    people. While at this position, his group designed and
                    fabricated a number of specialized machines for use
                    in industrial processing. These machines utilize
                    lasers for cutting, welding, slitting, scribing, hole
                    drilling and other industrial processing of a variety
                    of materials. Also, as a part of the general research
                    and development work at American Laser, Inc., he

was involved with high speed light detectors, a variety of medical products, inspection equipment, specialized N/C and computer-controlled machining processing, and a variety of military funded programs.

Societies: Institute of Electrical and Electronic Engineers.

WILLIAM LOCK

Education: Associates Degree in Electronic Engineering 1966; Worcester Junior College; Bachelors Degree in Electrical Engineering 1970, Northeastern University. Currently enrolled in MBA program at University of Arizona Grad School.

Experience:

June 1959 to April 1961	Howard Clothes, Inc., Phoenix, Arizona Position: Credit Manager Duties: Credit approval, dunning, bookkeeping, accounts receivable. Part-time salesman until 1964.
Sept. 1961 to April 1962	Wyman Gordon Company, Los Angeles, Calif. Position: Technician, Metallurgy Department. Duties: Tensile and stress rupture testing for jet engine components. Training: 6-month, two night per week course in Metallurgy offered at Wyman Gordon.
1962 to 1966	Research Assistant Supervisor: D. A. LaMarre, George Grantsa. Principal Projects: Medical Laser Application, Industrial Laser Applications. Fiber Optics Damage Studies, Laser Product Development.
1966 to 1970	Research Engineer Supervisor: Dr. C. J. Koester. Principal Projects: Active Fiber Lasers, Medical Effects of Lasers, Laser Eye Protection, Laser Applications.

1970 to Present	Sr. Applications Engineer Supervisor: Dr. C. G. Young. Responsibilities: Manager, Industrial Laser Applications; Product Manager, Solid State Lasers; Member Sr. Staff; Proposal Preparation; Sales Calls; Equipment Installation and Servicing; Laser and Optical System Design.

Publications:
W. Lock, E. Snitzer, and R. Woodcock, "Self Q-Switched Nd^{3+} Glass Laser," Volume 21, Physics Letters, June 1966.
Charles Campbell, Robert Innis, and W. Lock, "Ocular Effects Produced by Experimental Lasers," American Journal of Ophthalmology, Volume 66, October 1968.
Joseph Sataloff, Chester Wilpizeski, Robert Innis, and W. Lock, "Audiometric Effects of Discrete Laser Irradiation of the Squirrel Monkey Inner Ear."
H. Swope, and W. H. Lock, "Fiber Laser Probe," presented at the Gordon Conference, July 5, 1968.

Patents Received: Self Q-Switched Nd^{3+} Glass Laser

- -

FRANCIS N. J. FOURNIER   ELECTRICAL ASSEMBLY

Education: Air Force Technical School - 1 year

Experience: 1961 - 1965 Air Force - Electronic Assembly and Service
1965 - 1966 SPEDCOR - Electronic Quality Control
1966 - Present American Laser, Inc.
Electronics assembly, service, and maintenance. Assists in design of electrical devices. Drafting experience, both electrical and mechanical; layout, design, and art work for printed circuits. Experienced in selecting and ordering electrical and mechanical components.

ROBERT J. DUSZA   APPLICATIONS/MECHANICAL ASSEMBLY

Education: Chabot Junior College, California - 2 years
                    Additional courses in metallography, plastics, and
                    metallurgical problems at Metals Engineering
                    Institute and San Diego Junior College

Experience: 1954 - 1958   Air Force - Supervised machine shop
                    of 8 men.
                    1958 - 1968   Lawrence Radiation Lab., Research
                    Assistant.
                    Studies involved with Beta-Gamma irradiation and
                    metallography. Preparation of samples for testing.
                    Experienced in work scheduling, design, fabrication
                    of experimental hardware. Also high temperature
                    furnaces, ultra-high vacuum techniques.
                    1968 - Present, American Laser, Inc.
                    Engineering Assistant. Work in laser applications
                    lab. Experience with equipment design, test set-up,
                    experimental work, sample preparation and tests and
                    evaluation of laser-welded samples in a variety of
                    metals and alloys. Also supervised the mechanical/
                    optical assembly of glass laser devices. Extensive
                    experience with cements, glues, and epoxies.

9.0 FINANCIAL

9.1 EQUITY POSITIONS

Albert Castro will put into the company $15,000 cash and will be a 60% owner of the business. William Lock will put $10,000 cash into the company and will be a 40% owner of the business. There exists the option to American Laser, Inc. that they receive either a 5% equity position in LWD, Inc. or a portion of after-tax profits for the years 1976 and 1977 as a partial payment to them for the business. No other equity positions are contemplated at this time.

9.2 DEBT FINANCING

We have proposed to American Laser Corporation that they allow us to pay them $45,000 of the total we offer as a three-year note which would be senior to all other debt. In addition, a cash-flow analysis of our expected operation indicates a need for at least $50,000 additional cash. No other debt is contemplated at this time.

9.3 OPERATIONS (EXPENSE/SALES) SHEET

To collect sufficient data and assumptions from which proforma cash-flows, a break-even analysis, and P&L Statements could be devised, a proforma operating sheet was made for the period June 18, 1973 to December 31, 1975. We believe, in general, that this sheet, shown in this section, is self explanatory if we present the assumptions we made. Accordingly, they are:

— Assumptions —

1. American Laser, Inc. accepts our proposal as presented;
2. Outside funding group accepts our proposal as presented;
3. That our sales are as shown. That these sales estimates can be established by considering that:

   A) Torry Company will order two Model 11's for immediate delivery. Three more will be ordered within the first six months operation. We project six additional units in 1974, and up to eight more in 1975.
   B) Foxboro Company will order one Model 14 within the first six months operation. We project one additional unit in 1974, and another in 1975.

C) Xerox will order a laser module within the first six months operation.
D) Past sales of accessories has been approximately $2000 per month.
E) Applications work with Timex, Ethicon, Eastman Kodak, and Delco should result in some purchases in 1974 and 1975.

4. That no expenses other than those shown in the operations sheet be incurred.

9.4 PROFORMA CASH FLOW

Using data from the Operations Sheet, a proforma cash flow analysis was made and is also given in this section. In making this projection of cash flow, it was assumed that all bills owed were paid within 30 days, all accounts receivable to us were paid within 30 days, and no cash payouts other than those shown were to be made.

9.5 P&L STATEMENTS — BREAK-EVEN ANALYSIS

These projections are given also in this section.

Sales by Product — First 6-Month Period

Product	Number	Average Price	Total
Model 11	4	$12,500	$50,000
Model 14	1	14,000	14,000
Model 6	0		
LWD	0		
Laser Module	1	2,800	2,800
Optical Systems			2,600
Accessories			1,000
TOTAL SALES		(Six months only)	$70,400

Sales by Product — 1974

Product	Number	Average Price	Total
Model 11	10	$12,500	$125,000
Model 14	2	14,000	28,000
Model 6	0		
LWD	1	20,000	21,000
Replacement Parts			6,000
Optical Systems			10,000
Accessories			15,000
TOTAL SALES			$203,000

Sales by Product — 1975

Product	Number	Average Price	Total
Model 11	12	$12,500	$150,000
Model 14	7	14,000	98,000
Model 6	2	8,000	16,000
LWD	1	20,000	20,000
Replacement Parts			12,000
Optical Systems			10,000
Accessories			16,000
TOTAL SALES			$332,000

	June 28 June 30	July	August	Sept.	Oct.	Nov.	Dec.
				1973			
Sales	—	1,000	26,860	21,000	16,500	1,000	3,800
Cost of Goods Sold	—	400	13,400	10,500	8,800	400	1,800
Shipping Insurance	—	20	200	200	200	40	60
Total	—	420	13,600	10,700	9,000	440	1,860
Salaries							
R. Dusza & F. Fournier	1,000	2,000	2,000	2,000	2,000	2,000	2,000
Clerk Typist		430	430	430	430	430	430
Castro and Lock							1,500
Mech./Opt. Assembler				1,000	1,000	1,000	1,000
Machinist							
Salesman							
Assembly Man							
Consultant						200	
Total Salaries	1,000	2,430	2,430	3,430	3,430	3,630	4,930
Marketing							
Travel	150	150	200	200	200	200	200
Advertising				500	500	1,000	1,000
Promotion		50	50	50	50	100	100
Telephone & Mail		50	50	50	100	100	200
Total Marketing	150	250	250	800	850	1,400	1,500
Insurance	300						
Lawyer	500			500			
Accountant				500			
Debt Service							
AO							
Loaner							
Capital Equip.							
Rent							
Utilities						400	800
Board of Dir.				300		50	50
Misc. Equip.		200	200	200	200	200	200

	1974				1975		
1st Qtr	2nd Qtr	3rd Qtr	4th Qtr	1st Qtr	2nd Qtr	3rd Qtr	4th Qtr
35,800	45,500	50,000	62,000	65,000	75,000	82,000	90,000
35,800	45,500	50,000	62,000	65,000	75,000	82,000	90,000
11,700	(5,227)	(17,400)	(28,995)	(31,950)	(35,005)	(31,410)	(22,755)
47,500	40,273	32,600	33,005	33,050	39,995	50,590	67,245
12,000	11,200	11,000	13,000	15,600	18,000	19,000	22,000
26,062	31,868	34,190	34,690	34,740	35,340	35,920	35,920
5,700	5,700	5,800	6,300	6,300	6,800	6,800	7,200
		250				250	
500	250	250	250	250	250	250	250
4,315	4,315	4,315	4,315	4,315	4,315	4,315	4,315
		1,920	1,920	1,920	1,920	1,920	1,920
600	600	650	700	700	700	700	800
2,400	2,400	2,400	2,600	2,600	2,600	2,600	3,000
150	150	170	180	180	180	190	200
	300				300		
300	300	300	300	300	300	300	300
600	340	600	700	700	800	900	1,000
52,727	57,673	62,595	64,955	68,055	71,405	73,345	77,105
(5,227)	(17,400)	(28,995)	(31,950)	(35,005)	(31,410)	(22,755)	(9,860)
10,000	12,000	14,000	14,000	16,000	16,000	18,000	18,000
15,227	29,400	49,995	45,950	51,005	47,410	40,755	27,860

	1973						
	June 18 June 30	July	August	Sept.	Oct.	Nov.	Dec.
Cash Sources							
Sales			1,000	26,860	21,000	16,500	1,000
ADC & WHL	25,000						
Total Sources	25,000	—	1,000	26,860	21,000	16,500	1,000
Cash on Hand	—	(16,800)	(20,100)	(23,380)	(4,450)	9,700	20,040
Total Cash Available	25,000	(16,800)	(19,100)	3,480	16,550	26,200	21,040
Cash Payouts							
Purchase	40,000						
Raw Material		400	1,200	3,000	1,200	440	1,800
Salaries	1,000	2,430	2,430	3,430	3,400	3,630	4,930
Mkt/Expense		250	250	800	850	1,400	1,500
Lawyer	500				500		
Accountant					500		
Debt Service							
ALI							
Loaner							
Misc. Equip.		200	200	200	200	200	200
Rent						400	800
Utilities						50	50
Insurance	300						
Board of Dir.				300			
Shipping		20	200	200	200	40	60
Total Cash Payouts	41,800	3,300	4,280	7,930	6,850	5,960	9,430
Cash Position	(16,800)	(20,100)	(23,380)	(4,450)	9,700	20,040	11,700
Operating Reserve	10,000	10,000	10,000	10,000	10,000	10,000	10,000
Total Loan Required	26,800	30,100	33,380	14,450	300	(10,040)	(1,700)

1974				1975			
1st Qtr	2nd Qtr	3rd Qtr	4th Qtr	1st Qtr	2nd Qtr	3rd Qtr	4th Qtr
48,200	37,800	51,000	66,000	65,000	80,000	87,000	100,000
12,100	12,200	14,600	19,000	18,600	23,000	25,000	29,000
600	440	600	700	700	800	900	10,000
12,700	12,640	15,200	19,700	19,300	23,800	25,900	30,000
6,000	6,600	6,600	6,600	6,600	7,200	7,200	7,200
1,290	1,290	1,370	1,370	1,370	1,370	1,450	1,450
11,400	11,400	11,400	11,400	11,400	11,400	11,400	11,400
3,000	3,000	3,200	3,200	3,200	3,200	3,400	3,400
1,900	1,900	1,900	1,900	1,900	1,900	1,900	1,900
2,500	7,500	7,500	8,000	8,000	8,000	8,000	8,500
		1,900	1,900	1,900	1,900	1,900	1,900
	200	200	200	250	250	300	300
26,090	31,890	34,190	34,690	34,740	35,340	35,920	35,920
800	600	600	700	700	800	800	900
3,600	3,600	3,600	3,600	3,600	3,600	3,700	3,800
1,000	1,000	1,000	1,000	1,000	1,000	1,000	1,000
1,000	1,000	1,000	1,000	1,000	1,000	1,000	1,000
5,700	5,600	5,800	6,300	6,300	6,500	6,800	7,200
	300				300		
250	250			250		250	
250	250	250	250	250	250	250	250
4,315	4,315	4,315	4,315	4,315	4,315	4,315	4,315
1,920	1,920	11,920	1,920	1,920	1,920	1,920	1,920
						1,000	1,000
2,400	2,400	2,400	2,600	2,600	2,600	2,600	3,000
150	150	170	180	180	180	190	200
300	300	300	300	500	500	500	500
600	600	650	700	700	700	700	800

LWD Proforma P&L Statements

July 1973 - December 1975

	(6 months)	Year	Year
	Dec. 31 1973	Dec. 31 1974	Dec. 31 1975
Total Net Sales	$ 70,160	$203,000	$332,000
Cost of Goods, Total			
Materials			
Direct Labor, Burden & Overhead			
Misc. Equipment and Supplies	43,720	130,270	176,640
Gross Profit	$ 26,440	$ 72,730	$155,360
Operating Expenses			
Marketing/Selling Expenses	$ 5,050	$ 48,900	$ 59,300
General Administration	2,880	19,320	20,440
Engineering/Applications	11,900	15,760	26,740
Rent and Utilities	1,300	10,450	11,550
Lawyer and Accountant	1,500	1,500	1,500
Insurance	300	300	300
Debt Service	—	6,200	4,500
Capital Equipment	—	—	2,000
Total Operating Expense	$ 22,730	$ 87,270	$116,330
Net Operating Profit	$ 3,510	$(14,540)	$ 39,030

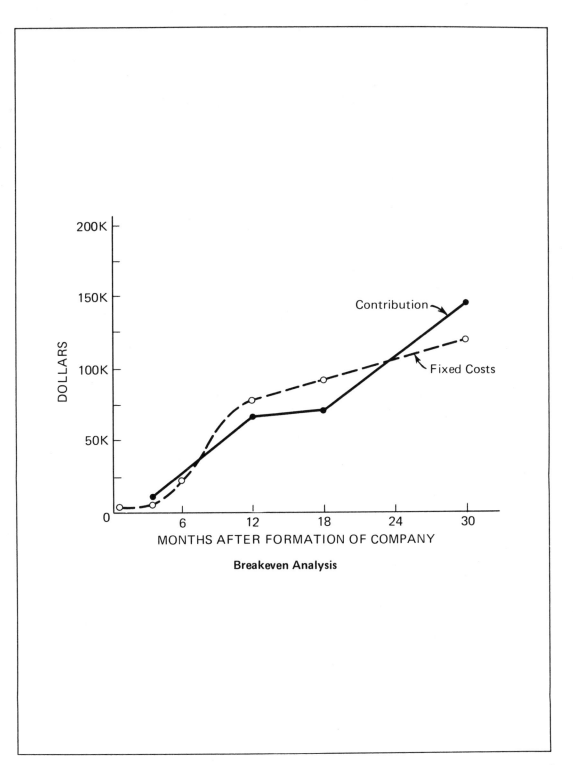

Breakeven Analysis

10.0 ADVANTAGES TO ALI OF OUR PROPOSAL

10.1 GENERAL

It may be felt that this proposal was made with consideration only being given to our interests. We, however, feel quite strongly that this proposal was carefully considered to benefit not only us, but American Laser Corporation as well. We fully recognize that the company must be concerned with getting the best possible offer that might be forthcoming for this business. We feel that our offer allows ALI to receive maximum benefit from its decision to leave the industrial laser market and wish, in this section, to point out to ALI some of the advantages of accepting this proposal.

10.2 SPLITS UP LASER BUSINESS

The Laser Products Department, up to its last day of operation, really was not in only one business, but rather in two quite different ones — glass laser devices and CO_2 laser devices. Our proposal asks ALI to recognize the fact that, indeed, these businesses are quite different: the customers are different, the applications are different, the people concerned with the products at AO are different, the advertising/promotional activities of the two are different and the competitive positions relative to products of other companies are completely different.

The glass laser line and accessories business we have discussed quite in length in this proposal. Let us now consider the CO_2 part of LVD. What does it consist of? How much is it worth? Who will buy it?

We contend that, such as this business is, ALI maximizes its potential return by trying to sell this portion separately. This CO_2 line consists of the ALI-45, ALI-55, and now the Ferranti laser. It is our belief that the Ferranti agreement was made to ALI only and that all agreements that ALI has (or had) with them are now broken. We do not believe, therefore, that ALI can pass along to whoever purchases this business the agreement that ALI had. If this indeed is the case, ALI's CO_2 line really consists of just the ALI-45 and ALI-55. These products being quite similar, can be considered to be the same for purposes of this discussion. What then do they offer a potential buyer? We contend that the only thing, other than the CO_2 laser inventory, that AO has to sell, is its process using starter strips. The use of these strips results in better laser operation and is really the only unique advantage that ALI's CO_2 lasers possess. This being the case, the line could be salable to other CO_2 laser manufacturers who would be able to make use

of the process in their existing products, or a non-CO_2 laser manufacturer wishing to enter the marketplace with a unique product feature.
Tying the sale of the glass laser line to the CO_2 line to either of the
above categories of potential buyers, we feel, decreases the probability
that they would be even interested. The advantages to ALI of choosing
not to sell this unique process and keeping it for possible exploitation
later as its medical laser business grows, should also be seriously
considered.

In summary, of the split we contend:

1. ALI has always had two different laser businesses - glass and
   CO_2.
2. Different ALI people were concerned with each of the two
   product lines.
3. By splitting LPD into two pieces, ALI maximizes its potential
   because the two businesses each have different appeal to different buyers; therefore, ALI gets maximum offer from each.
4. Ferranti Laser agreement really not ALI's to confer.
5. ALI should consider not selling CO_2 business, but adding it to
   Framingham's Medical Laser Group.

10.3 SPEED

We are prepared to present ALI with a check for $10,000 immed-
iately upon their acceptance of this proposal. We contend that it could
be months before another suitable buyer could be found. As this time
elapses, the business will rapidly decrease in value as potential customers find other solutions to their problems. The buyer then finds
that all he has is the inventory - glass, metal, etc. - not laser systems,
just metal, glass, etc. If ALI will accept our proposal with the timing
suggested, we can move quickly enough to insure that potential glass
laser customers might still purchase lasers from this product line
inventory. We have been able to quote the full inventory value to ALI as
part of our offer because we believe the inventory can be sold by us. A
delay, in which ALI searches for another buyer, cannot benefit anyone.
However, a delay in the sale of the CO_2 line might be borne without ill
effect because there are few near-in sales prospects and few systems in
the field. Further, the personnel involved with these CO_2 systems are
still employed at ALI's Research Center and therefore could be available
for servicing equipment as required.

10.4 SERVICE

All of the glass laser systems testing, installation and service has been, to date, performed by members of our proposed company only. We propose to continue servicing these systems for ALI. We believe that it is impossible to imagine that any other group could perform this service as well. We know the equipment; we know the customers; we know the customer's application; we know the history of his equipment, and its performance on the job.

10.5 CONTINUITY

Acceptance of our proposal will allow ALI to leave the laser business with dignity and honor, keeping its accessories line available for sale through LWD, Inc., and having no servicing and warranty worries on this portion of its laser business. If ALI wishes, it could retain an interest in the laser field by acceptance of the option to hold an equity position in our new company.

We have made a sincere effort to propose a viable plan to ALI whereby the Corporation as well as LWD, Inc. might benefit. We urge immediate consideration of this proposal.

"PERSPECTIVE"
Senior Citizens' Magazine

CONTENTS

SUMMARY OF BUSINESS PLAN   1

MARKET ANALYSIS OF TARGET AUDIENCE   3

    Audience Identification   3
    Needs of Middle Agers   3
    Prospective Advertisers   3
    Competition   4
    Supplementary Services   6

EDITORIAL OBJECTIVES   8

    The Communication Need   8
    Editorial Purpose   8
    Feature Articles   9
    Editorial Board   10
    Editorial Philosophy   10

THE CONSUMER MAGAZINE INDUSTRY   12

    Trends   12
    Risk Factors   13

PERSONNEL   14

    A Brief Statement of Business Philosophy   14
    Organizational Structure   15
    Resumes of Founders   17

SALES/PROFIT FORECAST   19

    Supplementary Cash Flow Data   19
    Year 1 Cash Flow   20
    Year 2 Cash Flow   21
    5 Year Cash Flow Summary   22

PLAN FOR FINANCING   23

    Seed Financing   23
    Secondary Financing   23
    Expected Return to Investors   24

APPENDIX

    Supplementary Cash Flow Data
    Market Survey Questionnaire
    Renewal Estimates
    Staffing/Salary Schedule
    Itemized Expenses for Test Program
    Article: "Stop Worrying! Magazine Publishing is a High
          Profit, Low Risk Business."

SUMMARY OF BUSINESS PLAN

A MULTI-SERVICE corporation will be established dedicated to serving the needs of 30 million Americans in the 50 to 65 age group -- a group that commands the largest discretionary purchasing power in the U.S.

The initial service will be the quarterly paid-subscription magazine, PERSPECTIVE. The editorial objectives of this specialized publication will be to put the middle years in their proper context -- to show why and how they can be an exciting, challenging and independent time of life. Retirement planning will also receive a great deal of attention, with special emphasis on financial planning. In all cases the approach will be of a practical "how to" nature, attempting to establish a deep seated rapport between staff and reader.

Advertising acceptance will be promoted by offering a comprehensive readership profile package. By utilizing its computer expertise, the corporation plans to generate in-depth psychographic profiles (i.e., life style, beliefs, attitudes, etc.). The decision to offer psychographics was confirmed by the corporation's recent survey which indicated that advertising executives of consumer oriented companies were looking to supplement the demographics which they felt did not fully describe their target markets. Psychographic data will fill this void. However, standard demographic descriptions including age, sex, income and education will be included also.

The attraction of advertising is further enhanced by the absence of media directed solely to middle agers. For those advertisers selling to middle agers, there is no cost-effective magazine alternative available. The only publication addressing itself solely to middle agers is a non-profit organization -- one that does not accept advertising.

Advertising will be solicited from a variety of national firms such as health/life insurance companies, airlines, pharmaceutical firms, investment counseling services, land development organizations, travel/leisure groups, book clubs, and home study.

After eighteen months, PERSPECTIVE will switch to bi-monthly publication while retaining the $6 annual subscription price.

Circulation objectives are:

>   500,000 subscribers at the end of 1st year
>   700,000 subscribers at the end of 2nd year
>   850,000 subscribers at the end of 3rd year
>   950,000 subscribers at the end of 4th year
>   1,000,000 subscribers at the end of 5th year

Another key innovation will be the guarantee to Charter subscribers that their subscription rate of $6 will NEVER be increased provided that they subscribe on a continuing basis. It is expected that this offer will have an extremely positive effect on subscription sales. Analysis has shown that this will be an economically feasible offer.

Once PERSPECTIVE has identified and cultivated a customer base, the corporation plans to expand its capabilities by offering additional services to its subscribers. Regular communications via the editorial pages will facilitate the promotion of services currently in demand by middle-aged citizens. Among these are mail order pharmaceuticals, group insurance programs, group travel, book clubs and investment counseling.

A two stage financing package is planned. The initial phase will require $60,000 to test readership acceptance. Once proven, $1,500,000 will be secured to launch operations and expansion.

The corporation plans to be profitable within two years. After five years a $1,500,000 profit (after taxes) is expected on revenues of $13,000,000.

MARKET ANALYSIS OF TARGET AUDIENCE

Audience Identification

The target audience of the corporation will be the 30 million American men and women between the ages of 50 and 65. This group has the largest discretionary purchasing power in the U.S.

The attractiveness of this audience should be obvious to consumer oriented companies. First, middle-aged persons are usually in the best financial positions of their lives. They are no longer subject to the economic strain of raising a family -- food, clothing and tuition costs are in the past. Most pre-retireds have paid off their mortgage and they are generally looking forward to the independence of middle age. They are also enjoying high salaries as their careers near a peak. With family obligations lessened, more time is available for leisure, hobbies, travel, etc., and more money is available for the accumulation of consumer goods.

Needs of Middle Agers

Middle agers have unique needs. Among them is the need to appreciate the opportunities that exist for middle agers. Unfortunately there is widespread apprehension toward this period of life. A fuller discussion of these needs will follow under the "Editorial Purpose" section. Suffice it to say that middle-agers should be concentrating on the positive aspects of the <u>now</u> and the <u>future.</u> A satisfying and productive life requires an excitement about what lies ahead; about new and challenging learning experiences, and it requires the setting of worthwhile objectives. There is also a distinct need for middle agers to plan for retirement. Unfortunately, a great number go out of their way to avoid thinking about retirement, no less planning for it. A great deal of unnecessary hardship could be avoided, both material and psychological, if a well-designed plan preceded retirement.

Prospective Advertisers

A questionnaire survey was conducted to identify advertising potential for the proposed magazine. Advertising managers and ad agency people of the largest consumer product/service companies were polled. (See Apprendix for sample questionnaire, methodology, etc.). Results indicated that insurance, land development, investment services, pet foods, hotels/motels and mobile homes are key prospects.

Another important finding was the confirmation that advertising people are looking for more psychographic data to describe their relevant markets. Psychographics tries to identify the life style, attitudes, values and beliefs common to a specific market segment. Once identified, finely tuned advertising can be used to promote a product that fits that segment's psychological needs. To help identify those segments, companies are calling upon statisticians, psychologists, behaviorial scientists, and computer technicians. The type of product will determine whether the promotional efforts should be focused on the "swingers", the "economy-mindeds", the "conformists", etc.. For example, Crest toothpaste found the "worriers" to be their target audience. These people are concerned with cavities, tend to be a little hypochondriacal and they prefer flouride toothpaste. The Crest ads show a concerned, responsible father looking after his son's healthy teeth.

With the increased marketing sophistication it is clear that demographic data is losing its importance. In the past, age, income, sex and education were sufficient to define a company's target audience. Many advertisers now find that demographics are unreliable -- or at best incomplete. The corporation recognizes the need for psychological data. By utilizing its computer expertise, it will provide psychographics to advertisers as part of the readership profile package.

Competition

Apart from T.V. and general interest magazines (e.g., Reader's Digest) with their attendant high advertising cost, there are no alternatives for advertisers who want to focus on the 50 to 65 year old audience.

Dynamic Maturity is currently the only specialized magazine directing itself solely to this audience. It is a relatively new monthly publication, having begun operations in November 1971. It is sponsored by Action for Independent Maturity (A.I.M.) which is a division of the American Association of Retired Persons (A.A.R.P.). Both A.I.M. and A.A.R.P. are non-profit organizations. Membership in A.I.M. is $3 per year and includes pharmacy, travel and insurance services in addition to the magazine. Dynamic Maturity does not accept advertising.

An editorial staff member of Dynamic Maturity indicated that they are still in the process of "putting it all together" and that membership is growing significantly. The current list of 50,000 subscribers was generated with minimal promotional expense by piggy-backing subscription advertisements in their sister publication Modern Maturity (A.A.R.P.). A brief summary of the magazine's strengths and weaknesses follow.

Strengths

- Due to the close relationship with A.A.R.P., Dynamic Maturity provides access to a host of well-established services such as travel, insurance, etc..

- The magazine can play on the excellent reputation of A.A.R.P.. With 4,000,000 members, A.A.R.P. is certainly an influential force and well-respected for its political muscle.

- Access to editorial subject matter is relatively easy. Perhaps because of A.A.R.P.'s acknowledged credibility, public figures participate readily. For example, Senator Jacob Javits contributed the keynote article in the initial issue of Dynamic Maturity.

- The staff appears enthusiastic and dedicated.

- Its non-profit status allows substantial savings in postage.

<u>Weaknesses</u>

- It appears that financing is limited and there is no opportunity for outside venture capital interests to participate.

- The marketing efforts are weak and lack incentive.

- The physical format of the magazine is unimpressive although improving.

- The staff is quite small, consisting only of an editor, associate editor, editorial secretary, art director, director of publications and a service consultant.

- There is no profit motive.

<u>Modern Maturity</u> which was mentioned previously is the bi-monthly magazine sponsored by A.A.R.P.. It is not direct competition to PERSPECTIVE since its audience is the retirement sector. However, some overlap will occur.

<u>Retirement Living</u> (formerly <u>Harvest Years</u>) also concentrates on the retirement group, although it has recently expanded its audience to include 58 year olds. It differs from the other two publications in that it accepts advertising -- although it has had very little. In existence since 1960, the current circulation numbers 100,000 paid subscribers (@ $6 per year). It is published by the Magazine Division of Whitney Communications Corporation.

Supplementary Services

The primary purpose of the corporation is to profitably serve the varied needs of middle-agers. And PERSPECTIVE is only the first step. To satisfy a wider range of those needs, the company plans to offer a cluster of supplementary services to its subscribers. A partial listing of the proposed services include:

- Mail order pharmaceutical services
- Group life and health insurance
- Group travel programs
- Leisure resorts

This approach will be advantageous to both the reader and the company. For the PERSPECTIVE reader, he will be offered a product or service that has been thoroughly screened and evaluated. Before the company endorses a service, it must prove to be appropriate, reputable and of exceptional value. Another advantage to the reader is an economic one. Because of PERSPECTIVE'S large customer base, the company will have considerable leverage when negotiating for the various supplementary services. As a result, PERSPECTIVE subscribers should realize significant discounts.

From the company's point of view, each service will provide additional revenue. And assuming that PERSPECTIVE establishes a strong rapport with its readers, and that it becomes a credible spokesman for middle-agers, it should prove relatively easy to market the recommended services via direct mail and within the pages of PERSPECTIVE.

EDITORIAL OBJECTIVES

The Communication Need

According to a recent Business Week Special Report,

> A rather stark fact confronts society today: People are retiring earlier, living longer, and having fewer children. The result is that in a nation that has long worshipped the youth cult, the retirement ranks are swelling, the overall population is actually growing older. This has created an enormous strain on an economy and social structure geared toward the young.

With 30 million Americans between the ages of 50 and 65, this group is fast becoming not only one of the country's largest minority groups, but one that wields significant financial leverage in the marketplace.

A vital communication need has emerged. Middle agers have no regular or convenient information source to help them get more enjoyment out of living NOW, or to help them plan for their approaching retirement.

Editorial Purpose

The basic editorial purpose of PERSPECTIVE is to show how middle age can be a tremendously rewarding period of life. The route to a successful, happy and active life will be charted through the regular columns, features, and special staff reports. In all cases, the editors will be taking a distinctly positive "how to" approach.

Middle agers have a lot going for them. Most Americans in their fifties have acquired a new independence after raising their children; they are in the best financial position of their lives; plus they have the advantage of fifty or so years of living experience behind them. In essence, they have the ingredients for a truly enjoyable life style.

Unfortunately, many Americans (including middle agers) do not view it in this context. Rather, they see the middle years as the beginning of the "downhill" phase. Contributing to this notion is our nation's obsession with youth. With Madison Avenue continuing to worship the 18 to 35 year old market, our economy is flooded with goods and services directed to the young or "young at heart". At the same time there appears to be a conscious denial of the existence of middle age. It is understandable why people view advancing years with apprehension.

However, PERSPECTIVE feels that middle agers should become more concerned with their own unique needs. They should be concentrating on the now and the future. Rather than looking back longingly at past successes, or enviously at the benefits of being young, they should be asking themselves such relevant questions as: How can we enjoy ourselves now? Where have we been, and where do we want to be in five, ten, or twenty years? What type of retirement life style do we want? Can we afford it? How should we plan for it?

By putting middle life in its proper perspective, it will be shown that it is a time of unequaled opportunities, a time for new and challenging learning experiences, a time to be enthusiastic. PERSPECTIVE will show how to exploit the independence of middle age, to take on self-development programs or even to consider new second careers.

For the future, continued satisfaction requires a hardnosed, sensible retirement planning program. This requires considerable thought and effort before meaningful objectives can be established. PERSPECTIVE will provide useful assistance by exploring all areas of retirement; again using a practical, easy-to-understand approach. The financial aspects of retirement planning will receive considerable emphasis.

Feature Articles

The feature articles proposed for PERSPECTIVE will consist primarily of staff written and staff-researched material with obvious appeal to the special needs, lifestyle, interests, and anxieties of middle agers. As such, PERSPECTIVE will have special significance to a very precisely defined segment of the population. It will not be a general interest magazine attempting to appeal to the mass audience (e.g., Life, Look, Saturday Evening Post, etc.).

The thought of a magazine designed to help people plan, particularly with respect to financial, insurance, and investment matters, immediately conjures up the notion of a very rigorous, tutorial editorial format. However, to avoid this potential drawback, all articles will be presented in practical, layman's language. Examples of representative feature articles include:

Middle Age -- A Time for Career Evaluation
A Guide to Staying Physically and Mentally Fit in Middle Age
The A, B, C's of Common Stock Investment (a series)
Change of Life -- A Positive View
How to Start Your Own Business
Investment Objectives for Middle Agers
Franchising -- A Second Career Opportunity?
Kids Gone, House Too Big, What are the Alternatives?
New Ideas in Traveling Abroad
Unusual Hobbies for Middle Agers
Planning for Retirement is a Must!
Middle Age -- A Time of Unequaled Opportunity
Looking for a New Job? A Checklist for Middle Agers
Plan for Financial Security -- NOW!
Social Security in 1980
How to Evaluate Supplemental Health Insurance -- A Checklist

Editorial Board

The corporation will establish a "blue ribbon" panel of editorial advisors to provide expert opinion, commentary, and guidance on such relevant topics as personal finance, health and nutrition, travel and leisure, and retirement planning. The editorial advisory board will consist of persons of national stature with expertise in finance, business, government, medicine, and education.

Editorial Philosophy

Advertising, circulation, and editorial are the three main supporting elements of any magazine. Assuming that a reasonable effort is channeled into selling advertising, and soliciting subscriptions, the most important task remaining for a new magazine is that of establishing a strong bond or empathy within the reader. This can only be done by starting with a valid editorial concept and building a deep-seated rapport with the reading audience. To accomplish this, the editorial staff must be totally committed to the needs of its readership. It must be sensitive to change and it must be flexible enough to respond to those changes. PERSPECTIVE will actively seek out the opinions, tastes and needs of its readers. It will seek active participation. (One method of accomplishing this will be the use of punch card questionnaires that can be computer processed, and will be periodically inserted in the magazine for the readers' use.)

PERSPECTIVE must create a personality for itself, one that is obvious and consistent. Hopefully it will project itself as a responsive, credible, and distinctive spokesman for middle agers. Above all, it must prove genuinely valuable to the reader. It must provide a worthwhile and continuing service if it is to retain its readership. In short, the ultimate success of a specialized consumer magazine such as PERSPECTIVE rests with its editorial product. PERSPECTIVE intends to achieve the highest quality editorial standards by attracting talented and highly motivated professionals to its staff. The corporation foresees no difficulty in assembling an experienced editorial team with proven records.

THE CONSUMER MAGAZINE INDUSTRY

Trends

Magazines compete with newspapers, television, radio and direct mail for advertising revenue. Although magazine advertising revenue has increased from $873,236,000 in 1962 to $1,251,388,000 in 1971 (a 4% compounded annual growth rate), magazines have actually lost ground with respect to market share:

Market Share of Advertising Expenditures

	Magazines	Newspapers	T.V.	Radio	Direct Mail
1962	7.9%	31.0%	13.3%	5.9%	15.3%
1971	6.9	30.3	17.2	6.7	14.4

Lately, however, magazines have been holding their own with respect to market share, while ad revenues have been hitting new peaks. Beginning in January of 1971, each month has seen an increase over the year earlier results. Through October, of 1972, $1 billion worth of ads had been placed in magazines -- a new ten month record. Favorable economic conditions, plus the banning of cigarette commercials on T.V. have been the main contributing factors.

Perhaps the most significant trend withing the industry has been the increasing success of specialized magazines vis-a-vis general interest magazines. The demise of Colliers, Look and most recently Life, clearly indicates that a major shift in reader interest and advertising has occurred. Why have general interest magazines failed? Primarily because they have been unable to compete effectively with television. Advertisers have come to demand a clearer definition of the readership audience. In many cases, only a small segment of the readership was relevant to the advertiser's product. Hence, the cost per relevant reader was prohibitively high. Compounding the problem was the practice of mass magazines to offer cut-rate subscriptions to maintain unrealistic circulation objectives. In many instances, these prices were not enough to cover the cost of obtaining and fulfilling the subscription. Focusing on the problems of general interest magazines unduly distorts the overall picture of the magazine industry. As a matter of fact, the industry is quite healthy. In the last ten years 753 magazines have been introduced while only 160 have been merged or discontinued -- a net add of 593 publications.

Year	Magazines sold, merged or discontinued	New magazines introduced
1962	10	41
1963	17	50
1964	6	41
1965	17	73
1966	18	70
1967	9	115
1968	22	101
1969	17	100
1970	24	86
1971	20	76
	160	753

A recent problem confronting magazines is the 144% increase in postal rates that will occur between 1971 and 1976. It is a major problem because magazines will not only see the increased cost of mailing the magazine, but they will also face a significant increase in their circulation promotion expense. Many publications use direct mail as the primary method of selling new subscriptions.

Risk Factors

The start-up of a new magazine involves certain risks. In most instances, advertising agencies and advertising managers show a reluctance to support a new publication, regardless of how viable they think the concept is. The magazine must first establish a track record. It must show that its readership offers significant potential for the advertiser's product, and that the magazine will survive the critical early years. A good rule of thumb is that widespread advertising support will take at least one or two years. Therefore, the importance of adequate financing is obvious.

PERSONNEL

A Brief Statement of Business Philosophy

Certain ingredients are necessary if a company is to enjoy long term success. The sum total of the following statements will provide an insight into the founders' operating philosophy.

People

If a firm is to profitably serve a selected market, it must attract and retain exceptional people. It is strongly believed that people are the company's most valuable asset, and that a climate must be established that will encourage individuals to contribute their best efforts. A growing, healthy company is characterized by highly motivated personnel who show a sense of urgency about their job and their company. They feel that they are contributing to the total effort and that their contributions are being recognized -- they feel they have an impact on their organization. The establishment of such an atmosphere does not occur by chance; it must be consciously planned and nurtured. To start, a great deal of time, effort and resources must be allocated to the personnel selection process. Once selected, talented people must be retained. Management is committed to a continuing program of people development. At the same time, a continuing search for new talent should be conducted if vital growth is to be sustained.

Planning

A great deal of emphasis will be placed upon the planning process. The setting of bold, but realistic objectives will serve to promote a clear understanding of the firm's purpose and direction. Good planning is both difficult and time consuming, but it usually results in efficient use of resources and a unity of purpose. There is a great deal of truth in the often quoted "If you don't know where you're going, any path will get you there". Successful planning requires input from all operating levels, from those who will be responsible for final implementation of the plan.

Organizational Structure

Marketing, Editorial, Production, Information Systems and Finance represent the basic operating functions of the corporation. The organization chart (Exhibit A. p. 16) identifies key job functions within each category. Consultants will be used to a considerable extent for legal, management, publicity, and direct mail assistance.

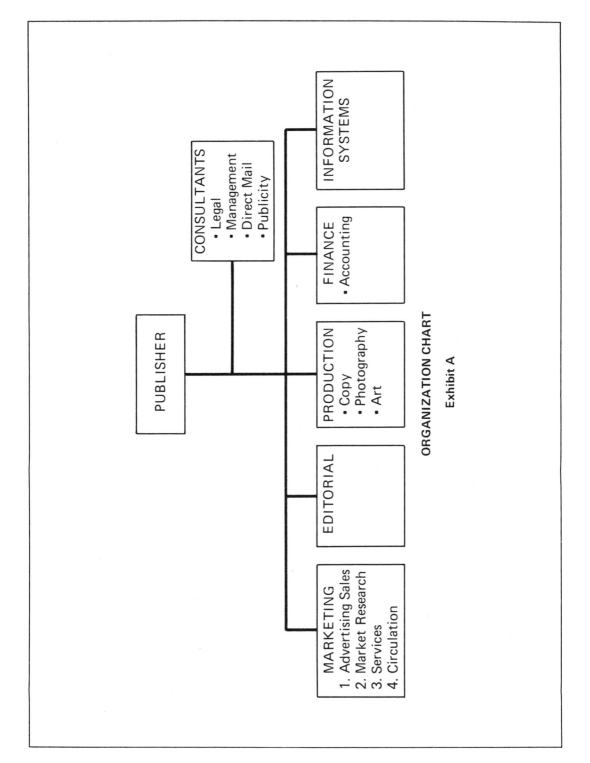

ORGANIZATION CHART

Exhibit A

With respect to the marketing function, a hybrid advertising sales organization will be used -- a direct sales organization plus commissioned
representatives. The company's own sales offices will be established
in New York and Chicago, while commissioned representatives will
be employed on the west coast and possibly Detroit, Michigan.

Resumes of the Founders

John C. O'Mara has held marketing positions with American Air Filter
Company, Spaulding Fibre Company and Fleetguard Division of Cum-
mins Engine Company. Mr. O'Mara is currently employed as Marketing Analyst for the Fenwal Incorporated division of Walter Kidde &
Company. His past experience includes:

- Acquisition studies including financial analysis.
- Long range planning.
- Market research.
- New product pricing, profitability, return on investment.
- Economic forecasting.
- Media analysis.
- Direct mail programs.

Beginning in 1968, Mr. O'Mara attended the University of Connecticut
on a full time basis. He received his M.B.A. in 1970 concentrating in
finance. Mr. O'Mara's undergraduate work was completed at Southern
Illinois University in 1963 where he received a B.A., with a major in
mathematics.

Mr. O'Mara is 36 years old, married, honorably discharged from the
U.S. Marine Corps and is in excellent health. He is currently residing
in Northboro, Massachusetts.

William A. Gannon is a co-founder and a director of Modern Data Services, Inc., a five-year old firm which publishes Modern Data. Modern
Data is a monthly magazine circulated to 90,000 data processing executives and computer professionals in the U.S. and Canada. The privately
held Framingham, Massachusetts firm also provides computerized
market information services and publishes various computer equipment
buyer's guides and market reports.

Mr. Gannon actively participated in the formulation of the initial editorial concept for Modern Data, developed advertising sales strategies,
and implemented several innovative and copyrighted techniques for the
conversion of subscriber records to marketable computerized data
files.

Prior to the formation of Modern Data Services in 1967, Mr. Gannon was with Computer Design Publishing Corporation where he served as associate editor of Computer Design magazine, and publisher of Computer Industry Annual. Mr. Gannon also held various sales and marketing management positions with two computer manufacturing firms; Computer Control Company (later acquired by Honeywell), and SEL, Inc..

Mr. Gannon is 36 years old; graduated from the University of Pittsburgh in 1958 with a B.S. in mechanical engineering; and served four years as a commissioned officer in the U.S. Navy. Mr. Gannon resides in Franklin, Massachusetts with his wife and two children.

PLAN FOR FINANCING

Seed Financing

A prerequisite to the $1.5 million funding necessary to launch PERSPECTIVE will be a test to determine readership acceptance. A limited partnership will be established to accomplish this. Discussions with James B. Kobak, Inc. (management consultants specializing in consumer magazines) have confirmed this strategy. Sixty thousand dollars will be required to perform the test. The seed investor(s) will receive up to 24% of the equity, depending on the size of their investment. An advantage to the investor is that test expenses incurred can be deducted from ordinary income. In this case, if the investor(s) fell within the 50% income tax bracket, the net cost of the investment would be $30,000. (See Appendix for itemized breakout of test expenses).

Secondary Financing

Upon successful completion of the test (e.g., 5% response) the limited partnership will be incorporated with the equity distribution remaining in the same proportion. At this point, James B. Kobak, Inc. will be in a position to secure the final $1.5 million that will launch PERSPECTIVE and will finance future expansion. They have an excellent track record in securing secondary financing once testing has proven successful.

It is expected that the venture capital people will require 50% ownership in return for the $1.5 million financing -- resulting in equity dilution for the founders and seed investors. The following table projects equity dilution of the original seed dollars invested.

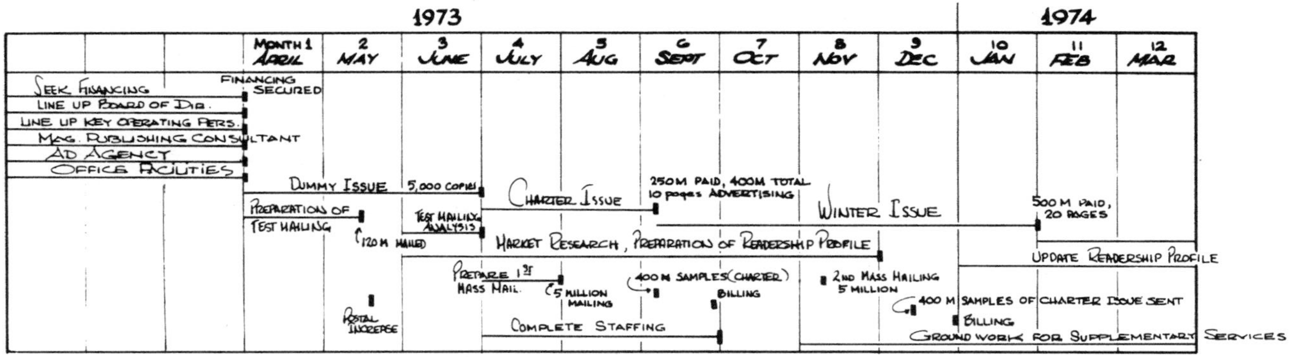

1973 / 1974

	Month 1 APRIL	2 MAY	3 JUNE	4 JULY	5 AUG	6 SEPT	7 OCT	8 NOV	9 DEC	10 JAN	11 FEB	12 MAR
SEEK FINANCING	FINANCING SECURED											
LINE UP BOARD OF DIR.												
LINE UP KEY OPERATING PERS.												
MAG. PUBLISHING CONSULTANT												
AD AGENCY												
OFFICE FACILITIES												

Annotations (left to right):
- DUMMY ISSUE — 5,000 COPIES
- PREPARATION OF TEST MAILING / 120 M MAILED
- 1ST MAILING JULY 15?
- PREPARE 1ST MASS MAIL.
- CHARTER ISSUE
- MARKET RESEARCH, PREPARATION OF READERSHIP PROFILE
- 250M PAID, 400M TOTAL / 10 PAGES ADVERTISING
- 400 M SAMPLES (CHARGED) / BILLING
- 5 MILLION MAILING
- COMPLETE STAFFING
- WINTER ISSUE
- 500 M PAID, 20 PAGES / 2ND MASS MAILING 5 MILLION
- 400 M SAMPLES OF CHARTER ISSUE SENT / BILLING
- UPDATE MEMBERSHIP PROFILE
- GROUND WORK FOR SUPPLEMENTARY SERVICES

PROJECTED CASH FLOW — YEAR 1

	APRIL	MAY	JUNE	JULY	AUG	SEPT	OCT	NOV	DEC	JAN	FEB	MAR	TOTAL
REVENUE													
1. SUBSCRIPTIONS						1,050,000*	1,050,000*	450,000		1,090,000	460,000		3,000,000
2. ADVERTISING							12,500*	7,000	6,000		51,000*	30,600	107,100
3. SERVICES													
4. TOTAL REVENUE													3,107,100
EXPENSES													
5. PRODUCTION	2,000*	2,000	4,000*	35,000	40,000*	12,000	7,500	40,000*	19,500	50,000*		7,000	114,000
6. CIRCULATION FULFILLMENT				10,000	60,000			67,500	2,000	15,000	15,000		211,500
7. EDITORIAL	1,000	1,000	2,000	2,000	2,000	2,000	2,000	2,000	2,000	2,000	2,000	2,000	21,000
8. MAGAZINE POSTAGE						16,000*		14,000*		20,000*		7,000	57,000
9. COST OF PRODUCT (5,6,7+8)	3,000	3,000	6,000	2,000	101,000	30,000	9,500	127,500	21,500	87,000	17,000	17,000	413,500
10. SALARIES	13,500*	13,500	13,500	35,000	35,000	35,000	35,000	34,000	36,000	36,000	49,000	38,000	364,500
11. PERSONNEL RELOCATION	6,000			10,000	4,000								20,000
12. OFFICE SUPPLIES & EQUIP.	1,000	1,000	1,500	1,500	1,500	1,500	1,500	1,500	1,500	1,500	1,500	1,500	16,500
13. SELLING EXPENSE	2,000*	2,000	2,000*	5,000	5,000	5,000	5,000	6,000	6,000	6,000	6,000	6,000	59,000
14. CIRCULATION PROMOTION	5,000*	51,000*	10,000*	904,000*		110,000	24,000*	912,000*	10,000*	28,000	14,000		2,184,000
15. ADVERTISING PROMOTION			5,000*	2,000	1,000	2,000	1,000	2,000	2,000			17,000	21,000
16. SERVICES PROMOTION													
17. EDITORIAL TRAVEL, ENTERTAIN.	500	500	500	1,000	1,000	1,000	1,000	1,000	1,000	1,000	1,000	1,000	10,500
18. ADVERTISING SALES COMMISS.								400	300		2,000	1,500	5,100
19. RENT, HEAT, LIGHT	1,600	1,600	1,600	1,700	1,700	1,700	1,700	1,700	1,700	1,700	1,700	1,700	20,100
20. TELEPHONE	500	500	500	1,600	1,800	1,800	1,800	1,800	1,800	1,800	1,800	1,800	19,100
21. TELEPHONE/LEGAL	1,000	1,000	1,000	1,000	1,000	1,000	1,000	1,000	1,000	1,000	1,000	1,000	12,000
22. AUDIT	600*	600	600	1,600	1,600	1,600	1,600	1,600	1,600	1,500*	1,900	1,000	3,000
23. FRINGE BENEFITS													17,100
24. TAXES (FED, STATE, etc.)	4,000*	4,000	4,000	3,000	3,000	2,000	2,000	2,000	2,000	2,000	2,000	500*	500
25. CONSULTANTS FEES	2,000	2,000	2,000	2,000	2,000	2,000	2,000	2,000	2,000	2,000	2,000	4,000*	34,000
26. ADVERTISING AGENCY						1,000	1,000	1,000	1,000	2,000	3,000	3,000	24,000
27. MISCELLANEOUS	1,000	1,000	1,000	1,000	1,000	1,000	1,000	1,000	1,000	1,000	1,000	1,000	17,000
28. SELLING, G&A (10-11...+21)	41,100	79,600	61,200	964,600		167,100	94,200	974,000	167,500	86,500	75,500	64,400	2,834,300
29. TOTAL EXPENSES (9-28)	41,100	82,800	68,200	968,600	163,600	197,100	103,700	1,095,500	189,440	173,300	90,500	81,400	3,317,800
30. NET INCOME (4-29)	(44,100)	(82,800)	(68,200)	(968,600)	(162,600)	(97,100)	958,800	(648,500)	(183,440)	876,100	410,500	(56,800)	(150,700)
31. CUMULATIVE	(44,100)	(126,900)	(195,100)	(1,163,700)	(1,326,300)	(1,523,400)	(564,600)	(1,203,100)	(1,186,500)	(510,400)	(99,900)	(150,700)	(150,700)

1974 — 1975 Timeline

	MONTH 13 APRIL	14 MAY	15 JUNE	16 JULY	17 AUG.	18 SEPT.	19 OCT.	20 NOV.	21 DEC.	22 JAN.	23 FEB.	24 MAR.
	SPRING ISSUE		SUMMER ISSUE		FALL ISSUE			JAN/FEB ISSUE			MAR/APRIL	

- TEST MAILING – HEALTH INSURANCE
- 500 M 40p
- HEALTH INSURANCE OFFERED IN SPRING ISSUE
- DIRECT MAIL PROGRAM OFFERING HEALTH INS
- POSTAL INCREASE
- 460M "LOOKSEE" COPIES OF SPRING ISSUE
- BILLING
- 5 MILLION PIECE SUBSCRIPTION MAILING
- 700M TOTAL 500M PAID 12p
- 700M TOTAL 500 PAID 40p
- 700M PAID 40p
- 700M PAID 40p
- UPDATED LEADERSHIP PROFILE
- NEW MERCHANDISING KIT
- 6.25 MILLION SUBSCRIPTION MAILING
- TEST MAIL HEALTH INS.
- 500M "LOOKSEE" COPIES OF FALL ISSUE
- DIRECT MAIL HEALTH INS 450 K
- RENEWAL MAILING 500M
- BILLING
- 2ND RENEWAL MAILING

PROJECTED CASH FLOW   YEAR 2

	APRIL	MAY	JUNE	JULY	AUG.	SEPT.	OCT.	NOV.	DEC.	JAN.	FEB.	MAR.	TOTAL
REVENUE													
1. SUBSCRIPTIONS	20,400	51,000	840,000*	340,000*	51,000*	600,000*	420,000*	1,230,000*	750,000	20,400*	142,800*	85,700	4,220,000
2. ADVERTISING			30,600	20,400	67,200	30,600	20,400	51,000	30,600	20,400	32,800	34,000	359,900
3. SERVICES						51,800	56,820	39,200	30,600	31,600			344,000
4. TOTAL REVENUE	20,400	51,000	870,600	360,400	118,200	682,600	497,220	1,320,200	811,000	52,000	175,600	119,700	5,098,900
EXPENSES													
5. PRODUCTION	99,000*			77,000*			152,000*			77,000*		71,000	442,000
6. CIRCULATION FULFILLMENT	75,000*	27,000	27,000	24,000	21,000	21,000	94,000	36,000	21,000	23,000	23,000	23,000	417,000
7. EDITORIAL	2,000	2,000	2,000	2,000	2,000	3,000	4,000	4,000	4,000	4,000	4,000	4,000	36,000
8. MAGAZINE POSTAGE	20,000*	20,000*	9,000	35,000*	23,000	60,000*	60,000	40,000	25,000	35,000	15,000	15,000	205,000
9. COST OF PRODUCT (5,6,7,8)	196,000	49,000	29,000	138,000	23,000	24,000	291,000	40,000	25,000	139,000	27,000	139,000	1,120,000
10. SALARIES	38,000	38,000	38,000	38,000	38,000	38,000	43,000	43,000	49,000	45,000*	45,000	45,500	491,500
11. PERSONNEL RELOCATION												4,000	4,000
12. OFFICE SUPPLIES & EQUIP.	1,500	1,500	1,500	1,500	1,500	1,500	2,000	4,000	8,000	2,000	2,000	2,000	21,000
13. SELLING EXPENSE	6,000	6,000	7,000	7,000	7,000	8,000	8,000	8,000	8,000	8,000	8,000	8,000	89,000
14. CIRCULATION PROMOTION	900,000*	110,000*	14,000			1,340,000*		36,000*					2,484,000
15. ADVERTISING PROMOTION	16,000*	17,000*	2,000	2,000		12,000	7,000	2,000	2,000*				60,000
16. SERVICES PROMOTION	7,000*	100,000*							2,000	84,000*			198,000
17. EDITORIAL TRAVEL, EXPERIM.	2,000	2,000	2,000	2,000	2,000	2,000	3,000	3,000	3,000	3,000	3,000	3,000	30,000
18. ADVERTISING SALES COMMISS.	1,000	2,000	1,500	2,000	2,600	1,500	1,000	2,600	1,500	1,000	7,000*	4,000	27,700
19. RENT, HEAT, LIGHT	1,700	1,700	1,700	1,700	1,700	1,700	1,700	1,700	1,700	1,700	1,800	1,900	21,000
20. TELEPHONE	1,000	1,800	1,800	1,800	1,800	1,800	2,000	2,000	2,000	2,200	2,200	2,200	23,400
21. LEGAL	1,000	1,000	1,000	1,000	1,000	1,000	1,000	1,000	1,000	1,000	1,000	1,000	12,000
22. AUDIT						2,000						2,000	4,000
23. FRINGE BENEFITS	1,900	1,900	1,900	1,900	1,900	1,900	2,500	2,500	2,500	5,000	5,000*	5,000*	33,500
24/25. TAXES (FED, STATE etc.)												239,900	239,900
26. CONSULTANTS FEES	5,000*	5,000	5,000	5,000	5,000	5,000	2,000	2,000	2,000	2,000	2,000	2,000	42,000
27. ADVERTISING AGENCY	2,000	2,000	2,000	2,000	2,000	2,000	2,000	2,000	2,500	2,500	2,500	2,500	25,500
28. MISCELLANEOUS	2,000	2,000	2,000	2,000	2,000	2,000	2,000	2,000	2,000	2,000	2,000	2,000	27,000
SELLING, G & A (10/14...,27)	98,900	291,500	59,400	80,900	66,500	1,430,400	81,200	109,800	74,700	172,600	82,200	320,300	3,783,100
29. TOTAL EXPENSES (9,28)	1,177,900	341,500	128,400	218,900	89,500	1,454,400	372,200	149,800	99,700	311,600	109,200	459,900	4,903,000
30. NET INCOME (4,29)	(1,157,500)	(290,500)	742,200	161,500	28,700	(771,800)	125,000	1,170,400	711,300	(259,600)	66,400	(340,200)	195,900
31. CUMULATIVE	(1,308,200)	(1,598,700)	(856,500)	(695,000)	(666,300)	(1,438,100)	(1,313,100)	(132,700)	578,600	319,000	385,400	45,200	

292

FIVE YEAR CASH FLOW SUMMARY

	1973/4	1974/5	1975/6	1976/7	1977/8
1. Subscriptions	3,000,000	4,200,000	5,100,000	5,700,000	6,000,000
2. Advertising	107,100	554,900	2,000,000	3,200,000	4,000,000
3. Services		344,000	1,000,000	2,000,000	3,000,000
4. TOTAL REVENUE (1+2+3)	3,107,100	5,098,900	8,100,000	10,900,000	13,000,000
5. Production	138,000	442,000	864,000	1,596,000	2,052,000
6. Circulation Fulfilment	211,500	417,000	500,000	588,000	617,000
7. Editorial	22,000	36,000	55,000	70,000	85,000
8. Magazine Postage	52,000	205,000	540,000	992,000	1,520,000
9. COST OF PRODUCT (5+6+7+8)	423,500	1,120,000	1,959,000	3,190,000	4,274,000
10. Salaries	366,550	493,500	598,000	640,000	700,000
11. Personnel Relocation	20,000	4,000	8,000	8,000	8,000
12. Office Supplies & Equip.	16,550	21,000	27,000	30,000	35,000
13. Selling Expense	35,000	89,000	120,000	150,000	160,000
14. Circulation Promotion	2,186,600	2,934,000	3,150,000	3,378,000	3,291,000
15. Advertising Promotion	27,000	60,000	65,000	50,000	100,000
16. Services Promotion		138,500	230,000	300,000	380,000
17. Editorial Travel Entertain	10,500	30,000	35,000	50,000	60,000
18. Advertising Sales Commiss	5,400	27,700	57,000	160,000	200,000
19. Rent, Heat & Light	20,100	21,000	23,000	24,000	30,000
20. Telephone	19,100	23,400	27,000	33,000	35,000
21. Legal	12,000	12,000	14,000	15,000	15,000
22. Audit	3,000	4,000	5,000	5,000	5,000
23. Fringe Benefits	17,100	33,900	60,000	100,000	114,000
24. Taxes (Fed, State etc.)	500	239,500	884,000	1,431,000	918,000
25. Consultants Fees	34,000	42,000	50,000	30,000	50,000
26. Advertising Agency	24,000	25,500	30,000	30,000	30,000
27. Miscellaneous	17,000	24,000	25,000	30,000	30,000
28. SELLING, G & A (10+11...27)	2,834,300	3,783,000	5,448,000	6,539,000	7,157,000
29. TOTAL EXPENSES (9+28)	3,257,800	4,903,000	7,377,000	9,729,000	11,431,000
30. NET INCOME (4-29)	(150,700)	195,900	723,000	1,171,000	1,569,000

Seed Increments Invested	% Equity in Limited Partnership	% Equity in Corporation*
$10,000	2.0%	1.0%
20,000	4.4	2.2
30,000	7.2	3.6
40,000	11.2	5.6
50,000	17.0	8.5
60,000	24.0	12.0

* After secondary financing

Since no follow-on financing is anticipated beyond the $1.5 million secondary funding, ownership will remain intact until the corporation goes public within five years.

Expected Return to Investors

When the corporation sells its stock to the public, investors should realize a significant return on their investment. It is expected that a Price-Earnings multiple of 25 will be reasonable based upon the company's earnings growth and the nature of the business. The corporation plans to vigorously identify itself with the leisure/service industry rather than with the publishing industry.

The following section derives the value of investments based upon equity distribution at the time of public sale.

Total Value of Corporation = $37.5 million
($1.5 million after taxes x 25)

Seed Investors

Seed $ Invested	Fully Diluted Ownership in Corp.	Expected Value When Going Public
$10,000	1.0%	$ 375,000 (37x)
20,000	2.2	825,000 (41x)
30,000	3.6	1,350,000 (45x)
40,000	5.6	2,100,000 (52x)
50,000	8.5	3,187,000 (64x)
60,000	12.0	4,500,000 (75x)

Venture Capital Investors

Venture Capital $ Invested	Fully Diluted Ownership in Corp.	Expected Value When Going Public
$1,500,000	50.0%	$18,750,000 (12x)

APPENDIX to Business Plan II

SUPPLEMENTARY CASH FLOW DATA
Year 1

(Month 1)

5. Cost of Production
   Dummy Issue $2,000

7. Editorial
   Contributing Editors. 1,000

10. Salaries
    See Appendix, Exhibit 13,500

11. Personnel Relocation
    Three employees @ approx. $2,000 each 6,000

13. Selling Expense
    Sales Manager and Publisher 2,000

14. Circulation Promotion
    ● Preparation of space ads for test.
    ● Preparation and research for FM radio and direct mail
      tests.
               5,000

19. Rent, Heat and Light
    Rent @ . . . . $1,500/mo.
    Heat and light @ . . . . <u>100/mo.</u>
               1,600

23. Fringe Benefits
    ● F.I.C.A. for 1973: 5.5% on 1st $10,800 = $594
               1974: 5.5% on 1st 12,000 = 660
               (See Staffing, Exhibit)

    Total F.I.C.A. for April . . . . $ 400
    Group health insurance 150
    State and federal unempl. etc. <u>50</u>
               600

25. Consultants Fees
    ● Consumer magazine consultant @ $2,000/mo.
    ● Direct mail consultant @ . . . . . . <u>2,000/mo.</u>
               4,000

26. Advertising Agency Fee 2,000
    *Primary function of advertising agency is to provide
    effective PUBLICITY.*

(Month 2)

14. Circulation Promotion
    A. Direct Mail Test
       - 120,000 pieces @ $150/M
       - List rental @   30/M

                      $180/M

       $180/M x 120 . . . . $21,600
    B. Space Advertising Test
       Total budget of $40,000:
       One-half to be used in May   20,000
       One-half in June
    C. FM Radio Test
       Total budget $20,000:
       One-half in May   10,000
       One-half in June

                                                 $51,600

(Month 3)

5. Production
   Print run of 5,000 dummy copies
   @ $.40 ea   2,000
   Other production expenses, ie. ast,
   layout etc.   2,000

                                                 $ 4,000

14. Circulation Promotion
    Space Advertising Testing @   20,000
    FM radio testing @   10,000

                                                 30,000

15. Advertising Promotion
    2,500 merchandising kits @ $2.00 ea 5,000

(Month 4)
All Ahead Full

10. Salaries
    See Appendix, Exhibit $35,000

11. Personnel Relocation . . . .
    Five employees @ approx. $2,000 ea 10,000

13. Selling Expense
    New York Office (Manned by National Sales Manager and Salesman)
    A. Rent . . . . $ 400/mo
    B. Telephone, equip., supplies   300
    C. Travel, entertain., (Nat. Sales
       Mgr.)   1,200

D. Travel, entertain. (Salesman) 500
E. Part-time secretary 100
F. Miscellaneous 100
$3,000

Chicago Office (Regional Sales Manager)
A. Rent 300
B. Telephone, supplies, equip. etc. . . 200
C. Travel, entertainment 500
$1,000

Home Office $1,000

Total $ 5,000

14. Circulation Promotion
Assuming that direct mail proves to be the most cost effective medium in soliciting new subscribers, a two-stage mailing will follow. The mail piece will offer a free, no obligation "look-see" at the Charter issue. It is expected that of the initial 5 million pieces, 400 thousand will want to see the Charter issue (8%). Of these, 250 thousand will eventually subscribe. Therefore, it is expected that two, 5 million piece mailings will result in 500 thousand new subscriptions.
Cost of mail piece, list rental and postage = $180/M
$180/M x 5,000M $900,000

15. Advertising Promotion
Personalized direct mail program directed at ad agency media, and account executives, plus advertising managers of key consumer product/service companies 2,000
(to be run for six consecutive months)

23. Fringe Benefits
Total F.I.C.A. $1,200/mo
Health insurance 300
State and fed. unemp. etc. 100
1,600

25. Consultants Fees
Consumer magazine consult. $2,000
Direct mail consultant 1,000
3,000

(Month 5)

5. Production
Charter issue print order of 400,000
400,000 x $.10 ea. . . . . $ 40,000

297

6. Circulation Fulfillment
   There will be an estimated one-time cost of $.15
   for each respondent. Maintenance of each subscriber will be approximately $.03 per month.

	Aug	Sept	Oct	Nov	Dec	Jan	Feb
Respondents*	400M	400M	250M	250M	250M	250M	250M
Respondents**				400M	450M	250M	250M
	400M	400M	250M	650M	650M	500M	500M

Fulfillment Expense

	Aug	Sept	Oct	Nov	Dec	Jan	Feb
Fulfill. Exp*	$60M	12M	7.5M	7.5M	7.5M	7.5M	7.5M
Fulfill. Exp**				60.0M	12.0M	7.5M	7.5M
	$60M	12M	7.5M	67.5M	19.5M	15M	15M

  * First mailing
 ** Second mailing

11. Personnel Relocation
    Two employees @ approx. $2,000 each . . . . $ 4,000

(Month 6)

8. Postage
   400,000 Charter issues mailed at $.04 each. This
   assumes that 1972 second class rates will increase
   by 33% -- from $.03 to $.04 . . . . $16,000
   400,000 x $.04

14. Circulation Promotion
    Approximately three weeks after sending sample
    Charter issue, a follow-up letter will be mailed
    outlining the subscription offer. The mail piece
    will include:
    - Cover letter
    - Order form
    - Inducement flyer
    - Return postage paid envelope

    The letter will offer a one-year subscription of
    four quarterly issues for $6. The Charter issue
    will be free and will not count as one of the
    quarterly issues. Inducements for subscriptions
    (especially long-term) will be offered i.e., paper-
    backs.

    Payment will be requested from those wishing to
    subscribe. Those not willing will be asked to
    simply write "Cancel" on the order form and

return in the postage paid envelope.

It is estimated that the 400,000 letters will cost
$.15 each including $.06 bulk postage. The $.06
represents a 20% increase over 1972 rates. Also,
it is expected that first class rates will increase
by 25% -- from $.08 to $.10.

Cost of circulation promotion mailing:

1. 400,000 letters @ $.15 each = $60,000
2. 400,000 replies @   .10 each = 40,000
3. 250,000 inducements @ .20* each = 50,000

* includes postage

However, actual cash flow is expected as follows:

	Sept	Oct	Nov
Cost of 1.	$60,000		
Cost of 2.		28,000	12,000
Cost of 3.	50,000		
	110,000	28,000	12,000

25. Consultants Fees
Consumer magazine consultant . . . . $ 2,000

(Month 7)

1. Subscription Revenue
The two-part subscription mailing of 10,000,000 pieces
will produce an estimated 500,000 subscribers @ $6
per year. The $3,000,000 revenue will be generated
over a five month period.

	Oct	Nov	Dec	Jan	Feb
Revenue from 1st mailing*	$1,050M	450M			
Revenue from 2nd mailing				1,050M	450M
	$1,050M	450M		1,050M	450M

* It is assumed that 70% of the subscription revenue
from each mailing will be received within 30 days
of billing, and 30% within 60 days.

2. Advertising Revenue
- Guaranteed circulation of Fall issue = 250,000
- Full page black and white @ $12/M = $3M/page
- Estimated 10 pages advertising
  10 x $3,000 $30,000
  less 15% agency comm.   4,500
                $25,500

It is estimated that 50% of advertising revenue will be received within 30 days of publication, 30% after 60 days, 20% after 90 days.

.5 x $25,500 = approx. $12,500 rec'd in Oct.
.3 x 25,500 = approx.   7,000 rec'd in Nov.
.2 x 25,500 = approx.   6,000 rec'd in Dec.
                        $25,500

15. Advertising Promotion
Readership profile study by independent research
company $10,000
Direct mail   2,000
                                                                         $12,000

18. Advertising Sales Commission
The corporation plans a hybrid advertising sales organization composed of direct salesmen (New York and Chicago) and commissioned sales representatives (west coast). It is estimated that 2/3 of the total space sold will be sold direct, 1/3 by sales representatives. A 15% commission will be paid to the representative organizations. The resultant commission rate on total advertising revenue equates to 5%. For example, advertising revenue expected for October (month 7) is $12,500 net after 15% agency commissions.

1/3 space sold by reps . . . $12,500/3 = $4,167
@ 15% commission. . . . . . 15 x $4167 =   625
$625/$12,500 . . . . =   5%

(Month 8)

5. Production
Print order for 400,000 additional Fall Charter
issues @ $.10 each. $40,000

10. Salaries (See Appendix, Exhibit)   36,000
Manager of Supplementary Services added

13. Selling Expense.   6,000
Add $1,000/mo. - Manager Supplementary Services

14. Circulation Promotion
2nd half direct mail subscription program (5,000,000)
$180/M x 500 M= $900 M
Return postage from 1st mailing*   12 M
                                       ──────
* See Sept. '73, #14   912,000

(Month 9)

14. Circulation Promotion $110,000
    (See Sept. 1973 Circulation Promotion)

(Month 10)

5. Production
   Print order Winter Issue, 500,000 copies
   500,000 x $.10 ea . . . . $ 50,000

8. Postage
   .04 x 500,000   20,000

10. Salaries   38,000
    Includes a 5-1/2% increase across the board

23. Fringe Benefits

    F.I.C.A. $1,400 (5.5% on 1st $12,000)
    Health Ins.   350 (15% increase)
    State & fed. unempl. comp.   ___150
                                                              1,900

(Month 11)

2. Advertising Revenue
   Guaranteed circulation of 500,000
   Full page black and white @ $12/M or $6,000/page
   Estimated 20 pages advertising

   20 pages @ $6,000/page = $120,000
   less 15%   __18,000
                             $102,000 net

   Assume income profile @ 50% within 30 days
   30% within 60 days and 20% within 90 days.

   .5 x $102,000 =   51,000 rec'd in February
   .3 x 102,000 =   30,600 rec'd in March
   .2 x 102,000 =   20,400 rec'd in April
                    $102,000

18. Advertising Sales Commissions

    .05 x $51,000 paid in February . . . $2,600
    .05 x 30,600 paid in March 1,500
    .05 x 20,400 paid in April 1,000

(Month 12)

25. Consultant's Fees

Consumer magazine consultant $2,000
Direct mail consultant* 2,000

$ 4,000

* Preparation for direct mail subscription program

Business Plan II SUPPLEMENTARY CASH FLOW DATA Year 2

5. Production
   - A 10% increase is expected in the cost of printing the magazine (from $.10 to .11 per copy).
   - It is estimated that 400,000 respondents will request a free copy of the Spring Issue via the 5,000,000 piece direct mail program.

   Total print order = 500M + 400M = 900 M
   900,000 x $.11 ea $99,000

6. Circulation Fulfillment
   In addition to the $15,000/mo. required to fulfill the current 500,000 subscriptions, the direct mail program will produce 400,000 additional names to be processed @ $.15 ea. initially, and .03 per month thereafter.

		Apr.	May	June	July	Aug.
1.	Current Subs	500M	500M	500M	500M	500M
2.	Respondents	400M	400M	400M	300M	200M
	Fulfillment of 1.	$15M	15M	15M	15M	15M
	Fulfillment of 2.	$60M*	12M	12M	9M	6M
	Total cost	$75M	27M	27M	24M	21M

   * @ $.15 each one-time charge

8. Postage (magazine only)

	April	May
Current Subscriptions	$20M*	
400,000 free copies		$20M**

   * 500,000 x $.04 = $20,000
   ** 400,000 x .05 = 20,000 (25% increase in postal rate)

14. Circulation Promotion/Subscription Solicitation
   Cost of mail piece, list rental and postage = $180M
   $180/M x 5,000M $900,000

15. Advertising Promotion
   Space advertising program 16,000

16. Services Promotion
   Test mailing for health insurance
   10,000 piece mailing @ $200/M 2,000

25. Consultants Fee
    Consumer magazine consultant = $2,000
    Direct mail consultant*   = 3,000

    * Development of two programs:
        1. Health insurance
        2. Subscription drive

                              5,000

(Month 14)

14. Circulation Promotion (See Sept. 1973)
    400,000 follow-up letters will be sent to those
    requesting a free copy of the Spring Issue. The
    same offer will be made as in the two previous
    mass mailings except that new subscribers will
    receive five issues rather than four. The extra
    issue resulting from the magazine going bi-
    monthly.

    It is estimated that the 400,000 letters will cost
    $.17 each including $.07 for bulk postage (a 17%
    increase over 1973 rates). Also included is an
    11% increase in the cost of the mail piece. It is
    also expected that first class rates will increase
    20% -- from $.10 to $.12.

Cost of Circulation Promotion Mailing

1. 400,000 letters   @ $.17 each = $68,000
2. 400,000 replies   @ .12 each = 48,000
3. 200,000 inducements @ .25 each* = 50,000

* includes postage

However, the cash flow is expected.

	May	June	July
Cost of 1.	$ 60,000		
Cost of 2.		34,000	14,000
Cost of 3.	50,000		
	$110,000	34,000	14,000

15. Advertising Promotion
    A personalized direct mail program directed at ad
    agency media and account executives; plus adver-
    tising managers of key consumer product service
    companies. Approximately $2,000 will be spent in
    May, July, September, October, November, Decem-
    ber and January. (Primary concentration on ad
    managers) . . . . $ 2,000

    Space advertising program . 15,000

                             17,000

16. Services Promotion
    Direct mail program offering health insurance to
    subscribers.

    Cost of mail pieces, list rental and postage = $200/M
    $200/M x 50M $100,000

(Month 15)

1. Subscription Revenue
    The 5 million piece mailing will produce an
    estimated 200,000 new subscriptions @ $6 each.

    $6 x 200,000 = $1,200,000

    However, the actual receipt of subscription revenue
    will probably occur over a two month period as follows:

	June	July
Subscription Revenue	$840,000	360,000

(Month 16)

5. Production
    It is estimated that the 5 million piece April mailing
    will result in 200,000 new subscriptions. Total print
    order equals 500,000 charter subscriptions plus the
    additional 200,000 = 700,000 copies.

    700,000 x $.11 . . . . $ 77,000

8. Postage (Magazine)
    700,000 x $.05   35,000

(Month 17)

3. Revenue from Services
    In the Spring Issue (approx. May 1) health insurance
    was offered to PERSPECTIVE subscribers. A follow-
    up direct mail program will be sent to all subscribers
    in May. It is assumed that 2% of the 500,000 total
    circulation will accept the offer (10,000 respondents).
    It is further assumed that the corporation will receive
    $50 for each policy sold at an average annual premium
    value of $100 ($5 per month per adult and $1.50 for each
    child).

    It is expected that the $500,000 revenue resulting from
    policy sales will flow in an irregular manner due to an
    expected three month lag -- from the time the customer
    signs up until the actual payment to the corporation.
    Another factor is that the customer has the option to

pay annually or monthly. The actual cash flow calculations are quite involved and will not be included here but are available as back-up data.

(Month 18)

1. Subscription Revenue
   50% of the original charter subscribers are expected to renew in response to two renewal mail programs and solicitation in the Fall Issue.

	Sept.	Oct.	Nov.	Dec.
# Renewals - 1st Notice	100M	40M		
Notification via Fall Issue		30M	30M	
- 2nd Notice				50M
	100M	70M	30M	50M
@ $6 each	$600M	420M	180M	300M

14. Circulation Promotion
    500,000 renewal letters to charter subscribers

    500,000 letters @ $.12* each = $60,000
    250,000 replies @ .12   each = 30,000
    $90,000

    * includes .07 postage (bulk rate)

    New subscription solicitation
    Cost of piece, list, postage @ $200/M
    $200/M x 6,250M = 1,250,000 $1,340,000

(Month 19)

1. Subscription Revenue
   New subscriptions from the 6.25 million mailing will produce an expected 250,000 new subscriptions.

   Cash flow from the renewal mailings will be super-imposed to get total subscription revenue through December

	Oct.	Nov.	Dec.
Cash via renewals	$420M	180M	300M
Cash via new subsc.		1,050M	450M
	420M	1,130M	750M

5. Production

Current subscriptions	=	700,000	
Requests for "looksee"	=	500,000	
Total print order		1,200,000 x $.11 ea.	$ 132,000

6. Circulation Fulfillment

	Oct.	Nov.	Dec.	Jan.*	Feb.
1. Current subscriptions	700M	700M	450M	450M	450M
2. 6.25 million mailing	500M	500M	250M	250M	250M
Fulfillment cost of 1.	$21M	21M	135M	135M	135M
Fulfillment cost of 2.	$75M**	15M	75M	75M	75M
	$96M	36M	210M	210M	210M
* add 10%				2M	2M
				212M	212M

** @ $.15 initial cost

1,200,000 x $.11 . . . . $132,000

8. Postage (Magazine)
   1,200,000 x $.05   60,000

10. Salaries   43,000
    Add $5,000 per month for expansion of staff

14. Circulation Promotion - Renewal
    500,000 renewal letters to charter subscribers

    500,000 letters @ $.12* = $60,000
    250,000 replies @   .12   =   30,000

    * includes $.07 postage   90,000
    (bulk rate)

15. Advertising Promotion

    Direct mail $2,000
    New merchandising kit =   5,000

                                                                         7,000

                          (Month 20)

14. Circulation Promotion/Subscription Renewal
    The second subscription renewal program will cost

    300,000 letters @ $.12 ea . . . . $ 36,000

    Reply postage has been accounted for in October.

                          (Month 21)

16. Services Promotion
    Test mailing/health insurance

    450,000 subscribers on board since last promotion --
    direct mail program will focus on this segment.

    10,000 piece mailing @ $200/M . . . . $ 2,000

5. Production
   Print order 700,000
   700,000 x $.11 . . . . $ 77,000

10. Salaries 45,500
    Approx. 5-1/2% increase across the board

16. Services Promotion
    Direct mail program to recent subscribers offering
    health insurance package.
    450M x $210/M 94,500

(Month 23)

2. Advertising Revenue
   Guaranteed circulation of 700,000
   Full page black and white @ $12/M or $8,400/page
   Estimated 40 pages advertising

   40 pages @ $8400/page = $336,000
   less 15%   50,400
                             $285,600 net

   Assume revenue inflow @ 50% within 30 days,
   30% within 60 days, 20% within 90 days

   .5 x $285,600 = $142,800 Feb.
   .3 x   285,600 =   85,700 Mar.
   .2 x   285,600 =   57,100 April
                    $285,600

18. Advertising Sales Commission

    .05 x 142,800 . . . . . 7,100 Feb.
    .05 x   85,700 . . . . . 4,300 Mar.
    .05 x   57,100 . . . . . 2,900 April

(Month 24)

24. Taxes (Federal, State, Local)
    Assuming an effective tax rate of 55% to cover federal,
    state and local taxes:

    Income before taxes: $435,400
    .55 x $435,400 . . . . $239,500

    Note: The corporation is due a tax credit on
          the loss for the preceding year. It has
          not been included in the cash flow projection.

Creative Professional Services, Inc.

36 Montvale Avenue
Stoneham, Massachusetts, U.S.A. 02180
Telephone: (617) 438-3838

May 4, 1972

Mr. Charles Pinkham
5 Horse Lane
Mansfield, Massachusetts

Dear Mr. Penkham:

We would like to know how we can help you reach your customers more effectively via Consumer Magazines.

Our client (a publisher) has assigned us the task of determining your satisfaction with current advertising alternatives. In short, do you feel that
your options allow you to reach your customers on a cost-effective basis?
If your answer is "no", please use the enclosed questionnaire to let us know
more about your problem -- if "yes", we'd like to know that too.

Since we have selected a very small (but significant) sample of advertising
managers, it is extremely important that we hear from you.

We'd be happy to send you a free executive report summarizing our findings
if you'd like one.

Sincerely,

John C. O'Mara

John C. O'Mara

JCO:oc

Enclosure

WALTER WEINTZ and Company, Inc. • 1100 High Ridge Road, Stamford, Conn. 06905
···

Telephone: 203 329-0931
NYC (212) 586-6730

June 28, 1973

Mr. John O'Mara
22 Cherlyn Drive
Northboro, Massachusetts 01532

Dear Mr. O'Mara:

The purpose of this letter is to give you in written
form a summary of the test proposal which I made you today
by telephone for your prospective new magazine, Perspective.

As you know, magazine circulation, for specialized
magazines of this sort, is generally secured through direct
mail.

Direct mail, as you also know, is a combination of
science and art. It's possible, in direct mail, to make
very scientific tests. At the same time, the copy that
you use to promote your product is decisive in determining
whether your mailings are a success or not.

The procedure, then, is to put together a test or a
series of tests, to mail out 50,000 or 100,000 pieces to
selected mailing lists, and to count the returns. On the
basis of the returns, you can then make a very accurate
financial forecast. You can say with great assurance that
if you mail so and so many thousands or millions of pieces,
you will get back so many trial subscribers at such and such
a cost per subscriber.

Walter Weintz and Company is a direct mail consulting
firm which specializes in the creation of such direct mail
tests. As you will recall, I was for some twelve years
Circulation Manager of Reader's Digest. I left the Digest
in 1958 to start my own direct mail consulting firm. Since
then I have done consulting work for literally dozens of
magazines, book clubs, and publishers. Last year, for
example, I helped Women's Wear Daily launch their new consumer newspaper, "W." Four years ago, I helped launch Family
Health Magazine, with a national guaranteed circulation of
one million.

Mr. John O'Mara   2   June 28, 1973

Our firm is currently doing consulting work for TV
Guide, Rodale Publishing Company (Organic Gardening Magazine),
Funk & Wagnalls Encyclopedia, Fuller & Dees Publishing Co.,
Meredith Publishing Company and Maclean's.

To put together a test program which would tell you
how big your market is and whether or not it can be reached
by direct mail, would require a budget of about $30,000.
This would break down into a $5,000 consulting fee for
Walter Weintz and Company, and $25,000 for a test of some-
where between 50,000 and 100,000 pieces. The elaborateness
of the mailing that we decide on would, of course, govern
the cost per thousand. I can't forecast this in advance.

In order to carry out such an assignment, we would
require four months. If retained by you, effective July 1,
we would be able to deliver a test plan with copy before
the end of July, and have this test in the mail around
Labor Day. Returns would come in during the month of
September, and we would write a summary and analysis with
recommendations, and wind down the test in October.

In order to carry out this assignment, we would meet
with you as necessary, setting aside one day a month for
regular consultation, with in-between meetings to submit
copy, review plans, and so on.

Our $5,000 fee would cover all our in-house services
and expenses -- copy and layout and travel. We would
carry copy up to the mechanical stage; out-of-pocket expenses for mechanicals, printing, lists and so on would
be passed on to you at cost.

If you wish to retain us, I suggest that you do so for
a period of four months, July through October, with the
option of continuing or cancelling the arrangement thereafter with one month's notice. Our fee would be $1,250
per month retainer -- a total of $5,000 for the four months
-- payable in four monthly installments at the start of
each month.

Telephone: 203 329-0931
NYC (212) 586-6730

Mr. John O'Mara   3   June 28, 1973

    If you wish to retain us for this job, you can do so
by signing and returning one copy of this letter, together
with your check for $1,250, in which case this letter be-
comes an informal letter of agreement between us.

    I wish you success with your new venture, and I hope
we will have a chance to work for you.

Very truly yours,

Walter Weintz

Walter Weintz

WW:mec

Accepted for Walter Weintz and Co., Inc.:   Date:

_____   _____
Walter Weintz   June 28, 1973

Accepted for <u>Perspective</u>:   Date:

_____   _____
John O'Mara

QUESTIONNAIRE
MAGAZINE ADVERTISING/CONSUMER MARKETS

1. For which of the following CONSUMER products/services do you buy or recommend MAGAZINE advertising media? (Please check the appropriate product/service.)

☐ Airlines ☐ Investment Services ☐ **Pharmaceuticals**
☐ Automobiles ☐ Mail Order ☐ **Real Estate**
☐ Banking ☐ Menswear ☐ **T. V. Sets, Radios**
☐ Books, Bookclubs ☐ Mobile Homes ☐ **Food/Nutrition Products**
☐ Health Aids (e.g. vitamins,etc.) ☐ Motels/Hotels ☐ **Other**_____
☐ Insurance ☐ Pet Foods _____

2. Which AGE GROUPS do you consider most difficult to reach through MAGAZINE advertising? (Please rank order from 1 to 5, using 1 as the most difficult).

MOST DIFFICULT AGE GROUPS TO REACH

PRODUCTS/SERVICES (As checked above)	Under 18 Yrs.	18–25	26–35	36–55	Over 55
A. _____	_____	_____	_____	_____	_____
B. _____	_____	_____	_____	_____	_____
C. _____	_____	_____	_____	_____	_____

3. For the products that you checked in Question 1, which INCOME GROUPS do you consider the most difficult to reach through MAGAZINE advertising? (Rank order 1 to 5, using 1 as the most difficult.)

ANNUAL HOUSEHOLD INCOME

PRODUCTS/SERVICES (As checked above)	Less than $10,000/yr.	$10,000 to $14,999/yr.	$15,000 to $19,999/yr.	$20,000 to $25,000/yr.	Over $25,000/yr.
A. _____	_____	_____	_____	_____	_____
B. _____	_____	_____	_____	_____	_____
C. _____	_____	_____	_____	_____	_____

4. Which COMBINATION of demographics (one or more) most accurately describes the market(s) that you now find most difficult to reach through magazine advertising? Simply insert the appropriate characteristics; add others if necessary.

DEMOGRAPHIC CHARACTERISTICS

PRODUCTS/SERVICES	Age Group	Income Bracket	Sex (MorF)	Education Level	Marital Status	Geographic Location	Other
A. _____	_____	_____	_____	_____	_____	_____	_____
B. _____	_____	_____	_____	_____	_____	_____	_____
C. _____	_____	_____	_____	_____	_____	_____	_____

5. Would you care to provide any additional comments or observations that might help in identifying other possible deficiencies in consumer magazine advertising?

_____
_____
_____
_____

****

Thank you for your help. If you'd like a summary of the results, please enter your address to the right.

NAME_____

ADDRESS_____

_____

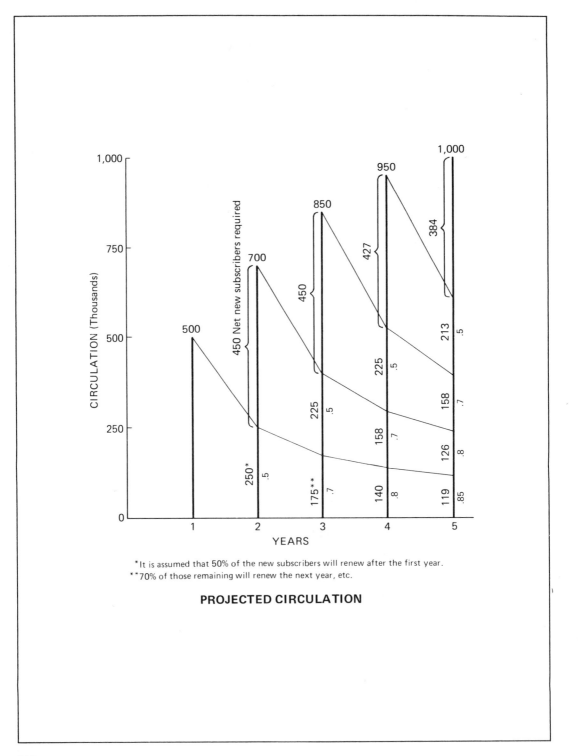

CIRCULATION (Thousands)

1,000

750

500

250

0

500

700   450 Net new subscribers required

850   450

950   427

1,000   384

250*   .5

175**   .7

225   .5

140   .8

158   .7

225   .5

213   .5

158   .7

126   .8

119   .85

1   2   3   4   5

YEARS

*It is assumed that 50% of the new subscribers will renew after the first year.
**70% of those remaining will renew the next year, etc.

PROJECTED CIRCULATION

STAFFING / SALARY SCHEDULE

	Month 1	2 MAY	3 JUNE	4 JULY	5 AUG.	6 SEPT.	7 OCT.	8 NOV.	9 DEC.	FILM '73	FILM '74
1. Publisher	$2,500									$574	$660
2. Editor	2,500									574	660
3. Sales Manager	2,000									574	660
4. Art Director	1,700									574	660
5. Production Manager	1,700									574	660
6. Market Research Dir.	1,500									400	440
7. Clerk / Typist	600									400	440
8. Clerk / Typist	600									574	660
9. Managing Editor				2,000						574	660
10. Associate Editor				1,500						574	660
11. Associate Editor				1,200						574	660
12. Copy Editor				1,200						574	660
13. Copy Editor				1,100						530	580
14. Staff Writer				1,000						574	660
15. Editorial Assistant				800						574	660
16. Editorial Assistant				1,500						574	660
17. Salesman (N.Y.C.)				1,500						574	660
18. Salesman (Chicago)				1,000						574	660
19. Assistant to Publisher				1,500						574	660
20. Assistant Art Direct.				600						400	440
21. Circulation Director				1,000						400	440
22. Clerk / Typist										574	660
23. Clerk / Typist										574	660
24. Accountant				1,000						574	660
25. Supplementary Service				700						400	440
26. Staff Writer								1,700			
27. Mail, Misc.											
	$13,500	13,500	13,500	35,000	35,000	35,000	35,000	36,700	36,700		

Reduce to 3,000 Per Cash Flow

ITEMIZED EXPENSES
FOR TEST PROGRAM

1. **Direct Mail Test**
   Includes the selection, acquisition and testing of
   appropriate lists, copywriting and consulting fees.
   See attached letter from Walter Weintz for
   details $30,000

   Artwork, production, miscellaneous 3,000

2. **Entrepreneur's Subsistence**
   Six months @ $1000/month 6,000

3. **Travel and Related Expenses**
   Estimated cost of $350/week when traveling.
   Estimated 15 weeks of travel. $350 includes
   air and auto travel, lodging, meals plus
   miscellaneous.

   15 weeks x $350/week is approximately 5,000

4. **Telephone**
   $150/month x 6 is approximately 1,000

5. **Consultants Fees**
   James B. Kobak, Inc. will be retained to assist
   in the test program, i.e., recommendations on
   editorial staff assistance, refining of financial
   projections, etc., and seeking secondary
   financing 10,000

6. **Legal**
   Drawing up documents for limited partnership, etc.
   Estimate of legal fees based upon discussion
   with Mr. Mark Thoman of Day, Lord & Day,
   N.Y.C. The firm specializes in magazine publish-
   ing ventures 4,000

7. **Miscellaneous**
   Postage, entertainment, etc. 1,000

   TOTAL $60,000

STOP WORRYING!

MAGAZINE PUBLISHING IS A HIGH PROFIT, LOW RISK BUSINESS.

By James B. Kobak
James B. Kobak, Inc.

The persistent myth that magazine publishing is a high risk, low profit business is widespread both inside and outside the industry. One successful publisher recently called investing in magazines "very slightly safer than betting on horses--sometimes."

The truth is that a new publication can begin with relatively little capital and go on to earn high profits with much less risk than in most other fields. Why, then, does the myth persist?

The first assumption, that publishing is risky, is fed by the nature of the business. The passing of Colliers, Saturday Evening Post, and Look, for instance, was headlined, analyzed, and minutely examined, not only in terms of their own business histories, but in relation to the state of the nation, its mores and its standards. Because by nature magazine publishing is a public business, the failure of a magazine gets more public attention that the event warrants. Bigger failures--RCA's and GE's abortive sallies into the computer business, DuPont's Corfate, Boise-Cascade's land ventures, Ford's Edsel, the Penn-Central's daily operations--make news briefly, but are not subjected to lengthy analysis anywhere except on the business and financial pages. They do not generate the same wide public discussion. The difference is that the individual subscriber has a personal and emotional relationship with a magazine that speaks directly to him and enters his home. When a magazine dies he feels that he has lost a friend. He has no such personal rapport with RCA, probably irrationally hates computers, and cares little about the company's problems.

Even when they do occur, magazine failures are rarely business catastrophes of the kind suffered in other industries. In 1971, for instance, only 17 periodical publishers went bankrupt, leaving liabilities of a little over $1 million. When you consider that these bankruptcies occured in an industry with total receipts of $3.64 billion you can see that these losses were miniscule.

Stillborn magazines that do not result in bankruptcies are not spectacular financial losses either. Show Business Illustrated cost less than $1 million before it died. Contrast this with some of the losses which companies in other fields are able to build up in just a year, such as Lockheed's $83.6 million in 1970.

Few realize it, but the industry has never been healthier than it is today, with about 3,750 trade and consumer magazines, a total which is constantly growing.

And there are more companies publishing magazines today than there have ever been, literally in the hundreds.

It is very difficult to kill a magazine that has at one time been a success, even though it may have outlived its life cycle. The Saturday Evening Post declined for many years with the handwriting on the wall. Advertisers continued to support it after the funeral cortege had passed, to a great extent out of loyalty.

And often magazines that fail are resurrected to go on in a somewhat more limited way than they had before--witness the Post itself, Liberty and Cosmopolitan. The same emotional attachment that causes so much talk when a magazine dies, remains in the public's consciousness to help bring immediate recognition and acceptance if it comes back to life.

Unfortunately, shooting down the first myth--that publishing is a high-risk business--only adds fuel to the second myth--that it can earn only small profits. Too many people assume that it is an iron-clad law of finance that only big risks bring big gains.

Even data compiled by the Magazine Publishers Association seems to support this theory, showing only small average magazine profits. But the truth is that recent MPA figures have been weighted by a few large magazines, such as Look, which were in trouble (after having been highly profitable in the past). Besides, the data does not include figures from a number of large, very successful magazines which do not report to the association, nor are the earnings of business magazines included. Statistics of the American Business Press show a very different picture.

The fact is that a great many magazines have made and still make very handsome profits. Time, Inc., McGraw-Hill, Meredith and a number of other well-known communications companies were built from the profits earned from magazines. The earnings of individual magazines have rarely been made public. It is not unusual for a successful magazine to earn 25-30 percent of its revenues (before taxes). Consider how this compares with large companies in other fields.

There are several reasons why magazines are high profit/low risk.

1. Most magazines have a built-in advantage over other businesses. There are often two revenue streams--one from advertisers and one from readers. Most modern publishers have multiplied this advantage by adding diversified activities built around the aura and image of the magazine and based on the loyalty and interests of its readers.

   These additional opportunities for profit can often come with minimal investment. A magazine can, for instance, take information it already owns and present it in another form--books, cassettes, microfilm, audio-visuals, seminars--and have an added source of revenue. Or it can use the resources and talents of its own staff to create newsletters, travel programs, yearbooks, special events and many other forms of communication.

   A magazine can create products which are marketed through its own pages, or via direct mail to its own circulation list. When a magazine launches a new venture it has the enormous advantage of knowing precisely who its customers are, and of having a sympathetic communications channel.

   Playboy Enterprises is an example of a thoroughly diversified communications company. Playboy operates clubs, hotels, a limousine service, and a modeling agency. It markets gift items, makes movies, owns movie theatres and a research company. It is planning a book club, greeting card company, and music publishing and record production division. All of this grew out of the magazine, and at this point magazine sales of $74 million are almost equaled by the $58 million from other enterprises.

2. Before the first issue of a magazine is actually published for a relatively small amount of money it is possible to find out whether the concept is viable. With a cash outlay of some $35-60,000 a prospective publisher can test public response to his idea. There are few businesses which can do this kind of pre-testing at such a low cost. Could you ask people to buy your new automobile in case you decided to put one out? Of course not.

   This testing process, which has been developed to a fine art, is normally done through direct mail, but can be accomplished in other ways.

   The point is that a major part of the risk can be eliminated through the testing process for a relatively small amount of money--and if the public responds positively you can go ahead with much greater confidence.

3. The costs for launching a magazine are not of the magnitude of those required for most major businesses. Sure, it is possible to begin a magazine by spending a great deal of money. You can invest heavily in promotion, create preview issues, and hire large staffs. It is said that Sports Illustrated began with some $40 million, and it has paid off. Psychology Today is more typical of a magazine in today's economy, requiring about $1.5 million before it reached a break-even. (Its present value is far above that, of course, having been sold several years ago for more than $20 million.)

The essential point is that you don't need the huge amounts of capital which are required to start most major enterprises. Publishing is people and ideas--there is no need for a building or machinery. All the services, such as printing, list maintenance, etc., are available from outsiders.

4. In the event that a magazine is not successful, the largest liability is the unexpired portion of the subscriptions in effect, and this can normally be eliminated. Most subscribers of magazines which have closed their doors in the past have been willing to accept other magazines to fill the unexpired portions of their subscriptions. There have always been publishers willing to take over these obligations. To date, no publisher has ever paid out a significant amount of cash to satisfy his liability to subscribers.

5. Investments in magazine publishing operations can be designed so that they are deductible against ordinary income. This serves to cut the real cost of capital, depending on the tax brackets of the investors.

All these points act to minimize the risk and enhance the return on the investment.

A last word of warning: While magazine publishing in general is a high profit/low risk business, it can be quite the opposite. Bad management, a lack of planning, an editorial product that does not meet a need or deliver the promise, a falling out among partners, lack of adequate financing and many other mistakes can render the best idea worthless. But this is no different than in any other business.

BLT CORPORATION
Car Wash/Gas Station Combination

THE B. L. T. COMPANY

PARTICIPATION IN A TECHNOLOGICAL AND MERCHANDISING REVOLUTION

THE AUTOMOBILE SERVICE INDUSTRY IS IN THE EARLY STAGE OF A TECHNOLOGICAL AND MERCHANDISING REVOLUTION. THE COMBINATION OF TWO ESSENTIAL AUTOMOTIVE NEEDS--CAR WASHING AND GASOLINE--HAS PRODUCED A HIGHLY PROMOTABLE AND EXTREMELY PROFITABLE SERVICE.

TECHNOLOGICAL REVOLUTION

The technological revolution is the result of the development and perfection of a new generation of car wash equipment. This equipment is highly automated and inexpensive to operate and maintain.

MERCHANDISING REVOLUTION

The merchandising revolution is the result of combining the purchase of gasoline with the car washing function. This combination has created a new and highly promotable service which offers the consumer distinct economic and convenience benefits previously unavailable.

PROFITABILITY

The profitability of the modern gas pumping-car wash unit is based upon the following fundamental business principles: Low labor, high gross margins, and minimal inventory and accounts receivable.

THE B. L. T. COMPANY CONCEPT

The B. L. T. Company was organized to capitalize on the technological and merchandising revolution and the fundamental business advantages outlined above. The B. L. T. Company intends to multiply the profitability of an individual car wash and gas pumping-car wash unit through the establishment of a national chain of wholly owned and franchised installations.

Each wholly owned car wash unit is expected to generate between $25,000 and $40,000 pre tax annual earnings on an investment of approximately $50,000. Each franchised unit is expected to generate initial income from the sale of equipment of between $5,000 and $10,000, plus continuing income of between $3,000 - $6,000 annually.

Each wholly owned gas pumping-car wash unit is expected to generate between $50,000 and $70,000 pre tax annual earnings on an initial investment of about $65,000. Each franchised gas pumping-car wash unit is expected to generate initial income from the sale of equipment of between $7,000 and $12,000, plus continuing income of between $5,000 - $7,000 annually.

THE COMMERCIAL CAR WASH MARKET

There are approximately 85 million passenger vehicles registered in the United States today. By 1975 this number is expected to reach 130 million. Only ten percent of the passenger vehicles on the road today are regular patrons of commercial car washes.

It is estimated that the total size of today's commercial car wash market exceeds $300 million annually, and has a realistic potential of over $1.0 billion in the next ten years.

* * * * *

The first commercial car washes appeared after World War II. Washing was accomplished manually by low grade labor. Mounting labor costs precipitated the development of mechanized equipment featuring a series of large rotating brushes which cleaned the car as it was towed through a tunnel. A team of mitters dried the car as another crew cleaned and vacuumed inside.

This system featured:

- Decreased reliance on low grade labor.
- Heavy initial capital investment ($75,000 - $150,000).
- High operating, overhead, and maintenance costs.
- Costly and time consuming to customer.

The tunnel wash has remained unchanged to this day, and has failed to capture a broad base of consumer patronage.

During the early 1950's the coin operated do-it-yourself wash was developed. By 1967, over 6,000 units were in the field. The do-it-yourself wash consists of a bay equipped with a coin operated pressure hose dispensing wash and rinse water.

This system features:

o Customer washes car himself.
o Time consuming and inconvenient.

The do-it-yourself system offers limited economic return to the investor.

During the early 1960's the do-it-yourself concept was mechanized by mounting the high pressure water source on a moving arm which circled the car. Many companies, all utilizing the same principal, entered the market with closely related equipment. Automatics grew quickly in popularity and now number over 5,000 units.

The features of the high pressure automatic are:

o Customer does not work.
o Minimal labor.
o Moderate initial investment ($50,000 - $65,000).
o Moderate operating and maintenance costs.
o Attractive price to customer (usually 50¢).

The principal shortcoming of the spray system is the basic inability to remove road film. In addition, the car is left wet.

Paralleling the growth of the high pressure spray was the development of the combination brush and spray automatic. The brush-spray automatic consists of five brushes mounted on a gantry which moves back and forth over the stationary car.

This unit combines the washing effectiveness of the brush with the simplicity of the high pressure spray. Its features are:

o Customer does no work.
o Minimal labor.
o Moderate initial investment ($50,000 - $100,000).
o Moderate operating and maintenance costs.
o Attractive price to customer ($.75 - $1.00).

The brush-spray system offers the desired merchandising advantages, while delivering a superior wash. In addition, a forced air blower removes about 70% of the water.

* * * * *

Throughout most of its 20 year history, the commercial car wash industry has been dominated by independent owner operators utilizing a variety of equipment and methods. To date, commercial car washing has been a high priced service featuring low grade labor, unattractive surroundings, and ineffective and backward merchandising.

In the entire industry only one company, Robo-Wash, Inc., of Kansas City, Missouri, has recognized and successfully capitalized on the untapped market and inefficient competition. In less than four years, Robo has built a chain of over 1,000 franchised car wash units and is currently evaluated by the investing public at over $35 million. This remarkable success was the result of a superior merchandising program. Despite its dynamic growth and merchandising success, Robo has captured less than 5% of the potential car wash market in the United States.

We believe that the B.L.T. Company can successfully duplicate and possibly exceed Robo's performance by combining the two most essential automotive needs, car washing and gasoline, in a national program of company owned and franchised gas pumping-car wash units. To successfully carry out this program, B.L.T. will implement the following three phase program.

Phase I. The construction and operation of six to eight wholly owned units in five distinct market areas of the southwest corridor.

Phase II. The execution of a franchise program built around the B.L.T. merchandising concept and operating results, demonstrated by company owned units.

Phase III. Expansion of territorial coverage of wholly owned and franchised units from funds internally generated and from the proceeds of a contemplated public offering.

EQUIPMENT SELECTION

The brush-spray automatic car wash equipment offers the best balance between washing ability, initial cost, and profit potential. The American Sterilizer Corporation produces the best brush-spray automatic on the market today.

The B.L.T. Company has entered into a working arrangement with American Sterilizer which will manufacture its basic equipment to our specifications under our name. American Sterilizer can meet our anticipated production needs, provide field installation service, engineering support, and supply backup.

In addition, the relationship with the American Sterilizer Corporation affords us the advantage and prestige of being associated with a large reputable company.

The equipment consists of a compact gantry which straddles the car. Five brushes mounted on the gantry wash, rinse, and apply wax as the gantry moves back and forth on rails. A high velocity, forced air blower removes about 70% of the water during a second pass back and forth. The car remains stationary and the driver stays behind the wheel during the entire operation.

THE DIAGNOSTIC PROCESS

CRITERIA

1) Differentiating Between Language and Events

2) Specifying the Degree of Precision in Available Information

    A) Fact vs. Opinion
    B) Verifying the Judgement

3) Specifying the Underlying Causes Rather than Blame

    A) Why
    B) How

4) Specifying Multiple Causality

5) Explicitly Formulating the Final Working Diagnosis

ROBO-WASH – B.L.T. COMPARISON

The following compares certain key investment and operating factors of the Robo-Wash, B.L.T. Car Wash Unit, and B.L.T. Gas Pumping-Car Wash Unit franchise program.

Concept:

All three operations are based upon an attractive package featuring a clean, open, and functional operation. The B.L.T. Gas Pumping-Car Wash Unit goes one step further by combining two essential automotive services.

Capital Investment Required:

	Robo-Wash*	B.L.T. Car Wash Unit	B.L.T. Gas Pumping- Car Wash Unit
Basic Equipment	$23,000	$27,500**	$27,500**
Boilers, Electric & Pumping Equipment	7,000	5,000	5,000
Reclamation System	5,000	–	–
Correlator	–	2,500	2,500
Land Improvements	8,000	8,000	8,000
Building and Foundation	11,000	12,000	12,000
Signs, Working Capital & Misc.	5,000	5,000	5,000
Gas Pumping Equipment	–	–	15,000
Total Cost to Franchisee	$60,000	$60,000	$75,000

*Based on actual experience of franchise operators in the northeast.

**The B.L.T. Company will offer an equipment leasing program requiring a downpayment of $10,000, reducing the franchisee's initial cash outlay to approximately $42,500, and $58,500, respectively.

THE B. L. T. COMPANY ACTION PLAN

The following outlines the major tasks to be accomplished by the B. L. T. Company on a month by month basis through May.

June

- o Identify locations for company owned units and conduct initial negotiations with owners for net leasing.
  - Three to four locations to be identified in the Bay Area.
  - Three to four additional locations to be identified in Los Angeles.
- o Finalize total merchandising and investment package to be used in all company owned and franchised units.
  - Equipment and building specifications.
  - Sign, image, site, and name specifications.
  - Franchise merchandising program.
  - Merchandising approach to investors and owner-operators.
- o Finalize management, control, and logistic systems.
- o Identify two potential manager-salesmen.
- o Conclude equity financing.

July

- o Finalize and close leases.
- o Begin construction of units, place equipment orders.
- o Begin implementation of full scale franchising program.
- o Hire and train two manager-salesmen.

August

- o Continuation of construction of company owned units.
- o Continuation of franchising program.

September

- o Installation of equipment in company owned units.
- o Continuation of franchising program.
- o Hiring and training of operators for company owned units.

329

<u>October</u>

- Company owned units operational.
- Continuation of franchising program.
- Deliver first packages to franchisees.
- Extend company owned unit program into new territory.

<u>November . . . . . May</u>

- Continuation of October program.
    - Operate company owned units.
    - Continue franchise program.
    - Extend company owned unit program as cash flow permits.

MANAGEMENT

The management function of the B. L. T. Company will be the direct responsibility of the Messrs. Bacon Lord, and Thompson.

H. Lloyd Bacon will serve as Board Chairman and will be responsible for financial planning and corporate development. He has spent eight years as an investment banker with Goodbody & Company, where his primary responsibilities included evaluating, structuring and negotiating corporate underwritings and mergers, as well as financial planning and consulting. He is currently on leave of absence from Goodbody to manage investments and engage in private financial consulting.

Donald A. Lord will have primary responsibility for adminis-tration and finance. He has been a tax consultant with Arthur Andersen & Company for four years and holds an LL. B. from Duke University. He is responsible for having set up a Robo-Wash area franchise program for a group of private investors.

Bradley E. Thompson has been with Booz-Allen and Hamilton, management consultants, for two years. He has been responsible for projects in a variety of industries with heavy emphasis on marketing and organizational problems. Prior to joining Booz-Allen he was with Eastman Kodak Company, as an industrial engineer. Thompson holds an M. B. A. from the Harvard Business School and a degree in mechanical engineering. As a member of the B. L. T. Company, his primary areas of responsibility will be operations and marketing.

PROPOSAL

To effect this program, the B. L. T. Company will raise $500,000 through the private placement of ten $50,000 B. L. T. Company Participating Units to a limited number of sophisticated investors.

Each unit will consist of:

    I. 1,000 shares Common Stock
   II. $40,000 Participating Convertible Preferred Stock, convertible into 1 000 shares Common Stock.

Upon completion of the financing, and full conversion of the Participating Convertible Preferred Stock, the Unit holders will own 44.5% (20,000 of 45,000) of the Common Shares then outstanding.

The B. L. T. Company will, as soon as practicable, seek to effect a primary public offering of common stock to raise additional working capital to accelerate and expand the programs outlined, and to create a market to facilitate the acquisition of going franchised units.

CAPITALIZATION

	May 31,	Pro Forma

Common Stock

Authorized:
  100,000 shares $1.00 Par Value
Issued and Outstanding:
  May 31, 1968 - 25,000 shares ... $25,000
  Upon completion of financing - 35,000 Shares
  Upon completion of financing and conversion
    of Participating Convertible Preferred
    Stock - 45,000 Shares ... $125,000

Participating Convertible Preferred Stock*

Authorized:
  $1,000,000 principal amount
Issued and Outstanding:
  May 31, 1968 - $0 principal amount ... —
  Upon completion of financing - $400,000
    principal amount ... $400,000

Total Capital ... $25,000 ... $525,000

*The Participating Convertible Preferred Stock will, in the aggregate, be entitled to receive 25% of the company's annual net earnings after tax up to $500,000, and 12-1/2% of net earnings between $500,000 and $1,000,000. The Board of Directors will have the right to redeem the stock at its discretion after two years.

B.L.T. CAR WASH UNIT — CASH FLOW ANALYSIS

Cars Washed Per Month	6,000	8,000	10,000	12,000
INCOME (at 75¢ per wash)	$4,500	$6,000	$7,500	$9,000
EXPENSES				
Direct cost of Wash*	600	800	1,000	1,200
Land-Rent & Taxes	1,000	1,000	1,000	1,000
Labor	800	900	1,000	1,100
Maintenance	100	125	150	175
Insurance	125	125	125	125
Advertising	400	400	400	400
Miscellaneous	200	200	200	200
Total Expenses	$3,225	$3,550	$3,875	$4,200
MONTHLY CASH FLOW	1,275	2,450	3,625	4,800
ANNUAL SUMMARY				
Income	54,000	72,000	90,000	108,000
Expenses	38,700	42,600	46,500	50,400
Cash Flow	$15,300	$29,400	$43,500	$57,600

*Direct cost of wash includes: Detergent at $.03 per car, wax at $.01 per car, electricity at $.04 per car, and water at $.02 per car.

B.L.T. GAS PUMPING-CAR WASH UNIT – CASH FLOW ANALYSIS

Cars Per Month	6,000	8,000	10,000	12,000
INCOME*				
Wash	$4,250	$5,000	$6,250	$7,500
Gas	15,250	21,000	26,250	31,500
Total Income	$19,500	$26,000	$32,500	$39,000
EXPENSES**				
Direct Cost of Gas	12,600	16,200	20,250	24,300
Direct Cost of Wash	600	800	1,000	1,200
Land-Rent & Taxes	1,000	1,000	1,000	1,000
Labor	2,000	2,300	2,600	2,900
Maintenance	100	125	150	175
Insurance	425	425	425	425
Advertising	600	600	600	600
Miscellaneous	500	500	500	500
Total Expense	$17,825	$21,950	$26,525	$31,100
MONTHLY CASH FLOW	1,675	4,050	5,975	7,900
ANNUAL SUMMARY				
Income	$234,000	$312,000	$390,000	$468,000
Expenses	213,900	263,400	318,300	373,200
Cash Flow	$20,100	$48,600	$71,700	$94,800

*Assumes: Of the total cars passing through the unit each month, 1/4 will purchase no gas and pay the full price - $1. per wash; 1/4 will purchase 5 gallons of gas and pay $.75 for the wash; 1/4 will purchase 10 gallons of gas and pay $.50 for the wash; 1/4 will purchase 15 gallons of gas and pay $.25 for the wash.

**Assumes: Average cost of gas at $.27 per gallon yielding $.08 per gallon gross profit.

THE B.L.T. COMPANY – QUARTERLY CASH FLOW ANALYSIS

	September	December	March	June	Total
			Year 1		
Income					
Company Owned Units	—	$36,000	$57,000	$69,000	$162,000
Franchise Operation	—	77,600	159,600	270,000	507,200
Total Income	—	$113,600	$216,600	$339,000	$669,200
Expenses					
B.L.T. Operating	$15,000	15,000	21,000	27,000	78,000
Const. B.L.T. Units	360,000	60,000	60,000	180,000	660,000
Franchise Operation	—	6,000	18,000	28,000	52,000
Total Expenses	$375,000	$81,000	$99,000	$235,000	$790,000
Estimated Income Taxes					
Net Cash Flow	(375,000)	32,600	117,600	104,000	(120,800)
Cash Balance	150,000	182,600	300,200	404,200	404,200
Net adjustment to Cash Flow					362,000
Net Profit (Loss) From Operations					$241,200
Units Opened During Period					
Company Owned		6	1	2	9
Franchised		10	20	30	60
Units in Operation at End of Period					
Company Owned		6	7	9	9
Franchised		10	30	60	60

THE B.L.T. COMPANY – QUARTERLY CASH FLOW ANALYSIS (cont.)

	September	December	March	June	Total
			Year 2		
Income					
Company Owned Units	$90,000	$117,000	$156,000	$207,000	$570,000
Franchise Operation	383,600	508,000	648,000	796,000	2,335,600
Total Income	$473,600	$625,000	$804,000	$1,003,000	$2,905,600
Expenses					
B.L.T. Operating	39,000	54,000	78,000	105,000	276,000
Const. B.L.T. Units	180,000	360,000	360,000	360,000	1,260,000
Franchise Operation	39,500	55,500	76,500	102,500	274,000
Total Expenses	$258,500	$469,500	$514,500	$567,500	$1,810,000
Estimated Income Taxes		250,000			250,000
Net Cash Flow	215,100	(94,500)	289,500	435,500	845,600
Cash Balance	619,300	524,800	814,300	1,249,800	1,249,800
Net adjustment to Cash Flow					122,000
Net Profit (Loss) From Operations					$1,217,600
Units Opened During Period					
Company Owned	3	4	5	6	18
Franchised	40	50	60	70	220
Units in Operation at End of Period					
Company Owned	12	16	21	27	27
Franchised	100	150	210	280	280

THE B.L.T. COMPANY – QUARTERLY CASH FLOW ANALYSIS (cont.)

Year 3

	September	December	March	June	Total
Income					
Company Owned Units	$261,000	$315,000	$369,000	$423,000	$1,368,000
Franchise Operation	958,000	1,054,000	1,150,000	1,246,000	4,408,000
Total Income	$1,219,000	$1,369,000	$1,519,000	$1,669,000	$5,776,000
Expenses					
B.L.T. Operating	120,000	126,000	135,000	135,000	516,000
Const. B.L.T. Units	360,000	360,000	360,000	360,000	1,440,000
Franchise Operation	112,500	112,500	112,500	112,500	450,000
Total Expenses	$592,000	$598,500	$607,500	$607,500	$2,406,000
Estimated Income Taxes		1,000,000			1,000,000
Net Cash Flow	626,500	(229,500)	911,500	1,061,500	2,370,000
Cash Balance	1,874,300	1,646,800	2,558,300	3,619,800	3,619,000
Net adjustment to Cash Flow					(1,092,000)
Net Profit (Loss) From Operations					$2,278,000
Units Opened During Period					
Company Owned	6	6	6	6	24
Franchised	80	80	80	80	320
Units in Operation at End of Period					
Company Owned	33	39	45	51	51
Franchised	360	440	520	600	600

IN-LINE TECHNOLOGIES, INC.
High Technology Investment

CONTENTS

Page

I.   INTRODUCTION (Exhibit A)   1

II.   COMPANY   4
         Application of Products   4
         History   5
         Organization (Exhibit B)   6

III. FOUNDERS AND DIRECTORS   7

IV.   PRODUCT LINE   11
         General   11
         What is Automatic Photo-Chemical Processing
             Equipment?   12
         Product Description   15
         Semiconductor Industry   15
         Thin Film Industry   16
         Electronic Manufacturing Industry   17
         Product Data:
             In-Line Wafer Processing System   18
             Conformal Coater System   19

V.   THE MARKET   20
         Market Response (Exhibit C)   20
         Competition   22
         Marketing Goals (Exhibit D)   26
         Customer List   30
         Potential Customer List   31

VI.   FINANCIAL   34
         Operating Plan and Projections   35
         Sales and Earnings Past and Future   37
         Projected Sales   38
         Projected Net Earnings   39
         Projected Stock Value   40
         Projected Balance Sheets (1973-1975)   41
         Projected Cash Flow (1973-1975)   66

I.   INTRODUCTION

The electronics industry today still offers great potential to the entrepreneur for the creation of sizeable, profitable business ventures
especially in the areas of <u>proprietary</u> product marketing. This is true
for several reasons. First and foremost, of course, is the fact that the
dynamic state-of-the-art technology existing in the electronics industry
today affords a greater ease of market entry for the innovator. New,
unique, and different approaches to the solution of old problems are
welcomed, and are, in fact, a requirement for a successful company
engaged in the marketing of proprietary products.

For such companies the rate of growth and, of course, the rate of
profitability are limited primarily by the financial structure and support
of the organization, assuming that dynamic leadership, superior marketing capability, and exceptional technical talent are available. With a
proper financial base the growth pattern of such organization in today's
growing and expanding electronics market is highly probable.

The purpose of this business plan is to present in significant detail a
plan whereby an organization fitting the above pattern can make a substantial impact on the proprietary product market in a short period of
time with a minimum of the type of entrepreneurial risk usually found
to be an integral part of such plans. The minimization of these risks
comes about because of the following basic facts:

1. In-Line Technology, Inc. is a thriving organization that
    exists and will provide the vehicle for this plan.
2. In-Line Technology has already designed and manufactured
    90% of its fiscal year 1974 product line and is in the process
    of beginning its initial phases of marketing production tested
    and customer proved equipment.
3. In-Line Technology is supplying equipment to a rapidly
    expanding market for semiconductors that is forecasted to be
    greater than $2 billion by 1976, *almost a factor of 2 greater
    than the 1971 total in just the United States alone.
4. In-Line Technology can accurately control and predict first
    year's bookings and shipments (with adequate financing) due to
    management's combined experience of over thirty years of
    marketing and engineering in the photo-chemical processing
    field.

---

*Market information from "Electronics' 1973 forecast of Electronics
 Markets.

340

In-Line Founders are in Tune with Photoprocessing Trend

A company that started as a part-time effort some 18 months ago has recently become its founders' sole business concern, and indeed, they appear in a good position to profit from semiconductor manufacturers' growing enthusiasm for automating their photoprocessing operations.

While Hendrik F. Bok and Eugene R. St. Onge worked together in the Systems division of EPEC Industries Inc., New Bedford, Mass., they saw the need for systems that could automatically handle cleaning, drying, etching, and developing. "There are a lot of different systems available," notes Bok, "but you have to buy the etcher from one company, the coater from another. To form a complete line of equipment, a plant manager needs to buy four or five makes of equipment that aren't always compatible."

The two men joined forces to make specialized turnkey photoprocessing systems, and In-Line Technology Inc. was born in Assonet, Mass. By now, In-Line has emerged from a custom-equipment phase with a number of standard items, including cleaners, coaters, dryers, developers, etchers, wet strippers, and plasma strippers, all of which are interfaced for either manual or automatic loading.

Cutting loose. During In-Line's first year, Bok and St. Onge kept their jobs at EPEC, but last October they were able to buy out EPEC'S Spray division and devote full time to In-Line, of which they are sole owners. Sales this year may reach $1 million.

Bok thinks part of their success is a result of "the imagination to come up with something new," but part of it is traceable to their backgrounds also. Bok, 47, founded his first company in 1954 in his native Netherlands. (He still speaks with a Dutch accent.) It made spray coaters, and in 1958 he brought the process with him to the U.S. where three years later he founded another company with expertise based on the same process. Joining EPEC in 1967 as a vice president, he gained experience in coating and first started to build integrated systems including sprayers, dryers, exposure equipment, and developers.

While Bok considers himself a "concept" engineer, St. Onge, 36, is a process engineer. One need they see is for better yields, and they believe their automatic production lines, which include automatic wafer handling, can help. Since wafers and plates are untouched throughout production, and the line is so timed that clean plates don't have to wait before being coated, dirt caused pinholes and other faults are cut down.

II. THE COMPANY

Applications of Products

In-Line Technology is primarily engaged in the manufacture and sales of highly sophisticated photo-chemical processing systems for the microelectronics industry. Application categories for this equipment are in the following manufacturing processes:

- A. Integrated Circuits
- B. Optoelectronic and Electro-Optical Displays
- C. Hybrid Circuits
- D. Transistors and Diodes
- E. Power Devices including Thyristors, SCR's and multiple devices

Additionally, In-Line Technology has also developed and sold an automatic conveyorized spray system for assembled printed circuit boards which are utilized in the following applications:

- F. Computers
- G. Industrial Instrumentation Systems
- H. Portable Test Equipment
- I. Air Pollution Control & Manufacturing Equipment
- J. Bio-Medical Instrumentation
- K. Communications Systems
- L. Geophysical Instrumentation
- M. Meteorological Equipment
- N. Oceanographic Systems
- O. Military Systems of all varieties

History

In-Line Technology was incorporated in Massachusetts on the 13th of July, 1971. Although the company was operated on a part-time basis by the founders, In-Line obtained a $101,000 order from Owens-Illinois in August of 1971. This system was installed during the month of January 1972, and has been operating satisfactorily, as evidenced by the subsequent purchase orders received from Owens-Illinois for additional processing systems.

In-Line became a full-time operation on October 1, 1972, when it leased its present 8500 sq. ft. of manufacturing and office space at 30 Mill Street, Assonet, Mass. 02702.

During the first half of 1973, In-Line placed most of its effort on the development, engineering and introduction of a line of "standard" automated products primarily aimed at the semiconductor manufacturing industry. The impetus for this direction was the demonstrated need of major semiconductor firms, such as Motorola, Zenith Radio, General Electric, I.B.M., etc.

Organization

The management team directing this Corporation will initially consist of four full-time managers, with supporting staff, supplemented by experienced part-time consultants. A brief description of the experience and capabilities of the four managers are contained in this document under Founders. Management has set exceptional goals for the organization. We believe these goals will be attained through the creation of an organization which stimulates and rewards contributions by each of its members. We intend to be a profitable, vibrant, growing organization, with character and high ethical standards, responsive to the diverse needs of its customers, stockholders, employees and the community in which it exists.

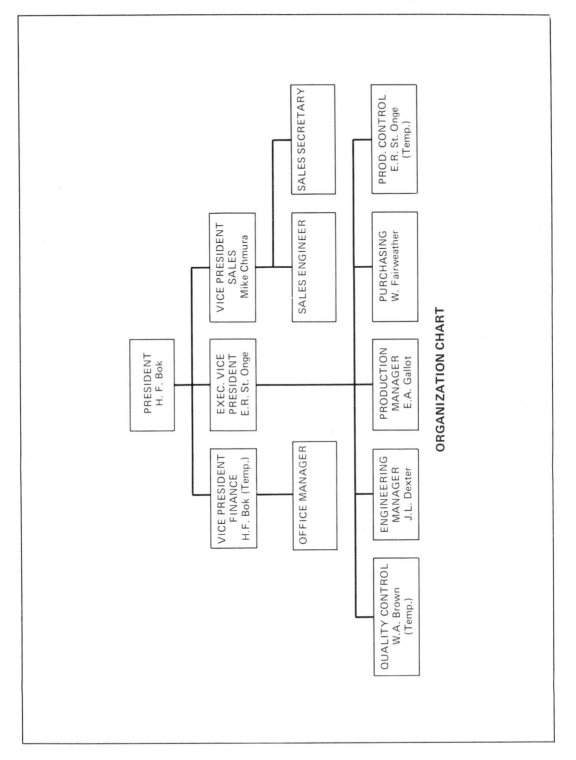

ORGANIZATION CHART

PRESIDENT
H. F. Bok

EXEC. VICE
PRESIDENT
E. R. St. Onge

VICE PRESIDENT
FINANCE
H. F. Bok (Temp.)

VICE PRESIDENT
SALES
Mike Chmura

OFFICE MANAGER

SALES ENGINEER

SALES SECRETARY

QUALITY CONTROL
W.A. Brown
(Temp.)

ENGINEERING
MANAGER
J.L. Dexter

PRODUCTION
MANAGER
E.A. Gallot

PURCHASING
W. Fairweather

PROD. CONTROL
E.R. St. Onge
(Temp.)

III.   FOUNDERS AND DIRECTORS

Director, Founder,
President, Treasurer

Hendrik F. Bok
52 Thompson Street
Fairhaven, Mass.
Phone: 617-992-5479

Personal:

Age: 47
Height: 6' 4"
Weight: 210 lbs.
Health: Excellent

Education:

Vincent V. Gogh High School

E. T. S. B. S. EE
1949 – Amsterdam, Holland

M. T. S. – Industrial Styling
1953   Electronics
Eindhoven, Holland

Patents:

Mr. Bok holds approximately 60 patents world-wide, including 20 patents exclusively in microelectronic process equipment. He receives substantial royalties on these patents at the present time.

Experience:

January 1967
to
October 1972

EPEC Industries, New Bedford, Mass.
Vice President of Engineering

His duties were to head up the Equipment Division for the design of various spray systems; in addition, a modular equipment line for printed circuit processes was designed and marketed; substantial application and field work was done with leading corporations to define systems for their production lines, e.g., coating equipment was developed and sold to IBM for their magnetic head production line, printed circuit board photo-resist sprayers were developed for Western Electric; eight patents were issued to Mr. Bok during this period on various methods of spraying, curing, developing, etc.

1960	Zicon (formerly Chemtronic)
to	Vice President of Engineering and Founder of
January 1967	Corporation

His duties included equipment development and field liaison with prime potential customers in terms of evaluating the chemical aspects of cleaning, exposure, etching and spraying; pioneered many of the basic processes of spraying photo-resist instead of the older spinning method; developed the conformal coatings for space vehicle equipment in conjunction with NASA as one of the few sole source suppliers to the agencies.

1954	Bok Research & Development Corp.
to	Holland
1960	

His work involved the development of spray equipment in terms of developing the basic processes for application, make-up and design; received several patents world-wide involving the above developments as well as work in other basic development areas.

- -

Eugene R. St. Onge
Denise Avenue
East Freetown, Mass.
Phone: 617-763-5012

Director, Founder
Executive Vice-Pres.
Operations

Personal:

Age: 37
Height: 5' 10"
Weight: 150 lbs.
Health: Excellent

Education

Msgr. James Coyle High School
M.I.T. (Evening Division)
S.M.U.

Experience:

July 1965	EPEC Industries, Inc.
to	Manufacturing Engineering Manager
October 1972	Sales Engineering Manager

Responsibilities included design, engineering, installation and service of printed circuit manufacturing equipment; included responsibility for customer training at Epec and process problem solving assistance to customers in the field.

Other positions at Epec were special projects eng. and mfg. eng. in the printed circuit division. Duties included the determination of methods and procedures to economically fabricate printed circuit boards in compliance with customer and/or military specifications and blueprints. Other duties included methods improvement, cost reduction, evaluation of new processes and process trouble shooting. The position also required a limited amount of jig, fixture and die design.

IV. PRODUCT

PRODUCT LINE DEFINITION

General

The company intends to pursue those markets where high-volume, automatic, photo-chemical processing equipment is needed, specifically for the semiconductor industry and the electronic manufacturing industry. Immediately the question will be asked, "Why the automatic process equipment market?"

- - - - Why, with all the tremendous choice of product direction, should we concentrate on this particular area? Putting it simply and logically, the answer is, because it is our opinion that today the automatic processing equipment market, more than most others, is ripe and poised for tremendous expansion. "Electronics" magazine, the most respected journal in the industry, says, "In semiconductor production equipment overall, the combined 1972-1973 improvement will add up to dollar sales two or three times better" than in 1971.

The semiconductor industry dollar volume is forecasted to reach a level greater than $1.6 billion in 1973, an increase of 20% over 1972 sales. However, the semiconductor industry must increase its output by 50% to effect a 20% growth in sales due to the ever present decline of 20% per year in the average selling price. With the rapid-volume expansion of integrated circuits, fueled by the needs of the automotive, calculator and computer markets, the requirement for automatic equipment that can increase throughput and also improve the yield, the all-important profit indicator for the semiconductor industry, will enjoy rapid growth.

Editor's Note: The next 60 pages of this business plan contained product information which has not been reproduced in this book. The product description actually comprised more than one-half of this original business plan.

THE MARKET

Although In-Line Technology's effort to date has been minimal (sales coverage estimated at five to ten percent of the potential market), and primarily consisting of introducing standard products to the selected customers, the rewards have been gratifying and encouraging. The company had sales of $174,803 during the first half of 1973, with only a slight loss of $14,243.45.

Market Response

The market reaction to this line of products may be described in the following manner:

a. Even with a very limited sales effort, In-Line has been able to sustain a production growth of 400% during the last seven months.

b. Over one hundred and fifty requests for additional information were received from visitors to In-Line's booth at the "Semicon III" Show in San Francisco. These requests included almost every major semiconductor manufacturer in the United States, as well as numerous requests from companies in Europe and Japan (see actual and potential customer lists which follow). Indeed, one of the largest semiconductor manufacturers in Europe, S.G.S. Ates-Italy, is scheduled to visit us shortly to see a demonstration and to further discuss the proposal they requested as a direct result of the show. Mr. Bok, In-Line Technology's President, was asked to participate in the Technical Program which ran concurrent with the show by describing the latest process techniques to engineers in a technical paper he delivered (Exhibit C).

c. Several trade journals have printed product releases concerning In-Line's conformal coating system. These product news releases have produced numerous inquiries from all over the United States, Canada, Japan and Europe.

d. One of the leading trade journals (Electronics Magazine) has discerned growing customer interest in In-Line Technology to prompt them to write a complimentary article about the company and its founders (Exhibit A).

e. Other leading trade journals, including "Solid State Technology" and "Electronic Packaging and Production," have also expressed interest in publishing articles about In-Line Technology and its products.

f.   Motorola, Phoenix, prior to placing an order for a new etcher which In-Line has developed, desired a 60-day option for nine more systems, at no specified price, to assure their availability at the top of the priority list upon the successful operation of the first etcher. (Sales price of the initial system was greater than $30,000.)

Competition

In-Line Technology is a corporation which holds a unique position in a dynamically expanding market. In-Line supplies integrated manufacturing equipment that is directed toward a complete processing system for integrated circuits. At the present time, there is no direct competitor for such an integrated process line. However, there are some competitors for certain portions of this system, especially in the area of applying photo-resist.

Companies Supplying Photo-Resist Coating Equipment

Companies	Method of Application
In-Line Technology, Inc.	Spray
Zicon	Spray
GCA/Industrial Modular Systems, Inc.	Spinning
Headway Research, Inc.	Spinning
I.I. Industries, Inc.	Spinning
Plat-General	Spinning

Except for Zicon and In-Line Technology, each of the above companies supplying photo-resist coating equipment sell spinners to apply the coating. This method of application uses the principle of centrifugal force to spread the photo-resist over the wafer. This application technique is subject to some inherent problems, e.g., because this method is dependent upon centrifugal force which is a function of speed, the spinning method is severely limited by the geometry of the substrate. Variations in consistency across the wafer as a result of the spinning process can cause additional yield loss. As integrated circuit manufacturers go completely to 3-inch wafers, and in some cases 4-inch wafers, the limitations of spinning become severe. The need to use spraying at this point becomes obvious. Zicon was the first to apply photo-resist by spraying, using techniques developed by Mr. Bok. However, since his departure

CONFERENCE REPORT

Semicon III Technical Program

May 22-24, 1973 San Mateo Fairgrounds, San Mateo, Ca.

This year's SEMICON III technical program features a limited
number of judiciously selected papers to allow for sequential rather than
simultaneous presentations. Bound abstracts of the sessions will be
available at the show. The third annual tradeshow for suppliers of
materials and equipment to the semiconductor industry, SEMICON III
will host over 320 exhibits, a 60% growth over last year's exhibition.

B, "Fully-Automated Photo Printing & Etching Systems for Thin
Film and Semiconductor Devices", Hendrik S. Bok -- In-Line
Technology, Inc.

The paper will discuss the most advanced process techniques,
associate with the photo printing and etching systems for thin film
and semiconductor devices.

The discussion will cover advanced, production volume substrate
feed systems, used with the following newly developed substrate processing equipment:
> a. Wet and dry, automatic substrate surface cleaning
> systems
> b. Automatic high-production photo-resist spray and
> dry systems
> c. Wet process developer and post bake units
> d. Wet and dry process etcher systems
> e. Wet and dry process photo-resist stripping systems

Emphasis is placed on process instrumentation required with
high-volume, close tolerance production systems.

in 1967, Zicon has not accomplished any significant upgrading of this equipment.

In-Line Technology has, within the last nine months, developed fully automated equipment to apply photo-resist by spraying, in addition to a series of modular process systems which have been designed to be combined into a single integrated process line.

In-Line Technology has in such a short time span been able to reach this unusual position by combining extensive experience with several disciplines of engineering to build their systems. This unique blending of engineering mechanics, fluidics, electronics, pneumatic mechanisms and chemistry, including plasma chemistry, make the concept of integration work in terms of an automatic photo-chemical process line. Customers have been forced up to this time to buy various pieces of equipment in hopes that they would function adequately in combination with each other, or re-engineer them in some way so that the interface becomes compatible between them. Pieces of equipment purchased from various manufacturers, although good of themselves, do not necessarily lend themselves to being interfaced with each other to form an optimum process line. In-Line Technology does, therefore, hold a strong, growing position in this market because it sells a totally integrated system concept and is striving to broaden this concept in the future. The final result may be reached when human hands never touch a wafer, so that automatic handling will be the case for an entire integrated circuit process line. At that time, the entire production and testing of integrated circuits can be controlled with this equipment and a suitable computer system. The result will be a dramatic increase in yield and precisely repeatable integrated circuits from batch to batch.

Marketing Goals

In-Line Technology has established a marketing program under their new Vice President of Marketing, which has the following goals:

1.   Select, hire and train direct salesmen to effectively penetrate the major concentrations of semiconductor manufacturers in California, Texas and Arizona. In-Line Technology's automated equipment varies in price from $30,000 to $300,000, depending upon the extent of the system. This relatively high value for the average sale requires a strong feeling of confidence on the part of the customer, as well as a direct link to the factory. The direct salesman can supply this interface most economically and effectively in these geographic areas where the amount of potential business justifies the overhead cost.

2.   Prepare a series of professional advertisements to be placed in the leading trade media.   The company has established an excellent reputation with the customers to whom they have directed their sales efforts. Approximately 90% of the market, however, does not have a distinct impression of the company or their products.   These advertisements will establish a communication to these potential customers and support the direct field sales activity.

3.   Establish representation for sales and service in Europe and Japan. Several semiconductor firms have announced plans to establish manufacturing facilities in various countries in Europe to serve that market only.   This new investment, plus the burgeoning pace of the European and Japanese markets, are untapped opportunities for In-Line Technology's products.   The recent devaluation of the dollar has made automated process equipment more attractive, especially in view of the accelerating inflation rates prevalent in these countries.

4.   Establish suitable sub-contractor in conjunction with management to manufacture a limited line of plasma systems for sale and distribution by In-Line Technology.   Plasma systems are used in conjunction with photo-chemical process equipment.   In-Line Technology's founders know the needs of these customers and plan to expand their integrated product line by offering this "dry chemical" processing system, which will be interfaced with the existing systems.   In this way In-Line can supply an optimum integrated system for certain unique applications at little investment to the company.

5.   Establish a network of representative firms to sell In-Line Technology's Conformal Coater to electronic manufacturing companies. Customers for this product line are not generally the same as those for photo-chemical process equipment.   A different network of "Reps" are required to reach this market.   This diversification by In-Line Technology across different markets, with a similar product using essentially the same manufacturing techniques, same materials and the same construction, assures the company a stable manufacturing base.

CUSTOMER LIST

Motorola SPD
Phoenix, Arizona

Western Electric Co.
Kearny, New Jersey

Western Electric
North Andover, Mass.

Owens-Illinois, Inc.
Perrysburg, Ohio

The Franklin Mint
Franklin, Pa.

General Electric Co.
Auburn, New York

Motorola
Vega Baja, Puerto Rico

Liberty Mirror Co.
Brackenridge, Pa.

Wellings Mint
Rexdale, Ontario, Canada

Zenith Corporation
Chicago, Illinois

I.B.M. E. Fishkill
Hopewell Junction, N.Y.

Dynell Electronics Corp.
Melville, Long Island, N.Y.

John Pinches, Ltd.
London, England

POTENTIAL CUSTOMER LIST (PARTIAL)

Semiconductor Process Equipment

A. M. I.
Cupertino, Calif.

A. M. I.
Pocatello, Idaho

Advanced Memory Systems
Sunnyvale, Calif.

Advanced Micro Devices
Sunnyvale, Calif.

Aerospace Corp.
Los Angeles, Calif.

Aertech Industries
Sunnyvale, Calif.

American Micro-Systems
Santa Clara, Calif.

Antex Industries
Mt. View, Calif.

Autonetics
Anaheim, Calif.

Beckman Instruments
Fullerton, Calif.

Bell Labs
Allentown, Pa.

Bell Northern Rsch.
Canada

Bell Telephone Labs
Murray Hill, N. J.

Burroughs Corp.
San Diego, Calif.

Cal Tex
Santa Clara, Calif.

Control Data
Minneapolis, Minn.

Dainippon Screen Mfg.
Toshima-Ku, Tokyo, Japan

Delco Electronics
Kokomo, Ind.

Dickson Electronics
Scottsdale, Ariz.

E C C Corp.
Euless, Tex.

Electronic Arrays
Mt. View, Calif.

Fairchild Semiconductor
Mt. View, Calif.

Fairchild
San Rafael, Calif.

Fairchild S/C
So. Portland, Me.

G T E Labs
Waltham, Mass.

General Instrument Corp.
Hicksville, Long Island, N. Y.

Heliotek
Sylmar, Calif.

Hewlett Packard
Cupertino, Calif.

Hewlett Packard
Palo Alto, Calif.

Hewlett Packard
Santa Clara, Calif.

Hewlett Packard
Loveland, Colo.

I.B.M.
San Jose, Calif.

I.B.M.
E. Fishkill, N.Y.

I.B.M.
Hopewell Junction, N.Y.

I.B.M.
Manassas, Va.

INTEL
Mt. View, Calif.

INTEL
Santa Clara, Calif.

Intersil, Inc.
Cupertino, Calif.

Microma, Inc.
Cupertino, Calif.

Microsystems Int.
Ottawa, Canada

Monsanto
Cupertino, Calif.

Motorola
Mesa, Ariz.

Motorola, Inc.
Phoenix, Ariz.

National Semiconductor
Santa Clara, Calif.

Nissho Semicon
Saitama, Japan

Nitron Corp.
Cupertino, Calif.

Raytheon Semiconductor
Mt. View, Calif.

Rockwell International
Anaheim, Calif.

Rockwell Int.
Newport Beach, Calif.

S G S Ates
Brianza, Italy

N.V. Philips
Nijmegen, The Netherlands

Signetics
Orem, Utah

VI. FINANCIAL

Plan of Operations and Projections

In-Line Technology completed its first full six months of operations on June 30, 1973, with a sales level of $191,862.00 and a small net loss of $14,243.00. During this period of time the company was essentially in the prototype stage of their products. The cost of goods sold was, therefore, initially high at 71% (first six months of 1973). This factory cost will decrease to 58% for the last six months of 1973, then to 50% and 48% in the second and third year due to these factors:

A. The experience of the first group of employees hired and trained has been increasing steadily.
B. Most of the products are now becoming fully standardized.
C. A new sheet metal facility, just completed, will lower sheet metal cost and provide delivery of material on schedule.

Research and Development

The company has capitalized a portion of the Research and Development that was undertaken in developing their product line. This capitalization has been shown on the balance sheet to clearly reflect the assets and operations of the company. A write-off of these initial expenditures was judged inappropriate for the following:

A. The lifetime of these standard products is expected to be greater than five years.
B. Year to year operating comparisons would not be meaningful.
C. A planned amortization would more clearly show expenses incurred in development against customer deliveries.

Statement Criteria

Projections made for the financial statements assume the following:

A. A ninety-day production cycle will exist.
B. Work-in-process inventory will be maintained at a level equal to one month's shipments.
C. Raw material inventory is maintained at the thirty-day use level.
D. Amortization of R&D will be accomplished in less than five years.

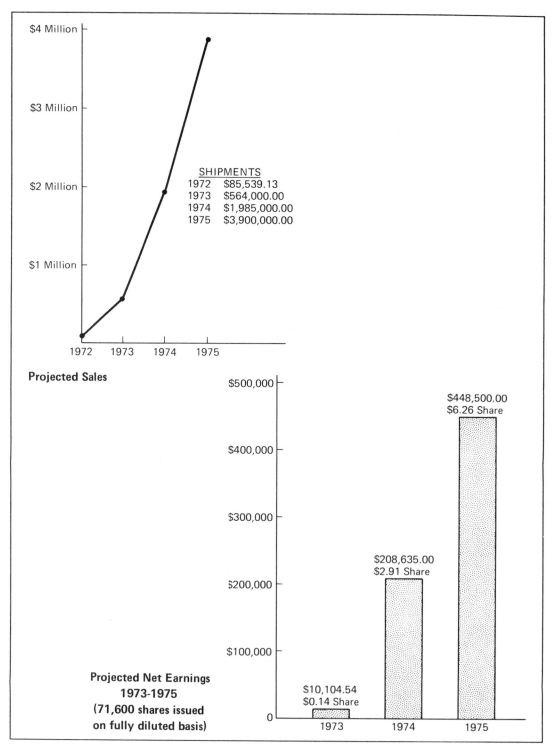

SHIPMENTS
1972 $85,539.13
1973 $564,000.00
1974 $1,985,000.00
1975 $3,900,000.00

Projected Sales

$448,500.00
$6.26 Share

$208,635.00
$2.91 Share

$10,104.54
$0.14 Share

**Projected Net Earnings
1973-1975
(71,600 shares issued
on fully diluted basis)**

1973   1974   1975

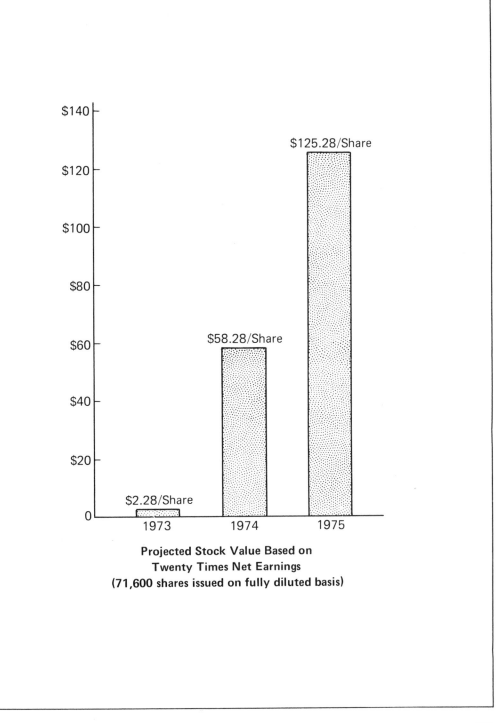

Projected Stock Value Based on
Twenty Times Net Earnings
(71,600 shares issued on fully diluted basis)

PROJECTED BALANCE SHEETS

1973 - 1975

IN-LINE TECHNOLOGY, INC.

Balance Sheet, June 30, 1973

Assets

Current Assets		
Cash	$ 6,931.74	
Accounts Receivable	62,239.95	
Inventory	75,331.74	
Prepaid Expenses	7,028.00	
Total Current Assets		$151,531.43

Fixed Assets			
Machinery & Equipment	78,557.64		
Less: Accumulated Depreciation	3,942.00	74,615.64	
Research and Development	44,807.82		
Less: Accumulated Amortization	698.85	44,108.97	
Total Fixed Assets			118,724.61
Total Assets			270,256.04

Liabilities and Capital

Current Liabilities		
Accounts Payable	90,900.05	
Notes Payable	82,781.49	
Deposit on Orders	7,217.10	
Federal and State Taxes	1,985.14	
Total Current Liabilities		182,883.78

Capital		
SBA Loan	43,101.85	
Common Stock	3,100.00	
Additional Paid-in-Capital	50,594.31	
Earned Surplus	4,819.55	
Retained Earnings	(14,243.45)	
Total Capital		87,372.26
Total Capital and Liabilities		$270,256.04

IN-LINE TECHNOLOGY, INC.

Projected Balance Sheet

Dec. 31, 1973

Assets

Current Assets			
Cash	$ 94,422.24		
Accounts Receivable	130,972.85		
Inventory	108,249.74		
Prepaid Expenses	5,128.00		
Total Current Assets			$338,772.83
Fixed Assets			
Machinery & Equipment	78,557.64		
Less: Accumulated Depreciation	7,884.00	70,673.64	
Research & Development	44,807.82		
Less: Accumulated Amortization	4,898.85	39,908.97	
Total Fixed Assets			110,582.61
Total Assets			449,355.44

Liabilities and Capital

Current Liabilities			
Notes Payable	46,800.00		
Deposits on Orders	56,000.00		
Federal and State Taxes	4,500.00		
Accounts Payable	58,679.50		
Total Current Liabilities			165,979.50
Capital			
SBA Loan	114,751.85		
Preferred Stock	100,000.00		
Common Stock	53,700.00		
Surplus	4,819.55		
Retained Earnings	10,104.54		
Total Capital			283,375.94
Total Capital and Liabilities			$449,355.44

IN-LINE TECHNOLOGY, INC.

Projected Balance Sheet

Dec. 31, 1974

Assets

Current Assets		
Cash	$368,615.99	
Accounts Receivable	183,472.85	
Inventory	149,664.00	
Prepaid Expenses	5,128.00	
Total Current Assets		$706,880.84
Fixed Assets		
Machinery & Equipment	78,557.64	
Less: Accumulated Depreciation	15,768.00	62,789.64
Research and Development	44,807.82	
Less: Accumulated Amortization	13,298.85	31,508.97
Total Fixed Assets		94,298.61
Total Assets		801,179.45

Liabilities and Capital

Current Liabilities		
Notes Payable	36,800.00	
Deposit on Orders	157,000.00	
Federal and State Taxes	55,658.75	
Accounts Payable	84,009.76	
Total Current Liabilities		333,468.51
Capital		
SBA Loan	90,451.85	
Preferred Stock	100,000.00	
Common Stock	53,700.00	
Surplus	14,924.09	
Retained Earnings	208,635.00	
Total Capital		467,710.94
Total Capital and Liabilities		$801,179.45

IN-LINE TECHNOLOGY, INC.

Projected Balance Sheet

Dec. 31, 1975

Assets

Current Assets			
Cash	$906,782.24		
Accounts Receivable	250,472.85		
Inventory	234,080.00		
Prepaid Expenses	5,128.00		
Total Current Assets			$1,395,463.09
Fixed Assets			
Machinery and Equipment	78,557.64		
Less: Accumulated Depreciation	23,652.00	54,905.64	
Research and Development	44,807.82		
Less: Accumulated Amortization	21,698.85	23,108.97	
Total Fixed Assets			78,014.61
Total Assets			$1,473,477.70

Liabilities and Capital

Current Liabilities			
Notes Payable	36,800.00		
Deposit on Orders	278,000.00		
Federal and State Taxes	127,125.00		
Accounts Payable	139,641.76		
Total Current Liabilities			581,566.76
Capital			
SBA Loan	66,151.85		
Preferred Stock	100,000.00		
Common Stock	53,700.00		
Surplus	223,559.09		
Retained Earnings	448,500.00		
Total Capital			891,910.94
Total Capital and Liabilities			$1,473,477.70

IN-LINE TECHNOLOGY, INC.

Statement of Operations

6 Months Ending June 30, 1973

Sales		$191,861.69
Cost of Goods Sold (Schedule A1)		137,885.70
Gross Profit		53,975.99
Operating Expenses		
Engineering Expenses (Schedule A2)	$14,512.46	
Sales Expenses (Schedule A3)	28,380.47	
General & Administrative Expenses	25,326.51	
Total Operating Expenses		68,219.44
Net Loss		($14,243.45)

IN-LINE TECHNOLOGY, INC.

Schedule of Cost of Goods

6 Months Ending June 30, 1973

Inventory — Jan. 1, 1973	$ 37,121.53
Material Purchased	111,817.28
Labor	46,997.43
Payroll Taxes	3,781.38
Blue Cross	2,424.50
Light and Power	706.40
Depreciation	3,942.00
Employment	2,165.00
Truck Expenses	1,108.22
Freight	2,423.34
Miscellaneous	730.36
Total	$213,217.44
Less: Inventory June 30, 1973	75,331.74
Cost of Goods Sold	$137,885.70

IN-LINE TECHNOLOGY, INC.

Schedule of Engineering Expense

For 6 Months Ending June 30, 1973

Salaries	$12,415.58
Payroll Taxes	975.84
Research and Development	698.85
Miscellaneous	422.19
Total	$14,512.46

IN-LINE TECHNOLOGY, INC.

Schedule of Sales Expense

For 6 Months Ending June 30, 1973

Salaries	$ 6,653.04
Payroll Taxes	548.77
Advertising	980.79
Travel	8,038.09
Telephone	3,884.24
Aircraft	3,782.34
Office and Postage	3,859.92
Entertainment	330.03
Other	303.25
Total	$28,380.47

IN-LINE TECHNOLOGY, INC.

Schedule of General & Administration Expenses

For 6 Months Ending June 30, 1973

Salaries	$10,257.50
Payroll Taxes	793.04
Professional	710.00
Equipment Lease	2,345.00
Life Insurance	4,133.65
Rent	3,492.00
Interest	2,182.64
Other	1,412.66
Total	$25,326.51

IN-LINE TECHNOLOGY, INC.

Projected Statement of Operations

For 6 Months Ending Dec. 31, 1973

Sales		$410,031.00
Cost of Goods Sold (Schedule B1)		237,433.63
Gross Profit		172,597.37
Operating Expenses		
Engineering Expenses (Schedule B2)	$25,056.27	
Sales Expenses (Schedule B3)	81,289.15	
General Expenses (Schedule B4)	41,903.96	
Total Operating Expenses		148,249.38
Net Profit		$ 24,347.99

IN-LINE TECHNOLOGY, INC.   Schedule B1

Projected Schedule of Cost of Goods Sold

For 6 Months Ending Dec. 31, 1973

Inventory — June 30, 1973	$ 75,331.74
Material Purchased	175,947.00
Labor	68,397.88
Payroll Taxes	8,007.45
Blue Cross	6,197.30
Light and Power	1,560.00
Depreciation	3,942.00
Truck Expenses	800.00
Freight	4,000.00
Miscellaneous	1,500.00
Total	345,683.37
Less: Inventory Dec. 31, 1973	108,249.74
Cost of Goods Sold	$237,433.63

IN-LINE TECHNOLOGY, INC.

Projected Schedule of Engineering Expenses

For 6 Months Ending Dec. 31, 1973

Salaries	$18,216.38
Payroll Taxes	2,024.95
Research and Development	4,200.00
Miscellaneous	614.94
Total	$25,056.27

IN-LINE TECHNOLOGY, INC.

Projected Schedule for Sales Expenses

For 6 Months Ending Dec. 31, 1973

Salaries	$26,892.36
Payroll Taxes	3,095.05
Commission	13,300.00
Advertising	2,500.00
Travel	15,711.84
Telephone	7,050.30
Aircraft	2,582.19
Office and Postage	4,557.41
Entertainment	800.00
Other	4,800.00
Total	$81,289.15

IN-LINE TECHNOLOGY, INC.

Projected Schedule of General & Administrative Expenses

For 6 Months Ending Dec. 31, 1973

Salaries	$17,559.00
Payroll Taxes	2,207.75
Professional	4,700.00
Equipment Lease	3,300.00
Life Insurance	3,000.00
Rent	6,715.00
Interest	3,422.21
Miscellaneous	1,000.00
Total	$41,903.96

IN-LINE TECHNOLOGY, INC.

Projected Statement of Operations

Year Ending Dec. 31, 1974

Sales		$1,987,000.00
Cost of Goods Sold (Schedule C1)		993,500.00
Gross Profit		993,500.00
Operating Expenses		
Engineering Expenses (Schedule C2)	79,480.00	
Sales Expenses (Schedule C3)	377,530.00	
General & Administrative Expenses (Schedule C3)	119,220.00	
Total Operating Expenses		576,230.00
Net Profit before provision for Federal Income Tax		417,270.00
Provision for Federal Income Tax		208,635.00
Net Profit to Retained Earnings		$ 208,635.00

IN-LINE TECHNOLOGY, INC.

Projected Schedule of Cost of Goods Sold

Year Ending Dec. 31, 1974

Inventory — Jan. 1, 1974	$108,249.74
Material Purchased	714,861.26
Labor	225,000.00
Payroll Taxes	27,000.00
Blue Cross	25,805.00
Light and Power	4,961.00
Depreciation	15,768.00
Truck Expense	2,775.00
Freight	13,883.00
Miscellaneous	4,861.00
Total	$1,143,164.00
Less Inventory Dec. 31, 1974	149,664.00
Cost of Goods Sold	$993,500.00

IN-LINE TECHNOLOGY, INC.

Projected Schedule of Engineering Expenses

Year Ending Dec. 31, 1974

Salaries	$57,750.00
Payroll Taxes	6,352.00
Research and Development	13,298.85
Miscellaneous	1,999.15
Total	$79,400.00

IN-LINE TECHNOLOGY, INC.

Projected Schedule for Sales Expenses

Year Ending Dec. 31, 1974

Salaries	$124,585.00
Payroll Taxes	14,346.00
Commissions	61,537.00
Advertising	11,326.00
Travel	72,863.00
Telephone	32,467.00
Aircraft	11,325.00
Office and Postage	21,141.00
Entertainment	3,775.00
Miscellaneous	24,165.00
Total	$377,530.00

IN-LINE TECHNOLOGY, INC.

Projected Schedule for General & Administrative Expenses

Year Ending Dec. 31, 1974

Salaries	$49,953.00
Payroll Taxes	6,199.00
Professional	13,352.00
Equipment Lease	9,299.00
Life Insurance	8,345.00
Rent	19,075.00
Interest	9,537.00
Miscellaneous	3,460.00
Total	$119,220.00

IN-LINE TECHNOLOGY, INC.

Projected Statement of Operations

Year Ending Dec. 31, 1975

Sales		$3,900,000.00
Cost of Goods Sold (Schedule D1)		1,872,000.00
Gross Profit		2,028,000.00
Operating Expenses		
Engineering Expenses (Schedule D2)	$156,000.00	
Sales Expenses (Schedule D3)	741,000.00	
General & Administrative Expenses (Schedule D4)	234,000.00	
Total Operating Expenses		1,131,000.00
Net Profit before provision for Federal Income Tax		897,000.00
Provisions for Federal Income Tax		448,500.00
Net Profit to Retained Earnings		$ 448,500.00

IN-LINE TECHNOLOGY, INC.

Projected Schedule of Cost of Goods Sold

Year Ending Dec. 31, 1975

Inventory — Jan. 1, 1975	$ 149,664.00
Material Purchased	1,318,898.00
Labor	462,791.00
Payroll Taxes	56,758.00
Blue Cross	48,333.00
Light & Power	9,502.00
Depreciation	23,652.00
Truck Expense	3,807.00
Freight	25,272.00
Miscellaneous	7,403.00
Total	2,106,080.00
Less Inventory — Dec. 31, 1975	234,080.00
Cost of Goods Sold	$1,872,000.00

IN-LINE TECHNOLOGY, INC.

Projected Schedule of Engineering Expenses

Year Ending Dec. 31, 1975

Salaries	$113,412.00
Payroll Taxes	12,480.00
Research and Development	26,052.00
Miscellaneous	4,056.00
Total	$156,000.00

IN-LINE TECHNOLOGY, INC.

Projected Schedule for Sales Expenses

Year Ending Dec. 31, 1975

Salaries	$244,530.00
Payroll Taxes	28,158.00
Commissions	120,783.00
Advertising	22,230.00
Travel	143,013.00
Telephone	63,726.00
Aircraft	22,230.00
Office and Postage	41,496.00
Entertainment	7,410.00
Miscellaneous	47,284.00
Total	$741,000.00

IN-LINE TECHNOLOGY, INC.

Projected Schedule for General & Administrative Expenses

Year Ending Dec. 31, 1975

Salaries	$ 98,046.00
Payroll Taxes	12,168.00
Professional	26,208.00
Equipment Lease	18,252.00
Life Insurance	16,380.00
Rent	37,440.00
Interest	18,720.00
Miscellaneous	6,786.00
Total	$234,000.00

IN-LINE TECHNOLOGY, INC.

Projected Cash Flow

Year Ending Dec. 31, 1973

	3rd Qtr. 1973	4th Qtr. 1973
Collections from Accounts Receivable	$180,234.61	$269,941.00
Disbursements		
Cost of Goods Sold	55,292.18	182,141.45
Selling Expenses	18,908.21	62,380.94
General and Administrative	9,549.60	32,354.36
Engineering Expenses	5,729.76	19,326.51
Loans Payable Stockholder		10,000.00
Notes Payable/S.B.A.	2,025.00	2,025.00
Notes Payable/Ins. & Accounts Receivable Loan	53,526.10	52,600.00
Taxes on Estimated Profit		
Payment on Accounts Payable	30,350.00	22,426.00
Total Disbursements	$175,380.85	$383,254.26
Excess or Deficit	4,853.76	(113,313.26)
Cumulative Total	11,785.50	(101,527.76)
Assumptions		
Collections		
New S.B.A. Loan		100,000.00
New Equity Capital		100,000.00
Disbursements		
Payments on S.B.A. Loan		4,050.00
New Excess or Deficit		94,422.24

IN-LINE TECHNOLOGY, INC.

Projected Cash Flow

For Year Ending 1975

	1st Qtr.	2nd Qtr.	3rd Qtr.	4th Qtr.
Collections from Accounts Receivable	$791,000.00	$935,000.00	$1,054,000.00	$1,174,000.00
Disbursements				
Cost of Goods Sold	370,560.00	445,440.00	499,680.00	556,320.00
Selling Expenses	146,680.00	176,320.00	197,790.00	220,210.00
General and Administrative	46,320.00	55,680.00	62,460.00	69,540.00
Engineering Expenses	30,880.00	37,120.00	41,640.00	46,360.00
Loans Payable Stockholder				
Notes Payable/S.B.A.	2,025.00	2,025.00	2,025.00	2,025.00
Notes Payable/Ins. & Accounts Receivable Loan				
Taxes on Estimated Profit	52,158.75	112,125.00	112,125.00	112,125.00
Payment on Accounts Payable				
Total Disbursements	$648,623.75	$828,710.00	$ 915,720.00	$1,006,580.00
Excess or Deficit	142,376.25	106,290.00	138,280.00	167,420.00
Cumulative Total	331,042.24	437,332.24	575,612.24	743,032.24
Assumptions				
Collections				
New S.B.A. Loan				
New Equity Capital				
Disbursements				
Payments on S.B.A. Loan	4,050.00	4,050.00	4,050.00	4,050.00
New Excess or Deficit	506,742.24	608,982.24	743,212.24	906,582.24

Accordion theory, 98–99
Accountants, 29–30, 107
ACE (Active Core of Executives), 125
Achieving Society, The (McClelland), 3–4
Acquisitions, 80
Adell Chemical Company, 103, 119
Adler, Fred, 68
Advertising agencies, 28–29, 107
Age of entrepreneurs, 6, 7, 20
Airport lounges, 148–49
Alberto-Culver, 59
Allen, George, 11, 118
Amana, 120, 140
American Motors Corporation, 124
American Research and Developent
     Corporation (ARD), 39, 68, 185
Analog Devices, Inc., 41, 137
Anderson, Abraham, 185
Anderson, Harlan E., 185
Angels, 31
Apple Computer Corporation, 20
Arnold's, 119, 140
ARP Instruments, 119
Assets, 63, 65
Atari, 161
Auerbach, Red, 11
Avon Products, 59, 185

Balance sheet, 62–65
Bangs, Andy, 54n
Bankers, 30
Bankruptcy, 24, 30, 62, 81, 131–36
Bankruptcy Act of 1898, 123, 132–33
Banks, 80, 84, 179–80

Barowsky, Jacob L., 103
Birth order of entrepreneurs, 4, 7, 21
B.L.T. Company, 59
Blue sky offering laws, 57
Blumenberg, Joseph, 103n
Board of directors, 30–31, 107
Book value of business, 51
Borgatti, Anthony "Spag," 8
Bottoms-up technique, 96
Bradham, Caleb, 186
Bread-board, 97, 98
Breakeven analysis, 99–102
Breakeven point, 100
Broken-field running, 38–39
BUMS (Boston Unemployed Men's Society),
     108
Bushnell, Nolan K., 161–62
Business brokers, 136–37
*Businessman's Guide to Capital-Raising Under
     the Securities Laws, A* (Coleman and
     Seldin), 48
Business plan, 53–77
  balance sheet, 62–65
  caliber of people in deal, 65–66
  characteristics of company and industry,
     59–60
  cover of, 67
  definition of, 53
  delivery of, 68
  five minute reader, 56–58
  information questionnaire for development
     of, 143–47
  reading process, 58–67
  reasons for, 54

Business plan (*cont.*)
  sample, 193–385
  sources of information on preparation of,
    76–77, 149–50
  summary, 67–68, 70
  table of contents, 58, 69–76
  terms of deal, 60–62
  uniqueness of deal, 66
  writing, 58, 69–76
Business trust, 105

Campbell, Joseph, 185
Campbell Soup, 185
Capital, sources of, 177–81
Capital gains tax, 183
Capitalism, 120–21, 138
Capital stock, 64
Carnegie, Andrew, 137
Center for Entrepreneurial Management, Inc.,
  The, 16
Certified public accountants (CPA), 29–30
Chandler Act of 1938, 132, 134
Chapter Eight-Chapter Ten, 133–35
Chapter Eleven, 81, 123, 134–35
Chapter Twelve, 133
Chapter Thirteen, 134
Charisma, 113
Cisneros, Gustavo, 158
Clayton Act of 1914, 122
Clipping services, 167–68
Coca-Cola, 185
Coleman, Michael M., 48
Collings, Robert, 21
Collins, O., 4, 5, 6
Common stock, 60, 61
Communism, 120
Company salesmen, 33
Compensation of advertising agency, 29
Competition, 73
Competitive pricing, 97
Compromise, 94
Conflicts, 27–28
Congressional Small Business Committees, 124,
  169–71
Constantine, William, 103*n*
Contribution analysis, 101–2
Control Data Business Centers, 175–77
Control Data Corporation, 160
Controllers, 33–34
Convertible debentures, 60, 61, 62
Cooper, Arnold, 6, 50, 120*n*
Corporate bankruptcy, 133–34
Corporations, 28, 105
Council of Small Independent Business
  Associations (COSIBA), 169
Crane Company, 157
Credit cards, 132
Creditors, 28
Cuisinarts, Inc., 160–61
Customers, 113, 117

Das Kapital (Marx), 120
Data General Corporation, Inc., 59, 68, 137

Daydreaming, 13
Deal (*see* Business plan)
Debt/equity ratio, 63–64
Debt financing, 42–43, 76, 78, 81, 126
Debtor in possession, 134
Debt with warrants, 60, 61
DeCastro, Ed, 20, 137
Delaware Floor Products, 120
Delegation, 11–12, 25
DeLorean, John, 23
Dible, Donald, 10*n*
Digital Equipment Corporation (DEC), 39, 59,
  68, 137, 139, 156, 185
Disney, Walt, 24
Drucker, Peter, 34, 111
DuPont, Eleuthere Irenee, 185
DuPont DeNemours, E.I. & Co., 185
Durant, William, 186

Eastman, George, 185
Eastman Kodak Company, 119, 139, 185
Ebony magazine, 157
Economic Development Administration funds,
  181
Economic Opportunity Loan (EOL), 126, 127
Education of entrepreneurs, 5, 7, 21, 150–56
Employee Retirement Income Security Act of
  1974 (ERISA), 49
Employee stock option trusts (ESOP), 49–50
Employee stock ownership trusts (ESOT),
  49–50
Enterprise profitability, 97, 98
Enterprising Man, The (Collins and Moore), 5
Entrepreneurial team, 25–34
  accountants, 29–30, 107
  advertising agencies, 28–29, 107
  bankers, 30
  board of directors, 30–31, 107
  choice of, 12, 22–23
  controllers, 33–34
  lawyers, 28, 107
  management consultants, 31–32, 106
  manufacturer's representatives, 32–33,
    164–65
  partners, 27–28
Entrepreneurs:
  age of, 6, 7, 20
  birth order of, 4, 7, 21
  characteristics of, 8–11
  defined, 3–4, 15
  delegating, 11, 25
  early development of, 4–5
  education of, 5, 7, 21, 150–56
  expense reports, 10–11, 23
  father-son relationship, 4–5, 21–22
  Hall of Fame, 156–63
  heroes of, 12–13
  individualism of, 8
  intuition, 13, 94
  life cycle, 25–26
  "love affairs," 13, 22
  luck and, 23, 94, 137
  management style, 11–14
  new research on, 7–8

optimism of, 8
organization systems, 13–14, 23
quiz, 15–24
risk-taking of, 8–9, 22
spouse of, 9–10, 21
time planning, 13–14
traits of, 5–7
venture capitalists and, 37–38, 56
women as, 5, 10, 188–89
(*See also* Entrepreneurial team; Leadership;
   Management of small enterprise)
Equity financing, 42–43, 48, 75, 78, 81, 126
Expense reports, 10–11, 23

Failure, 109, 129–40
  bankruptcy, 24, 30, 62, 81, 131–36
  lack of planning and, 54
  reasons for, 129–30
  selling business, 136–37
  taxes, 130–32
Family corporations, 85
Farmers Home Loan, 180–81
Father-son relationship, 4–5, 21–22
Federal Express Corporation, 163
Federal Trade Commission, 122
Federal Trade Commission Act of 1914, 122
Ferkauf, Eugene, 103
Fideli, Fred, 61
Finance companies, 84
Financial reports, 74–75
Finders, 86
Fixed assets, 179
Fixed costs, 99–100
Ford, Edsel, 102
Ford, Henry, 24, 109, 137, 186
Ford Motor Company, 130, 186
Forecasting new product sales, 96
Foreign-owned banks, 179
Foreign rights, 85
Form S-18, 48
Franchising rights, 85
Freeman, Howard, 103

Gamble, James, 186
General Dynamics Corporation, 130
General Electric Company, 139
General Motors Corporation, 50, 186
General partnership, 105
Gillete, King Camp, 186
Gillette Blades, 119, 186
Glamour fields, 59
Goal setting, 113, 114
Golden boy syndrome, 66
Goodyear Tire and Rubber Company, 186
Gordy, Berry, 156
Government legislation, 121–23
Grace, Peter, 157
Grants, 163–64
Gurnard, Inc., 103*n*

Haggerty, Pat, 139
Hall of Fame of entrepreneurs, 156–63
Hamilton, Ferris, 162
Hamilton, Frederic C., 162

Hammer, Armand, 159–60
Heroes, 12–13
Hershey, Milton, 24
Hewlett, William R., 27, 137, 186
Hewlett-Packard, 137, 186
History of company in business plan, 70
Homestead Act, 30
Honda, Soichiro, 156–57
Honda Motor Company, 156
Howard, James S., 151
*How to Form Your Own Corporation Without
   a Lawyer for Under $50* (Peterson), 28
*How to Lose $100,000,000 and Other Valuable
   Advice* (Little), 184
How to Read a Financial Report (Merrill,
   Lynch, Pierce, Fenner & Smith), 63
Hudson, Mary, 157
Hughes, Howard, 20
Hwang, Philip K., 20

IBM Corporation, 138–39
Idea, 97, 98
Incentive buying, 164
Income statement, 62, 63, 65
Incorporation, 28, 182–83
Individualism, 8
Inflation, 138
Initial public stock offering, 44–45
Insurance agents, 107
Intel, 120
Internal Revenue Service (IRS), 130–32
Internal Revenue Service (IRS) Code, 105
Intuition, 13, 94
Inventions, 165–66
Investment tax credit (ITC), 49–50
Issue pricing, 82–84
ITEK Corporation, 103

Jefferson, Thomas, 4
Jobs, Steven, 20
Johnson, John H., 157
Joint stock company, 105
Jonsson, John Eric, 157

Keogh plan, 183
Korvettes, E. J., 103
Kroc, Ray, 61, 186

Laboratories, 166–67
Land, Edwin, 12, 21, 137, 139
Landrum-Griffin Act of 1959, 123
Lanewood Laboratories, Inc., 59
Lawrence, Mary Wells, 157
Lawyers, 28, 107
Leadership, 111–21
  active and reactive actions, 112–13
  charisma, 113
  future expansion model, 113–17
  goal setting and resource allocation, 113, 114
  tasks of, 118–21
Lear, Norman, 120
Lee, Byung Chull, 157
Lee, Sara, 119, 140
Legal forms of business, 104–5

Lehrman, Lewis E., 157
Levitt, Theodore, 111, 116, 139
Liabilities, 63, 65
Life cycle concept, 98
Life insurance companies, 85
Limited partnership, 104–5
Lincoln, Abraham, 4
Liquidation value of business, 51
Liquidity, determination of, 63
Little, Royal, 156, 184–85
Litton Industries, 138
Lombardi, Vince, 11, 23, 93
Long term debt, 64
Lorber, Matthew, 41
"Love affairs," 13, 22
Luck, 23, 94, 137
Ludwig, Daniel, 22

Mail, missing, 183–84
Management by Objectives, 34
Management consultants, 31–32, 106
Management of small enterprise, 74, 93–110
  advice, 107–8
  avoiding mistakes, 107–10
  breakeven analysis, 99–102
  legal forms of business, 104–5
  name of enterprise, 102–4
  new products, 96–99
  organization chart, 95
  resource management and allocation, 106–7
Management style, 11–14
Mancuso, Joseph R., 6n, 97n, 112n, 116n, 119n
Manufacturer's representatives, 32–33, 107, 164–65
Manufacturing plan, 71
Marketing and sales, 72–73
Marketing Myopia (Levitt), 111
Marketing sources, 168
Market value of business, 51–52, 80
Massachusetts trust, 105
MBAs, 34
McClelland, David, 3–4
McConnell, David H., 185
McDonald's Corporation, 61, 98, 156, 186
McGraw, John, 11
McNair, Malcolm P., 98
Mello, Thomas, 157
Mergers, 80, 85
Merrill, Lynch, Pierce, Fenner & Smith, 63
Metzer, Arthur I., 103
Minority Business Opportunity Committee (MBOC), 125
Minority Enterprise Small Business Investment Corporations (MESBICs), 128, 178–79
Moore, D., 4, 5, 6
Moore, Gordon, 21
Motivation, 118
Motown Industries, Inc., 156
Multiple of earnings, 44–45
Murphy's Laws, 109–10

Name of enterprise, 102–4
National Labor Relations Act (Wagner Act) of 1935, 123
National Labor Relations Board, 123
National Science Foundation (NSF), 189–90
Net worth, 63, 64–65
New products, 96–99, 119–20
Newton, Dereck A., 113n
New York Stock Exchange, 79
Norris, William C., 160
Noyce, Robert, 21

Office of Minority Business Enterprise (OMBE), 125
Olivetti Typewriter, 138
Olsen, Kenneth H., 137, 156, 185
Olsen, Stanley, 185
Olson, Sherman, 103
Operation Business Mainstream (OBM), 126, 127
Optimism, 8
Organization chart, 95
Organization Diego Cisneros (ODC), 158
Organization Makers, The (Collins and Moore), 4
Organization systems, 13–14, 23
Outside and inside philosophy, 26, 27
Over-the-counter market (OTC), 45
Owner's equity, 64

Packard, David, 27, 137, 186
Packard, Vance, 4
Partners, 27–28
Partnerships, 104–5
Pastoriza, Jim, 102–3
Patents, 85, 165–66
Pearlman, Alan R., 103, 119
Pemberton, John, 185
Pension Reform Act of 1974, 50
Pepperidge Farms, 119, 140
Pepsico, 186
Perdue, Frank, 157
Perdue Farms Inc., 157
Personal bankruptcy, 133
Peterson, Nick, 28
Planning, 95
  (See also Business plan)
Polaroid, 12, 21, 119, 137, 139
Practice of Management, The (Drucker), 111
Pratt, Stanley, 187
Preferred stock, 60, 61
Premiums, 164
Price-earnings ratios (P/E), 44–45, 51
Pricing, 96–97, 100–101
Printer Technology, Inc. (P.T.I.), 115, 116
Private debt, 85
Private placement, 44, 84
Procter, William, 186
Procter & Gamble, 26, 186
Production and personnel plan, 71–72
Product notion, 97–98

Product profitability, 97, 98
Product sale, 97, 98
Profit-sharing plan, 49
Proprietorship, 28, 105
Prototype, 97, 98
Psychologists, 108
Publications, 181–82
Publicity, 167–68
Public stock offering, 43–48
  advantages of, 79–81
  disadvantages of, 81–82
  pricing the issue, 82–84
Purchase commitment, 87–88

Rabb, Sidney R., 162–63
Raising new money, 78–89
  banks, 84
  family corporations, 85
  finance companies, 84
  franchising and foreign rights, 85
  life insurance companies, 85
  mergers, 80, 85
  New York Stock Exchange requirements, 79
  private debt, 85
  private placement, 84
  trade credit, 85
  underwriters, 85–88
Raytheon, 120, 140
RCA Corporation, 120, 130, 139, 140
Recruiting process, 118
Reeves, Rooser, 66
Regulation A, 79, 88
Regulation D, 48
Related business, methods of determining, 113, 116
Repeat sale, 97, 98
Reps, 32–33
Research and development (R&D), 73
Resource organizations, 168–75
Retained earnings, 64
Retirement benefits, 49
Return on Investment (ROI) analysis, 57
Richman, Herb, 20
Rind, Kenneth W., 188
Risk-taking, 8–9, 22
Roberts, Edward, 5–6, 7
Robinson-Patman Act, 122
Robo-Wash, 59
Rockefeller, John, 137
Rolls Royce, 26
Roosevelt, Franklin Delano, 4, 26
Rotenberg, Jonathan, 20–21
Royal Typewriter, 138
Rubell, Stanley, 187
Run for Daylight (Lombardi), 93

Samsung Group, 157
Sanders, Royden, 103
Scandinavian Airlines Systems (SAS), 158
Schacter, Stanley, 4
Schwartz, Robert, 151–52

SCORE (Service Core of Retired Executives), 125–26
Sears, Richard Warren, 186
Sears, Roebuck & Company, 186
Section 1244 stock, 104, 130
Secured debt, 62
Securities Act of 1933, 50, 88
Securities and Exchange Commission (SEC), 44, 45, 57, 69, 135, 136
Seed money financing, 42
Seiberling, Frank, 186
Seldin, Irving P., 48
Self-development books, 149
Selling business, 50–51, 136–37
Senate Small Business Committee, 124
Service businesses, 98–99
7A term loan guarantee, 126
Sharing the wealth, 49–50
Sherman Anti-Trust Act of 1890, 121-22
Silver, A. David, 55n
Singer, Issac Merrit, 186
Singer Company, The, 186
Small Business Act of 1953, 123
Small Business Administration (SBA), 57, 84, 123-24, 171–72, 177–78
  areas of assistance offered by, 124–26
  Business Management Courses, 152–53
  Guaranteed Loan Program, 175–77
  loan vehicles, 126–28
Small Business Development Center (SBDC) Program, 154–56
Small Business Innovation Research Act of 1982, 189-92
Small Business Institute (SBI), 126
Small Business Investment Act of 1958, 127n
Small business investment companies (SBICs), 57, 84, 127–28, 177, 178
Small business publications, 181–82
Smith, Adam, 120
Smith, Brian, 151
Smith, Frederick, 20, 163
Smith Corona and Merchant (SCM), 138
Sole proprietorship, 105
Sontheimer, Carl C., 160–61
Sontheimer, Shirley, 160–61
Spouse of entrepreneur, 9–10, 21
Stata, Ray, 41, 102-3, 137
State Mutual Life Assurance Company, 61
Stengel, Casey, 11
Stock option plans, 49–50
Stone, W. Clement, 21
Stop & Shop Companies, 162–63
Straight debt, 60, 62
Subchapter S corporation, 105
Subordinated convertible debt, 60, 61–62
Summary of business plan, 67–68, 70
Suppliers, 113, 114–15
Swanson foods, 120

Table of contents of business plan, 58, 69–76
Taft-Hartley Act of 1947, 123

Taxation, 104-5, 121, 130-32
Tax Reduction Act of 1975, 49
TeleVideo, 20
Tennyson, Alfred, 40
Texas Instruments, Inc., 120, 137, 139, 157
Textron, Inc., 156, 184
T.H.E. Insurance Company, 179-80
Time planning, 13-14
Tops-down technique, 96
Trade credit, 85
Trademarks, 165
Trade shows, 168
Trump, Donald, 20
1244 stock, 85
Two-tier lending rate, 179

Underwood Typewriter, 138
Underwriters, 44-45, 48, 85-88
Underwriting proposal, 86-87
Unemployment, 138
Unique Selling Proposition (U.S.P.), 66
University Business Development Centers
        (UBDCs), 126, 153-54
Unrelated business, expanding into, 113, 117
Unsecured debt, 62

Variable costs, 99-100
Venture capital, 37-48

public offering (see Public Stock offering)
raising, 38-41
resource publications, 187
sources, 59, 188
structure of, 41-43
(See also Business plan)
Venture capitalists, entrepreneurs and, 37-38,

Vor   urg, Diane, 157

Wal   arcus, 158
Wal   159
War   21, 158
War   ories, 7, 158
War   61
Was   George, 4
Wa   nas, 20
We   tions, The (Smith), 120
Wh   iling concept, 98
Wh   lfred North, 6
Wil   ldes, 119
Wi   h C., 186
Wi   lrow, 4
Women entrepreneurs, 5, 10, 188-89
Worcester Polytechnic Institute (WPI), 8
Working capital, 63
Wozniak, Steven, 20

Xerox Corporation, 137, 139, 186